THE CONFESSIONS OF AN ANTI-FEMINIST

THE AUTOBIOGRAPHY OF ANTHONY M. LUDOVICI

EDITED BY JOHN V. DAY

Counter-Currents Publishing Ltd.
San Francisco
2018

Copyright © 2018 by Counter-Currents Publishing
All rights reserved

Cover image by
Antony M. Ludovici

Cover design by
Kevin I. Slaughter

Published in the United States by
COUNTER-CURRENTS PUBLISHING LTD.
P.O. Box 22638
San Francisco, CA 94122
USA
http://www.counter-currents.com/

Hardcover ISBN: 978-1-940933-32-0
Paperback ISBN: 978-1-940933-33-7
E-book ISBN: 978-1-940933-34-4

Library of Congress Cataloging-in-Publication Data

Names: Ludovici, Anthony M. (Anthony Mario), 1882-1971. | Day, John V.
Title: Confessions of an anti-feminist : the autobiography of Anthony M. Ludovici / edited by John V. Day.
Description: San Francisco : Counter-Currents Pub. Ltd., 2018. | Includes bibliographical references and index.
Identifiers: LCCN 2013037560| ISBN 9781935965886 (hardcover : alk. paper) | ISBN 9781935965893 (pbk. : alk. paper) | ISBN 9781935965909 (ebook)
Subjects: LCSH: Ludovici, Anthony M. (Anthony Mario), 1882-1971. | Essayists--Great Britain--Biography. | Philosophers--Great Britain--Biography. | Critics--Great Britain--Biography. | Authors, English--Biography.
Classification: LCC CT788.L7645 A3 2015 | DDC 920.92--dc23
LC record available at http://lccn.loc.gov/2013037560

THIS
COMMEMORATIVE·WINDOW,
DESIGNED AND ERECTED BY A.M.L.
To Celebrate Hys Friends' and Hys Owne
"RETREAT FROM PARIS" A.D. 1900
Was Presented to, and is still in the House
of Hys especial FRIEND GUY DREW.

Contents

Editor's Foreword ❖ iii

Author's Preface ❖ vii

1. My Family ❖ 1

2. My Mother ❖ 39

3. My Education I (1882–1910) ❖ 63

4. My Education II (1910–1916) ❖ 98

5. My Education III (1916–1959) ❖ 131

6. My Friends I ❖ 158

7. My Friends II ❖ 176

8. My Life Work ❖ 224

9. Final Reflections ❖ 314

Appendix ❖ 323

Select Bibliography ❖ 327

Index ❖ 335

About the Author ❖ 352

Editor's Foreword

Anthony M. Ludovici, the author of this present book, was a British writer who died in 1971, having left a will instructing his Trustees—the two executors of his will—

to pay the cost of publication at the lowest price compatible with the cost of production of a decent and presentable edition of the following works if they have not already been published:

THE ENGLISH COUNTRYSIDE
MY AUTOBIOGRAPHY (The Confessions of an Antifeminist)

and I DIRECT my Trustees to send complimentary sets of the said publications to the Public Libraries of Edinburgh, Glasgow, Dublin, Belfast, La Bibliotheque Nationale, Paris, and the National Libraries of Berlin, Amsterdam, Stockholm, Rome, New York and Zurich. I leave the details of these publications otherwise to the discretion of my Trustees, but the quality of the editions should not be inferior to that of THE QUEST OF HUMAN QUALITY (published by Riders in 1952). The typescripts of the books will be found among my papers in the study of my house in Ipswich.[1]

After the estate duty was paid on his estate and a few minor bequests were made, Ludovici had left over £36,000. According to Government statistics, such a sum of money would today be worth more than ten times that figure. In short, Ludovici had bequeathed plenty of money for the publication of these two books. But for reasons best known to his executors, both of

---

[1] Ludovici's will in full is on the Internet at www.anthonymludovici.com/will.htm.

whom were trained lawyers, neither work was ever put into print and then sent to the designated libraries.

Typescripts of the two works are currently held by the Special Collections Division of Edinburgh University Library in Scotland.² According to the library, its 'Papers of Anthony Mario Ludovici (1882–1971)' are 'composed of 3 pieces of typescript material, being *The confessions of an antifeminist*, *The English countryside today*, and the considerably shorter *Juvenile delinquency and sex*.' These three works, the library says, were 'acquired from executors, in Diss, Norfolk, January 1997.'

One presumes that Ludovici's executors handed over these works to Edinburgh University because Ludovici's will had bequeathed the bulk of his estate to Edinburgh. He wanted Edinburgh University to conduct 'research into the influence of miscegenation on man's quality and well-being' and to award an annual Ludovici Prize for the best thesis on this subject, although, in the event, the university declined Ludovici's bequest and, after discussions with his executors, used most of the money available to study the hereditary disease of Huntington's chorea.³

But the good news is that Ludovici's *Confessions* have not remained under lock and key in a university library, because a second typescript of this work recently cropped up in the public domain. Apparently with safe-keeping in mind, Ludovici gave a copy of the work to Ron Creasey, a friend and neighbour in Suffolk, and as an old man Creasey passed it on to his friend and neighbour, Nick Griffin, who in turn lent it to people he knew were keen on publishing it.

This typescript must predate the Edinburgh one, because Ludovici declares in the final chapter that 'I am not sorry to have reached the end of my eightieth year in 1962,' whereas the

---

² Regarding Ludovici's papers, see www.archiveshub.ac.uk and search for Ludovici.

³ For further details, see R. Gayre of Gayre's article, 'The late A. M. Ludovici's bequest to the University of Edinburgh,' *The Mankind Quarterly* 8, 1972-3, pp. 191-4 (which is on the Internet at www.anthonymludovici.com/bequest.htm).

corresponding sentence in the Edinburgh version concludes with 'my eighty-eighth year in 1970.' Nevertheless, Edinburgh's 1970 typescript has only three passages that add anything substantial to the 1962 typescript—the first passage has Ludovici apologizing for his behaviour when younger; the second describes his father in a much better light than before; and the third says a little more about Anthony's own appearance and character.[4] Equally, though, this present book has several passages that the 1970 typescript either omits or tones down.

Now, more than four decades after Ludovici's death, it is thanks to Mr Creasey, Mr Griffin and several of Ludovici's admirers in the United States that the public at large has the chance to read these present *Confessions* – the autobiography of one of the twentieth century's most perceptive and outspoken thinkers.

John V. Day

---

[4] The three passages are discussed in the Preface, note 1; in Chapter 1, note 12; and in Chapter 1, note 13. (A few more minor amendments from the 1970 typescript will be mentioned in other footnotes.)

Preface

'I believe that every man who has written anything whatsoever is bound by the most compelling duty to supply material for his biography.'

— Friedrich Hebbel, *Diaries and Letters*

After translating the above quotation for this preface, I was not certain whether Hebbel meant that an author owes the duty in question to himself or to posterity. I incline to the belief that he owes it chiefly to himself. A man writes to be understood, and the dread of failing here has probably led to many of the autobiographies of literary men.

At all events, when a man has been misunderstood and misrepresented as consistently as I have been, he owes it to himself to try to clear the fog that has settled about him. For in England, and London above all, fog is notoriously the danger. Careful clarity of expression is no protection against it, because long ago, centuries before fighting armies and fleets had thought of the use of artificial fog, literary critics, professional rivals and all those whose advantage was served by obscuring an author's message had discovered the tactical advantage of smoke-screens in the war of ideas and, more especially, in the struggle for power.

Besides, many quite innocent readers carry their own fog about with them and, without malice prepense, allow it to settle on the printed pages before them. This would be more easily forgiven if only they would refrain from subsequently ascribing to the work itself and not to their own private nebulosity the false impressions they have gathered.

Occasionally, even in the densest fog, the Englishman finds his way. But, as a rule, only his own way home. Beware, then, all those who invite him to grope through his murk along unwonted paths!

It has been my fate always to offer him hitherto untrodden, uncharted itineraries. Naturally, he lost his way. What is far more serious, he usually lost his temper. In my sixty years of literary work I have had to put up with an extraordinary amount of bad temper. As most of it was quite undeserved, I owe it to myself, rather than to my readers, to follow Hebbel's advice.

But, in a sense, I also owe it to the public. For supposing that the many ideas and messages in my books are, as I believe, valuable, what then? Could I in charity depart from the scene before trying to correct these errors of judgement on the part of my critics which have prevented the majority of my fellows from making my acquaintance? Not to speak of my enemies and envious rivals! They would be only too pleased if the fog they spread hung over my work eternally.

I have therefore decided to describe the kind of life I have led. A good deal about this matter already lies recorded between the covers of my various books. This was inevitable. Had they told the whole story, however, I should have failed dismally to realise my ambition, which was to write objectively. True, much could not help leaking out. Because all did not leak out, I am writing these *Confessions*. But I shall not try to duplicate information.

A shrewd Jewish medical man once said to me: 'Had you loved women more, you would have described them less accurately.'[1]

I quote this as an aid to those readers who may already be wondering what I am driving at. It was a penetrating remark and a clue which all may follow who wish to draw correct inferences from the more objective passages in my works, or to interpret the subjective ones exactly. For, if the Jewish doctor's

---

[1] In the 1970 typescript Ludovici maintains that in old age one finally sees oneself objectively, and he therefore chastises himself as 'a repentant sinner.' Specifically, he regrets that he lacked tenderness with women, attributing his coldness to his mother spoiling him and thereby making him selfishly accept love without giving too much in return. —Ed.

reasoning was sound, other features of my writings must also unmask me to the alert reader.

These *Confessions*, then, are but additional information. They will explain much that my books leave in obscurity.

Among my more obscure works I include my contribution to the symposium *Gentile and Jew*, my *Four Pillars of Health* and my treatise on the Jews, *Jews, and the Jews in England*, the latter of which I published under the pseudonym of 'Cobbett.' Not that I mean that these books are hard to read, for they are as lucid as the multiplication tables. But all three were written when the air in England was exceptionally thundery; when, for the first time, I discovered that the Englishman's much boasted and boosted right of private judgement and of free speech had, all along, been only fair-weather principles. Given the change in the wind, they went by the board. The reasons for many of the bitterest implications and imprecations in these three treatises, all those who can put two and two together will find in the pages of these *Confessions*.

One last word, and about sincerity. It is a great virtue, especially in an author, and one with which I hope every reader will not hesitate to credit me. Before the general public, however, it has to be exercised with a caution not necessary in friendly conversation. Even if in the end he sells only one copy out of a whole edition, an author has to write as if he were addressing a wide public. There is the law of libel. Besides, his readers, as strangers to him, will be prone to suspect personal motives for his least subjective remarks. In this sense, I could not look on my *Personal Reminiscences of Auguste Rodin* as a wholly sincere book, even in its tone. It is all true, but it is by no means the whole truth. Its very innuendos are muted. For, had I written differently, what thanks should I have got? The Rodin fans everywhere would have proclaimed not that I spoke the truth, but that I bore my former employer some grudge for which I wished to pay him out when he could no longer defend himself.

If critics could darkly hint at the smell of a rat in my timely attack on the 'healthy food and healthy soil evangelists' of the third and fourth decade of this century,² heaven knows what gigantic rodent they would have scented had I written all I knew about Rodin!

Some countenance is lent to these remarks about the reminiscences in question by the review the book was given in *La revue des deux mondes* by Louis Gillet. He was knowledgeable enough to hint at some tactful insincerities. In the issue of December 1926, after describing my book as 'un livre charmant'³—words he would hardly have used had I written differently—he goes on to say: 'C'est une justice à rendre à M. Ludovici que son livre est celui d'un homme bien élevé. Il n'a pas profité de la confiance d'un grand artiste pour le trahir. Il n'a pas cru faire preuve d'indépendance en déchirant un maître pour prix de ses bontés.'⁴

You can guess under what circumstances he would have spoken of my book as 'celui d'un homme mal élevé.'⁵ And what did he know that made him hint at the possibility of a betrayal? Enough, at any rate, to be able to pat me on the back for not having 'déchiré'⁶ the Master.

In the confessional, however, one betrays chiefly oneself. Although baptised as a Catholic, this is my first confession. All the confessions I might or should have made are here crammed into my last literary production. Nor do I expect absolution. The English reading-public are, in any case, not qualified to absolve. Nor even if they were, will they feel inclined to do so when they have read these pages.

Anthony M. Ludovici

---

² See my *Four Pillars of Health*, London, 1945.
³ 'A charming book.'—Ed.
⁴ 'It is a tribute to Mr Ludovici that his book is that of a well-mannered man. He hasn't profited from the trust of a great artist to betray him. He hasn't thought to prove his independence by disparaging a master in reward for his kindnesses.'—Ed.
⁵ 'That of an ill-mannered man.'—Ed.
⁶ Disparage.—Ed.

MY FAMILY

The reader who knows my work will not need to be told that I hold strong views on the deplorable psychophysical effects of random breeding. As I show with enough cogency in the first chapter of *The Four Pillars of Health*, it means ill health both of the spirit and of the organism as a whole. For, owing to the independent inheritance of bodily parts—including, of course, brain and ganglia—from disparate parents and their stocks, it leads not only to disharmony and conflict in the inherited passions, bents, gifts and tastes, but also in the various organs, controls and, therefore, functions of the whole system. The reader to whom all this sounds new and, consequently, either difficult or ridiculous—above all, the reader who, like most moderns, has been reared on the sophistry that 'opposites should mate'—will find it worth his while to glance at the scientific grounds which, in my *Four Pillars of Health*, I advance for the above unfashionable and unpalatable conclusions.[1]

Nor am I unqualified to speak with inside knowledge of the disharmonies of spirit and body which result from the random breeding I condemn, for, as a child of the period during which random breeding began to reach its apogee in Europe, including England, I have been able to observe its manifold evil consequences both in those about me and in my own person. I know the *Ding an sich*[2] of the condition.

I say 'in my own person' with some justification, for I am derived from stocks which must inevitably have transmitted to me all the disharmonies and conflicts implicit in their having been largely disparate and possessed of different constitutions, vocations, gifts and so on.

My paternal grandfather, Albert Johann Ludovici, was born at Zittau in the extreme eastern corner of Saxony in 1820, and

---

[1] My *Quest of Human Quality* (London, 1952) should also be consulted.

[2] Thing in itself. — Ed.

my paternal grandmother, Marie Caroline Grenier, who came of French agricultural stock, was born in Paris in 1821.

My mother's father, Antoine Mario Cals, was a Basque, the oldest race in Europe, and her mother, Marie Méhaye, was a Parisian. My paternal grandfather was an artist, and my maternal grandfather was a businessman, with artistic gifts displayed chiefly in jewellery design, an amateur poet and a political biographer, whilst his wife was the daughter of parents in business in the French capital.

Accordingly, I should be half-French, a quarter-German and a quarter-Basque. As, however, some doubt exists about my grandfather Ludovici's nationality, and neither my grandfather nor my father were ever able to trace his origin, it may be that my German blood is a myth. But this I doubt. Their investigations into the matter led them to conclude that my grandfather's forebears probably migrated into Germany from Italy sometime during the second half of the eighteenth century. I have, however, long suspected that there was much wishful thinking behind this theory, and from the first it struck me as bogus. For, in the first place, both my grandfather and father had a wholly irrational dislike of both Germany and her people, and were always suspiciously anxious to pass themselves off as Latins. Secondly, the family on my great-grandmother Ludovici's side, whose pedigree we possess, can be traced right back into the early eighteenth century, and they were all German. Thirdly, it is by no means unusual to find Latinised forms of German names in Germany, and as in Bouillet's *Biographical Dictionary* and in the authors' catalogue in the British Museum reading-room the name Ludovici occurs in front of works, both philosophical and otherwise, all published in Leipzig or elsewhere in Germany and written by Germans for German-readers throughout the eighteenth and early nineteenth centuries,[3] it seems rather far-fetched to look for an Italian origin for my great-grandfather Ludovici simply because an allegedly careful search made in the late nine-

---

[3] For example, the eighteenth-century German authors Christianus Theophilus Ludovici, Jacob Friedrich Ludovici and Carl Guenther Ludovici. — Ed.

teenth century by two amateur and none too zealous genealogists failed to reveal any of his immediate forebears in south-eastern Saxony. Fourthly, it is very doubtful whether Ludovici is an Italian form of the name at all. Ludovico is common in Italy and seems to be the Italian equivalent of Lewis in England, Louis in France, Ludwig in Germany (and hence Latinised as Ludovicus, and in the genitive as Ludovici, as in the book of one called Ludovicus), and Lodovigo in Spain. Fifthly, there was very little trace of any Italian blood either in my paternal grandfather himself or any of his children, my father least of all. On the contrary, those who resembled the old man looked distinctly German; and I remember him perfectly well, for I was twelve years old when he died and, owing to my deep admiration and love of him, I had spent much time in his company. So it is exceedingly probable that I am a quarter-German.

My paternal grandmother was a fine, tall woman of majestic bearing, and whatever good looks the family possessed came chiefly from her. Her forebears were very tall. My great-grandfather on her side, Antoine Sebastian Grenier, who died in Paris in 1871, was over six feet in height, and my father remembered feeling dwarfed beside him as they took walks together. His mother, one of my great-great-grandmothers on my father's side, Madame Louis Grenier (née Marie Delahaye), who was married twice and bore each husband four children, lived at Lieuvillers in the department of Oise.

It was doubtless from these ancestors that my eldest brother derived the tall stature which was exceptional in us of the third generation.

Notwithstanding the good grounds we all had for regarding ourselves as at least partly German, my father always favoured the Italian pronunciation of our name and would always speak of himself as 'Ludovichi.' This pronunciation therefore became traditional with us, and only my mother's Gallic loyalty accustomed us to the simultaneous use of the pronunciation, 'Ludoveesee.' In later life I favoured this pronunciation, as I saw no point in trying to pass myself off as of Italian descent, for I was much more proud than ashamed of my German blood. My brother George and his English wife, who looked on this blood as the skeleton in our cupboard, were inclined to stress the legend of our Italian origin and to insist on my father's pronunciation of the name, especially during the War of Belgian Independence (1914–18), and one cousin, my uncle's eldest son, under pressure from his English wife, actually changed his name by deed poll to Hibberd.

When I recall my paternal grandfather's studio, his consummate skill as a draughtsman, his virtuosity as a painter, and his mastery of every branch of his craft (for he even made his own pastels), I cannot help thinking that whatever thoroughness and pains I may have shown in my treatment of some of the abstruse problems with which from time to time I have dealt have been due to that quarter of German blood of which I gratefully acknowledge him to have been the source.

He had studied at the Atelier Drölling in Paris in the forties of the nineteenth century, and was a contemporary of Henner, the celebrated French painter. He witnessed the revolution of 1848 and married in 1850. He left Chemnitz for Paris in 1843, and after five years of hard work settled in England as a portrait-painter, a profession for which he was admirably gifted. After staying first of all in Margate, where he was most successful, he was able to return to Paris and, at Notre Dame de Lorette on 7th February 1850, to marry my grandmother, whom he had met six years earlier. On returning to England he was soon able to make a comfortable income, and he brought up a family of five children — two boys and three girls — to all of whom he gave a costly education. Incidentally, among the portraits he painted were those of King Edward VII and Queen Alexandra as Prince and Princess of Wales, and he often regaled me with interesting reminiscences of the sittings they gave him.

I never knew my grandfather Cals. He appears to have been of medium height and slim, and my mother always said that I reminded her of him. A liberal in politics, he was a great admirer of Béranger and Victor Hugo, and at the time of his first marriage, circa 1848, he was a partner in the firm of Boucheron, the jewellers of Rue de la Paix. He died when he was about fifty-nine of heart disease.

Both my paternal grandparents died when over seventy — my

grandmother of cancer in 1893, and my grandfather of a severe internal chill in 1894 at Vevey in Switzerland. I remember seeing the latter as late as August 1893 dashing into heavy breakers on the shingle beach at Quiberville, and during that holiday with us he was able to take long walks in our company.

Enough has now been said to make it clear that in my hereditary make-up there is such a wealth of conflicting strains that few could be better qualified than I am to exclaim, with Goethe's Faust, 'Zwei Seelen wohnen, ach! in meiner Brust!,'[4] although in my case it would be more accurate to speak of four rather than two souls.

To those who knew my parents, different lights and moods make me look like either of them. More than any other of their children, I was a blend of both, and after their death I grew used to first one and then the other being recalled whenever an old friend or relative met me. I also seemed to have gathered up, in a way my brothers and sisters did not, the abilities which distinguished my father and mother respectively. Except for my sister Lily, fifteen months my senior, I was the only child who inherited any of my father's and his father's artistic gifts; and Lily and I were the only children who displayed any of my mother's interest and ability in literature.

She was the more highly endowed of my parents. Allowing for my strong bias in her favour, I think this a fair statement and one which most of my family circle would confirm. She had an excellent memory, and had only to read three or four times a long speech like Auguste's in Act V of Corneille's *Cinna* in order to know it by heart. My father's memory, on the other hand, was poor. She knew her own language very well, had the command of a large vocabulary, and she taught and wrote in it with success. My father's English, however, although the only language he spoke with perfect ease, was elementary, and his vocabulary small. My mother could recite whole passages from her native classics and sing all the traditional nursery and other songs of France. My father knew nothing by heart at all, and I never heard him quote any author, English, French or German. He

---

[4] 'Two souls, alas, dwell within my breast.' — Ed.

taught us no English lore, and we left our parental roof essentially French in spirit and outlook. It was not until I reached my teens that I grasped the reason of the English proverb, 'One swallow does not make a summer.' Until then, I had always thought of swallows as the harbinger of spring, having from my earliest childhood heard that 'Une hirondelle ne fait pas un printemps.'[5]

But, although French thought and sentiment certainly preponderated, it is not strictly true to say that 'we left our parental roof essentially French in spirit and outlook,' for, thanks to the interest taken in us by some of my father's pupils, we were introduced to much English lore, subjected to a good deal of English influence, and made acquainted with many classical English works of fiction. I knew and enjoyed *Robinson Crusoe* before I was twelve, and Lily and I both loved *The Swiss Family Robinson* and read it through more than once. At the hands of our governesses, moreover, we became familiar with some of the English poets, and before our teens we had already written essays on some of Tennyson's works. I remember particularly *Enoch Arden* in this respect.

The two English books which did most to give our minds a contemporary English stamp were, however, *Alice's Adventures in Wonderland* and *Through the Looking-Glass*, which Lily and I adored and got to know pretty well by heart. Yet, in relishing these two English masterpieces, our French blood and upbringing asserted themselves, for, in quickly apprehending and in applying what we learned from Lewis Carroll, we insensibly required a yardstick with which to measure and judge the people, young and old, about us. Because, at bottom, as every intelligent English reader knows, despite the general opinion to the contrary, these are by no means essentially nonsense or children's books. I remember perfectly the kind lady pupil of my father's who introduced them to us and, with much deliberate and persuasive laughter, dilated on the scenes she felt sure would most appeal to us — the famous game of croquet with its flamingos for mallets, its hedgehogs for balls and its contorted soldiers for

---

[5] 'One swallow does not make a spring.' — Ed.

hoops; the equally famous Cheshire Cat, and the baby that turns into a pig. Yet, had the kind and well-meaning lady only known, these features of the two fairy tales were those that appealed to us least of all, and I don't believe any intelligent child over nine years of age ever finds them as funny as the average adult imagines they should be to him. At any rate, what chiefly attracted Lily and me, and never ceased to amuse us, were the more probable and less laboriously fun-provoking features of the two books — those both true to life, plausible and yet implicitly critical of the English cast of mind. For, when once we had recognised that both books were extremely clever skits on English people and their foibles — i.e., their congenital lack of logic, their utterly unconscious lack of intellectual honesty, their inveterate mental indolence and habit of loose thinking — we never ceased to enjoy reading and rereading them. But it is important to note that this aspect of Carroll's two tales was revealed to us only when we were too old to be entertained by incongruities alone. Only then did we understand that most of the uproarious fun to be derived from reading about Alice had very little to do with the glaring and far-fetched nonsense of the croquet scene, the Cheshire Cat, the pig-baby and the like, but consists chiefly in the sharp corrections which the characteristic infirmities of the English mind constantly provoke in the course of the two stories.

Thus, throughout the two books, Alice is repeatedly pulled up short and made to perceive the logical, if not necessary, implication of all that she and her interlocutors say. She is baffled and bewildered by being incessantly made aware of her own and other people's habit of loose thinking and her careless use of language. She is constantly made to recognise the difference between intellectual uprightness and its converse in facing difficulties and problems, whilst no-one in the books is forgiven for using a cliché or a tag as an ersatz for a thought.

But all this, although tremendously funny to anyone aware of the prevalence of these shortcomings among even the educated in England, and to my mind constituting the principal attraction of the two books, is quite above the head of the average young child and is the very last feature which endears them to him. Yet I have found that many an adult English reader who professes to be fond of these works of Carroll enjoys them largely owing to their nonsensical passages—the passages assumed to appeal most strongly to infants—and often misses the ironical castigation of English mental habits which gives the books their peculiar humour and charm.

Although Carroll may be unique in the witty and allegorical form he has given to his jibes at certain English foibles, he is, however, by no means alone in having recognized them. As recently as 1958, F. L. Lucas, in his *Search for Good Sense,* has admitted that 'we have a reputation for mental dishonesty,' and he adds: 'And it is an unpleasant one.'[6] English illogicality is also proverbial, and the Anglo-Saxon tendency to loose thinking, and to the use of a tag or cliché where a thought would be more appropriate and helpful, has been noticed by all good observers of English life. Even the English love of nonsense *per se*, which is so characteristic of English humorous literature, is well-known to indicate mental sloth, for nonsense obviously affords a respite to mental effort; it suspends the need for accuracy and rigid rational thinking. It is equivalent to throwing the reins of reason over the horse's neck, and to a temporary truce granted by the higher mental faculties to the lazy impulses of the mind. Thinkers like Renouvier,[7] Penjon[8] and John Dewey[9] all agree that nonsense is a favourite refuge not necessarily of stupid, but certainly of lazy, thinkers.

Now, in Carroll's two famous works all these characteristics are repeatedly and most amusingly ridiculed, and it was probably the tincture of logicality in our French minds that helped Lily and me, relatively early, to appreciate and enjoy this aspect of the books, an aspect which I still think constitutes their principal charm, originality and claim to rank as works of genius.

Outstanding examples are the way Alice is pulled up when she uses tags like 'you know' or 'you see'; her perplexity when the characters and she herself are caught assuming complete

---

[6] P. 126.

[7] *Le rire.*

[8] *Revue philosophique*, Number 8, 1893.

[9] *The Psychological Review*, Volume 1, 1894.

analogies when there is but one common feature, as when the pigeon classes little girls with serpents because both eat eggs; and when they give explanations that are logically inadequate, as when the Cheshire Cat explains why it is mad; or when Alice is shown the danger of assuming a similarity of meaning when the terms are reversed. The March Hare, for instance, rebukes her for maintaining that to say what you mean is the same as to mean what you say.

An excellent example of the snare of using popular tags is the King's remark to Alice in *Through the Looking-Glass* that, when he said there was 'nothing like' eating hay when you're faint, he by no means wished to be understood as saying 'there was nothing better,' which Alice quite illogically took to be his meaning. And so on *ad infinitum*. In fact, in no other country than England and no other language than English could these two books have been written. Because only in England are the foibles they illustrate and ridicule so essentially indigenous. This explains the dire failure of the French translation, and although the German translation, especially the rendering of 'The Jabberwocky,' is brilliant, much of Carroll's subtle denigration of his country's mental sloth and illogicality is lost, because it has no foreign equivalent.

In his own line my father showed great ability, although he was a much better colourist than draughtsman. This explains why he was never really capable of producing a portrait that bore any likeness to his sitter, and I remember that when he was commissioned to paint a life-size portrait of Edna May[10] she complained bitterly about the defective likeness. I went with him to her house or flat, somewhere in the region of Sloane Street, to discuss the matter, and was mortified by her disparaging remarks. He was best at work in which fine draughtsmanship was not so necessary, as for instance in landscapes and urban scenes quickly sketched in water-colour. In this respect he was quite unlike his father, who was a first-class draughtsman. His whole family was, in every sense of the word, *tüchtig*.[11] His eldest sister was a graduate of the Royal Academy of Music, the

---

[10] British actress and singer (1878–1948). — Ed.
[11] Able. — Ed.

next in age was equally gifted as a painter, musician and cook, and the third was a competent musician besides being an excellent linguist.

My parents' constitutions were as disparate as they well could be. My mother, about five feet six inches in height, was supple and fleet, and all her children were born without any difficulty whatsoever. Her bones were gracile, but her general appearance, although always beautiful to me, was less prepossessing than my father's. She wrote a clear firm hand, an accomplishment usually associated with good bodily coordination; she always breathed through her nose; and swam, walked and ate well. Like my father, too, she was naturally abstemious. Her death at the age of sixty-four was, I suspect, the result of the absurd tight-lacing which was the fashion during her youth and middle age.

My father was stiffer and heavier, and just about her height. He was a good walker, swam well and loved the sea. Always well-upholstered, he never in his worst illness looked as thin and bony as I have looked all my life. He had an excellent back (better than my mother's and mine) with no trace of lordosis, yet, strange to say, all his life he was subject to costiveness—an unusual combination of traits. He wrote a pointed hand, much influenced, no doubt, by his early training in a Swiss school. Generally considered handsome, he had what passed for a very becoming aquiline nose but, as there was little in his immediate forebears to account for this comely feature, it is quite possible that it was due chiefly to adenoids. For this affliction often does embellish a face in this way, and the eminent silk D. N. Pritt, who had such a nose, assured me that, although he was originally snub-nosed, adenoids alone had been responsible for his noble Roman profile. Lending some support to this explanation of my father's attractive nose is the fact that he always breathed through his mouth (hence the terrific snoring which shook the house to its foundations and soon led to my mother's having to use a separate bedroom). Another of his infirmities was his perpetual flatulence. Although it never ceased to afford him much amusement, had he, like a high court judge, a magistrate or any public official, been compelled to remain for long spells at a stretch within earshot of his fellows, I cannot think how he could possibly have survived. As a monarch, he would have had no other alternative than to abdicate, and one wonders how many of the royal abdications in history may have been due to this affliction, not excluding those of Emperor Charles V, Christina of Sweden and John Casimir of Poland. His death at the age of seventy-nine from rectal cancer may not have been unconnected with his constant straining at stool and the irritation caused by accumulations of desiccated faecal matter in the colon.[12]

Together with my mother's mental gifts, I, my parents' third child and second son, probably inherited those of her features which made her less good-looking than my father. From her side, with her fifty per cent of Basque blood, I also derived my suppleness of body.

As to type, I am a dark schizothymic leptosome, five feet eight inches in height, and light of build. My nose—none too handsome—and my slightly prognathous lower jaw I got from my mother. My eyes and mouth are my father's, whilst my ears, brow and (mesocephalic) skull are my mother's. I am what Léon MacAuliffe termed 'economically organised,' and am a light engine able to run on small amounts of fuel. Probably because I hail from artistic stock on both sides I am acutely sensitive, and my skin becomes easily inflamed if I am stung by any of God's smaller creatures. This may be due partly to my allergic constitution, for, like Goethe's sister, I have suffered all my life from urticaria.[13]

---

[12] In the 1970 typescript Ludovici sees his father in a much better light, realising that Albert's strikingly good looks matched a noble and dignified personality. Anthony explains that a 'marked Oedipus complex' had prejudiced him against his father and made him abandon a career in art.—Ed.

[13] In the 1970 typescript Ludovici describes himself as having always been fond of women—or, in his own words, 'an inveterate mulierast.' Even so, he regards himself as 'fundamentally an androgyne with many marked feminine traits,' such as an upright forehead, a somewhat high-pitched voice and what he calls his 'tendency to poetical and intrepid mendacity.' Women have been attracted to him, he suggests, because his feminine traits stimulated their heterosexual

I was never eupeptic. As a child I shunned rich cakes and pastries, and the very sight of iced fruit and *marrons glacés* turned my stomach. Thus, although, like Montaigne, 'On a eu en mon enfance, principalement à corriger les refus que je faisais des choses que communement on ayme le mieux en cet age: sucre, confitures, pieces de four,'[14] I was unlike him in never being able to go to stool, as he did regularly, 'au saut du lict.'[15]

Whether owing to my acute sensitiveness, or to my early awareness of my poor physique, I have all my life been pestered with inferiority feelings. On Adlerian grounds I favour the second of the two suggested causes of this condition, and it was certainly my intimate knowledge of it and the result of watching the effects of it in myself that enabled me to recognise its presence in others and assess its influence on their conduct and on modern life in England and western Europe in general. For it ultimately became clear to me that if Adler is right, and I believe he is abundantly so, then, in view of the deplorable prevalence of morbidity and physical defect in millions of modern people, most of my contemporaries must be, like myself, sufferers from this mental infirmity.

My birth on 8th January 1882 is said to have been 'spontaneous'—i.e., it followed an unusually short labour and was uneventful. It occurred about two in the morning whilst my father was on his way to the doctor, and I was received into the world by a sleepy general servant.

As I have already explained, I was my parents' third child and second son. Two more boys and another girl followed me. Coming as we did from parents who, although racially akin, were, like the vast majority of modern couples, morphologically and constitutionally disparate, we six children, like the offspring of all randomly-bred people, were quite unlike one another.

My eldest brother, Albert, grew up to be the tallest, and my

---

and latent homosexual feelings.—Ed.

[14] *Essais*, Book III, Chapter 13: 'Of Experience.' 'In my infancy, what they had most to correct in me was my refusal of things that children usually love best, such as sugar, sweetmeats and marzipans.'—Ed.

[15] *Ibid*. 'Upon leaping out of bed.'—Ed.

eldest sister, Lily, by far the best-looking of the family, for she inherited more of my father's handsome features than any of us. Five of us—all except George, the third son—were mesocephalic like my mother, whilst he, who had inherited my father's brachycephaly, was the most Teutonic-looking of us all.

Very early we tended to form ourselves into clans, and for a while the girls with Edward (the Benjamin) were opposed to George and me. Though when I say 'opposed,' it should not be understood too literally. All it meant was that the two groups thus formed chose different pastimes and different scenes. But this original order soon changed, and, thanks to the common gifts and tastes that united us, Lily and I ultimately became permanently united vis-à-vis of the rest. My eldest brother, Bert, who was three and a half years older than Lily, seemed in the early days so far ahead of us all that insensibly we acquired the habit of not reckoning with him, an attitude that remained with us even after our ages had increased sufficiently to obliterate much of the distance that separated him from us. On this account, he perforce led a comparatively lonely existence. Thrown on the company of any friends he was able to make in the neighbourhood—people who were often strangers to the rest of us—he shared few of our interests, and we were familiar with none of his. These conditions, coupled with the psychological trauma he had suffered when, after three and a half years of bliss as the only child of adoring parents, he was jostled off his little throne by five importunate usurpers, probably caused him much secret unhappiness and may account for the unsteadiness and lack of sound judgement which marked his early business life.

I can remember no occasion, whether in our play or at our work, when we five either expected him to join us or to have a voice in our councils. When, moreover, I recall how tolerant he was in those early days, and how little he used his superior size and strength to domineer over or bully us, or make us pay for our galling invasion of his little realm, I cannot help concluding that he must have been the best-natured of us all. The fact that he was the favourite of our paternal grandparents, our aunts and uncles, and our more intimate friends is certainly a tribute to his character and personal charm, whilst the testimony of those of his friends whom I came across later in life has confirmed my belief that he must have been a good mixer, excellent company and possessed of the sort of nature that flourishes best amid warm human relationships.

It is therefore hardly to be doubted that the lonely path he trod outside the family circle must have been the source of much bitterness and perplexity to one so highly endowed for a cordial and positive relationship to his fellows, and if his early attempts to become self-supporting, in this country at least, ended in failure, it seems highly probable that the peculiar circumstances of his life from the age of four to late adolescence and early manhood were largely to blame. In the treatises on juvenile psychology there is much evidence which confirms this supposition. Besides, was he not the offspring of disparate parents and therefore, like the rest of us, a hybrid with all the conflicts and psychophysical disharmonies of the mongrel? For, as I have already indicated, although our parents were not racially very different, like most couples today their types and forebears were morphologically and constitutionally so disparate that, besides being themselves typological hybrids, their disparity alone could hardly have failed to make their progeny psychophysical mongrels.

This hybridity of the offspring of parents disparate in their stock and type is so constantly overlooked in estimating the quality and character of modern Europeans, and so little account is usually taken of its role in causing unpredictable, if not actually unbalanced, behaviour, that it is as if present-day psychologists and sociologists, despite their expertise, were blind to the influence of biological factors on human conduct.

In all my reading, which on this subject has been extensive, I have come across only one thinker who so much as mentions hybridity as a possible factor accounting for juvenile or adolescent waywardness in modern Europe and America. I refer to that grossly neglected Scandinavian genius, Thorstein Veblen, who in *An Inquiry into the Nature of the Peace*, when discussing the popular motives behind a war policy, refers to 'that appreciable contingent of morally defective citizens that is to be counted on in any hybrid population.'¹⁶ Nor do his other works leave unsupported the claim here made that we—i.e., modern Europeans and our kindred overseas—are a mongrelised population.

Countless travellers and explorers have in the past spoken of the unreliability, obliquity and instability of racial hybrids, and although this point of view is now unfashionable and generally frowned upon, it may be found expressed, and in wholly uncompromising terms even as recently as 1957, in Francis Toye's *Truly Thankful*,¹⁷ a book which on its every page proclaims not only the writer's fair-mindedness but also his absence of xenophobia. But, in considering modern Europeans and their kin all over the globe, not only does nobody except Veblen stress their random breeding, but he is also alone in mentioning as a source of characterological unsteadiness the peculiar hybridity which results from the random mating of people not necessarily different in race, though radically disparate in type and constitution.

Yet when we who belong to this modern hotchpotch of heterogenes, and are members of this population composed of men and women conspicuously different in size, shape, pigmentation, endocrine balance, type, temperament and character—when, I say, we contemplate ourselves and our fellow-beings in the light of the increasing anarchy and disorder of our societies, and recognise our lack of both rigid principles of conduct and of any compelling impulses of rectitude and honour, it is difficult to avoid the conclusion that, even if we may individually escape detection and conviction as the outcome of our inveterate instability, we are all at least potential liars and deceivers. When, moreover, we at last understand that this fundamental lack of character and of ineluctable impulses of steadfastness is due less to defective standards than to the intricate chaos and confusion of our hybrid natures, we appreciate that the disorder resulting from the convergence and amalgam in ourselves of the disparate types and stocks in our ancestry, together with their own corresponding conflict of proclivities, tastes and impulses, probably

---

¹⁶ New York, 1919, Chapter 2.
¹⁷ Chapter 8.

constitutes a determining factor in staging the human world as we find it in our time. For if at the present day we can no longer deny the interdependence and inseparability of bodily and mental attributes, we are compelled to acknowledge that, owing to our hybrid natures and the complex mosaic of discordant mental and bodily features of which we are composed, we are all harlequins of variegated sentiments and motivations, rudderless, unstable, plural- and not single-minded, and therefore prone at any moment and opportunity that offers to go off the rails and, especially if detection seems unlikely, to behave, if not asocially, at least in a manner revealing our indecisive, many-sided constitutions. And this is true of both the so-called 'highest' as well as the 'lowest' of the land.[18]

It will be remembered that, as early as 1891, Herbert Spencer had felt entitled to maintain that 'the system under which we live fosters dishonesty and lying.'[19] Much later on, the Dean of Bristol, speaking in that city, said: 'There is far more dishonesty at the present moment than there ever was before. . . . it was the terrible truth that dishonesty and immorality were rife in Britain.'[20] Dr C. M. Chavasse, Bishop of Rochester, is also reported to have remarked about the same time that 'every section of society is corrupted by an epidemic of dishonesty and by untruthfulness and moral laxity.'[21]

The compilers of that hair-raising treatise, *Our Towns*, declared in 1944: 'Dishonesty is unhappily widespread in our society'[22]; whilst in 1951 Viscountess Milner expressed the belief that 'we have lost our love of truth,' and, after giving examples of mendacity in the so-called upper classes, she added: 'Looking at

---

[18] In the 1970 typescript Ludovici complains that Freud downplays random breeding as a cause of conflicts and disharmonies — an error which accounts for Freud continually having to modify his doctrines and methods and for the relative failure of Freudian psychotherapy. — Ed.

[19] *A Plea for Liberty*, Introduction.

[20] *Daily Mail*, 23rd April 1943.

[21] *Ibid*.

[22] The Hygiene Committee of the Woman's Group in Public Welfare.

all this one wonders whether these are signs of national decay or only of the mortal sickness of a caste.'[23] Two years later, Mr Rowland Thomas, QC, the Marlborough Street magistrate, observed that 'the sense of honesty seems to have passed from a large number of our people,'[24] and twelve months later, Bertrand Russell, writing in the Stockholm newspaper, *Dagens Nyheter*,[25] admitted that he found 'among many people at the present day an indifference to truth,' which he could not but think 'extremely dangerous.'

Can the sense of all this approaching falsity and obliquity have been Renan's reason for remarking over a century ago that 'L'honnêteté est la véritable aristocratie de nos jours'?[26]

I wonder how many people were shocked by a certain passage in Judge Gerald Sparrow's book, *The Great Swindlers*, where, speaking 'after a lifetime spent in the law, either on the Bench or in private practice,' he says: 'Most children are natural thieves ... Small boys usually cease to be thieves at quite an early age; around eight, even earlier. Girls develop much later, and often so great is their individuality, they never really accept the man-made world where the distinction between my property and yours — and that of the state — is sharply drawn. The majority of women, even adult women, will steal if given the opportunity.'[27]

That a sense of humour and laughter should be respectively the quality and social expression of choice in present-day society, especially in England and America, is therefore not surprising, particularly when we reflect that, of all expressions of feeling, laughter is the most easily counterfeited. On that account alone it is the expression most likely to be favoured by any fundamentally dishonest, insincere and mendacious generation. Even the peculiar staccato notes of laughter lend themselves to

---

[23] *My Picture Gallery*, 1951, Chapter 30.
[24] *News of the World*, 21st June 1953.
[25] 9th November 1954.
[26] *Essais de moral et de critique*, 1859. 'Honesty is the true aristocracy of our time.' — Ed.
[27] 1959, Chapter 23. I write this in 1961.

faultless imitation by the least competent of actors, and no frequenter of cocktail parties can fail to have noticed this.

In order to understand the great change that has overtaken our society in this respect, it is only necessary to look at the photographs of leading personalities of the nineteenth century and compare them with the photographs of similarly ranking people of the present day. The contrast is striking.

In the nineteenth-century photographs, whether of merely popular figures, leading politicians or royal personages, we behold an unbroken sequence of placid, uncontorted faces, all expressing an air of dignified composure. In the photographs of the later period, on the other hand, especially in those belonging to the decades following the death of Edward VII, we see no face that is not broadly smiling or actually distorted with laughter. The Prime Minister photographed with a colleague is always seen in the throes of enjoying an immensely funny joke. Lord Morrison, or any other member of the Labour Party, cannot stand beside Mr Gaitskell without both of them looking as if they were discussing something uproariously amusing. Every member of the Royal Family feels it *de rigueur* to look as if life and the world at large were irresistibly comic. If we may assume that a broad smile and a prompt gust of laughter are now among the public duties of royalty, they certainly perform these duties with impressive regularity, although in this they may be wholly outclassed by President Eisenhower, who seems never to have been photographed except when convulsed with laughter.

All the lesser folk follow suit, and although much of this resolute merriment, especially among models, film stars, actors and actresses, may be due to dental pride—or what Madame de Cambis wittily described as 'une gaieté de jolies dents,'[28] when she heard people praising Madame de Genlis' good cheer—it indicates a significant contrast between the people of the two periods. For widespread pride over a good physical feature suggests its rarity, rather than its prevalence.

At all events, we do not need to be aware of the various reasons for the marked changes in our society during the last fifty

---

[28] 'A cheerfulness of pretty teeth.'—Ed.

years in order, when contemplating a photograph of Queen Victoria, Edward VII, George V, Kipling, Gladstone, Joseph Chamberlain or Henry Irving, to feel some difficulty in imagining them laughing into the camera, or even smiling broadly at it. And if we ponder why we feel this way about it and why as a matter of a fact we should be slightly shocked if such people were represented as having just listened to some exceptionally amusing anecdote, we may reach interesting conclusions concerning our own epoch, especially if we bear in mind that, of all expressions of the emotions, laughter is the most easily and convincingly feigned and counterfeited.

At all events, it is extraordinarily significant that this modern addiction to resolute hilarity at all costs should have remained uninfluenced by the almost universal toothlessness of all classes of the population in England, from teenagers upwards. For nowadays all English people display their false teeth with just as much assurance and aplomb as Madame de Genlis did with her own excellent natural dentition.

To return to my family, in my elder brother's case, besides all the fatal consequences of a hybrid nature, there was also, as I have suggested, the psychological trauma caused by his dethronement from the place of honour and supremacy in the family. Thus, it was only when he went abroad and had to suffer the hard discipline of adversity and privation that he ultimately made good and was able to rear a family in decent comfort.

His gruesome end as a victim of general paralysis of the insane at the age of thirty-five was the result of a venereal infection contracted after he had left England, and was a cruel aggravation of the hardships that exile had already inflicted upon him. But it was only long afterwards, by eventually piecing together the circumstances of his sad life and recognising the extent to which he had been wronged by conditions no-one could have foreseen or prevented, that I deplored having done nothing to mitigate the dangerous emotional aridity of his lot. For he was a creature of ardent sensibilities whose heart expanded to every fellow-being, and his inability to find complete adaptation for his affections in the bosom of his family must have been a serious blow to him. Truth to tell, I alone could hardly have done much to relieve his lot, but nothing seems to have been done by any of us, including the senior members of the family. He was the third close relative whose death-agony I had the unhappiness to witness, and I cannot forget the harrowing spectacle of one succumbing to general paralysis of the insane.

* * *

My elder sister Lily was never a lonely figure. Always the centre of every family gathering, no programme, whether of work or play, could ever be thought of in which she did not take a prominent part. Owing to our common interests and tastes, she and I naturally gravitated towards each other comparatively early in life and, as we two alone inherited our parents' literary and artistic gifts, we were united in an unusually close and satisfying partnership. The others, not blind to the bonds that held us together, and aware of the powerful influence our early performances in art and literature exerted over the elders of the family, looked on us rather as backbenchers probably look on their party leaders. This was bound to be so, because, in view of the negligible role played by our eldest brother, we were the virtual chieftains among the siblings and insensibly acquired all the privileges and prestige of our position. It became important to secure our backing for any scheme or project our juniors had in mind, and even more indispensable was our support if any conflict arose between them and our parents. Even their pleasures and recreations were to some extent dependent on us; nor do I think we often failed them in this form of leadership. We were always ready for any kind of spree or frolic, and we two, together with my mother, were for many years the *boute-en-train*[29] of the household, the acknowledged *Ton-Angeber*,[30] and what we proposed or devised, because it was usually known to be rewarding, was always accepted without demur.

Lily was a sensitive, passionate girl who, according to the English standards of the time, developed precociously. At thir-

---

[29] The life and the soul of a party. — Ed.
[30] Tone-setters. — Ed.

teen she was exceptionally mature in body and mind, and Egan Mew, a minor poet of the day, was already giving her encouragement in her early attempts at versification. As is not unusual with young women of her type, the very ardour of her sensibilities forced upon her a habit of secrecy and reserve which successfully misled everyone in her circle. Thus, from her fourteenth year onwards, few of us, least of all her parents, uncles and aunts, had any inkling of the fires she tried daily to damp down in her innermost being. They could not guess what terrific storms probably raged in her breast when she met a youth who attracted her, or witnessed a scene which bore in any way on a problem with which she happened to be wrestling at the time. She read a great number of English and French books and, like me, was particularly fond of listening to my mother reading to us aloud. Nor in this connection can I forget some of Amélie Perronet's poetry, which my mother always read with so much feeling that Lily and I would often be utterly shattered before the last verses were reached. And when I point out that all this poet's poems were known to us, besides many by Victor Hugo, through having heard them again and again, the fact that they hardly ever failed in their effect, and that we were always ready to be once more subjected to their spell, is at once a tribute to my mother's dramatic skill, for she was a born actress, and an indication that as children and adolescents Lily and I must have been voluptuaries of emotional excitement. I recall one particularly poignant poem by Amélie Perronet, 'Comment on devient brave,' which always left all three of us broken-hearted and bathed in tears, and my mother's reading of *La dame aux camélias* had the same effect.

As already explained, Lily developed early, or certainly at an age which in England of the late nineteenth century was considered so. Although at fourteen she was still a schoolgirl, she was also a young woman, and in this dual role was moved by many deeply conflicting impulses. Today, owing to the universal overfeeding of the children of all classes, this precocity, especially in the female, is a commonplace—a fact which pours ridicule on the recent agitation fomented by ignorant Labour romantics for the extension of the school-leaving age,[31] for, even as things are, the school-leaving age for girls is absurdly late. One has only to stand at the gates of any girls' school at the dinner-hour in order to note the high percentage of mature, if not matronly, figures among the senior girls, in order to be satisfied on this point. Even a medieval English spectator would have to laugh, let alone an ancient Greek or Roman. Yet it is really no laughing-matter, because the anomalies created by the situation may, and often do, have tragic consequences. As a park-keeper said to me, not so very long ago, 'If they do extend the school-leaving age, it will simply mean that most senior girls will go to school pregnant.'

The world says 'child' and acts accordingly, whilst Nature, more realistically, says 'woman,' and the so-called child, subconsciously sensing her nubility, acts with a determination that shocks and alarms her deluded elders. Society, especially when prompted by puritanical prejudices, tries by every means in its power to prolong what it believes to be the 'innocent' and halcyon period of immaturity, and the extension of the school-leaving age is but one of these means. But the effort is romantic and wasteful, because the importunate impulses of Nature in the more normally-endowed girls, at a time when, as we have been assured, sexual appetite is at its zenith, render concentration and application in the classroom, if not actually impossible, at least difficult.

At all events, this was the situation in which my sister Lily found herself at the age of fourteen, and I cannot help suspecting that it was her condition at that time — together with the intense reserve which it induced her to maintain, rather than his deliberate callousness — that made the young man who was the major influence in her life miscalculate the effect of his behaviour. For although a casual observer might have got the impression that he was exerting himself unduly to attract her, he was after all behaving in exactly the same way to every one of us. He was the Pied Piper of our family. Boys and girls alike, we were all devoted to him, and only in my sister Lily did this attitude acquire an

---

[31] I am writing in 1961.

awkwardly passionate character.

At any rate, happy and cloudless as her life had been up to her fourteenth birthday, from about that time until her death four and a half years later an ominous change came over her which, gradual though it may have been, was soon noticeable enough to cause us grave alarm. For a long while, however, only my mother was aware of the severe blow that had initiated Lily's decline.

It is my belief that the young man, who was about ten years her senior, either misunderstood the nature of her attachment or else — what amounts to the same thing — failed to allow for the fact that she was no longer a child. It is a very common error, especially in England, where the whole of the public bias favours this sort of misconception about female adolescents. My mother, who claimed to have probed the affair to the bottom, thought differently. She believed that prompted by vanity — and the young man in question was certainly vain — the object of my sister's affection had been too glad to bask in the flattering warmth of her fierce adolescent infatuation to dream of discouraging her, and had too late appreciated the conflagration he had kindled. One circumstance, which I shall relate in due course, lends some colour of probability to this explanation, for the young man's most unwise and ultimate action seems to indicate that he wished to measure and taste to the full the ardour he had managed to inspire.

The gentleman in question was Frederick Hobday, Professor of Materia Medica and Therapeutics at The Royal Veterinary College, Camden Town, the future Dean of the institution, who subsequently became famous and was knighted. He was a good-looking, most engaging and in many respects brilliant young fellow, excellent company and an enchanting entertainer. We all adored him. Whenever he called upon us, he used to come armed with some fresh trick or hoax, and, as he always managed to persuade us that his new so-called experiment involved a startling scientific phenomenon, we were invariably taken in and thoroughly enjoyed his joke at our expense. One such experiment consisted in our being invited to watch the blood course through a strand of human hair. A large basin full of water was produced, and in it Lily was asked to drop a hair from her head. Then, the moment all five of us were eagerly bent over the basin, trying our hardest to discern the flow of blood through Lily's hair, Hobday would plunge his two hands into the basin and smother us with water.

He often came in the evening and would then join us in taking down the French dictations my mother was in the habit of giving us. His French improved greatly under her tuition, and there was always intense excitement when Lily, he and I passed up our exercise-books to my mother to be corrected. The number of his mistakes dropped to a figure so alarmingly near our own that Lily and I, who rather prided ourselves on our proficiency, began to grow anxious about a rivalry which at first we had imagined we could safely scorn. As, moreover, he was not the sort of person to miss such a chance of chaffing us, these evening dictations soon became most thrilling competitions, more especially as his scientific training gave him advantages which Lily and I thought rather unfair. Any medical term that happened to occur in a passage my mother dictated was, owing to the international uniformity of most learned terms, generally known to him, although to Lily and me it might be completely unknown, and I recall one dictation containing the word 'torticollis' which, while it delighted him, left us utterly baffled. The more we protested, however, the more he hooted with joy, and my mother, crying with laughter, had to put down her book and wait for the storm to abate.

Meanwhile, unbeknown to us all, Lily must have been growing more and more infatuated. I was, perhaps quite naturally, unaware of what should have been obvious to any experienced observer not obsessed with the idea that childhood extends to the thirties or thereabouts. Yet even my mother and father, probably deluded by the rollicking mood that prevailed whenever Hobday was with us, never suspected the truth until it was too late to do anything about it. Whether, when Lily and Hobday were alone together, he gave her any encouragement, led her to hope that she might one day be his wife, or ever went so far as to kiss her, none of us knew. Fond as I was of her, and prone to pangs of jealousy at any challenge to my prescriptive right to come first in her affections, I should have been quick to resent any undue familiarity on Hobday's part. On the other hand, like the others, I was so much inclined to overlook any unconventional behaviour where he was concerned that I may well have failed to notice what in any other man would have given me umbrage. In 1894, for instance, when he followed us down to Hythe, where we went for our summer holidays, he and Lily must have had many opportunities for private walks and talks. But even if they made abundant use of them, I can think of no occasion when Hobday's immense popularity with my father's female art-pupils on that holiday appeared to cause my sister any visible grief or anxiety. If it did, her habitual reserve successfully concealed the fact.

At all events, to cut a long story short, one evening, whether late in 1894 or early in 1895, Hobday called on us and, during a few minutes spent alone with Lily, showed her an engagement-ring he had just bought and asked what she thought of it. Apparently, or so my mother subsequently maintained, Lily's heart leapt for joy. Instantly inferring that the ring must be meant for her, she was speechless with delight. Her ecstasy was, however, short-lived, for to her consternation Hobday hastened to explain that the ring was intended for the widow of an old veterinary friend of his in Herefordshire, whom he was going to marry. Lily, who, like the rest of us, had never heard of this widow, or of his wish to settle down, strove her utmost to conceal the shock these tidings caused her and, struggling to dissemble her disillusionment, contrived to stammer a few incoherent words of congratulation. But the wound she had been given only sank the more deeply for being nursed in secret. In any case, from that day to the hour of her death in 1899 her health steadily declined. She ceased to take any interest in life, and the youths who subsequently tried to court her, among whom were a Frenchman, Louis Lamotte, who was by way of being some sort of cousin, and an Englishman named Frank Hopkins, ultimately withdrew, estranged by what they took to be her natural frigidity.

Apparently, for months after that last interview with Hobday she cried herself to sleep every night, and by the middle of 1897, when our family doctor diagnosed disquieting symptoms in her lungs, she was already doomed, for in those days artificial pneumothorax was unknown and very little could be done in such cases. She certainly spent several months at a sanatorium for consumptives at Woking. But it was all to no purpose. Her health continued to deteriorate steadily, and in the autumn of 1898 she had to be confined to bed. In December of that year, and throughout January 1899, recurrent attacks of haemorrhage warned us of the approaching end, and my mother and I were panic-stricken. We took it in turns to attend her at night, and I can never forget the torture of having for weeks on end to be the constant witness of the slow dissolution of one so attractive and deeply loved.

I had earned a little money by illustrating a book of nonsense verses by Lord Alfred Douglas,[32] and I remember with what tremendous pleasure I managed to obtain in early January a basket of strawberries, which I brought to Lily's bedside. (The shop in which I had seen them exposed was, I believe, in Bond Street.) I also remember that, unbeknown to my mother and father, I paid a call on the young chest specialist in Harley Street who had been called into consultation about the case by our doctor. (I seem to recall that his name was Robinson or Rawlinson.) I implored him to try to do something to spare us the calamity that threatened and to mobilise all the resources of medicine to save my sister. But he assured me that there was nothing that could then be done, and he held out no hope of a recovery.

In those days, apart from the open-air treatment given at the various sanatoria for consumptives, there was no known remedy for pulmonary tuberculosis. Nowadays, the collapsing of a lung in the early stages of the disease often leads to a complete cure.

At all events, on the evening of 13th February 1899 a rather extraordinary thing occurred—a phenomenon which has puzzled me ever since and inclined me willy-nilly to lend, if not a wholly credulous, at least a willing ear to any account of an occult happening. I was sitting alone in the breakfast-room on

---

[32] The Belgian Hare [Lord Alfred Douglas], *The Duke of Berwick: A Nonsense Rhyme*, London, 1899. — Ed.

the ground floor of our house, engaged in writing a one-act playlet which I proposed to offer to the headmaster of our school for one of the items in his next winter's prize-giving entertainment, and, although I was only seventeen at the time, I can remember all the circumstances as if they had happened yesterday. Suddenly, I heard quite distinctly a curiously faint piping sound, as of a distant muted violin. It seemed to rise from under the boards of the floor and persisted long enough to command attention. Had it been but momentary, I should have assumed that it was negligible—possibly some transient effect of the blood circulating in my ears. It was only when, to my astonishment, it lasted and left me in no possible doubt as to its external reality that I laid down my pen to listen intently and to try to think what it could possibly be. I could not today give a musician any idea of the very few notes composing the sort of piping whine that broke the stillness of the room; all I can say is that the feeble voice sang in long-sustained breves or semibreves and more or less in a monotone. Being quite conscious and fully aware that no obvious explanation could be found for the phenomenon, I naturally felt rather scared, and as the voice continued in fits and starts, as if pausing for breath, I racked my brains to think of some means of accounting for it. Ultimately, it struck me that I had heard from my nurses or from our maid-servants the old wives' tale about singing mice and the tragic events their vocal efforts usually portended, and as I naturally associated this memory with the calamity that was awaiting us upstairs I wondered whether I could reasonably connect my strange experience with the disaster we were all most dreading. All my inveterate scepticism boggled at the idea, for even then I was already inclined to scorn superstitious beliefs, especially when their source was illiterate young women. However, I was too deeply stirred by the undeniable reality of the sounds to which I had been listening to dismiss lightly the possibility of their possessing some obscure significance. What, therefore, if the legend were true and the significance consisted of a warning of death? Quickly gathering up my papers and turning down the gas, I therefore left the room and hurried upstairs in search of my mother, for, although I was still not wholly convinced that I had not been deluded, I decided that it was my duty to mention my fears to her. I knew that she would be anxious to take a last farewell of Lily, and I could never have forgiven myself if, by scorning the premonition I had so mysteriously received, I had failed to give her the chance of this last leave-taking.

I found her, as I expected, in Lily's bedroom, and, beckoning to her to come to the door, I told her without explaining why I very much feared that Lily's end must be near and would probably occur that night. If, therefore, she wished to say anything to her and bid her good-bye, there was no time to lose. She made not the slightest attempt to question my warning or to ask me to explain it. On the contrary, although terrified and broken-hearted, she accepted it unhesitatingly, and together we went to stand by Lily's bedside. It was then a little after ten o'clock, and we each said all we had to say to Lily. Although she uttered only an occasional whispered word, I believe she heard and understood most of what we said to her. Soon after eleven, my mother asked me to fetch my father, and shortly afterwards all of us, including my two younger brothers and our two maid-servants, were standing at Lily's bedside waiting in silence for the end, which came a little after midnight.

I used certain main features of her life story in constructing the plot of my first novel, *Mansel Fellowes*, published nineteen years later, but as Hobday was then still living, and had meanwhile become well-known, I made considerable alterations in the circumstances in order to make any identification of the characters difficult. Never since that unhappy night, however, have I been able to obtain any explanation of the strange phenomenon which I appear to have interpreted correctly, or to come across any trustworthy person who has had a similar experience. Yet I cannot believe that it was all purely imaginary.

Unlike my mother, I was never convinced that Hobday had acted with deliberate heartlessness, although one or two facts seem to favour her point of view. For instance, in spite of his long and very intimate connection with our family, he ceased entirely from visiting us after the day when he showed Lily that engagement-ring, and in his autobiography[33] there is no mention of his close association with us or of Lily and her tragic end. These omissions may have a perfectly innocent explanation, but certain facts connected with his behaviour as Dean of the college, which many years later were reported to me by a veterinary friend, are not inconsistent with the view that in his relations with the female sex he tended to display weaknesses which, although never actually immoral, indicated a nature prone to take pleasure in feminine adulation.

Be this as it may, if he really was guilty of trifling with a girl whose passionate nature could ill survive the disappointment he ultimately caused her, it certainly brought him little luck. For the first child — a daughter, I believe — his wife bore him was either a congenital cripple or in some way gravely incapacitated, and my mother never doubted but what this was a heavenly judgement.

* * *

Before concentrating on my own career, which, as that of the third child, should properly be related here, I will now as briefly as possible dispose of the lives of my brothers and sisters who came after me — namely, George, born on the 22nd of May 1884, Dorothy (Dolly), born on the 10th of May 1886, and Edward, born on the 21st of June 1887.

George, slightly taller and bigger-boned than I am, grew into a robust type inclined to plumpness, and is the only one of us six children who inherited my father's brachycephalic Teutonic head. Neither a particularly good scholar nor much given to studious pastimes, he was not without aesthetic and literary interests, although quite early he showed a *terre à terre* or ultra-practical turn of mind by objecting to being beguiled by romances such as Dumas' *Comte de Monte Cristo* into sharing the tribulations and miseries of some hero of fiction, only to enjoy the ultimate triumph of his virtue and nobility in the sequel. Anticipating the author's intention of lacerating the reader's feelings

---

[33] Sir Frederick Hobday, *Fifty Years a Veterinary Surgeon*, London, 1938. — Ed.

simply in order to relieve them in the final chapters, George preferred not to undergo the gratuitous torment and to take the happy ending for granted. To Lily and me, who had always listened with rapt attention to my mother's reading of this very story, George's attitude seemed decidedly odd. But it was in keeping with his essentially practical nature, which had stronger affinities with the shrewd farming and commercial, than with the artistic, strains in our ancestry, whilst his singular skill at games such as draughts and his precocious flair for good business were all part of the same inheritance.

Despite defective schooling, he was successful in his business career, was able to retire fairly early in life possessed of comfortable private means, and throughout his business and married life displayed many solid and steady qualities. Of us all, he was perhaps the most happily integrated and the least affected by the conflicts and disharmonies incidental to a disparate parentage. This lent him a steadfastness and single-mindedness which, quite properly, the world ascribes to strength of character, and his long and successful business career in the employment of only two firms, to the latter of which he transferred comparatively early only to improve himself, bears out this estimation of his personality. Without any brilliance, but endowed with sound judgement, he always contrived to please those about him, chiefly because, being well-pleased with himself, he was always urbane, affable and gracious.

He married a fairly well-to-do widow, fourteen years his senior and the daughter of wholly plebeian parents. Although masterful and self-centred, she was inclined, as so many Englishwomen are, to stress the need of 'unselfishness' in others, especially in those composing her immediate circle. Nevertheless, George seemed to be very happy with her, probably, as I always thought, because of a slight strain of masochism in his constitution. He cheerfully complied with her every wish, and anyone who could have suspected him of chafing under her dominion would have confessed himself an untrustworthy reader of the human heart.

She died in July 1948. For months before her death she had been totally incapacitated, and I understand that George had, as long as was humanly possible, attended to her wants himself. They had no children; nor, indeed, in view of her age at the time of her second marriage, could any have been expected.[34]

*　*　*

As my younger sister Dolly was not quite eight years old when she died on 3rd March 1894, there is not much to record either about her life or character. There were indications that her tastes and gifts, like her looks, leaned more towards her mother's than her father's side of the family, while her bright sunny nature made her a favourite with us all. I cannot recall that she was ever seriously ill, and her lithe active little body inclined her to take part in all our outdoor pastimes with a gusto that argued both health and stamina. Like the rest of us, she was bilingual and could read English and French with equal dexterity. Truth to tell, however, and deplorable as it may seem, at the present moment — that is to say, in May 1960 — my most vivid recollection of her is connected with the circumstances of her sudden and tragic end, the unforgettable horror of which has, perhaps not unnaturally, dimmed, if not blotted out, all my less sensational memories of her.

It was about six o'clock on the evening of 3rd March 1894 when, just as my mother was on the point of handing me a warm towel to dry myself after a bath, to our great surprise Dolly came running into the bathroom, her mouth agape, and pointing desperately to her throat. She had an agonized expression and stood imploringly before my mother.

'Qu'y-a-t'il? Qu'est-ce qu'il y a?'[35] cried my mother frantically, for, apart from the sinister significance of Dolly's irregular invasion of the bathroom at such a moment, her muteness and anxious gesticulations were terrifying.

The poor child continued to point to her throat, and there was a look of such despair in her face that my mother and I were frozen with dread.

---

[34] In the 1970 typescript Ludovici records that George died from cancer of the larynx on 6th February 1967. — Ed.

[35] 'What do you have there? What's there?' — Ed.

'Mais qu'est-ce qu'il y a, ma Dollée, qu'est-ce qu'il y a?'[36] cried my unfortunate mother, taking Dolly in her arms and trying to look down her throat.

In the extremity of my alarm, forgetting all about my towel and that I was still wet and completely naked, I stood up in the bath and for a few moments watched the most bloodcurdling scene it has ever been my lot to witness. For, unable to obtain any enlightenment from Dolly, who was obviously growing weaker every moment, my mother had started exploring the poor child's throat with her finger and was meanwhile calling for help. Our French maid, Julie, startled by the sound of my mother's cries, dashed into the room, and I can still hear the distracted and quite futile appeals she addressed to Dolly, when once she thought she had grasped what had happened.

'Crache, ma Dollée! Crache!'[37] she repeated. But, alas, that was not the remedy. No amount of spitting, even if Dolly had been capable of it, could have saved her then.

At that late stage in the poor child's struggles there is not the slightest doubt that she could still have been saved, if only one of us had known the right, the only sensible, thing to do. But none of us did know, and Julie's repeated exhortations, as if stifled by the sickening evidence of their futility, died down, leaving the three of us in utter consternation.

Only a few seconds later, to our horror, the poor little girl lay limp and motionless in my mother's arms. I leaped from the bath and, seizing my towel, dashed out of the room and on to the landing of our first floor and started shouting to the walls of the house all kinds of useless and quite irrational instructions, among them, if you please, an appeal for some emetic. As if that could have helped! But I was only twelve at the time.

Our cook, wondering what the uproar was about, came hurrying upstairs and was instantly sent in search of a doctor, although it must have been fairly plain to both my mother and Julie that it was then already too late.

The two of them carried Dolly into the room adjoining the

---

[36] 'But what's there, Dolly, what's there?' — Ed.
[37] 'Spit, Dolly! Spit!' — Ed.

bathroom and laid her on a bed. She was lifeless, and my mother, still completely mystified, yet hoping against hope that something must remain to be done, was distractedly attempting to rouse the child by slapping her hands, shaking her and lifting her body into a sitting posture.

At last the doctor arrived. He was not our family physician, but an old retired army surgeon who lived a few doors away. He pronounced Dolly dead, and my mother, Julie and I heard the words as if they betokened our own doom.

I have often wondered since, whether even at that late moment Dolly might not have been saved, if only the proper first-aid expedients had been tried, followed by persevering efforts to apply artificial respiration. But the trouble was that nobody knew exactly what had happened, and, what was equally unfortunate, none of us attempted to act on the promptings of a shrewd guess.

This certainly proved to be the cruellest experience of my whole life, for, although Lily's and my mother's deaths left me disconsolate, there was in Dolly's tragic end a note of such baffled helplessness and ineptitude in the presence of a young healthy life rapidly reaching dissolution, and the terror was concentrated into such a brief space, that no nightmare could have proved more horrifying.

The post-mortem examination, by revealing the cause of death, added to our misery, for we learnt from the findings not only that it would have been possible to save the poor child, but also that to do so would have been well within the power of either my mother or Julie alone, not to speak of the two together. All they need to have done would have been to grasp Dolly by the ankles and suspend her head downwards, while at the same time administering a few sharp slaps to her back. This would have expelled the object that had become lodged in her trachea and she would have rapidly recovered.

And what was the obstruction?

It proved to be part of a most unwise child's toy, which in those days was not infrequently found in a Christmas cracker and consisted of the short wooden mouthpiece belonging to a small bladder which, when blown out and allowed to deflate, caused a whining sound that was supposed to please the child who played with it. As must often have happened in other families, this mouthpiece had through long use become separated from the bladder, and Dolly, in order to produce the whine in question, had evidently placed the vocal stem to her lips and inhaled as she did so, for it was this wooden mouthpiece that was found in her trachea by the doctor who conducted the autopsy.

The whole catastrophe should have been widely publicised as a warning to parents. In any case, it left my mother convinced that no young couple should think themselves entitled to rear a family who had not first acquired an elementary knowledge of first-aid to the injured. Yet to this day, I believe, it is still considered more essential for engaged couples to receive religious instruction than to be initiated into the elements of first-aid.

A day or two after the post-mortem, Dolly was buried in Highgate cemetery and my mother chose for her epitaph the following four lines from Malherbe's 'Consolation à M. du Périer':

> ... elle était du monde où les plus belles choses
> Ont le pire destin;
> Et rose elle a vécu ce que vivent les roses,
> L'espace d'un matin.[38]

* * *

My youngest brother, Edward, born on 21st June 1887, was, I believe, the most Gallic, if not altogether the most foreign, of us all. He lived to the age of sixty-six, and yet, although married to an English wife and in business in London from the time he left school, he never spoke English with a perfectly native accent. There was always a marked thickness, a *grasseyement*, about his r's which proclaimed him a stranger in the land of his birth. He was the most Gallic of us all also in other respects, for he was a typical *bon viveur* of the Paris boulevards, inclined to be slightly

---

[38] '... she was of the world where the fairest things / Have the worst fate; / And like a rose she has lived as long as roses live, / The space of one morning.' — Ed.

Rabelaisian in his conversation and jokes, and, whilst generally amoral in outlook, displaying the *désinvolture*[39] and unburdened conscience of which only born Latins are capable. He had, too, the natural Gallic gift of quick and often witty repartee, and his high spirits, combined with the qualities of a good mixer, made him popular wherever he went. When I say he was amoral in outlook, that is not to say that he was in any sense unscrupulous or reckless, for his surprising success in a class of commerce in which the utmost integrity is expected in all those who are engaged in it argues, on the contrary, a character essentially steady and reliable. But it does mean that he was not his own best friend, for his generally unwise way of life and his devotion to conviviality often shocked me. His relatively early end was, to an extent imperfectly appreciated by his family and not at all by himself, certainly due to his intemperate habits. Not that he was an alcoholic or a womaniser. He was simply a great lover of life and of *bonne chère*,[40] and, if he paid the penalty for these dangerous tastes, at least he enjoyed his life to the full.

He was my favourite brother, and, although he remained strangely illiterate to the end of his days, he was perhaps the only surviving member of my family who took an interest in my lighter literary work. He was particularly fond of my novel, *The Taming of Don Juan*, for instance, and always showed me the most touching deference. Yet I was never able to exert the least influence over him, and it is typical of our relationship that, although he was well aware of my anti-Christian attitude, and knew me too well to suppose that I had not the most serious grounds for it, he himself, like the characteristic Frenchman that he was, and in spite of his extreme worldliness, remained loyal to the Church of his ancestors, brought up his children as Catholics and prevailed upon his wife to become a member of the Holy Catholic Church.

When I say that he was strangely illiterate, I should not like it to be inferred that, for his particular calling and compared with business competitors, he was in any sense handicapped. On the

---

[39] Casual manner. — Ed.
[40] Fine cuisine. — Ed.

contrary, his good knowledge of French gave him an advantage which many of his colleagues and commercial rivals probably envied. It may even be said that it gave him also a cultural advantage over them, for, although he spoke French only with limited fluency and correctness, he understood it perfectly and was therefore often selected for business journeys abroad, which must have widened his knowledge both of men and of life in general. For, by a curious freak of atavism, he had chosen for his career precisely the trade in which his maternal grandfather had distinguished himself—jewellery, a class of commerce in which the French notoriously hold the lead.

I need hardly say that women easily fell for him, and I cannot doubt but what his business success may have been in great part due to the facility with which he won the confidence, if not the attachment, of his female customers. He had what is known as 'a way with him,' and it is not therefore surprising that the charm he exerted extended even to men. One or two fabulously wealthy Indian princes were his devoted friends, and men like Hatry[41] would not buy their more expensive presents from anyone else.

He had early warnings of his unsatisfactory physical condition, and cannot have been more than fifty when he already began to have disturbed nights and to complain of being unable to sleep after four or five in the morning. Headaches were also frequent, and, as is commonly the case nowadays, these premonitory signs were consistently overlooked or misinterpreted. Instead of calling his attention to his imprudent habits, and prompting modifications in his regime, they were ascribed to business preoccupations and excessive mental activity, and he continued to live as before, without any attempt to mend his ways.

These misunderstandings of middle-age disorders are so universal today that Edward could hardly be charged with eccentricity for being guilty of them. The man or woman who lies awake during the night, or wakes up long before the dawn and

---

[41] Presumably, the infamous English financier Clarence Hatry, jailed for forging securities in 1929. —Ed.

is unable to fall asleep again, naturally tends during the hours of wakefulness to dwell on domestic, business or professional problems, and when this happens it is easy to mistake the thoughts thus occupying the mind for the cause, instead of the consequence, of the wakefulness. Indeed, doctors often encourage this sort of error, for modern people prefer to hear that their brain is 'too active,' rather than that they have plied their knife and fork too assiduously. What is more, whilst most people will listen without impatience to a diagnosis that impugns only their mental habits, they less easily tolerate any advice that threatens to interfere with their gastronomical pleasures.

Thus, sedatives and even narcotics are often administered when the only sound and effective procedure would be to tell the patient that there is probably some grave disproportion between his feeding habits and the amount of exercise and fresh air he is able to enjoy. On the same principle, headaches, which if not caused by eye trouble or blood pressure are usually the result of intemperance either in drink or diet, are nowadays too often treated by the sufferer himself or herself with self-apportioned doses of aspirin or some popular analgesic, whilst the unwise regimen probably answerable for the morbid symptom is persisted in without any attempt at salutary reforms. Indeed, I know of whole districts in rural England where no shopgirl, setting off for her work in the morning, dreams of leaving home without arming herself with a bottle of Aspro or aspirin tablets.

I am afraid my poor brother was guilty of all these deplorable practices, and with the inevitable result. His health steadily deteriorated soon after he had reached his middle fifties. For some years before he was actually incapacitated he was receiving daily injections of insulin for his diabetes, and very soon his heart also began to cause trouble. The faulty circulation of blood in his legs gave rise to disquieting symptoms if ever his feet suffered any abrasion or wound, and not long after he had to leave his work he was sent to King's College Hospital for treatment. There he remained for some time. They amputated one of his legs, but this prolonged his life for only a month or two, and it was whilst performing the exercises intended to accustom him to the use of the artificial limb that was being prepared for him that he ultimately collapsed at 6.15 pm on Wednesday, 13th January 1954.

He remained jolly and witty to the end, and shortly before his death was joking with the sister who was superintending his exercises. His resilience and high spirits, by endearing him to the doctors and nursing staff of the hospital, were doubtless instrumental in procuring him much happiness during his last months of life, although I always felt that his complete ignorance of the very elements of medicine and pathology, in mercifully blinding him to the gravity of his plight, was also a major factor in sustaining his courage and preserving his cheerfulness.

My Mother

My earliest clear memory is of a disordered ground-floor room, the garden doors of which were screened by folding wooden shutters, securely closed and fastened. Furniture, books, rolled carpets, crockery of all kinds, fenders and cushions were lying higgledy-piggledy all about, and it was late evening. I was four years old, and my mother, who had me on her lap, was taking sips from a cup of freshly brewed tea. We had just moved into a new house in the northwest of London, and my brother George was then the youngest of the family. He must have been two years old at the time, and I seem to remember that he was sitting on my father's knee.

Why was he not on my mother's lap? As the Benjamin, this was his prescriptive right. But, as it was in the beginning, so it was to be until the end. I was my mother's boy, and from that evening to the day twenty-eight years later, when I was the last to see her alive, I was the one member of the family who spent most time in her company and whose existence was most closely interwoven with hers. We were rarely separated, and even when circumstances forced us for a while asunder it was a necessity of our lives to keep in almost daily touch. As soon as I was old enough I accompanied her on her outings, especially to the shops. When my head could hardly have reached halfway above a shop-counter she accustomed me to stay behind to spell out our outlandish name and give our address to the shop-assistants, whilst she sailed majestically on to another department of the store to place further orders

The store she chiefly patronized was James Shoolbred's in the Tottenham Court Road, and it was there that I first learnt one or two things about our family and the character of English people which remained indelibly imprinted on my mind. To begin with, I had it deeply impressed upon me that we were a queer people with an odd name that no-one seemed to like and which was a perpetual source of difficulty. Thus, early in life I felt our position in England was in some way different from that of the natives. Only my mother's calm assumption that the shop-men owed us the same attention as they owed other customers reassured me on the score of our conformity. I was deeply interested in observing the fluster and embarrassment which my mother's departure from a counter invariably provoked in the assistant who had been attending to her. For there was in those days, and still is today, in spite of the hundreds of thousands of refugees from all corners of the globe that have meanwhile been foisted on the population, a formidable barrier in the minds of all English shop-assistants of both sexes against any name less familiar than Jones, Smith or Brown. The consequence was that, at the mere sound of any name they had never heard before, they showed every symptom of extreme panic. I remember one assistant in particular at the Normandy butter-counter who became strangely agitated when the moment arrived for me to spell out our name and give our address.

Faced with having to choose one of her six children to accompany her on a visit or any other outing, the chances were strongly in favour of her selecting me, or at most Lily and me. Thus our circle of friends grew so used to seeing us together that insensibly we came to be thought a single unit, a state of things which procured me many a stolen holiday from school as well as many an enchanting experience. Whether the sense of importance that this gave me was salutary for my character is, however, another question.

Yet I regarded the company of my mother less as a luxury than as a right conferred by natural law—a right I was determined to retain by performing every possible duty that would give it validity in her eyes. In this sense alone, if in no other, it inured me to a valuable discipline, for it taught me to associate right with obligation.

Inclined all my life to a pessimistic outlook—a trait which has meant that only for short spells have I ever been free from thoughts of suicide—I always looked on the blackest side of any contretemps. I could not have been more than five or six years old when one day, through some fault in the lock of the door, I found myself imprisoned in our nursery with Lily. We exerted all our strength to try to let ourselves out, but in vain. It was not long, therefore, before I lost all hope of ever seeing the outside world again. We should inevitably perish before they could rescue us. I began to shriek with horror and could not understand Lily's comparative calm, nor could I believe her repeated assurances that it was bound to be all right. Had I known the words, I should have characterised her attitude as absurdly sanguine and unimaginative. Even the voice of our French maid who was on the landing outside did not comfort me, and it was only when our greengrocer's roundsman, summoned upstairs by my mother, put his shoulder to the door and burst it open that I was at last satisfied that Lily and I would still be able to enjoy a few more years of life.

This is by way of introducing another incident and to offer some explanation of it. I must have been about eight at the time, and I was supposed to be accompanying my mother to lunch with friends. We were expecting to start off about noon. But long before noon I had wandered off to a school-friend who I knew possessed a toy railway. I was uncommonly fond of trains and had become deeply absorbed in playing with his railway set. Unfortunately, I had failed to let my mother know my whereabouts, for it had never entered my head that I might forget so important an event as lunching out with her. Consequently, it was with a chill of terror that I heard my friend's mother tell him to put his toys away as it was dinner-time. If this was intended as a hint for me, I did not need to have it repeated, for without a word of thanks or farewell I left the house in a flash and rushed home. Filled with the darkest fears, I hardly dared to ask whether my mother had already gone; nor did I need to, for our French maid covered me with reproaches. But nothing she said could have increased my utter dejection. My mother had gone off without me! I should never see her again! I was unworthy of ever seeing her again! In a trice I was once more out of doors, bolting up the road in pursuit of her and not daring to lift my head lest I should have to slacken my speed. At last I reached the high road where she would catch her tram. But there was no trace of her; not a sign of any figure remotely reminiscent of her; only a mocking stream of heedless strangers and hard, indifferent horse-traffic. I could have dashed out my brains on the kerbstone.

Broken-hearted and feeling utterly abandoned, I returned home and had some difficulty to avoid making an exhibition of myself on the way. This was probably the first time thoughts of self-immolation occurred to me. But my hopeless exaggeration of the mishap did not make it easier to bear, and it is significant that I never quite forgave the school-friend who had been the means of withholding me from my mother, and never again did I take the same pleasure in trains. My interest henceforward turned to lead soldiers, of which I soon possessed several hundreds.

I have spoken of my abnormal sensitiveness, and now I cannot help suspecting that my lifelong thoughts of suicide may have been but the natural reaction to it. For this reason I was easily convinced of the truth of Freud's thesis in his admirable monograph entitled *Jenseits des Lustprinzips*,[1] because in my own lifetime I have too often experienced the connection between a harrowing event and an intense longing for a return to the peace and insensibility of that stage in our evolution which preceded our emergence from inorganic matter. People who do not know what abnormal sensitiveness means in the form of mental anguish cannot, I suspect, read this relatively late Freudian treatise with complete understanding.

From what I have related about my attitude to my mother in my childhood, the reader may infer the passions that animated it, and decades before Freud became known in England my innocent parents were already circulating as a family joke a remark of mine which, fifty years later, would probably have struck them as much less funny. I must have been seven or eight years old when one day I said grudgingly to my father, 'I do wish I had married Maman instead of you.'[2]

I have tried to describe what was fundamental in my childhood; it will therefore not surprise the reader to learn that, comparatively early, I used every artifice and exploited every

---

[1] *Beyond the Pleasure Principle.*—Ed.
[2] Ludovici had already mentioned this love for his mother in *The Choice of a Mate*, pp. ix, 302.—Ed.

gift I possessed in order to steal a march on my brothers and sisters in winning my mother's favour. Whenever she and my father went to a theatre, dined with a friend or had any other reason for spending the evening out, she invariably found on returning home a drawing or some illuminated message from me lying on her pillow. This was 'sucking up' with a vengeance, yet I have no reason to believe that my brothers and sisters resented the villainy of it; at least, I was never aware of their showing any rancour because of it.

Sitting or standing at her knees, Lily and I used to spend much time listening to the popular songs of the Paris she knew in the sixties and seventies of the nineteenth century. We learnt by heart many of the numbers out of Offenbach's most famous operettas and the soldier ditties of the Marlborough and Franco-German wars and of the Commune. Some of these songs were distinctly *scabreux*,[3] but we enjoyed them all the more for that. There was one about the Commune, which began 'Quand j'étais mobile à Paris et qu'il s'agissait d'une sortie,'[4] etc., to which we never tired of listening.

It cannot have been long after my eighth birthday when my mother began reading aloud to Lily and me and acquainting us with the treasures of her national literature. For many years she had been giving us lessons in her language, and we had long been familiar with La Fontaine's fables, Perrault's fairy tales and the traditional French children's songs so superbly illustrated by Boutet de Monvel. But now was the turn of more adult pabulum, and we listened entranced to the works of Dumas, Victor Hugo, Alphonse Daudet, Balzac and even Gyp. When we were in the mood for a good laugh, she would read a play of Molière or a novel by Paul de Kock, and eventually we were introduced to the sonorous majesty of Corneille and Racine. She also encouraged us to act charades to recite in French and to entertain visitors in singing part-songs. I remember still the earliest poem we learnt to recite in this way. It was called

---

[3] Obscene. — Ed.
[4] 'When I was a mobile [the nickname for a National Guard] in Paris and they organised a sortie.' — Ed.

'Le petit doigt de maman'[5] and was calculated to cultivate a guilty conscience in a crocodile.

Religion was never very rigorously insisted on. Occasionally we might be taken to the little Catholic Church of Notre Dame in Leicester Square or to the Dominicans in Hampstead, but religious observance played no routine role in our lives. Indeed, it was not until a certain Miss Mary Walker, a sister of a well-to-do and well-known organ-builder of the day, joined our circle of friends that religion played an important part in our lives. She was a pillar of Trinity Church, Finchley, and rather high-handedly she resolutely took Lily and me in hand, gave us Bibles and urged us to read them. Nor did my mother appear to resent in any way this sudden impact of a Protestant, Low Church and evangelical influence on our lives. On the contrary, she watched with extraordinary complacency Miss Walker's cool and determined appropriation of this part of her parental role, and even accepted a richly bound copy of the Bible in French from her. Thus, in the end, Lily and I, instead of receiving our first communion as Catholics, were prepared for confirmation at Miss Walker's church. Of the ceremony as a whole, however, I have only two distinct memories, which are that we had to learn by heart, among other things, the first sixteen verses of Matthew, Chapter 5, and that the curate who had charge of our preparation bore the name of Bevan and had lost the first phalange of his left or right thumb.

My mother's unruffled acceptance of this exotic and heretical influence over us may I think be ascribed to her unshakable confidence in our loyalty and devotion, but it seems to me now that she was probably also more amused than provoked by Mary Walker's usurpatory and missionary zeal, whilst her loose attachment to the Church of her fathers helped her to tolerate the denominational change in a calm spirit. Nevertheless, a faint trace of indignation at Mary Walker's importunate meddlesomeness may have been present in her mind all the same, for I remember how scornfully she laughed and rebuked the poor old spinster when informed of the substantial sum

---

[5] 'Mother's little finger.' — Ed.

that it cost the Mission to the Jews (or some such society which Mary Walker supported) to recruit every individual Jewish convert.

Thus were the boundaries of my early life demarcated and entrenched. It was emotionally warm and passionate, with all my attention concentrated on the only two beings who had thoroughly captured my heart and imagination—my mother and Lily. We seemed to make an ideal trinity, and no-one could have been better prepared than I was for a belief in the mystical unity of three in one and one in three. Indeed, it has sometimes struck me that my fundamental lack of acquisitiveness and of any eye to the main chance in matters material, which predestined me to a life much poorer in this world's goods than that of my two younger brothers, was probably due to the early and long-lasting sense of security and abundant wealth I derived from my relationship to my mother and elder sister. It made other forms of wealth seem paltry and insipid. Victor Hugo hinted at something of the sort when he wrote (I forget exactly where):

Je serai grand et toi riche
Puisque nous nous aimerons.[6]

These conditions lasted until my early adolescence and a little beyond, although I could not have been fourteen when a new and sinister factor entered our life which, later on, was destined to impair its harmony. For, repeat as often as you may with Socrates that 'if there be any merely bodily defect in another, one will be patient and love the same,'[7] the plain truth is that sickness is the great wrecker of all human charity and love. I say this, fully aware though I am of the indignation it will provoke in my contemporaries. Yet, because it is the plain truth, Heinrich Heine was abundantly right when, in a letter to J. Campe on 19th December 1837, he said, 'The greatest evil is

---

[6] *La légende des siècles*, première série, 1859: Eviradnus XI. 'I shall be great and you, rich, / Seeing that we shall love ourselves.' —Ed.

[7] *Republic*, III, 402.

sickness.'⁸ No candid and penetrating psychologist could ever grant to illness, as our morbid nineteenth century did, the role of rearing saints out of invalids and their attendants. The first magisterial psychologist of modern times, Montaigne, certainly considered health as 'le plus beau et plus riche present que nature nous sache faire,' and maintained: 'C'est une precieuse chose que la santé et la seule chose qui mérite à la verité qu'on y emploi non le temps seulement, la sueur, la peine, les biens, mais encore la vie à sa poursuite.'⁹

To have exalted the sickroom into an incubator of angels will probably stand as nineteenth-century England's most morbid aberration.

But I am anticipating. During my early teens only rare and relatively negligible harbingers of sorrow crossed my cloudless sky, but the shadow they cast was never so faint as to leave Lily's and my own peace of mind unstirred. For it was then that a sudden disquieting frequency in Dr Bryce's visits gave us the first warnings about the state of our mother's health. Apparently—and we whispered the words to give them less reality—she was showing signs of diabetes and of a heart affection diagnosed as pericarditis.

Owing to my inveterate pessimism, I was more alarmed than Lily, whose love for our mother, though in no respect inferior to mine, was coupled with a superior sense of proportion which put the matter in better perspective. At all events, to me, for whom there was never to be any *juste milieu*, the whole future seemed suddenly to have clouded over. Yet our mother had still eighteen years of active life before her—years in which she enjoyed much happiness, had many delightful adventures shared by Lily and me, and scores of numerous triumphs in the concert- and lecture-hall and even the theatre, of which we were the proud witnesses. At concerts she would often give

---

⁸ See, for instance, Charlotte M. Yonge.

⁹ *Essais*, Book II, Chapters 16 and 37. 'The finest and richest present that Nature gives us,' and 'It is a precious thing, health, and the only thing in truth that merits one use not only sweat, effort and wealth, but also life in its pursuit.' —Ed.

recitations she herself had composed, and they were always very well received. Her acting in Pailleron's *Le monde où l'on s'ennuie*, under Grein's management at the Royalty Theatre, was excellent, and she had a good press. Occasionally for her recitations she would borrow one of Madame Thénard's, but she excelled in monologues of her own creation, and Lily and I never tired of hearing them. On the occasion of a lecture she once gave, Lily behaved in a manner approaching the heroic and in circumstances eloquently illustrating her filial piety and devotion.

As president of the women's section of the Société Nationale de Professeurs de Français en Angleterre, my mother was to give a lecture at Westminster Hall. My father and I had set off for the hall by horse-bus, but my mother and Lily had taken a hansom-cab. When settling themselves in the cab, however, the folding doors had in some way, which I cannot now describe, caught and injured the fingers of Lily's left hand. Yet, although suffering excruciating pain, her determination to spare her mother any anxiety before the lecture caused her to conceal all knowledge of the accident until she was on the homeward journey.

I was thirteen at the time of this event, which took place on Saturday 8th June 1895, but adolescence and puberty had wrought no change in my attachment to my mother. I still spent as much time as possible in her company, visiting friends or shopping. Moreover, on half-holidays I often acted as her junior assistant at the French classes she was then holding at Miss Walker's in Elsworthy Road, Primrose Hill. Sitting at a small table near the window of Miss Walker's large dining-room, I would be given charge of the few children who accompanied their mothers to these classes, and I was expected to teach them their first steps in French reading and writing.

It was, however, in the later period of adolescence that the first strains began to be felt between the outside interests now claiming my attention and my former single-minded concentration on my mother and Lily, especially on the former. The period in question is always critical for the parent–child nexus, and although there continued to be no abatement in my devotion, it would be idle to deny that it was assaulted from many quarters. The steady and inexorable encroachments made upon former interests by what Macaulay rightly called 'the mightiest of human instincts' inevitably directed my mind towards matters and people unconnected with my home circle.

In retrospect, one hopes and prays that the change gave no pain to her on whom one was insensibly loosening one's grip, especially as in the parent–child relationship this relaxation is always unilateral and confined to the junior's tendrils. In regard to Lily, I had no need of caution, for, like myself, she was engaged in exploring a new world and had indeed been long so occupied. Each of us therefore took for granted that the other sympathised with and condoned the sharp divergence of paths. With my mother, it was different. She was aware of no reasons for discontinuing the old close relationship. The consequence was that—inadvertently, no doubt, and inevitably—she committed what seemed an indiscretion or breach of tact in making demands which, a few months previously, would have seemed to me quite natural and would probably have filled me with delight. Thus, to my deep subsequent regret, I would show impatience and speak roughly to her. An impulse compounded partly of a desire for freedom and a suddenly-whetted appetite for independence would force expressions from me which, though harmless in any other context, rang harshly against the sound-board of our former harmony. Such discords cannot really be helped. They occur because, as Hazlitt rightly observes, 'no young man believes he shall ever die,'[10] but also and above all because no loving son thinks of his mother except as eternal. But, although we may excuse ourselves in this way, the plain truth is that there really are no means of letting a devoted mother down gently. A heartless world, professing psychological enlightenment, speaks disdainfully of 'possessiveness' in this connection, forgetting that we owe our survival to the very quality which, when it becomes inconvenient, we pompously dismiss with this pseudo-learned term. But at bottom it is only a conscience-comforter,

---

[10] 'On the Feeling of Immortality in Youth.'

for, although we know that apron-strings must be cut, the operation, like any other intervention of surgery, cannot be painless.

Feebly, I have tried to convey some impression of this unhappy situation, both in my novel, *The Taming of Don Juan*,[11] and in the verses prefixed to my novel, *The Goddess that Grew Up*.[12] But when we reflect that in millions of homes, especially in the working classes, the prestige suddenly acquired by becoming a breadwinner in the home adds truculence to the expression of independence with which an adolescent confronts an adoring mother, who too often is also a drudge, this distressing scene, annually rehearsed without any hope of comfort or compensation for the bereaved senior, must constitute a formidable sum of human misery.

Meanwhile at school, my gifts as a draughtsman and painter inherited from my father and paternal grandfather procured me many a success which had little to do with scholarship, whilst the command of French which I owed to my mother, besides enabling me to shine on the modern-language side of the curriculum, also gained me easy popularity with schoolfellows whom I helped with their French preparation. It was now that my mother's influence over me proved most decisive, for although it had long been agreed that, like my father, I should go to Paris to be trained in the craft for which I was gifted, my interest in the project and my desire to take up art as a career were greatly outweighed by the taste and love for literature and literary pursuits which my mother had so sedulously inculcated upon me from my infancy onwards.

There was also another factor in my life which at that time powerfully confirmed my mother's influence, and this was my great admiration and affection for one of my masters, Sidney H. Wright, who was himself literary and who, soon after his joining the teaching staff at my school, took charge of my reading of English, which of course had been badly neglected. He gave me much private and wholly friendly tuition in English

---

[11] London, 1924, Chapter 15.
[12] London, 1922.

composition at a time when I was perhaps better equipped to write in French than in English, and it was through him that I first became acquainted with such English authors as Malory, Spenser, Sterne, Swift, Smollett, Fielding, Fanny Burney, Dr Johnson, Thackeray, George Eliot, Blackmore, Thomas Hardy, Charles Reade, Kipling, etc., and the poets Pope, Byron, Wordsworth, Coleridge and Cowper—in fact, most of the outstanding English literary lights except Dickens, whom he did not admire and whom I learnt to appreciate only when I was in hospital during the latter part of World War I.

All this reading helped to settle my taste. It led to my drawing comparisons, apportioning merit and sketching a provisional order of rank among English authors, based at least on personal feelings. I was soon able, for instance, to understand the reason for the superior fascination of novelists like Fanny Burney, the Brontës, Fielding and even Thackeray (in some of his purely humorous works) over writers like Smollett, George Eliot, Charles Reade and particularly Meredith. For although in the case of Fanny Burney, above all, the matter might be trivial, the appeal hardly profound and the psychology elementary, such authors displayed a spontaneity, impetuosity and luxuriance of invention which suggested hidden riches effortlessly tapped. It is convincing because, as the French might say, 'cela coule de source,'[13] whereas in such ponderous, laboured and arid writers as Meredith, whose works were the more disappointing for being so extravagantly praised, one was aware of a perpetual straining after effect, a constant maximum of effort and a tedious poverty of improvisation which were hardly mitigated by a style both precious, far-fetched and often obscure. I could never understand his fame. Was it perhaps due to a form of highbrow snobbery which, like the present exorbitant admiration for the more outrageous of the abstract painters and sculptors, owes its vogue to the dread of appearing undiscriminating, reactionary or benighted? In any case, it would be difficult to defend Meredith against the charge of tastelessness, for he is one of the few European authors I know who, as an artist,

---

[13] 'It flows from the spring.' —Ed.

was unwise enough to guarantee the anticlimactic effect of his stories by quite gratuitously promising in his prefaces feasts of witty sallies and *bons mots* which, however, were never served. One searches *Diana of the Crossways* in vain for any evidence of the sparkling, scintillating and *spirituelle* personality he assures us she undoubtedly was. As F. L. Lucas so shrewdly observes, 'The wits of history are sometimes like the wits of Meredith's fiction. We are constantly assured they were wonderful; yet the specimens provided are apt to disappoint.'[14] Mark Twain was infinitely superior in this respect, though to have dared to say so in the nineties of the nineteenth century was to risk being scalped or at least ostracised. Much later on, I always felt that writers like Henry James, Charles Morgan and even T. S. Eliot resembled Meredith in this fatal lack of spontaneity and improvisatory exuberance, both of which characteristics may be enjoyed at their best in Rousseau's *Confessions* and Goethe's *Hermann und Dorothea*.

Thus, if in the end I became reconciled to the idea of neglecting artistic gifts which were acknowledged to be pronounced, my mother's influence, heavily backed by Wright, was certainly paramount, although minor factors, such as my distaste for following in the footsteps of my father, whom I never wholly respected or loved, and feelings about performance in the graphic arts, which, as I was to discover later, I shared with Hazlitt and George Moore, no doubt also played their part. It will be recalled that in one of his essays—I cannot remember which—Hazlitt mentions his dissatisfaction with painting as a medium of expression because of its limitations, or words to that effect, whilst Moore, in his *Confessions of a Young Man*,[15] expresses much the same sentiments. I suffered the same revulsion of feeling, and my wide and long experience of artists has often made me suspect either that the persistent practice of their craft had ultimately infected them with its peculiar limitations, or else that their choice of it was in itself contingent on their own restricted congenital endowments. This would not,

---

[14] *The Search for Good Sense*, 1958, Chapter 3.
[15] 1886, III.

of course, apply to men like Leonardo and other geniuses of the same rank, whose versatility extends beyond their ability in the graphic arts.

Lily and I had long been having music lessons, but she alone had reached any proficiency, and when in our teens we ceased to be taught she could read music tolerably well at sight, whilst I could only play by ear. Nevertheless, it was by ear that I then began accompanying my mother whenever she sang one of the songs from her large repertory, and one summer at Cancale, for instance, she and I were able to give the people of the place an impromptu concert in the restaurant of the Hôtel du Centre, which caused a large and appreciative crowd to collect outside. But only the older visitors of my mother's generation from Rennes and Paris were able fully to enjoy the songs that had chiefly a historical interest. This was within four years of her death and seven years after the serious illness she had suffered in the autumn and winter of 1903-4.

As this severe attack of illness constituted an important milestone in our lives, considerably coloured (or discoloured) our subsequent relationship, and is therefore not without psychological interest—or so at least it seemed to me—I cannot pass it over without some comment and explanation.

In 1903 we had all spent our summer holidays at Étaples (Hôtel Ioos), and when, early in September, George, Edward and I returned home with my mother's maid, Ellen Gent, my parents had remained in France with the intention of spending a week or two in Paris. We had not been home very long, however, before we began to get disquieting news from Paris about my mother's health. Apparently, she had suddenly been seized with the most violent pains in the stomach and had had to be put to bed. A Jewish medical man, Dr David, the family doctor of the friends with whom my mother had enjoyed her last meal before the attack, was in charge of the case, and we gathered that, although she was very ill, there was every hope that in a week or so she might be able to return to London.

But instead of any improvement her condition steadily deteriorated, and the pains were so severe that Dr David decided to give her subcutaneous injections of morphia. My father, who could not possibly remain longer in Paris and who, on the other hand, did not feel that my mother could be left alone there, suggested that one of us boys should come over to Paris to relieve him. Naturally, the choice fell on me, and with all possible speed I packed up and crossed the Channel. I went most eagerly and without the slightest hesitation, but on arrival I was deeply shocked by the marked change in my mother's appearance. Having first seen her but a fortnight or so earlier, looking radiant and refreshed after her holiday in Étaples, the ravages wrought by her brief illness, and the suffering they implied, were all the more startling. I was, moreover, much perplexed by her symptoms as they were described to me. Ignorant though I then was of the most elementary medical facts, I could not help doubting whether so sudden and grave a disorder could possibly be the outcome of any spontaneous fulmination of a deep constitutional affection, and suspected a more transitory and accidental source of the trouble. Had I been as well-informed as I am now, I should have expressed the belief that her illness was less organic than functional.

Dr David's diagnosis, however, was gallstones. This seemed to explain the acute pains in the epigastrium and to account for the morphia injections.

Madame Rosset, the friend at whose apartment at 67 Rue du Faubourg St Denis my mother had been staying when she fell ill, was hospitable and generous enough to brush aside all my parents' and my own protestations and to insist on keeping both my mother and me in her flat until my mother had sufficiently recovered to go home, and never since that day have I come across a more staggering example of magnanimity and kindness. For she was a very busy woman, engaged in a skilful trade — the manufacture of artificial flowers — which at that time supplied goods that were in great demand; she had three children (two girls and a boy), with one still at school; and all her business was conducted in a part of the same flat in which my mother and I occupied the largest bedroom. It must have been terribly inconvenient for her to have us there, yet she never demanded a penny from my father for our keep and for all the trouble we caused, and not once were my mother and I made to feel that we were unwelcome.

She was only a year or two younger than my mother and was very good-looking, affable and intelligent. Such were the symmetry and beauty of her features that it was during this autumn of 1903 that, as the result of seeing her constantly at my mother's bedside, I found myself eventually and most reluctantly compelled to abandon the belief that my mother's looks were *hors concours*.[16] It was a hard blow, but one which my draughtsman's eye compelled me to suffer, though only after a struggle.

The three children were as uncomplaining and kind as their parents. Charlotte, the younger girl, used I know behind my back to help herself copiously to my Keiller's marmalade, which was one of the few contributions my mother and I made to the family table. But I said nothing, for, in addition to the fact that she was a very beautiful creature, her small depredations were negligible compared with what her family was doing for us. In my heart of hearts I could only hope and pray that, after taking her first spoonful and licking the spoon, she did not immediately delve for another lot, though, judging from the speed at which the stuff vanished, I always strongly feared that this was in fact her usual practice. The elder girl, Germaine, was much less attractive, for, besides having inherited her father's palpebral ptosis, which always made her look more dull, stupid and sleepy than she really was, she was plump and squat, and had none of Charlotte's natural elegance and grace. Nevertheless, although I was not in the least attracted by her, this did not prevent her typically French father from harbouring the darkest suspicions concerning our relationship, and he was wont to burst suddenly in upon us, if he knew us to be together, and seemed to me to look more crestfallen than gratified when he discovered us sitting safely and decently apart. Truth to tell, however, even if I had felt drawn to Germaine, I should never have abused the hospitality of my benevolent hosts by attempting any clandestine courting, for during the whole of that sojourn in Paris I was in a much too ex-

---

[16] Without competition. — Ed.

hausted state as the result of my constantly disturbed nights, and too deeply depressed by the spectacle of my mother's suffering, to feel disposed for any philandering.

It was not my first experience of nursing her. In the autumn of 1900, as a youth of eighteen, when I was in Paris representing a firm of art and commercial engravers, she had wished me back in London in order to take the place of a trained nurse whom she disliked, who was looking after her when she was recovering from an operation for a mastoid abscess. The wound had to be washed out at intervals with a syringe and kept open by means of a draining tube which had to be reinserted between the lips of the fast-growing proud tissue after every irrigation. But compared with what I had to do in Paris three years later this was trifling, and I was particularly glad to be able to do it, as my mother's delight at having me instead of the trained nurse was an abundant reward for my trouble.

Nursing her during her long illness in Paris in 1903–4 was a much more exacting business, for, whether mistakenly or not, under the impression that her trouble was gallstones, Madame Rosset and I thought that the passing of a gallstone would put an end to her suffering. Whether Dr David encouraged us in this belief, I cannot remember. But it is hardly likely that we should have persisted in the routine and very disagreeable procedures it suggested, had we not had his authority for doing so. Besides, after a few weeks of quite unsuccessful treatment, it was agreed that a second opinion should be obtained, and a tremendous swell — an *Agrégé en Médecin* — came to examine my mother. Unfortunately, he appeared to agree with Dr David's handling of the case, with the result that our high hopes fainted once more, and the disagreeable procedures were resumed.

Only after Dr David's treatment had been continued in vain for what seemed an eternity did I begin to feel convinced that the diagnosis had been at fault, for although, after her long spell in bed and the *régime lacté*[17] which she hated and which disagreed with her, she was alarmingly weak and emaciated,

---

[17] Milk diet. — Ed.

and although the morphia injections which Dr David had taught me to administer were doing her a good deal of harm, the attacks of pain in the epigastrial region had long ceased. Madame Rosset and I had come to the conclusion that this must be so, for when, owing to inadvertence, the morphia injections were forgotten for twenty-four hours or more, there was never any recurrence of pain. Reviewing the whole history of the illness, we therefore argued that if from the start my mother's indisposition had been properly diagnosed as merely a violent attack of indigestion she would probably have recovered quickly and been able to return home with my father. In view of these suspicions, I wrote to my father, told him that Madame Rosset and I had lost faith in Dr David's treatment, and as the only hope of any recovery seemed to depend on my mother being treated by her own English doctor I suggested that at all costs she must be moved to London. I was well aware that this would mean ambulance conditions all the way, but I was so deeply convinced that this was the only sane course that, after much difficulty, I was able to make my view prevail.

My mother heartily approved of the plan, and it was a pleasure to see her wan features light up at the prospect of relieving her friends of the burden she had so unwillingly inflicted on them and at the thought of escaping from the care of her native medical men. Like Madame Rosset and me, she had by then satisfied herself that her long illness, if not wholly iatrogenic, had been considerably aggravated by faulty medical treatment.

The preparations for the journey were complicated and lengthy, but everybody helped and, ultimately, on a morning in January 1904, I found myself at the *Gare du Nord* in a reserved first-class compartment of the boat train, sitting beside my mother, whose stretcher occupied the whole of one seat. The window of the compartment had had to be hastily dismantled to allow the stretcher to be lifted in, but the *Chef de Gare*,[18] his staff and the passengers in the adjoining compartments, de-

---

[18] Stationmaster. — Ed.

spite the delay all this caused, remained amiable and good-tempered throughout, and I marvelled, as I have often done since, at the extraordinary power illness can exercise in our civilisation in promoting the secretion of the milk of human kindness in circumstances where everything else would fail.

Dr David had given me both caffeine and morphia for use *en route* if necessary. But I had no need to administer either, for my mother bore the strain of the journey surprisingly well. The sea was, fortunately, perfectly calm; my father met us at Dover, and at Charing Cross he and I both accompanied my mother home in the ambulance that had been provided.

When once she reached home her recovery was a matter of only a few weeks, and in due course she resumed her normal life without any trace of gallstones or any biliary trouble. It was my firm belief that the whole nightmare had been entirely gratuitous, and I wrote a sharp rebuke to Dr David in which I hotly disputed his excessive professional charges.

Although my mother's recovery seemed complete, she had hardly survived unscathed, for apart from the untoward effects of the morphia injections, which had threatened to become an addiction, her digestion continued disturbed, probably owing to the prolonged *régime lacté* which she had so much disliked. There was, however, an even more deplorable consequence of this most unhappy stroke of fortune, and that was its effect on our relationship — or, to be quite accurate, its effect on me personally.

Too faint to be noticed at once, and felt only when the passage of time made it impossible any longer to overlook its cumulative effects, the insidious consequence of those gruelling Paris days, during which I had often been reduced to tears of desolation by the spectacle of my mother's sufferings and the heartbreaking ravages her illness had wrought, not to mention the merely physical hardships her illness had caused me — the insidious consequence of all this, I say, was the hardly perceptible but ultimately undeniable formation over the once tender and immaculate surface of my filial piety of ugly callosities and defensive armour. I no longer looked on her with the same old disinterested devotion. The unsullied bloom, the bright responsiveness as of a reflector, the punctual simultaneity of feeling, which had composed our harmony hitherto, had become impaired. Was it my inveterate and acute sensitiveness that had made it impossible for me to survive the Paris ordeal without building up some protective carapace against further raids on my powers of compassion and sympathy, especially from the quarter whence the most persistent forays had come? Or was the change of which I very gradually became aware an experience common to all those who have been exposed for any length of time to the sight of helpless suffering in a beloved object?

At all events, whether unique in this, or merely human, I felt that something precious in my relationship to my mother had been irrevocably lost through those painful weeks in Paris. The fine edge of my sensibility had been blunted. The promptings of my devotion became less spontaneous and unreflecting. In time, if any differences occurred, I became capable of feeling and expressing sentiments which, some years earlier, I could never have formed in my mind. Whenever my mother again became indisposed, the old wells of copious sympathy and compassion, although by no means dry, had sunk to much greater depths. What was even worse, my patience with the infirmities of age and their accompanying impairment of agility steadily diminished.

I feel all this cruelly now. But I must not exaggerate. It would be inaccurate to give the impression that we were not still a deeply united couple, always happiest in each other's company. The outcome of our Paris misadventure, although known to ourselves alone as deplorable, was not catastrophic. Only against the cloudless sunshine of former days could our sky be recognised as overcast. Nor is it unlikely that, had it not been already somewhat darkened by the subtle estrangement caused by the advent of puberty, its diminished purity would have been much less noticeable.

Nevertheless, whether or not it was magnified by the circumstances attending puberty, the untoward change that came over my relationship to my mother at this time has always seemed to me the necessary — aye, the natural and automatic —

reaction to the ravenous inroads the prolonged spectacle of suffering in a loved one makes on the inborn fund of sympathy, and on the innate capacity for compassion, with which each one of us is more or less endowed. For it is a matter of succumbing to or of surviving the repeated appeal to one sentiment and one emotion alone. One knows, for instance — I have known — potential hospital nurses who have succumbed while yet merely probationers. Is it reasonable to suppose that those who do not succumb ultimately qualify as State Registered Nurses without their hearts having undergone some hardening, however slight? And when we reflect that these invalid attendants are by no means always necessarily witnessing suffering in a loved object, how can we doubt that, when the spectacle of physical anguish is presented by a loved one and is unduly protracted, Nature reacts with measures of defence which are proportionately more drastic?

I am not seeking excuses for behaviour of which I disapprove, nor am I trying to relieve feelings of guilt connected with my attitude to my mother in the later years of our relationship. I am only adducing one of the many reasons life has taught me for agreeing with Heinrich Heine's dictum: 'The greatest evil is sickness.'

At all events, the first great psychologist of Europe, Montaigne, entirely supports the view I have here outlined concerning the inevitable wearing down of the capacity for compassion and sympathy through the protracted spectacle of a sick or suffering friend or relative, and as a sick man himself he knew what he was talking about.

'Vous apprenez la cruauté,' he says, 'par force à vos meilleurs amis durcissant et femme et enfants par long usage, à ne sentir et plaindre vos maux. Les soupirs de ma colique [he refers here to the renal colic from which he constantly suffered in middle age] n'apportent plus d'ennoy à personne.'[19]

---

[19] *Essais*, Book III, Chapter 9: 'Of Vanity.' 'You teach your best friends to be cruel perforce; hardening wife and children by long use neither to regard nor to lament your sufferings. The groans of the

As I had never forgiven the harmful effect illness had had on the most enchanting relationship of my life, my heart leapt when I first read this passage. Yet how philosophical and free from all resentment is Montaigne's admission that his long illness necessarily hardened his nearest and dearest. Is it perhaps only the power of our prevailing morbid values, always antagonised by realism, that, together with our fundamental insincerity, makes us spontaneously question the truth of Montaigne's awkward disclosure?

For many years after that eventful journey from Paris to London—in fact, until her death in May 1914—my mother and I continued the fastest friends, spending our summer holidays together, whether in England or France; reading aloud to each other and visiting friends; going to the theatre and attending lectures and concerts. Indeed, I remember as if they happened yesterday our summer holidays at Cancale, Étaples, Rye, Alfriston, Folkestone, etc. I also remember vividly the night we saw Matheson Lang together in *Mr Wu* at a theatre near Kingsway, and my mother's intense pleasure, as we left the theatre, on hearing the newsboys shouting that Carpentier had beaten Bombardier Wells. Throughout my employment as Rodin's secretary, moreover, I lodged her at the Hôtel de la Mairie in Meudon Val Fleury and spent all my leisure hours in her company.

When in 1907 I went to Germany we corresponded almost daily, and there was a revival of the old intensity of feeling. On my return to London in 1908 I was again called upon to nurse her during a fresh illness which prevented her from attending my first Nietzsche lectures at University College London, and from that day until her death we were never again parted.

The end came swiftly, and she remained wonderfully brave and active until almost the eve of her death. She had been reading St Simon's *Mémoires* to me within about a week of having to take to her bed, and when at last she was incapacitated I sat at her bedside reading Fanny Burney's *Evalina* to her. This was

---

stone are grown so familiar to my people, that nobody takes any notice of them.' — Ed.

the last book we read together, and she enjoyed it immensely.

She died at a nursing home in Osnaburgh Terrace on 12th May 1914. I had spent the last night beside her at the home, and I was the last to speak to her. I never hoped to experience again the delightful moments our relationship had given me, nor to enjoy once more the constant companionship of a nature so gifted, versatile and perpetually inspiring. Perhaps that is why I have always been so exacting and extortionate in my relations with my fellow-men and -women as never to have made many friends. At all events, in my eightieth year I must confess that the pessimistic forecast her death inspired seems to have been abundantly fulfilled, for, apart from the companionship of my wife, on the whole I have since 1914 led a singularly lonely existence.

I chose for her epitaph a few lines from her favourite poet, Victor Hugo, and a happier and more accurate summary of her personal qualities could hardly have been found:

Paix à vous, bon cœur utile,
Beaux yeux clos,
Esprit splendide et fertile![20]

In his letter of condolence to me, an old, intimate and very intelligent friend, Dr G. T. Wrench, author of various successful medical works, writing to me from India on 4th June 1914, said:

> Your mother was in love with you, more than any other mother I know with son. That love of hers was the one guidance of her life, and like all love cared often more for itself than you. When my mother died I could not think of her for months afterwards, death seemed so infamous, and yet a few hours after I realised my freedom, for I was fatherless, as you know, and had been brought up with women. So I feel about your mother's death the loss — a tremendous loss to you — and yet in

---

[20] 'Peace to you, kind helpful heart, / Beautiful closed eyes, / Magnificent and fruitful spirit.' — Ed.

some ways a gain to you as a man. I can't write otherwise. Forgive me if I pain you.

Your mother was in many ways a wonderful woman. I shall always remember her acting a little piece of mine, her motion, her gestures, her voice were infinitely significant. She had gaiety, wit and quality; would, I think, have become a great artist had her path lain that way. She gave all this up, not for your father, but for you, Ludo. She gave all she had to you and imprisoned you in some ways with her gifts.

Dear boy, I always think of you with an affection I bear to few or none of my friends.

Yours ever,
G. T. Wrench

There seems to me to be some overstatement in all this, but Dr Wrench was such a shrewd and trained observer that it is impossible to dismiss it out of hand.

MY EDUCATION I
(1882–1910)

In the conventional sense of the term, I received no education. Apart from the training my mother gave me in the language and literature of France, my schooldays were unprofitably frittered away in a local private school where the teaching bore no relation to any reputable means of paying one's way as an adult. It was run and owned by an amiable, good-looking and relatively illiterate man, G. F. Carr Vernon, whose highest scholastic attainments entitled him to state on his circulars and on the large board adorning the entrance to his school that he was an Associate of the College of Preceptors and a Fellow of the Educational Institute of Scotland. His greatest claim to distinction was his excellent voice, which he used to great effect when reciting the prayers with which the day's work started.

Fortunately, he employed six assistants, two of whom, owing to their superior erudition, rather redeemed his deficiencies, and were consequently much respected in the school. Incidentally, too, they happened to exert a powerful influence over me and my destiny. They were, first of all, a very fascinating, handsome but unsuccessful aspirant to the medical profession, S. H. Wright, who, owing to drink, had failed three times to obtain his medical degrees, and who, as he informed me later, had had delirium tremens when still under thirty years of age. Apparently, however, shortly before joining Mr Vernon, he had formed an attachment to a young lady and completely mended his ways, and, except for a rather ugly premature stoop and a slight tremor in both of his hands, nothing about him betrayed his unhappy past. Passionately interested in literature, and with a useful knowledge of Greek and Latin, he was also very much preoccupied with religious problems—as may be gathered from his novel, *Chasma*[1]—and he was well-read in natural science and

---

[1] Published by Hutchinson in 1903 under the pseudonym of H. W. G. Hyrst.—Ed.

philosophy. He was in any case an excellent teacher, possessed the rare gift of being able to impart knowledge, and knew how to stimulate interest in every subject he taught. It did not take me long to grow very fond of him, and he did much to confirm my literary tastes and my deep interest in biology and natural history. Nevertheless, strange as it may seem, even when I was still in my early teens his influence over me was never strong enough to overcome the instinctive resistance with which I confronted his efforts to inculcate a belief in Christianity upon me. Indeed, it was only when he began his determined assaults on my congenital unbelief that I recognised how superficial and contingent on merely social claims and curiosity had been the brief spell of religiosity which, together with my sister Lily, I had undergone through the friendly agency of Miss Mary Walker.

The other assistant master whose influence on my life was also decisive was a delightful, erudite and distinguished old German, Dr Heine, whose military bearing, unmistakable *Schmisse*[2] and charming manners were all redolent of 'Alt Heidelberg' and stamped him at once as a person of breeding and education. Well-known in army circles as a good German coach, he had a lucrative clientele among young officers wishing to acquire the coveted title of Interpreter, which carried with it certain added emoluments. Every inch a gentleman himself, he had little understanding for the crude and vulgar jokes which many of the words in the German language suggest to English boys, and in dignified silence would wait for the gusts of laughter to die down before he attempted, with a pained expression, to continue the lesson.

He loved his national heroes — Goethe, Schiller, Heine, Kant, Lessing, etc. — and could always quote passages from them to illustrate a point of grammar or syntax. His enthusiasm was infectious, and my progress in German was to no small extent attributable to his compelling charm and discriminating taste.

The reverent admiration I had always felt for my deceased German grandfather had in any case predisposed me in favour of everything German, and in view of Dr Heine's attractive and

---

[2] Dueling scars. — Ed.

aristocratic bearing it is not surprising that I should have been stimulated to make rapid strides in his native language and literature. Nor is it without significance that this happened despite the fact that my mother, who had suffered greatly during the siege of Paris in 1870–71, had never concealed from Lily and me her loathing of the Germans. My complete emancipation from this point of view is but a further tribute to the powerful influence Dr Heine must have exercised over me.

The various authors which these two men, Wright and Heine, prompted me to read introduced me to wholly new and hitherto undreamt-of worlds, and I began to follow paths which, though they led me away from my early home atmosphere, yet succeeded in confirming the strong bias in favour of literature which my mother had implanted in me. Thus, I neglected ever more and more my gifts for the graphic arts, and even when, as a youth of nineteen, necessity compelled me to turn these untrained gifts to some profit by applying them to commercial engraving, my principal preoccupation continued to be literature.

Although still ignorant of Dickens, of all Shakespeare's works except those which school had spoiled for me (*Henry V* and *Henry VI*), and of Chaucer, Rabelais, Montaigne, Bunyan, Milton and the more famous of the later English poets, I was rapidly becoming acquainted with the works of all the outstanding English and German authors recommended to me by my two favourite masters. Among these, the half-dozen which did most towards settling my literary taste and framing my outlook on life at that time were Fielding, Andrew Lang, Emily Brontë, Schopenhauer, Schiller (especially his admirable essays) and Herbert Spencer. The influence of Emily Brontë, Schopenhauer and Schiller proved permanent.

I was so much uplifted by Fielding's *désinvolture*[3] and freedom from cant and sentimentality that my dread of reaching the end of his works too soon made me curb my greed and limit my reading of them to a certain number of pages a day. I followed the same principle years later when, on a wooded height between Étaples and Paris Plage, I read what I still think is Kip-

---

[3] Casualness. — Ed.

ling's greatest book, *Captains Courageous*.

But the book that most thoroughly shook and staggered me, owing to the intensity of its passion and its psychological accuracy in the handling of a couple of human beings who live throughout their lives at white heat, was Emily Brontë's *Wuthering Heights*, which I read with bated breath; which I have read many times since; and which, at every fresh reading, I have admired more and more.

Here was a book which to my mind outclassed everything, French, English or German, that I had so far read. I could not believe that anyone who had really understood it could have handed it to me in the cool and detached way Wright had done when he first told me to read it. Nor to this day, in spite of all the reading I have meanwhile done, have I found any reason to depart from the opinion of this work which I held when I was nineteen.

When, however, I turned, as I soon did, to every source of information I could find about the authoress, her masterpiece and the reception it had been given by the so-called authorities of the day, I was shocked at finding no-one, male or female, who had shown the faintest sign of having grasped the meaning of this stupendous work. Indeed, I discovered that *Wuthering Heights* had not only been misunderstood and condemned by Emily's own sister and many of the established literary celebrities of the day, but also that even those who had praised it most highly had always added some reservation or saving clause which indicated that they had missed the essential qualities of the book.

In my opinion, *Wuthering Heights* is not merely, as Clement Shorter maintained, 'a monument of the most striking genius that nineteenth-century womanhood has given us'; it is not merely, as Sir William Robertson Nicol declared, the work of 'the greatest woman genius of the nineteenth century,' it is the greatest work of fiction by any man or woman Europe has produced to date—and I am writing in the year 1961. Let it be remembered, moreover, that, if even those of its champions who praise it most highly cannot refrain from implying some disparagement of the authoress's choice of characters and of the situations in which she displays them in action, it is because in England there is no adequate yardstick, no set of scales, by which such characters and situations may be measured and their quality assessed.

The English are a deeply Socratised people who tend instinctively to judge everything at the first hasty glance from a moral point of view, and as their long democratic tradition has conditioned them to passing snap judgements on all things, no matter how complex and unfamiliar, their hasty and superficial is usually their final and lasting judgement.

Thus, if in a story one or more characters, especially the leading and prominent ones, deviate conspicuously from the accepted pattern of what they consider 'decent' and 'respectable' behaviour, the story itself, together with its principal characters, is straight away dismissed as 'satanic' or, more usually, as 'morbid.'

In the case of *Wuthering Heights*, such an attitude is more particularly conducive to error, because, besides being narrated throughout by an ignorant serving-woman, who has not the ghost of a notion with whom she is concerned in the persons of the elder Catherine and Heathcliff, and who therefore constantly misrepresents and denigrates them, these two same characters are cruelly maimed and mutilated before even the evidence of their 'satanic' or 'morbid' traits is presented to the reader. What is more, the history and causes of their injuries are essential to the plot. Unless, therefore, we understand the extent of these injuries and their cause, we miss the purport of the narrative. We are like people who, coming upon two victims of a mishap that has metamorphosed their natures, ascribe their distorted minds to their inherited constitutions and not to their unfortunate accident. And among the pitfalls which make it difficult for the unalerted reader to discount the effects of the traumata they have suffered, perhaps the most important consists in the reiterated condemnation of the hero and heroine of the story by most of the other characters, including the serving-woman who is the narrator.

Thus, the two magnificent personalities around whom the action of the story takes place—the elder Catherine and Heathcliff—are called wicked and devilish by Ellen Dean, Hareton

Earnshaw, Isabella, Edgar Linton and Catherine junior. Isabella asks, 'Is Heathcliff a man? If so, is he mad? And if not, is he a devil?' Hindley Earnshaw calls him 'the hellish villain.' Edgar Linton dubs him 'a degraded character . . . a moral poison,' etc.

The likelihood of misunderstanding a hero and heroine thus maligned by those about them is shown by the universality of the misunderstanding in question. No English critic of *Wuthering Heights* has escaped this snare—not even Somerset Maugham, who discussed the book at length and appeared to have no understanding of its fundamental theme.[4] All of them tend to ascribe to the hero and heroine's original dispositions, to their inborn natures and not to the calamities of their lives, the wildly unconventional traits they display. It is true that these traits would hardly have been evoked, even by the very same calamities, in people less passionate and less capable of deep feeling, but here again is a pitfall which no critic seems to have escaped.

Hence Charlotte Brontë's silly comment: 'Whether it is right or advisable to create beings like Heathcliff, I do not know; I scarcely think so.'[5] Hence, too, Aldous Huxley's similar silliness in classing Heathcliff with Cain and Dostoyevsky's Stavrogin as a 'satanist,' and adding that he is also a 'figure of fun.'[6] Even Clement Shorter's unstinted praise of the book is marred by his reference to 'its morbid force and fire,' whilst Dante Gabriel Rossetti, in a letter to William Allingham in 1854, says of *Wuthering Heights*, 'The action is laid in hell—only it seems places and people have English names there.'

Reread *Wuthering Heights*, however, in the light of the remarks I have made about its two deeply ardent leading characters and their disfigurement through suffering, and the novel will assume a new complexion. But, before discussing what I believe to be the explanation of the fiendish behaviour of the hero and heroine, let me briefly summarise the essential features of the plot.

The whole book is concerned with the burning mutual love of

---

[4] *Sunday Times*, 19th September 1954.
[5] Editor's Preface to new edition of *Wuthering Heights*, 1850.
[6] Essay on Baudelaire in *Do What You Will*, 1929.

the elder Catherine and Heathcliff. They are shown as having grown up together and, from their early childhood, as having been so passionately attached to each other as to have formed that composite or entire human being which Aristophanes imagined and described in Plato's *Symposium*.

This exceptionally passionate attachment endured long after their youth and adulthood; so much so that, as a nubile young woman, the elder Catherine, speaking of Heathcliff, tells Nelly Dean (the illiterate narrator of the story): 'he shall never know I love him . . . he's more myself than I am. Whatever our souls are made of, his mind and mine are the same . . . Nelly, I am Heathcliff.'[7]

When, owing to the hatred felt for him by Hindley Earnshaw — Catherine's brother, who, on the death of his father, Hareton Earnshaw, who was Heathcliff's foster-father, inherited Wuthering Heights — Heathcliff suffered persistent and degrading humiliations and was reduced to little more than an ill-used drudge at the farm, Catherine was so cruelly afflicted that, disastrously as it turned out, she conceived the desperate plan of giving herself in marriage to a wealthy local JP, Edgar Linton, for whom, despite his ardent attentions, she cared not a rap, in order, as she said, 'to aid Heathcliff to rise and place him out of my brother's power.'

This marriage she eventually effected. Meanwhile, however, because he had overheard only misleading snatches of her explanation of this plan to Ellen Dean, and had failed to hear what would have put it in its proper light, Heathcliff, profoundly shocked and wounded, fled from the house. In vain did Catherine, in frantic distress, spend the whole of a wet and stormy night out on the moors looking for him; he was nowhere to be found, and he remained a fugitive from Wuthering Heights for three whole years.

During these years, Catherine, always hoping he would return — indeed, feeling certain he would do so — carried out her plan, married Edgar Linton and went to live at Thrushcross Grange as its mistress.

---

[7] Chapter 9.

When Heathcliff at last came back, we are not told what he did during his absence or how he acquired the means he now appeared to possess, but we learn that he 'had grown a tall athletic well-formed man,' beside whom Edgar Linton 'seemed quite slender and youth-like. His upright carriage suggested the idea of his having been in the army. His countenance . . . looked intelligent and retained no marks of former degradation . . . and his manner was even dignified.'[8] Later on, Ellen Dean says that 'he would certainly have struck a stranger as a born and bred gentleman.'[9]

To cut a long story short, when, after much manoeuvring, Heathcliff with Ellen Dean's help at last succeeds in having an interview with his former idol, now Mrs Linton, both recognise with horror the desperate situation they are in, and in the course of a harrowing scene Heathcliff tells Catherine the bitter life he has led since he last heard her voice, and that all his long struggle had been only for her.

Tender and unaltered as are his passionate feelings for Catherine, Heathcliff is resolved to wreak his revenge against her brother, Hindley, and to this end settles down at Wuthering Heights, for which he pays his former tormenter handsomely, and by encouraging him to drink heavily, and steadily relieving him of all his money at cards, he succeeds in his object. In addition, in order to punish Linton for having deigned to marry Catherine, he contrives to win the affection of Linton's sister, Isabella, whom he heartily dislikes, and very soon induces her to marry him. Eventually, Edgar Linton denies Heathcliff all access to Thrushcross Grange and threatens him with violence at the hands of his male servants if he dares to return there.

The insuperable difficulties thus brought about only increase the despair of the adoring couple, and Catherine, at last compelled to see the tragic hopelessness of their plight, asks only for her torment to end, even if death be the only solution. To hasten her release from the intolerable pain she is suffering, she deliberately exposes herself, almost naked, to the wintry blast blow-

---

[8] Chapter 10.
[9] Chapter 14.

ing in at her bedroom window and, 'careless of the frosty air that cut about her shoulders,' she 'leant right out.'

Needless to say, she now fell seriously ill, and to Heathcliff's consternation rumours of her condition reached Wuthering Heights. It was, however, in vain that he tried to persuade Ellen Dean, in defiance of her master's orders, to contrive another meeting between himself and Catherine. She refused to be a party to any such treachery, and it was only when the seriousness of his threats thoroughly alarmed her, for she was too well aware of his recklessness, that she consented at last to smuggling him into the house and upstairs to Catherine's room. But she had to wait three days before a favourable opportunity presented itself, and then at a prearranged signal, whilst Edgar Linton was at church, Heathcliff was at last secretly admitted into the house and hurried into Catherine's presence.

> In a stride or two [he] was at her side and had her grasped in his arms. He neither spoke nor loosed his hold for some five minutes, during which period he bestowed more kisses than ever he gave in his life before; but then my mistress had kissed him first, and I plainly saw that he could hardly bear, for downright agony, to look into her face—she was fated sure to die.
>
> 'Oh, Cathy! Oh my life!' he cried in despair, 'how can I bear it?'
>
> 'How many years do you mean to live after I am gone?' Catherine asked him. 'I wish I could hold you till we were both dead . . . will you say 20 years hence, "That's the grave of Catherine Earnshaw. I loved her long ago and was wretched to lose her, but it is past" . . . will you say so Heathcliff?'
>
> 'Don't torture me until I am as mad as yourself!' he cried . . . 'Are you possessed with a devil to talk in that manner to me when you are dying?'

Then, after reproaching her—mistakenly, as it happened, but he did not know that—with having been untrue to him, he added: 'It is hard to forgive and to look at those eyes and feel those wasted hands ... Kiss me again and don't let me see your eyes. I forgive what you have done to me. I love my murderer—but *yours*, how could I?'

Ellen then warns him that her master must be on the point of returning home, and he tears himself away.

Catherine died that same night, and when Heathcliff is told he goes mad with grief. Repudiating the possibility of living without her, he exhorts her not to hesitate to haunt him, if necessary, provided only that she remains by him. 'I know,' he cried, 'that ghosts have wandered on earth. Be with me always—take any form—drive me mad! Only do not leave me in this abyss where I cannot find you. Oh God, it is unutterable. I cannot live without my life! I cannot live without my soul!'

Then, Ellen Dean tells us, 'He dashed his head against the knotted trunk, and lifting up his eyes, howled, not like a man, but like a savage beast being goaded to death ... He was beyond my skill to quiet or console.'

For yet another eighteen years or so Heathcliff lived on, but he was hardly alive, scarcely aware of what happened about him or conscious of the least exacting duties he owed to his dependants. His mind concentrated only on the object of his inconsolable grief, and, his behaviour to all men betraying by its indifference and harshness the ravages his one great and frustrated passion had wrought in his humanity and capacity for human fellowship, he lingered on, dreaming only of how he could become reunited with his idol.

Shortly before his death he told Ellen Dean that, night and day, his memory of Catherine disturbed him 'incessantly—remorselessly, till yesternight; and yesternight I was tranquil. I dreamt I was sleeping my last sleep by that sleeper, with my heart stopped, and my cheek frozen against hers.'

And what had brought him this little tranquility at last? Merely that, when Edgar Linton had been buried some short time before, Heathcliff had succeeded in bribing the sexton to loosen one side of Catherine's coffin, and in pledging him to pull it away and then slide open one side of his coffin, too, so that he would be 'dissolved with her.' For he had contrived, by means which we need not enter into, to make sure of his own burial in the Linton grave, and to have his own coffin made in such a way as to allow for the removal of one of its sides, as he desired.[10]

Very soon after this, still happy at the thought of what he had done to be sure of rejoining her, he starved himself to death and was buried as he had wished. 'He might have had a monomania on the subject of his departure,' Ellen Dean comments here, 'but on every other point his wits were as sound as mine.'[11]

Now, what can be the secret message of this tragic story, all the dramatis personae of which, together with their impulses and sentiments, are so exotic in the English scene as to seem created *de toute pièce* by a foreign hand?

I suggest the following interpretation of the plot.

Emily Brontë, as her poems and the testimony of her contemporaries lead us to believe, was a young woman of noble character. She had never met a man who inspired her love, and her ancestral instincts and fertile imagination led her, as is often the case, to picture to herself the kind of man who would be her ideal mate.

As no mere catalogue of her desiderata could satisfy her, she lighted on the plan of revealing this lover as a character in a work of fiction and not as a husband—her artistic good sense made her eschew such unexplored territory—but as a worshipper in some way cheated of his chance to be united with her, cruelly robbed of his reward after having done more to win her than could be expected of any other man in his station of life.

Her instincts made her see him as one whose love could neither temporise nor suffer to be trifled with. He could not be her ideal if, after having failed to win her, he could be consoled, reconciled to his loss and resigned. He must be shattered, body and soul; and, more important still, he must not be the sort of man who is easily shattered. He must be of steel; the twists and dents the catastrophic blow inflicted must leave permanent and ineffaceable traces. No other kind of love was worthwhile.

The damage of a locomotive in collision varies as the square of the speed at which it is travelling. Likewise, if a passionate

---

[10] Chapter 23.
[11] Chapter 33.

lover be hopelessly thwarted, the extent of his undoing will be commensurate with the depth of his feelings. Emily Brontë shrank from none of the implications of such a situation. At the risk of discrediting her hero in the eyes of superficial people, she faithfully recorded every detail of the damage he suffered as the result of his frustration; and, as a counterpart to the sour negativism which, through the violence of his calamities, slowly perverted his original positive nature, she made her heroine, who is surely herself, seek death in the frosty winter air at her casement window, when once the impossibility of becoming united with her lover could no longer be doubted. Except for Balzac's *Roman de deux jeunes mariées*,[12] this means of self-destruction is, I believe, unique in European literature.[13]

Then, after falling mortally ill through her own act, without ever revealing to Heathcliff the true reason why she had not waited for him when he had fled from Wuthering Heights, she ultimately succumbed to her disease, and left him to the slow death of an inconsolable grief.

The reader may be wondering what this long digression about a great English novel has to do with the story of my own life. What justifies it in an autobiography? Strange as it may seem, the answer is that the reading of this masterpiece of fiction constituted a milestone along the road of my education. It taught me two lessons, opened my eyes to two truths, which, I believe, are of the utmost importance. At all events, their influence on my life was considerable, especially when, later on, I started to write about the relationship of the sexes and about woman in particular.

Apart from the intense beauty of the story and the daring and high-handed way in which the plot is unfolded—i.e., through the reminiscences of an ignorant serving-woman, incapable of understanding the people whose actions she is recording—the

---

[12] *Story of Two Brides*. —Ed.

[13] One or two suicides in fiction are similar. In D. H. Lawrence's *Women in Love*, Gerald Crich walks off into the snowy mountains and dies, and in James Joyce's short story, 'The Dead,' Michael Furey walks in the winter rain and dies. —Ed.

individual psychology of the leading figures, owing precisely to the narrator's inability to do more than relate (often with horror) all that she heard and saw, is so accurate, convincing and consistent that the book might serve as a textbook illustrating the inevitable pattern of human behaviour in certain well-defined situations. Its lessons are therefore extremely valuable, and among them the most essential I learnt from it over fifty years ago were, first and foremost, that, when her reproductive impulses are engaged and promise to be gratified, woman is always quite unscrupulous, lawless and anarchical. In other words, as I pointed out in my *Woman: A Vindication*,[14] the purposes of life and its multiplication become the directing force, and every other consideration is not merely sacrificed, it is not even thought of. Hence the emphasis I have laid in all my works about woman on the anarchical character of the human female, a view which I subsequently found abundantly supported by James Corin in his *Mating, Marriage and the Status of Women*[15] and Dr Fritz Wittels's *Die sexuelle Not*.[16] Hence, too, the belief I have held, ever since my early twenties, that feminism, which ultimately means female dominance, would necessarily lead to an anarchical society—a belief which the last sixty years of English history, with the steady decline of discipline in every department of the national life, has proved to be only too well-founded.

The second vital lesson I learnt from *Wuthering Heights* was that woman's major orientation is not and cannot be, as the sentimentalists of the nineteenth century supposed, to the child or children she bears, but to the male, to man. It is almost always forgotten, even by scientists aware of the facts, that in the evolution of the human race the relationship of the sexes to each other is immensely older than their relationship to their offspring—a fact to which I first called attention and supported with scientific evidence in 1927.[17] That this fact is really self-evident can be shown by simply comparing the duration of the Mammalia with

---

[14] London and New York, 1923; 2nd edition, London, 1929.
[15] London, 1910.
[16] [*The Sexual Need*—Ed.], Vienna, 1909.
[17] See my *Man: An Indictment*, London, 1927.

that of the creatures that preceded them, among which the parental nexus was largely absent.

Thus, assuming that the Mammalia first appeared at the beginning of the Jurassic period, some 152 to 167 million years ago, and that the preceding reptiloid quadrupeds first appeared in the Cambrian and Ordovician periods, 430 to 510 million years ago, we see immediately that, for about 300 or more million years, sexual reproduction occurred without any serious concern about progeny. The egg-laying female enjoyed an independence and a freedom from bodily handicaps differentiating her much less from the male than the female mammal is differentiated. More important still, in respect of the depth of the impulses concerned, is that her inclination and attachment were directed solely to the male and had no competing objective. We may therefore justifiably assume that her orientation to the male must have deeper roots than her orientation to her offspring — roots owing their strength to hundreds of millions of years of seniority over those connected with offspring. Thus, it must be clear that the maternal has shallower foundations than the venereal instinct.

When, therefore, horror is expressed because some woman has forsaken her children to abscond with a man not their father, and when astonishment is felt that such an 'unnatural' desertion should be at all possible, it is well to remember the relative ages and strengths of the two sets of roots in question — those which for 500 million years have been concerned only with the male-female, and those which have been concerned with the male-female plus the parent–child nexus. Briefly stated, it is well to recall that the impulse to venery is deeper than that to maternity.

All this, however, applies with even greater force to man, in whom the love of offspring is much less deeply rooted than it is even in woman. Not only is it in him a recent acquisition, but even today it is also far more a conventional product than a naturally conditioned emotion. As Margaret Mead so truly remarks: 'Man's desire for children is learned, learned in perhaps all cases as a very small child.'[18] Thus, here again, the orientation of the

---

[18] *Male and Female*, New York, 1949, Part III, Chapter 11.

sexes to each other is seen to be based on deeper impulses than the orientation to offspring, and in man, as Margaret Mead should have known, attachment to progeny is more often due to the support they give to his self-esteem as a potent male than to any conventions his society may have taught him.

Now, every fact I have stated about the relationship of the sexes may without effort be deduced from Emily Brontë's great work, beside which the best novels of the later Victorians — Dickens, Thackeray, Blackmore, Hardy, Phillpotts and, above all, Meredith — strike one as flat, timid and tame. None of them grasped the fundamental truth that in a properly organised society, where disparities of character and type are neither too frequent nor too conspicuous, the completest happiness is to be sought in a sound partnership of male and female, with the relationship towards progeny felt only as a possible second-best. But, naturally, where men have lost their stamina and virility, this happiness cannot be realised, even if there are few disparities between a couple.

* * *

From about my seventeenth year, my reading of science, especially biology, zoology and astronomy, became regular and assiduous. I read every book by Darwin, Haeckel, Huxley, Romanes, Spencer and Proctor that I could lay my hands on. With great avidity, I also read Huxley's famous controversy with Wace, following the arguments on each side with breathless interest and becoming a convinced agnostic in the process. But the two authors that probably exerted the greatest influence on me in my early twenties were Schopenhauer and Schiller. The former enlightened me enormously on psychology, and I still regard him as the greatest European psychologist who appeared between Montaigne and Freud. Indeed, there is much in his work that anticipates Freud's discoveries, a fact to which I have more than once called attention, and Nietzsche owed him many a profound observation, the source of which, however, is rarely acknowledged.

I can never forget the surprise and excitement with which I

started to read the *Parerga und Paralipomena*.[19] I can have hardly been more than nineteen at the time, and on my way home from Fleet Street one day, happening to pass through old Holiwell Street, Strand, a detour I constantly made so as to have a look at the bookshops there, I was lucky enough to pick up a copy of this book. Impatiently, I started reading, and for days thereafter could not put the book down. Only those who know this brilliant series of essays can appreciate what they must have meant to me at this time. For no-one can read them and remain the same person. Nor does it now seem possible that such a work can have been refused by three leading publishers in succession before A. W. Haym of Berlin at last undertook its publication, though without paying the author anything for it. Schopenhauer was then sixty-two years of age, and had already suffered the mortification of seeing the greater part of the first edition of his masterpiece, *Die Welt als Wille und Vorstellung*,[20] turned into waste paper.

Every page of the *Parerga und Paralipomena* is packed with ideas and suggestions that have preserved their interest and sometimes their novelty to this day. It is in itself an education, and I felt as Nietzsche declares he did when he first started reading Schopenhauer. 'I understood him,' he says, 'as if he had written for me alone.'[21]

Schopenhauer's style is not difficult, and I had, in any case, prepared myself as a reader of German by sedulously working my way through most of the more or less second-rate fiction of France and England in their German translations issued by the Engelhorn Bibliothek—such works as Georges Ohnet's *Les dames de croix-mort*[22] and Charles Reade's *It's Never Too Late to Mend*—for I found a German translation of a French or English work easier to follow than a book written originally in German. I used to take these translations out with me on my journeys through London and would often stop at a bookstall and pick up a dic-

---

[19] *Additions and Omissions.*—Ed.
[20] *The World as Will and Representation.*—Ed.
[21] *Schopenhauer as Educator*, 1874, II.
[22] *The Ladies of Dead Cross.*—Ed.

tionary to find the meaning of a word or expression I did not understand.

My mother, who was quick to notice the change Schopenhauer had wrought in me, signified her disapproval of many of my views, and particularly of their German source, by constantly referring to my philosophic hero with playful scorn, and with a hint at his gloomy pessimism, as 'Chapeau Noir.'[23] But I was not to be moved by banter, even from her, for Schopenhauer was in many respects a finishing school for me. When I agreed with him it was not necessarily because he said things I had long felt to be true, but for which I had so far failed to find the right expression, but because the moment I read them, and looked again on the world, I at once perceived their truth, unfamiliar though they had been a moment previously.

When, in addition, I began to read such profoundly stimulating essays as those by Schiller, for instance—especially the brilliant and little-known *Über naive und sentimentale Dichtung*[24] (1796), in which, for the first time in the history of European literary criticism, the exaltation of Nature and children is traced to a moral and puritanical source—I obtained an insight into the genesis of shallow and unreflecting popular prejudices which was to serve me in great stead in later years. For this essay of Schiller's might be regarded as a criticism written in anticipation of Wordsworth's 'Intimations of Immortality,' written ten years later.

The ground I covered thereafter, especially by my reading of science, prepared me with surprising thoroughness for the major enlightenment which was awaiting me in my twenty-fifth year. Meanwhile, I turned to Goethe. I disliked his *Werther* wholeheartedly and found it nauseating, but I greatly enjoyed and admired his *Faust*, his autobiography, *Aus meinem Leben*, and *Die Wahlverwandtschaften*.[25] In the last-named book, I sympathised with his hostility to ephemeral unions between the sexes and the way he made his hero and heroine prefer to die in a hunger

---

[23] Black Hat.—Ed.
[24] *On Naïve and Sentimental Poetry.*—Ed.
[25] *From My Life* and *Elective Affinities.*—Ed.

strike against their fate, rather than yield to the temptation of breaking up a happy marriage. It is a great pity that he does not attempt to describe narrowly the physical type of his characters, for this omission might lead many readers to infer that, for marital harmony, all that is needed is an affinity of souls. But I do not believe that this was his intention, especially as in the early part of the story he clearly states that the affinity he has in mind finds its equivalent in chemistry. On the other hand, a passage in one of his letters to Charlotte von Stein certainly indicates that he held the soul alone as important, for he says: 'Dauer der Liebe ist immer ein Beweis der seelischen Ähnlickeit.'[26] On the score of the present well-established inseparability of psyche and soma, this is tantamount to admitting that the type and morphology of lovers must be alike if their love is to endure. But, unfortunately, Goethe nowhere says this. His story contains no detailed morphological description of his principal characters, and the matter is thus left rather vague. The only person in the novel whose physical features are narrowly defined is a young architect who, however, plays no decisive role in the plot.

Nevertheless, one important doctrine is plainly enunciated in the story — that a permanent sexual anchorage can be secured by every man and woman if only they mate with their affinity.

Meanwhile, with the object of improving my English, which had been so sadly neglected both at home and at school, I thought it would be a good plan to try by means of my own unaided researches to compile a glossary and explanatory notes for an unannotated edition of Spenser's *Faerie Queene* which I happened to possess. This I proceeded to do and found the work most rewarding, though undoubtedly tedious. Indeed, at the end of it, I could not help agreeing with those French critics who think the poem a grossly overrated work. I still fought shy of Chaucer, but read Malory, Shakespeare, Dryden and most of the Restoration drama. Incidentally, in reading Malory I was struck by his extraordinarily frank picture of women in the days of chivalry, their sadism and their means of gratifying it. The picture left me wondering how these sadistic impulses in the fe-

---

[26] 'Enduring love is always a sign of spiritual affinity.' — Ed.

male can find expression now that the days of knight errantry are over—a question which I attempted to answer many years later in the antepenultimate chapter of my *Choice of a Mate.*

I must have been about twenty-three years of age when, owing to some trouble with my eyes which I believed to be due to the close work I had long been doing as an engraver, I decided to give the work up and turn wholly to literature. I had little success with my early attempts, but hardly had I recovered from my disappointment when inquiries reached us from Paris about my readiness to fill an important secretarial post that had just fallen vacant.

Apparently, Auguste Rodin had recently quarrelled with his private secretary, Rilke, the German poet, and was looking for someone to take his place. A knowledge of English, German and of course French was required, together with some familiarity with art and artistic questions. My name and qualifications were submitted to him and, without any preliminary interview, I was forthwith engaged.

Apart from the many interesting people I used to see, and whose conversation at table I was in a position to enjoy, the time I spent in 1906 at the Villa des Brillants in Meudon Val Fleury as Rodin's secretary did not contribute much to my education. It certainly widened my knowledge of mankind, confirmed my tendency to realism and fortified my congenital antipathy to any form of mysticism, because, as Saint-Beuve so correctly points out, the French race is 'peu idéale et peu mystique de sa nature'[27]; but otherwise I came away from the experience only moderately enriched, and in my *Personal Reminiscences of Auguste Rodin* have stated the utmost that can be said in its favour. Besides, as Rilke discovered before me, Rodin was neither an easy nor a too pleasant person to get on with. Uneducated, coarse, ill-mannered and intimately associated in his home life with a woman, 'Rose,' whom he ultimately married and who, as to intelligence and cultivation, was very much beneath him, his companionship was not always edifying. At all events, I was kept

---

[27] *Causeries de lundi*, VIII: La Fontaine. 'Not very idealistic and not very mystical by nature.' — Ed.

very busy, so that I had little time for private reading and, had it not been for my mother's presence at the Hôtel de Mairie in the town close by, I should have had no congenial companionship whatsoever.

Reading between the lines of Rilke's own account of his life at Meudon, I can only assume that his days as Rodin's secretary ended very much as mine did — i.e., in a violent quarrel over a trifling misunderstanding in which Rodin was insufferably rude, though I gathered from Bourdelle when I visited him in Paris a few years later that Rodin quarrelled with most people in the end. Nevertheless, I readily admit that I was never too well-endowed to be anybody's private servant, for, when my affection is not engaged, I am what is popularly regarded as 'too selfish' for such a position.

My mother and I returned to London early in 1907, and I immediately decided to employ my savings by spending a year in Germany to perfect myself in the language and to study some of the post-Kantian philosophers.

From the point of view of my education and future, this was certainly the most momentous decision of my life, for it was responsible for determining the whole of my subsequent career. Before explaining how this came about, I must, however, relate one circumstance connected with my departure from England which is too singular to be omitted here.

Among our friends at the time was a rather interesting and well-to-do widow named Mrs Dufresne, whom I used sometimes to oblige by giving her the morphia injections that had been prescribed for her neuritis. Her doctor approved of my doing this, as it was not always convenient or possible to summon him when she was in most urgent need of relief. Needless to say, this lady cherished a friendly regard for me and when I paid her my farewell visit, after presenting me with a handsome fountain-pen, said she very much wanted to read my hand. I don't believe she was an expert palmist, but I had much evidence of her powers as a clairvoyant.

She told me a good many things about my character which were more or less true, and then, as if suddenly struck by some conjunction of signs she had not previously noticed, she said:

'D'you know, Tony, in Germany you are going to come under the influence of someone whose name I can't quite make out, but which certainly begins with an N.'

At the time I paid little heed to this remark, for, although I firmly believed in the feasibility of character-reading from hands (because no physical feature can be insignificant and unrelated to temperament and mental traits), I doubted very much whether details about the future could be precisely foretold in this way, although I was ready to acknowledge that, to the extent to which character may determine future, a forecast on broad lines was perhaps possible. But Mrs Dufresne's prophecy of an influence coming to me through someone whose name specifically stated as beginning with the letter N was a different matter, and I dismissed it as unworthy of notice.

Yet, if her choice of the letter N was not a mere coincidence, no prophecy could have been more accurate and more punctually fulfilled. For not only did a name beginning with N greatly influence me at that time, but the bearer of it also proved to be the principal cause of most of the subsequent events in my life, from my start in literature to my marriage and ultimate literary output.

Apart from taking a few letters of recommendation to friends of my family, I arrived in Cologne without having booked any accommodation. I therefore put up at the first moderately cheap hotel that my *Droschke*-driver[28] stopped at, but I stayed there only one night, as my bedroom was infested with bugs, and I was hardly able to sleep at all. After moving into a cleaner and equally cheap hotel, I lost no time in getting an advertisement published in the *Kölnische Zeitung*, stating that I should like to hear of some family in the city who would be prepared to give me board and lodging. I received about forty replies and at once started the round of visits which ended in my ultimately finding comfortable quarters.

Strange to say, I made the fateful choice less on account of the appearance of the place and the appointments of the room I was offered than because of the extremely favourable impression the

---

[28] Cab-driver. — Ed.

old landlady made upon me. It was evening, I was exhausted, and as I climbed the three storeys at 34 Am Duffesbach I prayed that this might be the end of my long quest. I was not left in doubt very long. Indeed, I had hardly exchanged a couple of words with Frau Nippel before I had made up my mind to become her lodger. She was a very beautiful and dignified old lady; her voice was most attractive, and she spoke good *Hochdeutsch* with a faint lisp which, together with the absence of wrinkles on her face, gave her a charming air of youth and ingenuousness. I did not really need to inspect the room she offered me, and within twenty-four hours I settled in as one of her family.

In addition to the comfort and good fare she provided for a monthly charge which now seems risible, she and her daughters enjoyed the society of a wide circle of interesting friends chiefly drawn from the musical and scholastic members of the community, among whom Ferdinand Schmidt, a blind and very gifted musician, was the most distinguished. He and I did not take long to become fast friends, and he was my principal companion throughout my twelvemonth's stay in Germany. I used to take him about with me on my walks, and he showed his gratitude for the healthy exercise I thus enabled him to enjoy by helping me on with my German and even initiating me into some of the mysteries of his art. He had a stepbrother, Otto Schmidt, who was an *Oberlehrer*[29] — a tall handsome man who, to my astonishment, although he had never been outside Germany, spoke English without any trace of a foreign accent, simply as the result of his study of English phonetics. He, too, very kindly gave me some expert tuition for which he refused to accept any payment. But what I had chiefly to thank him for was the warm and deep devotion to Nietzsche with which he infected both his stepbrother and me. He lent us many of the Master's books, which at that time were taboo in all public libraries in Germany; helped us to understand some of the more obscure passages, and secured seats for us at lectures on the philosopher. Thus on one occasion we had the opportunity of listening to Horneffer on the

---

[29] Secondary school teacher. — Ed.

subject of Nietzsche's life and works.

In this way, Mrs Dufresne's extraordinary prophecy was fulfilled literally 'to the letter,' and I had obtained the constant company of two delightful men whose friendship I enjoyed until their death only a few years ago.

Nietzsche has been much maligned in England, especially during the two World Wars, and chiefly by people who knew his views only from hearsay or else from an odd line or two quoted on a calendar or in a newspaper. He was mistakenly supposed, for instance, to have been the source of most of the less commendable features of National Socialism under Hitler, and many a remark of his regarded as likely to inflame public opinion against him was torn from the context which would have explained it, and was bandied about as if it was typical of his whole system of thought. He was accused, for example, of condemning all pity, when he only wished to point out that today it is too lavishly and exclusively confined to the weeds and rubbish of the human community, instead of being, after the fashion of the farmer's and horticulturist's practice, extended particularly to the nobler and more valuable plants whose survival and welfare were seriously endangered by the spread and multiplication of the psychophysically inferior elements in the population.

Such was the prejudice excited against him that many of his major and more valuable contributions to thought have been completely overlooked or distorted. Nothing to my mind could have been more revelatory and enlightening than his idea that the genesis of all moral codes is the subjective judgement of the kind of man most likely to flourish under them. In other words, his persistent question in respect of every morality was always: The welfare and survival of what type of man was it calculated to secure? Whose interest was best served by it? Who would be likely to flourish under it? For he believed that every morality was but a means of survival and dominion for a particular type of man, and that 'good' and 'evil' were the weapons with which a group or a community secured victory or predominance for their kind. Yet these very important and illuminating doctrines only earned him the reputation of being hostile to all morality in general.

At all events, when I returned to London I made it my principal concern to bring this particular feature of his teaching clearly to the notice of English readers, and although I was obliged in my account of his works to explain his superman ideal, his theory of eternal recurrence and his aesthetic and anti-Wagner doctrines, I did not, like Bernard Shaw and others, exalt the more sensational aspects of his teaching above the less popular but pregnant ideas concerning epistemology and morals.

Had his detractors but thought dispassionately for one moment, they would have seen for themselves how the process of creating new moral precepts still operates in their world, and always to the advantage of those who produced them. The child of yesterday, taught to regard empire-builders as good, learns as an adult, at the bidding of powerful nations jealous of existing empires, to call empire-builders bad. That same child, who in pre-feminist days was taught to regard women as not 'good' as politicians, police officers, magistrates, etc., learns, after women's fight for what they conceived to be their advantage, that members of his mother's sex are 'good' (or alleged to be so) for all these callings. But the most conspicuous example of the sort that has occurred under the very noses of the people who dispute Nietzsche's generalisation is the recent volte-face that has marked the popular attitude to alien races, even in the matter of wedlock.

Promoted in the interest of a small and powerful minority in the population who wished to secure their own unquestioned acceptance by the British people, the propaganda against every form of xenophobia was actively prosecuted, and in order to conceal its main object (which was to safeguard the right of permanent *séjour*[30] for the powerful minority in question) was deliberately extended to include ever more and more exotic types until, if you please, the slogan 'No colour bar,' loudly broadcast throughout Great Britain, led the gullible and easily-governed English masses (indifferent to any change that does not seem to present a direct threat to their incomes) not only to regard as 'good' the dilution of their ranks by coloured and

---

[30] Residence. — Ed.

black people of all climes, but also to call 'good' even their own connubium with such people. And whose interest did this moral metamorphosis serve? Obviously that of the powerful minority in the land who, sheltered behind this far-reaching tolerance, thus established their own right to be accepted as the legitimate and unmolested compatriots of the people among whom they settled. All of the very small handful of Englishmen who protested against this dangerous hoax were instantly denounced, with the wholehearted approval of the thoughtless British mob high and low, either as certifiable lunatics or else as 'fascists' and 'Nazis.'

In view of such radical changes in the concepts 'good' and 'evil' applied to phenomena and behaviour, and effected at the instance of particular groups or bodies for their own advantage, how can anyone continue to doubt Nietzsche's claim that the worth and ultimate effect of every moral code is to be sought in the quality and value to the world of the men in whose interest it was created?

Soon after my return to England I was fortunate enough to make the acquaintance of Dr Oscar Levy just at the very time when he happened to be contemplating the production of a complete edition of Nietzsche's works in English, and he not only solicited my help in this venture but was also chiefly responsible for arranging the two courses of lectures on Nietzsche which I delivered at University College London in the late autumn of 1908 and December 1910.

Dr Oscar Levy was a Jewish medical man of exceptional intelligence and charm whose superior gifts really unfitted him for the routine drudgery of medical practice. By this I mean no disparagement of the general medical practitioner. I merely wish to call attention to the fact that even those callings which demand high mental qualities and exceptional skill may, owing to the extreme specialisation of the faculties they call into play and the narrow limitations of the interests they offer, prove unsatisfying to men of versatile gifts. This has always been so, and from Rabelais to Smollett, Conan Doyle and Somerset Maugham has led to the same result—the pursuit of letters by a man who found medicine tedious.

At all events, Levy always frankly admitted that his patients bored him, and, although his great gentleness, extreme urbanity and considerable gifts of sympathy and perspicacity might easily have secured him a large and lucrative practice, he preferred the less busy life of a police doctor and the ample leisure this left him to indulge his principal tastes, which lay in the direction of literature, social intercourse and philosophic meditation. In my first novel, *Mansel Fellowes*, I tried to depict him for posterity, and the fact that he was delighted with the book, and, I believe, presented copies of it to numerous friends and acquaintances, seems to indicate that my portrait of him was at least no caricature.

He used to spend a good deal of his time in the reading-room of the British Museum, and it was there that, after having had his attention drawn to me by the large number of books on Nietzsche which I daily appropriated, he ultimately made my acquaintance.

He gave me several of Nietzsche's works to translate, including the first *Unzeitgemässe Betrachtung, Götzendämmerung, Der Antichrist, Der Wille zur Macht* and *Ecce Homo*, and these I did in the order stated.[31]

There has been much severe criticism of this translation, but I think that when the immense difficulties of the work are taken into consideration and due allowance has been made for the relatively small number of discrepancies, many of which are obviously the result of careless proof-reading or even of original typescript-reading, it will be granted that those who, like Dr Levy himself, Friedrich Sternthal (the brilliant Berlin critic) and others, including Dr G. T. Wrench, have only praise for the translation, were not only more discerning but, above all, more fair than its detractors. This does not mean that I fail to deplore the fact that my versions should contain flaws, or that I do not regret the excessive haste and carelessness with which my translations were prepared for the press. But I think it is only right to point out that there has been gross exaggeration, if not actual

---

[31] *Thoughts out of Season, The Twilight of the Idols, The Anti-Christ, The Will to Power*, and *Ecce Homo* (Behold the Man). —Ed.

malice (the source of which I believe I know), in describing the translation as 'scandalously inaccurate.'

What were the circumstances under which, for instance, Volume 16 of the authorised English translation came into being? When these have been examined, the reader will be in a position to measure the justice of its wholesale condemnation.[32]

To begin with, we translators, working as a team, were expected to read and check each other's work before it went to press, so as to ensure accuracy by eliminating typing and printing errors, repairing omissions and oversights, and correcting actual mistranslations. It may be difficult to explain how and why, but this provision against error was certainly seldom conscientiously put into practice. We were all over-anxious to get our work through quickly and inclined to look on this extra unpaid duty (which really amounted to performing one's own translation of another man's book) as rather a tiresome *corvée*.[33] The consequence was that, whilst the arrangement inspired a certain amount of confidence and appeared to guarantee some security against inaccuracy, both of these aims were in fact defeated owing to the enormous labours such revision entailed and the perfunctoriness with which they were usually performed. This is not to suggest that the neglect of which we were all to some extent guilty was deliberately practised to reduce the credit of our colleagues as translators, but I do know that I for one, in revising other men's translations, often worked at a speed incompatible with perfect vigilance.

Secondly, Levy himself was inclined to be much too trustful and lenient. He was too much of a gentleman and too little of a martinet to take his editorial duties as strictly and as seriously as a less amiable and more industrious man would have done. He was, moreover, often too diffident and considerate about compelling the adoption of improvements suggested. I, for instance, had to revise Common's *Zarathustra*, and as an example of the procedure I see from my notes that I found altogether twenty errors in Part I alone, although few of these were ultimately ac-

---

[32] See Appendix. — Ed.
[33] Unpaid labour. — Ed.

cepted. Moreover, in Section XX of Part I[34] I strongly recommended a modification which, although warmly approved by Dr Levy, he declined, out of regard for old Common, to force upon him. It related to the seventh verse of the section. Nietzsche's words are: 'Nicht nur fort sollst du dich pflanzen, sondern hinauf!'

Common's version of this read: 'Not only onward shall thou propagate thyself, but upward!' I maintained that no English Nietzsche would ever have used such terms to express the idea in question and suggested that a better translation, more in keeping with Nietzsche's epigrammatic style, would have been: 'Let your descendants be your ascent.' As I say, however, Levy was too loth to risk hurting Common's feelings to insist on the necessary alteration. This was by no means an exceptional occurrence, and it was hardly encouraging.

Dr Levy's handsome acknowledgement of my services in his Preface to the third edition of *The Will to Power* may, in view of the way in which my translation has been vilified, sound strange and undeserved, but at least it shows that opinion regarding the quality of my work is divided.

It would be difficult, if not impossible, to relate all I owe to Dr Oscar Levy and to express the gratitude I feel for the substantial advantages I enjoyed through my close association with him during the six years preceding the First World War. Only through him and the remunerative employment he gave me early in my literary career was I able to obtain the leisure and opportunity for that extended study and increased knowledge of the world which I so much needed to repair the worst defects in my education. It was also entirely to him and the influence he wielded in certain literary and academic circles in both London and the provinces that my first lecture courses were arranged and received public attention. He was, moreover, responsible for finding me my first publishers, Foulis and Constable, and for introducing me to the *New Age* circle, whose leader, A. R. Orage, soon appointed me art critic of his famous weekly.

Nor does this list of benefits which I owed to Levy, formida-

---

[34] 'Child and Marriage.' — Ed.

ble though it may seem, exhaust the counts of my indebtedness to him, for, thanks to what some of my more bitter critics may regard as his 'inexplicable' fondness for my company, he began very early in our acquaintance to invite me to join him on holidays at various coastal resorts and often to give me the means of taking such periods of rest alone. Thus, we would go off to Bournemouth, Westgate, Folkestone or Eastbourne together, and sometimes even take a little work with us.

What I owed to him above all, however, was the grand tour which I made as his travelling companion in 1910, when we stayed at, among other places, Dresden (Hotel zum Prinzen?), Munich (Hotel Leinfelder), Venice (Hotel Victoria), Florence (Hotel Bonciani), Athens (Hotel Minerva), Smyrna (Grand Hotel Huck), Jerusalem (Hotel Fast), Jaffa (Hotel Jerusalem) and Cairo (Khedivial Hotel).

I thus was able to visit all the principal art galleries, museums and monuments of southern Europe and the Near East, and to complete more or less my knowledge of the art treasures of the modern world. It was an unforgettable and invaluable experience and coincided with what was certainly the highlight of my friendship with Levy. He was a delightful companion, as most clever Jews always are, understanding instantly what one said and not holding up the conversation, as so many Englishmen will, in order to have elementary psychological truths explained. (He was, moreover, a most generous host throughout, displaying that aristocratic unconcern about expenditure which sets dependants completely at their ease and is one of the more pleasant by-products, if not the best proof, of a long tradition of power in a family line. The behaviour of a parvenu in similar circumstances at once reveals the relative recency of his affluence.)

Strange to say, and quite contrary to our expectations, the place which in the course of our travels made the deepest impression upon both of us was not Venice, Florence or Athens, but 'Jerusalem the golden,' whose beauty and majesty, possibly because unexpected, we both found staggering. No epithet could be more apt than 'golden' to describe the picture this city presents to the traveller, and on the strength of that word alone the Rev. J. M. Neale, who wrote Hymn 228 in *Hymns Ancient and*

Modern, or else Bernard of Cluny, the author of the original hymn of which Neale's is an English version, may confidently be suspected of having seen the Holy City at some time in his life.

At all events, it was the only place throughout our journey where I felt irresistibly tempted to do any sketching, and I brought back several water-colours, one of which—that of the eastern view of the city, crowned by the beautiful Omar Mosque built on the site of the ancient Temple of Solomon—I painted from Siloa, the little hill village lying on the height opposite Jerusalem, across the Valley of Kedron. Levy liked the picture so much that when we returned to England I had to make several copies of it for him and friends.

I knew perhaps too much about Greece and the baneful influence its more famous and later philosophers, especially Socrates, had exerted over European thought to feel strongly prepossessed in its favour, and the time we spent at Athens afforded me very little pleasure. Both Levy and I were depressed rather than edified by the ruins of the Acropolis, for nothing can look more desolate and ugly than classical architecture dismembered and disintegrating. We therefore found the sight of the Parthenon, like a gigantic decayed molar crowning the city, anything but exhilarating, and this impression certainly accounted for our exceptional behaviour on a certain occasion at our Athens hotel. When we were all sitting at dinner one evening, our landlord announced that the Minister of the Interior had just kindly sent round to say that he had arranged for a party to view the Parthenon by moonlight that night and, in order that the necessary transport could be provided, he invited us to signify by a show of hands whether we wished to avail ourselves of the offer or not. The response was enthusiastic. All but Levy and me signified their assent, and it was not difficult to sense the perplexity, not to say the *froid*,[35] which our indifference to the romantic prospect provoked in our fellow-guests.

The incessant chatter of the population, their shrill wrangles and noisy street calls, the buzz of which remained audible even at the summit of the Lycabettos, were also exasperating. They

---

[35] Chill.—Ed.

were a constant reminder of the querulous, loquacious and hybrid stocks composing the local inhabitants—all Levantines of dubious origin, indescribably ugly and bewilderingly heterogeneous. The streets, moreover, were in a deplorable state of age-long neglect, and it was odd to see a low jerry-built structure bearing the words γυναίκες at one end and άνδρες[36] at the other, whilst in front of the palace the king's carriage had got stuck fast in a deep rut.

The Royal Gardens at the back of the palace were then perhaps the most attractive part of Athens, at least to me, and on 14th February 1910 we sat there in glorious sunshine, as hot as on a June day in England, amid orange trees, beds of violets and pleasant lawns, and we watched the king's grandchildren playing under the eye of an attendant. For although Wednesdays and Fridays were supposed to be the only public visiting-days in the gardens, the guard who had at first barred our way soon proved more accommodating when Levy handed him a handsome tip.

It is not surprising, after this, that we were perhaps unduly overawed by the medieval grandeur and beauty of Jerusalem, although when I now dwell on all the experiences of that grand tour I cannot help suspecting that it was the wholly unanticipated splendour of Jerusalem, its almost mint medieval state and the dignity and picturesque old-world charm of its inhabitants that made it so disproportionately attractive to Levy and me. For, after all, although chiefly through the medium of books and other sources of information, we knew Greece before we got there. We had studied its monuments and its art, and we had long ago become familiar with the Elgin Marbles. Jerusalem, on the other hand, I, at least, knew nothing beyond what is said about it in the Gospels.

Everything I saw was strange and new to me—not that novelty alone necessarily has charm. In Jerusalem, however, it was coupled with so much of antiquarian interest, beauty and calm, primitive industry that at every step one seemed to draw nearer and nearer to the heart of a bygone culture. Another probable

---

[36] Women and Men.—Ed.

cause of the greater pleasure that Jerusalem gave us was its convincing air of superior genuineness and authenticity. Although its inhabitants, their daily chores and their environment transported us both at one stroke to a period almost barbaric, at least every feature of Jerusalem life was in keeping; nothing jarred the harmony of the scene or jolted one by its incongruity. Few, if any, discordant notes, and hardly any anachronisms, marred the picture of a homogeneous medieval culture. Athens, on the other hand, struck one as offensively bastard. There, surrounded by the decrepit monuments of a glorious past, the scene was crowded with the tawdry and vulgar excrescences of a modern city. Like an Earl's Court travesty of some Western metropolis, Athens in 1910 looked counterfeit. With its ancient background in ruins, it had the air of a centenarian tricked out to resemble her own great-grandchild. I have no idea what it looks like now, but that was certainly how it appeared to me fifty years ago.

Nor, after Jerusalem, could I place even Cairo and Egypt uppermost among the memorable experiences of my tour. The vast distance of time separating the monuments of Egypt from her modern cities certainly gave a less discordant impression than the shorter interval did in Greece, and, odd though it may sound, these monuments seemed to present a less striking contrast to the upstart styleless buildings about them. Their austere and simple silhouettes, not unlike natural features, blended more perfectly with the urban landscape. But there could be no question about the relative beauty of the two places, and I doubt whether any traveller would dispute the justice of handing the palm to Palestine's capital.

Two strange adventures we had in Smyrna and Egypt are worth recording. When, on 16th February, we had found accommodation at the Hotel Huck in Smyrna, we were about to set off on a tour of the town when the hotel porter approached us to offer us his services as a guide, if we wished that evening to be shown one or two places of interest. Then, lowering his voice, but without any embarrassment, he asked us whether we would prefer a male or a female brothel. Levy did not appear in the least astonished by the question, but I confess that it rather took my breath away, particularly as the manner in which it was put suggested a routine rather than an exceptional practice. However, we did not commit ourselves and simply asked to be directed to the baths. I then had my first experience of a Turkish bath and thoroughly enjoyed it. On the 17th we walked to Mount Pagus to view the ruins of a mighty citadel belonging to the Byzantine period, and in the evening we went unaccompanied to a local brothel. Strange to say, the young girl who first came to sit on my knee was wearing a sort of loose bed-jacket over her nightdress. She was very attractive and could hardly have been out of her teens. When, however, I asked a friend of hers who understood French why she was so exceptionally clothed, she replied that the girl was 'indisposée.'[37] Then why appear at all? Did her presence among the rest, in spite of her condition, indicate that certain perverse tastes had to be provided for?

When we were on the point of leaving, Levy, very properly as I thought, refused to pay the exorbitant sum demanded by the *Puff-Mutter*[38] for our entertainment, and, after handing her what he thought quite adequate payment, beckoned to me to lose no time in following him out. But before we could reach the stairs, the proprietress gave the alarm and the most evil-looking ruffians suddenly poured in upon us from all sides. With commendable coolness, Levy dashed down the stairs with me close on his heels, and only one of the rascals who had contrived to forestall us, and was already at the door of the house when we reached it, made frantic efforts to shoot its bolts as he barred our way. With one prompt thrust from the shoulder Levy sent him sprawling; then, quickly unbolting the door, pushed me out and followed me into the street. It was a providential escape, for we had probably been most imprudent to venture into such a place alone. On the other hand, the idea of taking a stranger along with us on such an errand, even if he did happen to be the hard-boiled cynic whom we knew as the hotel porter, had hardly appealed to us.

The other strange adventure, which had features even more providential, happened in the Lybian Desert between the Pyra-

---

[37] Menstruating. — Ed.
[38] The brothel's madam. — Ed.

mids of Giza and the Step Pyramid of Saqqara. Having, on this two and a half-hour journey, left the Pyramids of Zayet el-Aryan on our left, we had passed the Pyramid of Abusir when, suddenly, at the very moment when the stench from a camel's carcase lying to windward was so overpowering that our one thought was to push on as quickly as possible into more wholesome air, I was seized with the most intolerable colicky pains which forced me to dismount and to seek a spot where I could immediately relieve nature. I therefore anxiously inquired of my German-speaking dragoman whether by any chance he had any of the toilet accessory which I should of course need. He regretted to say he had not; neither had Levy, nor his own dragoman. As I had nothing in my own pockets that would serve, I glanced helplessly at the endless waste of wind-blown sand about us, fully aware though I was that only desperation could have inspired any hope of thus finding what I wanted. Then, just as I was resigning myself to an unpleasant expedient suggested by Levy, there presented itself to my incredulous gaze what appeared some distance away as a strand of fluttering tissue paper, rising and falling in the breeze. Hardly trusting my senses, I hurried to the spot, and then to my speechless wonder saw lying at my feet not a strip or streamer of light buff paper, but an almost brand-new roll of excellent toilet paper, perfectly clean and dry!

Never before or since have I known or heard of such an extraordinarily happy coincidence, and, were the circumstances and the occasion more edifying, one can imagine such an occurrence giving rise to the sort of legend on which the belief in miracles is based.

We were both greatly depressed by the prevalence of eye disease in Syria and Egypt and, in a desperate attempt to awaken the adult women at least to the importance of hygiene in this respect, I remember that I used to go about the market-place in Jerusalem and wave a fan over the faces of their babies to scare away the clusters of flies that collected on their eyes as they lay sleeping beside their mothers' display of vegetables and fruit. But it was no good. Although the mothers did not seem to resent my action, they looked upon it merely as the vagary of an eccentric foreigner. Indeed, when Levy and I visited the German hospital and spoke to Dr Wallach about the matter, he said the situation was almost hopeless. The fellahin had no notion either of cleanliness or hygiene. I suggested that the girls, at least, might be made accessible to more enlightened ideas by appealing to their vanity. If it were pointed out that the terrible disfigurement of trachoma could be avoided by proper care, surely they would be anxious to learn what they should do. But Dr Wallach said he had found even that expedient of no avail.

Except for the journey from Jaffa to Alexandria, which we performed, *malgré nous*,[39] in a disgusting Russian steamer, the *Cezarevich*, full of pilgrims and vermin, whose captain had the effrontery to sit at the head of our dining-table and, under our very eyes, to eat a specially cooked meal very much superior to our own, we travelled on the liners of the Messageries Maritimes, the Portugal and the Saghalien, and I thought them excellent in every respect. The *vin ordinaire* at meals was *ad lib.*,[40] the cooking was first-class and the cabin accommodation most comfortable. There was, however, a brief exception to this rule, for we performed the trip from Trieste to Patras in a very fine ship of the Austrian Lloyd Line which also provided us with every comfort and excellent food.

---

[39] In spite of ourselves. — Ed.
[40] The house wine was free of charge. — Ed.

MY EDUCATION II
(1910–1916)

My art criticisms for Orage's *The New Age* reintroduced me to the world in which I had been brought up, and as a matter of course I had to attend most of the private views of pictures and sculpture in London. As a conscientious art critic, I had gradually come to feel the necessity of reaching definite conclusions concerning what I believed to be the essentials of quality in the graphic and plastic arts. Hating the anarchy that prevailed in this sphere, which ever since my schooldays had struck me as not only bewildering but also and above all as discouraging to all young aspirants striving to attain to a high standard of performance in art, I had for many years tried to arrive at some sort of canon of taste, or at any rate at an approximation thereto. For I felt that even if such a personal canon could never give my judgements universal validity (an impossible ideal in matters of taste, as I well knew), it could at least serve to lend them consistency—i.e., make them conform to reasoned and well-defined principles which could be appealed to if they were challenged.

As I hope to show in the chapter dealing with my life work, I was from the start suspicious of the doctrines held by the art school led by Whistler, the methods of which were influenced by the plausible, trumpery and fallacious views expressed in his famous *Ten O'Clock*[1] and especially in his letter to *The World*.[2]

For reasons which I have since made abundantly clear in my Introduction to *The Letters of a Post-Impressionist*,[3] in the later chapters of my *Personal Reminiscences of Auguste Rodin*[4] and particularly in an article contributed to the *Contemporary Review*,[5] I

---

[1] 1885.
[2] 22nd May 1878.
[3] London, 1912; Boston, 1913.
[4] London and Philadelphia, 1926.
[5] 'Confusion in the arts,' *The Contemporary Review* 192, 1957, pp.

felt there was something radically specious and irrational in Whistler's reiterated claim that in art 'the subject does not matter,' and I foresaw with prophetic clarity all the mischief to which such a doctrine must inevitably lead. It seemed to me that any art movement animated by such a principle must culminate in abuses of all kinds and in the degradation of the graphic and plastic artist's role. From being by tradition the pictorial or sculptural perpetuation or enshrinement of an 'état d'âme'[6] inspired in a peculiarly sensitive and gifted observer by some aspect of life, an enshrinement supplying common men with an interpretation of life raised to a key unattainable by their own unaided contemplation and therefore a new revelation of beauty or grandeur, the work of artists who followed Whistler's shallow ruling and obsessive insistence on the supreme importance of 'arrangement' and 'composition' (*lisez*: 'pattern') was, at a stroke, made to rank with that of a mosaicist, or a wallpaper- or carpet-designer. From being a means of exalting and intensifying his fellow-men's joy and exhilaration over some selected facet of the natural world, the so-called artist was demoted to a mere kaleidoscopist, a mere juxtapositor of varicoloured patches. For whether or not we choose to warn our generation against the charlatanry, humbug and fraud which such degraded art forms may promote among the less scrupulous art-aspirant of every generation, let alone the less highly endowed and less competent, the fact remains that no process of reasoning could justify us in setting the skill, gifts and technical mastery necessary for the designer of a patchwork quilt on the same level with those of the artist who enshrines for us ordinary folk his exceptionally vital, penetrating and tasteful interpretation of some aspect or feature of the world about us. When we appreciate the revelatory quality of such an artist's products and how they transcend our own impressions of the world about us, we immediately understand that no mere 'arrangements' and 'patterns' can compete with them for quality and enchantment.

106–10. — Ed.
  [6] Mood. — Ed.

On this account I could never see how anyone, after examining Whistler's shallow, tawdry and heretical dicta on art, could fail to dread their inevitable and dangerous consequences. Nor at all events does their ultimate logical conclusion in the production of what the modern world now recognises as 'abstract art' do aught but confirm and justify the suspicion and fear with which they first inspired me.

Thus, very early in my work as an art critic I was aware of the dangers attending the adoption of Whistler's corrupt teaching, for, accepting as I did Goethe's view that the subjectivity which abounds in all spheres today is a sign of degeneracy, I deplored any aesthetic doctrine which was bound to foster subjective forms of artistic expression having little meaning except to the artist himself and bearing no relation to any objective reality.

Meanwhile, I read a great number of treatises, both on aesthetics and the history of art, and thus became acquainted with the views of many of the leading art historians and philosophers (including Hegel) who had helped to mould European standards of taste. But although these studies brought me no nearer to a valid aesthetic canon, they widened my view of the problems and introduced me to the more important key thinkers on the subject of art. Through them, for instance, I came across the essential contributions made to my subject by Ananda Coomaraswamy and had the advantage of meeting this gifted Oriental aesthete and of discussing with him some of the most burning questions relating to art and art criticism.

The years immediately preceding World War I therefore covered a period of social contacts which, apart from those made through the English Mistery after 1930, were perhaps wider and more varied than I was ever to enjoy again, for, besides the Nietzsche group to which I belonged, I was more or less prominently associated with the *New Age* clique, and thanks to my articles and public lectures I had become acquainted with a number of societies and movements, among whose members I found many supporters. Of the various circles in question, I might mention above all the Sesame Club, many of whose members remained my friends until their death. I refer to such people as the Waggets, the Hunts and the Cosways.

In this traffic with my fellow-men I gradually learnt, albeit imperfectly, the art, if not the science, of human intercourse. That is to say, I learnt above all the importance of treading cautiously, of acquiring the behaviour which makes for a good mixer — a role for which I was from the start miserably endowed — and of avoiding the dire perils of too hasty speech. For, as Fontenelle so aptly remarked, 'Il y a peu de choses aussi difficiles et aussi dangereuses que le commerce des hommes.'[7] Not that I always succeeded! On the contrary, I can think of many a contretemps and setback in my life which I owed to words imprudently uttered and, as I imagined at the time, spoken safely and in confidence to a trusted relative or friend.

Much later on, when through the small stir caused in political circles by my *Defence of Aristocracy*, *A Defence of Conservatism* and *The False Assumptions of 'Democracy'* I became enrolled as a leading member of the English Mistery, a political organisation of the extreme Right, I came into almost daily contact with an even wider circle of men of all classes, among whom were numbered Conservative peers and Members of Parliament, lawyers and even scholars. At our dinners we often had foreign ambassadors, diplomats and sometimes even members of the Royal Family as guests, and as the speeches made on these occasions were never reported — the press being rigorously excluded from all our meetings — and as in other respects a certain air of mystery hung over both our aims and our proceedings, our group contrived during the period of its existence in full strength (i.e., from 1930 to about 1937) to attract a good deal of notice and to provoke considerable curiosity and interest. Nor was this confined to England, for our fame spread abroad, particularly to Germany and Italy, and with consequences which, as far at least as I was concerned, proved of the utmost educative value.

Nevertheless, my position as one of the foremost members

---

[7] 'There are few things as difficult but also as dangerous as dealing with men.' — Ed.

of this political society was by no means an easy one, and it was as a Mistery man that I learnt the hardest lessons of my life concerning the 'commerce des hommes,' an art for which I had few natural gifts and which in the Mistery was rendered all the more difficult because of the position of relative authority which I held by tacit consent under the executive of the organisation.

But in any case, whether my political philosophy and my claims to some authority in this field were justified or not, it can never be easy, especially in political circles where the struggle for power is prosecuted more nakedly than in any other department of social life, to live in harmony, friendship and loyalty with a large body of one's fellows; and when, as in modern England, there is in any event a certain tendency to negativism among middle-class people in particular, one has only to be prominent in any group in order to be the target against which most of the criticism and latent misanthropy are directed. And I believe this to be especially true of England, because of the fundamental particularism of the Anglo-Saxon character which, from the moment any party is formed and attracts recruits, gives rise among its members to centrifugal forces that tend to destroy every impulse of solidarity and loyalty. The result is that, instead of presenting with their fellow-members a united front against a common enemy outside, the men composing the average political group concentrate all their energies, not to mention their venom, on discovering reasons and weapons with which to fight and rout one, two or more of the members of their own group. Indeed, it makes one wonder how a leading politician is ever able to hold any body of supporters together long enough to exert effective power in Parliament.

I suggest that this happens chiefly in England owing to the inveterate particularism of the Anglo-Saxon character. But apparently the French cannot be far behind us in this respect—a fact which may explain the deplorable tendency of French political parties to break up into numerous hostile schisms. At all events, this tendency appears to have been already familiar to de Retz in the seventeenth century, for we find him saying: 'On a plus de peine, dans les partis, à vivre avec ceux qui en sont qu'à agir centre ceux qui y sont opposés.'⁸

This is certainly true of most political groups in England, and very early in my membership of the English Mistery I began to notice this splitting up of our society into small cliques composed of men who, on the score of some paltry difference, thought it worthwhile to break loose from the main body and thus to weaken and ultimately to destroy it. Invariably, too, this process of disruption was preceded and accompanied by whispering campaigns directed against some other section of the party or one of its members. Meanwhile, of course, the common enemy outside remained not only immune, but usually also utterly forgotten. No wonder an experienced politician like de Retz felt able to say: 'Je suis persuadé qu'il faut plus de grandes qualités pour former un bon chef de parti que pour faire un bon empereur de l'univers.'⁹

It was certainly this sort of internal canker, coupled with many dubious procedures on the part of the Party's executive, that ultimately brought about the complete dissolution of the English Mistery, and although I retained until the end the support and loyalty of a few members, some of whom are still my friends, I had long been aware of the denigration of both my person and my doctrines which seemed to constitute the favourite pastime of the congenital secessionists in our midst. In fact, so deeply rooted is this habit of disparagement in our Western society that it makes one wonder whether the proverbial love or animals, in England at least, may not be due to the knowledge that dumb animals are incapable of it.

But this unhappy experience was but a grandiose repetition of many such already undergone by me, although on a smaller scale. For among both the early Nietzscheans and the members of the *New Age* group the same inveterate schismatic tendencies prevailed, and my discovery that these tendencies were appar-

---

⁸ *Mémoires*, 1935 edition, Preface. 'In political parties, living with those who belong to them is more difficult than taking action against those who oppose them.' —Ed.

⁹ *Op. cit.*, Part I, p. 25. 'I believe that it needs greater qualities to make a good party leader than a good emperor of the universe.' —Ed.

ently endemic in England constituted one of the hardest parts of my education in the ways of the world.

In this respect, one of the bitterest jars I ever had was that which I suffered whilst writing for *The New Age*. I was of course well aware of the existence of factions in the group around A. R. Orage, but it never once occurred to me that my chief himself would ever be capable of siding with any of them against me, one of his own contributors. Yet this is what actually came to pass. But to make the whole incident clear, I must first explain how I innocently provided my enemies with the opportunity of injuring me. Above all, I must in brief outline describe my relationship to Orage.

The letters Orage wrote to me from time to time, many of which may still be found among my papers, in which he makes clear the price he set by some of my contributions, suffice to testify to our cordial relations. This did not, however, mean that we were unaware of fundamental differences of opinion on many matters. For instance, I feel sure that I disappointed Orage by showing insufficient interest in C. H. Douglas's monetary-reform doctrines. Nor did I ever doubt that my pronounced leanings to the Right in politics made it difficult for me to see eye to eye with him on matters of social reform. I never could believe, as many Fabians, including above all Shaw, maintained, that poverty was the major cause of both social discontent and crime. This, a favourite tenet of Marx, always struck me as shallow and heretical. The very fact that both adult and juvenile delinquency has increased rather than diminished under the benevolent institutions of the welfare state has surely confirmed rather than invalidated my point of view. I was therefore never one of the devoted and intimate coterie that used to foregather round Orage's table in the tea-shop opposite Cursitor Street, where policies and programmes were hatched. I went there but rarely — certainly not often enough to please our editor — although, of course, he never so much as hinted that my aloofness offended him.

Foremost among the reasons preventing me from wholly sympathising with his views was my dislike of his boundless catholicity. He seemed to me to throw his editorial net too wide and to be almost dissolute in the diversity and even the incompatibility of the doctrines and policies to which he granted the hospitality of his columns. Nor is it unlikely that I must often have voiced this objection to men who were in a position to repeat it to him. Yet I doubt whether any impartial judge could, after examining the various issues of the *New Age*, help concurring with this criticism. I respected his intellect, but, just as he doubtless deplored my 'narrow-mindedness,' so I regretted his sprawling sympathies.

Much later on a serious clash occurred over the Ouspensky-Gurdjieff teaching, for I was quite unable to accept his belief in its indispensability for life mastery, and, strange as it may seem, it was his fanatical faith in these two men that marked not only the end of the *New Age* period but also, as I half-suspected at the time, sowed the seeds of his own premature death. Because, if he had not joined Ouspensky in France at a time of life when the rigorous disciplines Gurdjieff imposed on his disciples constituted a grave danger, it is unlikely that he would have died when and how he did.

I can vividly recall the urgent summons he sent to me in the first days of March 1922. I was to come to see him in Cursitor Street immediately as he had something of the utmost importance to tell me. This must have been on Wednesday, March the 1st. He said: 'Ludovici, drop everything you happen to be doing and join us in the Ouspensky group! You will find it abundantly worthwhile to give all your time to the study of the way of life Ouspensky undertakes to teach us' — or words to that effect. I pointed out that it would be extremely difficult for me to do what he proposed. I was a married man and had not the means to abandon my work. Although I was prepared to attend Ouspensky's lectures, for I was always anxious to learn, and felt sure Orage was too intelligent and well-informed to be hoaxed by a charlatan, I made it clear that I could not possibly enrol myself as one of Gurdjieff's whole-time *chelas*.[10]

As early as 3rd March 1922 I accordingly went to hear Ouspensky, who was addressing a small and select circle in a

---

[10] An Anglo-Indian term for a disciple or novice. — Ed.

private house either in Kensington or Chelsea. I confess I understood very little of what he said and often failed to appreciate the relevance of many of his illustrations. But I could not help admiring his technique as a lecturer. The way he handled his audience and dealt with the ubiquitous and benighted interrupters, who at all such gatherings betray their inattention and stupidity by the futility of their questions, seemed to me, who had so often suffered at the hands of such people, exceedingly impressive. Anybody who by his, or particularly by her, misunderstandings revealed that further attendance on their part would be quite useless was unmercifully snubbed and humiliated, and if such a person protested, as one or two outraged listeners, unused to such rough handling, sometimes did, he or she was invited to withdraw altogether. Indeed, the very first time I heard Ouspensky lecture a female listener was thus summarily fired. This I found most exhilarating.

On 7th March I attended a second lecture and on that occasion actually saw Gurdjieff, who, opulently attired in a magnificent astrakhan overcoat, made his way straight to the front row of the audience and sat down immediately opposite me. (I should explain that presumably, as a friend of Orage and recommended by him, I had been allowed a seat on the platform.)

I cannot say I was favourably impressed by either the person or manner of Ouspensky's master and guru. Rightly or wrongly, I felt repelled rather than attracted. His air of truculent self-complacency, his unfortunate resemblance to one's image of the typical impresario, and the palpable obviousness, not to say shallowness, of some of his remarks on bodily control and economy of effort destroyed all hope of any rapport between us from the start.

When I now read accounts of him, and see the eminence and achievements of some of the men who took his teaching seriously (Dr Kenneth Walker, for instance), I appreciate that a sweeping dismissal of him would probably be unjust. But such pronounced initial feelings of antipathy as he inspired in me are difficult to overcome, and as I had meanwhile come to the conclusion that there was no chance of my being able to devote enough time to the teaching in order to benefit from it I decided to inform Ouspensky and Orage that, to my profound regret, I could not possibly undertake to join them.

Orage was greatly shocked and, like many another whose advice has been rejected, he most probably felt slighted. But I have never for one moment regretted this resolute act of defection. I never pretended to be a dedicated *chela*, or to lead either Ouspensky or Orage to suspect that I was withdrawing from their group because I thought little of the teaching. Indeed, had I done anything of the sort I should have been insincere, because I never professed a proper understanding of Gurdjieff's aims or how he expected to achieve them. Only long afterwards, when I was in a position to judge some of the unmistakable results of the Gurdjieff regime, did I feel entitled knowledgeably to question its value.

Thus, when after his spell at Fontainebleau and the frantic agitation raised by his friends to rescue him from the labours of the life there, and when after the conclusion of his activities in America, he at last returned to London and started the *New English Weekly*, I was among those who were invited to meet him and to learn about his future plans. As I was quite ready to forgive the injury he had done me, the full story of which I shall relate in a moment, I decided to go and thus had the opportunity of observing the marked changes that had come over his appearance since I had last seen him. The deterioration in his physical condition seemed to me conspicuous, and I felt I had every reason to congratulate myself on having escaped the rigours of Gurdjieff's training camp. What made me all the more confident of the justice of this conclusion was the fact that meanwhile—i.e., during the years of Orage's absence from England—I also had undergone a thorough course of physical rehabilitation, or rather normalisation, which had not only greatly improved my condition but had also supplied me with valuable criteria for knowledgeably assessing the physical status of my fellow-men. Instead of my judgements in this sphere being, as they had been in the past, chiefly guesswork and matters of opinion, I was now equipped to give at least valid reasons for classing a fellow-being as either able or unable to maintain his sound condition if he enjoyed such a blessing, or to improve his condition if it was faulty. This was not an assessment in the medical sense, which of course I was quite unqualified to attempt, but rather an estimate of a man's chances of keeping sound if soundness and health were already present. And I owed the knowledge for such judgements to the thorough schooling in the correct use of the body which I had undergone at F. M. Alexander's teaching centre in Westminster. Indeed, I may truthfully claim that this course of training in conscious control proved to be the principal turning-point in my life and, above all, in my education. Nor do I believe that anyone who has had the good fortune to leave Alexander's hands fully conditioned, as I ultimately became, to apply his methods in every kind of bodily activity, throughout every day of the year, would charge me with exaggeration or overstatement in making the claim I have made about his teaching. From the year 1925, when I first became his pupil, to the present day, I have not ceased to rejoice in the good fortune which led me to him. It resulted in my being as it were 'born again' and, what is more, enriched me with an armoury of new standards by means of which, henceforth, I could with substantial authority assess the psychophysical condition of my fellows, together with their chances of preserving any health they happened to enjoy.

Now, it was when I was thus equipped that I renewed my acquaintance with Orage, and I confess that I was genuinely shocked by the changes I noted in his appearance. These changes were probably also observed by others, but are unlikely to have been given the significance which I felt justified in giving them. For one thing, I could not help noticing how conspicuously he had begun to stoop and how rounded his back had become, and, remembering Alexander's shrewd adage that 'it is the stoop that brings on the infirmities of old age, and not vice versa,' I naturally felt alarmed at his appearance. His bodily coordination also struck me as in every respect what Alexander called 'villainous,' and I did not need more to convince me that, no matter what its other merits may have been, Gurdjieff's regimen could hardly have included conscious control, in Alexander's sense, as one of its disciplines. When, therefore, not long after the inauguration of *The New English Weekly*, Orage was reported to have died suddenly of a heart attack, I was not in the least surprised. His death at the comparatively early age of sixty-one occurred, I believe, on the night of 3rd–4th November 1934, when by a strange coincidence he and I both made our first BBC broadcast, and it was on returning home in the evening of the 3rd that he retired to bed, never to rise again.

But I am anticipating and must resume the thread of my account of some of the reasons why he had probably long felt secretly hostile to many of my views. For, although this hostility was never openly expressed, it had, as I have attempted to show, several possible roots, and is in any case the most charitable way of accounting for the act of gross disloyalty which constituted the gravamen of my charge against his character.

To explain the circumstances under which this breach of loyalty occurred, I must as briefly as possible describe at least one aspect of the aesthetic theory my studies and meditation had at last enabled me to reach. As an intransigent Nietzschean, I classified artists into three orders: 1) the major artists who were the legislators or the establishers of a culture's values; 2) the minor artists — poets, musicians, painters, sculptors and architects — who performed their works under the influence of the values established in their culture; and 3) the inferior artists — skilled craftsmen, decorators, designers, moulders etc., who likewise, under the influence of the values dominating their culture, carried out their various skills. This was more or less carefully explained in my introduction to *The Letters of a Post-Impressionist*.[11]

Now, it was in accordance with this purely taxonomic distinction that in a *New Age* article on Epstein's sculpture I spoke of the sculptor as a 'minor artist,' meaning, of course, that he belonged to the order next to the artist-legislators.[12] I had not the slightest intention of thereby implying that vis-à-vis of his fellow-sculptors Epstein occupied an inferior rank. All I meant

---

[11] London, 1912, pp. v–xlvii.
[12] 'The Carfax, the Suffolk Street, and the Twenty-One galleries,' *New Age* 14.7, pp. 213–15. — Ed.

was, as the reader can now at once appreciate, that in the hierarchy of artists he was one of those who came next to the artist-legislators. It was perhaps imprudent to use the term without a full explanation of the special meaning I gave it, and I do not for a moment suppose that either Epstein or his champion, Hulme, were aware of this special meaning, and the grossly abusive and gratuitously offensive attack on me which Hulme proceeded to write for the *New Age* had therefore at least the excuse of ignorance.[13] The vituperation in Hulme's article was absurdly exaggerated and spiteful, for, after all, even if I *had* meant to disparage Epstein's sculpture, as many others were doing, I was perfectly entitled to express my independent opinion about it. But in his impatient zeal to defend Epstein against a supposed denigrator, and doubtless too in his human, all-too-human, eagerness to find a good opportunity to hurt a fellow-creature, Hulme could always plead that he knew nothing about my hierarchy of artists and had consequently misunderstood my remarks.

But Orage knew better. When Hulme submitted his insolent article to him, therefore, not loyalty alone, or even ordinary friendliness, but his knowledge of the customary thoughtfulness of my aesthetic judgements should have made him hesitate before publishing such an unjust diatribe against one of his most constant contributors. Despite his natural editorial eagerness to have some sensational matter for the next issue of his journal, and in view of his knowledge of my art theories, he should have felt it his duty to protect a faithful colleague and friend from the gratuitous public insult Hulme's article was intended to administer. Although he might quite properly have allowed the publication of a temperate protest, it was surely incumbent upon him to refrain from flinging a friend to an angry mob. The fact that he did not refrain, but published Hulme's article exactly as it had been written, thus constituted an act of treachery which, as far as I was able to judge, could only have been due to a long history of differences between us

---

[13] T. E. Hulme, 'Mr. Epstein and the critics,' *New Age* 14.8, pp. 251-3. — Ed.

which had estranged us more than I suspected at the time. But one circumstance casts doubt upon this interpretation of his behaviour, which is that, although nothing quite as monstrous as the Epstein–Hulme episode ever came to my notice, I was aware of many facts which pointed to a streak of disloyalty and of the typical Anglo-Saxon incapacity for solidarity in Orage's character. It is significant, moreover, that I cannot recall any instance of his having allowed an attack, let alone one as scurrilous as he had sanctioned against me, to be made against anyone higher up in the ladder of fame and power than I was at the time of Hulme's onslaught.

I duly replied to the abusive article and explained in what sense I had used the term 'minor.' But I took no other steps to counter Hulme's extravagant effort to humiliate me. I never met or knew the man and assumed that, in view of the obvious exorbitance of his language and sentiments, the reading public would not take him too seriously. I must say, however, that when later on Epstein published his book, *Let There be Sculpture*,[14] and reproduced verbatim the whole of Hulme's attack on me, just as if I had never offered any explanation of the misunderstanding, I was genuinely astonished. Nor did the discovery of this further act of deliberate spite tend to enhance my opinion either of the sculptor himself or of the race to which he belonged. I was strongly advised to take no legal steps to redress my legitimate grievance. The issues were so likely to be misunderstood by both judge and jury that I should probably only have incurred further victimisation had I attempted to appeal to the law. I cannot truthfully say, however, that I was altogether displeased when, early in World War I, I heard that Hulme had been blown to pieces somewhere on the Western Front, and, like Norman Douglas's Italian bookseller, G. Orioli, when he heard of his business enemy Warburton's mortal paralytic stroke, I liked to think that there was a connection between Hulme's tragic demise and the perfectly unprovoked abuse he had levelled at me.[15]

---

[14] London, 1940.
[15] For Orioli's account of the annoyance Warburton had caused

As for Orage, who was the principal culprit in the whole affair, the fact that I ultimately forgave him is shown by my having actually become a constant contributor to *The New English Weekly*, the journal which succeeded *The New Age*, and by the letters which passed between us after his return to England.[16]

* * *

My next and perhaps most profitable discoveries about the nature and ways of men, and the school in which, I may say, I almost finished my education (for I had yet another rich crop of lessons to learn after World War II), were both the gift of that admirable monarch, Kaiser Wilhelm II, to whom I now belatedly tender my most grateful thanks. Because all the novel and immensely valuable experiences I had as an army officer from October 1914 to the autumn of 1919, including the priceless privilege of being able to witness at first-hand at least one infinitely minute facet of the prodigious world-tragedy that was to cut European history in two, were due entirely to this gifted and picturesque ruler—that is, of course, if his responsibility for World War I was as great as many Allied statesmen, above all Lloyd George, believed.

Nor can I now dare to think what would have been my loss, both in the knowledge of military life, the understanding of men, the experience of actual warfare, and insight into at least the gunner's side of World War I, had I, owing to a more rational and less childish handling of the world crisis of July 1914 by Western statesmen, been deprived of my five years in uniform.

Even in my wildest dreams I had never imagined myself a soldier; nor, except for my passion for Napoleon, had I ever been much interested in the military life. Whenever, in my life at home, I had displayed a fastidiousness and fussy concern about the cleanliness of table implements and utensils which

---

him, of his satisfaction over his rival's sudden death, and of his hope that there was some connection between it and the injury Warburton had done him, see G. Orioli, *The Adventures of a Bookseller*, 1938, Chapters 15 and 16.

[16] Many of these letters will be found among my papers.

struck my family as obsessive, my mother had always exclaimed: 'Dieu sait mon pauvre ami ce que tu aurais fait si tu avais été soldat!'[17] But I accepted the rebuke with complete equanimity, feeling certain that the chances of my squeamishness ever being put to a military test were too remote to cause me any concern. When, therefore, war broke out in August 1914, and I found myself seriously thinking of offering my services to the nation, it was in complete ignorance of what I was letting myself in for, and without any vainglorious hopes of distinguishing myself as a warrior or hero. Had my motives been narrowly scrutinised, they would have revealed that what chiefly actuated me when I went to Whitehall on 7th September 1914 to offer myself to the military authorities was in the first place sheer curiosity, and secondly a feeling of utter despair and despondency.

Curiosity was certainly a paramount factor. Distrusting, as I had learnt to do, the testimony of others, especially about any complex problem or event, I did not expect to obtain any trustworthy information about World War I, or about warfare in general, unless I witnessed both at first-hand. As, therefore, the circumstances presented me with a unique chance of doing this, it seemed to me foolish not to take it. Secondly, I say, I was at the time feeling deeply depressed and listless. My mother had died in the previous May, and I really did not much care what happened to me. What aggravated my feelings of despair was that they were accompanied by a persistent sense of guilt. Try as I might, I could not cease from rehearsing with harrowing detail the many scenes in which, during the thirty-two years of our life together, I had behaved unkindly or disrespectfully. The many services I had performed for her, and the precious memories of innumerable happy experiences in which I had played no shameful role, seemed forgotten beyond recall. It may be that such self-reproaches invariably torment the survivor of a couple that has long been deeply attached, but this does not make them more easy to bear.

---

[17] 'God knows what you would do, my dear friend, if you'd been a soldier!' — Ed.

Be this as it may, it was certainly with no patriotic ardour or public-spirited zeal that on 7th September I visited the Recruiting Office in Whitehall, and on 9th September, after being stripped, sounded and generally overhauled, I was, at 12 pm precisely, pronounced 'medically fit.' From there I was driven with six other fellows to the Civil Service Examination Centre at Burlington House, where at 1 pm an official informed us that, as the examiner could see only two of us before lunch, he would like us to toss for admission. I was one of the two to win and, as I had every reason to expect, passed the French examination without a hitch. In the examination for German, I soon became aware of the fact that my examiner knew less German than I did, and to my astonishment I actually had to suggest a few of his participles to him when at the end of a sentence he hesitated and fumbled for a word. Incidentally, this was the first jolt my illusions about British army efficiency received. It was soon to be followed by many more serious ones.

Having passed the German examination, I was told that I should now require for my commission the recommendation of three men of substance who would vouch for my trustworthiness, and that I must return on the following morning with their testimonials.

Mr Bowlby, an old friend in Erlanger's Bank; our family GP, Dr James Bryce; and Mr Baker, an accountant in the Duke of Portland's estate office, supplied me with the letters of recommendation I required. But it was only by chance that I found them accessible, for the afternoon of September 9th was all the time I had to collect the vouchers I needed, and as I rushed round London I not unnaturally found many friends out. I duly submitted the letters to the authorities next day, but there still appeared to be much hesitation about enrolling me in the Interpreter Corps—the unit I chose, not only because I possessed the necessary qualifications for it, but also because it was the surest means of being sent overseas without delay. Apparently, they did not like the sound of Nietzsche's name and still less my connection with him. Not that they knew anything about him, but they could not believe that anyone with such a name, and anyone who had translated his works, could possibly be up to any good. However, they very soon overcame their scruples, and I subsequently learnt that they were more or less compelled to do so, as their attempt to recruit interpreters exclusively from university undergraduates had, owing to these young men's deplorable ignorance of the languages they professed to understand, made it necessary to turn to less academic strata of the population. This, however, did not by any means signify that all the men they ultimately recruited were competent linguists, for, as I soon found out when the batch to which I belonged reached the Continent, only a very few had what I should have regarded as a good knowledge of French, still fewer knew enough German to be of use, and, out of the score or so which formed our batch, only two—myself and another fellow—were able without difficulty to make themselves understood by, and to understand, the French telephone operators at St. Omer when transmitting messages from the General or Field Officers to whom they had been attached. This surprised me very much, for accustomed though I was in private life to preposterously bogus claims to proficiency in some foreign language, I hardly expected to meet with them in members of a unit specially selected and tested for the job of interpreting. It occurred to me at the time that what the War Office examiners should have done was to converse with the examinees on the telephone—a most drastic test!—and as a matter of fact, as I discovered on the outbreak of World War II, this was the practice ultimately adopted.

When, early in October, our batch embarked at Folkestone for Ostend, each of us was first allotted a batman, and we gathered that we should not be attached to any unit before we reached the Continent. We stayed in Ostend about ten days, and those of us who were not allotted to any cavalry or infantry formation on its way to the Front were attached to some old 'dug-out' who was performing an administrative function in the port. I, for instance, became the assistant to the Military Landing Officer, a charming old Scots major called Ayrton, whose business it was to see to the landing of the 7th Division. As, however, I have in *The Nineteenth Century* magazine described all the essentials of my association with this excellent officer, together with the details concerning my first impressions of the old army veteran and the hair-raising experiences I had of hardly credible mismanagement on the part of the departments in Whitehall responsible for the landing of the 7th Division on the Continent, I need not expatiate at any length on these matters.[18] The lack of foresight in providing for the disembarkation of the cavalry, for instance, greatly shocked my chief, Major Ayrton, and it was in hastily improvising the means of making good such errors on the part of the General Staff that I was able, as my *Nineteenth Century* article shows, to be of particular help to him.

Only when Ostend was ultimately evacuated, and we all drifted along the coast to Le Hâvre, was I given a permanent billet. But, to my regret, this did not mean that I was attached to any unit moving up to the Front, but only my appointment as third officer in charge of prisoners of war. I owed this job to my knowledge of German, but it proved much more interesting and pleasant than I expected. My chief, Colonel Cooper, CMG, was a charming old 'dug-out' and his second-in-command, Captain W. C. Hunter, son of Sir William Hunter of the *Gazetteer of India*, remained a close friend of mine until his death shortly before the outbreak of World War II. They were both delightful people to get on with. Colonel Cooper, however, soon left us, and Captain Hunter became CO. We had charge of everything connected with prisoners of war—censoring their letters home, extracting any useful information contained in their letters from home, meeting batches of them arriving from the Front, sorting and checking the personal effects of German dead and wounded, and wherever possible identifying the owners of the articles so as to restore them to the relatives concerned. We also had to superintend the camps in which POWs were temporarily accommodated before being dispatched to England or allotted as working parties to various sectors of the Front.

I was often much impressed by the honesty shown by the front-line men responsible for collecting and forwarding the

---

[18] 'The return of the veteran,' *The Nineteenth Century and After* 91, 1922, pp. 349–64. — Ed.

belongings of German dead and wounded. It was not uncommon to find as much as ten pounds in gold (in German currency) among the articles sent to us, not to mention banknotes, watches and other valuables. Evidently the work of collecting these belongings must have been done under the supervision of officers or senior NCOs. When, however, in 1916 I was transferred to a combatant unit, and my battery was close enough to the front line for me to observe what often happened there, I certainly saw another side of the picture. For, although the practice was quite rightly forbidden and severely frowned upon by the high command, there is no doubt that a good deal of rifling of German dead bodies by our troops occurred with the object of securing what were euphemistically called 'war souvenirs.' One may be sure that these illicit practices took place on the German side as well, and after the war, in thousands of homes in both England and Germany, there must have been many valuable articles which were thus illegitimately obtained.

At Le Hâvre, I lodged at 36 Rue Fontenelle with a family consisting of a grandmother, her divorced daughter and her granddaughter—Mesdames Morillon and Charreau and Fernande Charreau. They made me quite comfortable and fed me well, and, as my batman came every morning to polish my buttons and belt and clean my boots, they did not find me much trouble. This servant of mine was a typical Kipling Tommy Atkins. He was quite illiterate, and although he had been ten years in the army the discipline had been unable to rid him of his high-handed and independent treatment of military terms. Ordnance, for instance, he always spoke of as 'audience,' and no matter how often he saw it written up nothing would shake his confidence in this purely personal way of designating it. In the same way, he always spoke of the Belgians as 'Belgiums,' and as for my name, from the very first he never hesitated about it for one moment. I was 'Bull Davis.' There could be no such word in the language as 'Ludovici.' But 'Bull' and 'Davis' were both familiar; therefore, I remained throughout 'Mr Bull Davis.' He was both trustworthy and willing and performed his duties with great punctuality and thoroughness. Sometimes, on my free afternoons I would get him to row me out to sea so that I could get a swim, but I could never induce him to follow suit. On leaving Le Hâvre in January 1916 in order to join a combatant unit I was obliged to part with him, but I was fortunate enough to get two other excellent servants in the artillery and never had to complain of my batman and groom.

At 36 Rue Fontenelle I not only had all my meals with the three ladies but often spent my evenings with them, and as Fernande was as irresistibly fascinating as only a good-looking French flapper can be, and was in addition very bright and intelligent, I inevitably fell a victim to her charms. Nor is it surprising that, in view of the stealthy persuasiveness of propinquity, she should have reciprocated my feelings. At all events, it was not long before we both knew that we were what is commonly called 'in love,' and the situation thus created in a French household has to be experienced in order to be believed. Accustomed to the freedom allowed to young couples in England, the Englishman in France soon discovers that his girl's family are the most obstructive, vigilant and indefatigable custodians of her virtue that it is possible to imagine, and only the fact that Fernande was a scandalously spoilt child and used to having her own way accounted for our being occasionally able to steal a few moments alone. Indeed, how this attractive and infinitely resourceful girl of seventeen often openly defied her elders in order to keep me company could but enhance my respect for her ability. As I always breakfasted before the three ladies, she somehow contrived as often as possible to creep into the dining-room to keep me company, being careful to spring to her feet and to wander about as if in search of something the moment we heard the sound of approaching footsteps. As on these occasions she was usually clad only in her nightgown and a light peignoir, the strain often imposed on my self-control was not easy to bear. Like the pretty little Charlotte mentioned in Chapter 1, Fernande also unscrupulously helped in the dispatch of my Keiller's marmalade, which always formed part of my *petit déjeuner*,[19] as well as of many other dainties—cakes, fruit, chocolates and ginger—which I used to get from friends in England, Switzerland and the

---

[19] Breakfast.—Ed.

West Indies. But I was too much enamoured of her to complain. Nobody could have been more aware than I was that the whole of our mutual attachment was what Johnson called 'mere sexual appetite' or concupiscence, for, had we been united for good, the marked disparities in our ages and natures would very soon have caused irreparable rifts in our relationship. I was old enough to know this. But had I been ten years younger I should doubtless have mistaken the powerful emotions I felt for the love which only affinity can inspire. I painted her portrait, which, probably owing to my infatuation, turned out to be a wonderful likeness. Even her grandmother and mother, despite their nascent suspicions and dislike of me, were loud in their praises of it, and when I ultimately left Le Hâvre and insisted on taking the picture with me — it still hangs in my bedroom — they were genuinely displeased. Meanwhile, we were already arranging clandestine meetings outside the town, and whenever possible we used to favour a secluded part of Sainte Adresse where, I confess, it was often only by superhuman feats of restraint that I was spared the consequences of the courses that the situation suggested and invited. I knew only too well that, if I resigned myself to the pleasures that recklessness would have secured me, I should inevitably expose myself to the severest penalties a puritanical base commandant and his staff could devise. Nor had the delirium of my surrender to Fernande's charms so far led me to forget that in England there was a young woman, much nearer to me in age, general tastes and interests, to whom I had already 'plighted my troth.'

My situation was in any case becoming most precarious, because in spite of the ostensible friendliness of Mesdames Morillon and Charreau I knew perfectly well that they were watching the girl's growing attachment to me with increasing anxiety, and would soon be questioning me about my intentions. I therefore began to turn over in my mind some means by which I could decently and quietly extricate myself from the tangle. Captain Hunter, to whom I confided my troubles, strongly advised me to find some excuse for leaving Rue Fontenelle as soon as possible. He pointed out that if any untoward development occurred and Fernande's elders reported me to the base commandant, although the army authorities might possibly take into account that there had been culpable complicity on the part of Mesdames Morillon and Charreau in allowing Fernande to join me at breakfast in the flimsiest of clothing, my marked seniority and the fact that I had been a willing party to her immodest conduct and to those clandestine meetings in the environs of Le Hâvre would all tell very much against me; and it was not unlikely that, if the worst came to the worst, I might be reduced to the ranks and dispatched to some infantry battalion at the Front. In any case, the prosecutor would be sure to point out that, even if Fernande's seniors *had* been imprudent, they had probably been prompted to adopt a lenient attitude because of their faith in my honour as an Englishman and, above all, as an English officer.

All this struck me as very cogent, and as for some time I had in any case been thinking of applying for a commission in a combatant unit—for, after all, interesting as my base job was, it was not fulfilling my desire to witness war at first-hand—I saw in this change of status a possible means of withdrawing gracefully from my awkward situation, I determined with Hunter's help to press forward my application as quickly as I could. Meanwhile, of course, I thought it only prudent to apprise Fernande of the probable change in my army role, and to come to some understanding with her which would reconcile her to our separation. And here I immediately encountered the most surprising difficulties.

Fluent and angry protests accompanied by torrents of passionate tears was her immediate reaction, and it all came so suddenly and was so word-perfect that it might all have been carefully rehearsed beforehand. It was impossible to appease her, and as we were at tea in a cafe at Sainte Adresse I was not a little embarrassed. In an instant her minute handkerchief became a sodden rag. She would go to Captain Hunter and implore him to intercede for us and declare me absolutely indispensable to him. This should be easy, as I had told her often enough that even in the Interpreter Corps English officers able to read the Gothic script of German prisoners' letters did not abound. Even if it meant appealing to the base commandant to get the order cancelled, her mother and grandmother would be only too ready to do so. (For I had felt obliged to tell her that my transfer to a combatant unit was not of my own seeking, but was an official order aimed at getting all able-bodied base personnel into the fighting forces.) This was far worse than I expected!

After each burst of eloquence, her face, which had quickly become inflated with grief and indignation, would be turned towards me with an expression of hope and supplication, as if seeking in my features a trace of the eager agreement she evidently expected. And when each such mute appeal ended in disappointment she would start a fresh chain of arguments and proposals calculated to defeat the alleged War Office order.

Meanwhile, I could but cudgel my brains to discover some plausible and convincing means of reconciling her to the inevitable. At last, by the time her fertile brain seemed to have exhausted all its resources, and the dumb apathy with which I had listened to all her schemes had probably led her to infer that I must have serious and only too well-grounded reasons for regarding the alleged order as irrevocable, I decided on the following daring course.

I was too conscious of my foolish responsibility for the jam I was in to try to free myself at Fernande's cost. I knew that the chief cause of my present awkward entanglement was the powerful appeal to his vanity which the attachment of an attractive adolescent girl can too often make in a man in his thirties. It constitutes a sort of biological guarantee that, judged by Nature raw and unsophisticated, he is still a desirable mate, still sex-worthy, still able to convey to the female of his species the impression of potency. In short, it constitutes a flattering certificate of enduring youth to a man on the threshold of middle age that, if he is as vain as I am, it may easily turn his head.

Persuaded as I was, on the other hand, that Fernande was the victim chiefly of propinquity and would need a month or two, not to say weeks, of separation from me in order to regain her *sang-froid*[20] and fancy-freedom, and feeling sure that her

---

[20] Composure. — Ed.

ardent adolescent impulses would not be indefinitely sustained by memories alone, no matter how tender; aware, moreover, of the fact that in her present mood nothing short of a dramatic and solemn gesture would be likely to make her lift her fingers from my person, I thought it not only politic, safe and humane, but also, and above all, imperative, to take the bold step of formally proposing to her and undertaking that very evening to obtain her mother's and grandmother's consent to our engagement.

The intrepid duplicity of this expedient would have been unpardonable had I not been certain that, when once the warm radiance of propinquity had been shut off, means would easily be found of insensibly expediting the healing of any wounds the wrench might have caused. At all events, this struck me as the most merciful method of unravelling the tangle, and I proceeded to apply it.

She listened with obvious signs of intense interest. For the first time in this painful interview the fire of indignation in her eyes died down, and by the time I announced my intention of speaking to her mother and grandmother she was smiling. It then struck me that probably she had for some time, maybe for weeks, been wondering when I would declare my intentions to her elders, and that this explained her sudden expression of complete relief. In short, as I had more than half-expected, the rash expedient answered admirably. Everybody seemed satisfied. I managed to persuade the old people that, in view of her youth and the long separation my transfer to the artillery would involve, it would only be wise to allow this period of separation as a test of her enduring affection for me, and that therefore I did not propose to tie her down by giving her a ring and thus publicly proclaiming our engagement. They thought this very reasonable, and I then immediately ordered a silver reticule from London which I gave her as a New Year's gift — she had expressed her wish for such an article — and celebrated our *fiançailles*[21] by entertaining the three ladies to dinner and then taking them to witness, from one of the best boxes in the

---

[21] Engagement. — Ed.

house, an excellent performance of Bizet's *L'Arlésienne*.

Thus did I pave the way for the peaceful, though not tearless, parting that took place in early January 1916. All three came to the docks one evening to bid me farewell before I climbed aboard the ship for England, and it was with a feeling of inexpressible relief that from the upper deck of the vessel I waved good-bye to the dark, shadowy and rapidly diminishing forms grouped on the quay. I was conscious of having escaped a most serious danger.

I had to report for training to the CO at the artillery barracks in Ipswich soon after reaching England, and from that day to this I have never seen anything more of those three women. If she survived World War II and my reckoning is correct, Fernande must now be sixty-four years old and, I trust, a prosperous matriarch of a large and flourishing family. She is hardly likely to have remained single, and it is probable that she married an English or American officer. But whatever she did, of this I am sure—she never died of a broken heart.

How I ultimately weaned her, and without undue fuss brought about our final and irrevocable estrangement, was the outcome rather of accident than design, for although I had envisaged the end before leaving France, it was only in Ipswich—town of magic inspiration—that the means whereby suddenly occurred to me.

I once explained the whole process to an intelligent Scotswoman in Edinburgh, and she so heartily approved of it and thought it so merciful and ingenious that I have no hesitation in describing it here.

On settling down at the barracks at Ipswich, where, I may say, I thoroughly enjoyed the life, it did not take me long to discover that, although the art of gunnery had many interesting sides, it was also riddled with boring details which to one like myself, unschooled in mathematics and mystified by such instruments as clinometers and such terms as 'ballistic coefficient,' made the training not an unmixed pleasure.

Now in my weekly letters to my fiancée, about whose existence I had not breathed a word to anyone, I used, perhaps not unnaturally, to describe some of the features of my training. At least such matters helped to cover the four pages which I thought it my duty to write, and, if only to check the French, I made a practice of always rereading a letter before I sealed it up. Five or six weeks had elapsed, and I happened one day to be thus engaged in rereading my sixth or seventh letter to Fernande, full of excruciatingly tedious details about my training, when I was suddenly struck by its deadly dullness and wondered whether I ought to dispatch it. Then an extraordinary thought crossed my mind. What if the intensely boring matter with which I had, as if by chance, hitherto filled my letters were henceforth made their dominant theme? What if I made explanations about indirect laying, range-finding, the angle of sight, etc. their principal contents? And I thought of the aching tolerance with which desperate English girls often listen to their young men's monologues about their hobbies — the minutiae of photography, the problems connected with the housing and rearing of carrier-pigeons, and so on. I knew, moreover, that if there was one thing a Frenchwoman, let alone Fernande, could neither endure nor forgive, it was boredom.

Instantly, I appreciated the supreme importance of my idea, and with the help of an English–French dictionary of military terms my duty letters became the most abstruse treatises on gunnery and its manifold aspects. I wrote two or three letters of this kind without, however, noticing any marked change in the answers I received. Then, after a while, subtle signs of irritation began to appear and the spaces left on the fourth page of Fernande's letters increased ominously. At last, a letter from Madame Charreau herself reached me, in which the note of exasperation was but imperfectly concealed beneath its perfunctory expressions of affection. Did I imagine that my letters were the sort of missives a warm-hearted fiancée expected from her betrothed? Interesting though my descriptions of my work undoubtedly were, could I be altogether unaware of the unfortunate impression they were likely to make on a sensitive and loving creature such as I knew Fernande to be? 'Madame Morillon,' so Madame Charreau informed me, 'searched my letters in vain for any sentiment or expression which would have seemed but natural, not to say essential, in view of my relationship to her granddaughter.'

I was then approaching the end of my most inadequate training as a gunner—at least, according to one of our favourite instructors, Lieutenant W. Kennard (a promoted NCO of the regular army), I understood it to be so, for he was always telling us that he could not answer for what we Kitchener gunners would be up to when once the war of position became a war of movement. Be this as it may, in a week or two I found that I was one of a batch to be sent overseas, and there followed all the adventures and vicissitudes which in my novel, *The Taming of Don Juan*,[22] are related of the hero, Gilbert Milburn. As there can be no point in burdening these pages with details already recorded in Chapters 12, 13 and 14 of the novel in question, the reader who wishes to know something of my life at the Front, and about World War I as I saw it, need but refer to what is recorded of these matters in the book I have mentioned. A small contribution to the subject will also be found in *The Nineteenth Century* magazine for April 1921, in the article entitled 'The British war horse on the Somme.' In both of these sources, however, the reader may rest assured that all I have related about Gilbert Milburn's war career, as also about the horse in war—i.e., from the rifling of Gilbert's kit by the rascally camp orderlies of Le Hâvre, down to the monstrous conduct of certain hospital nurses in charge of gas-gangrene cases, and the sharp rebuke Gilbert administered to a proudly bereaved father on a train from Harwich to London—is all based upon actual facts drawn from my own experiences during the period 1914 to 1916.

On my outward journey to the Front, I did not avail myself of my passage through Le Hâvre to make a call at 36 Rue Fontenelle, although I should have had time to do so in the evening if I had wished. But I thought it best not to rekindle embers which I believed to be dying, and, as the few hours we spent at the base provided an excellent excuse for not calling, I kept aloof. When, therefore, at Nielle les Bléquins I reached the battery to which I had been posted (C Battery, 79th Brigade), I

---

[22] London, 1924.

wrote to Fernande to announce my arrival at the Front and to explain why I had been unable to call on her on my way. I received another rather indignant letter from Madame Charreau in reply. Apparently, she had heard from a friend who had recognised me among the officers dining at the Hôtel de Normandie that evening that there would have been ample time for me to visit them had I wished to do so.

From that time henceforward I thought it politic, if not indicated by the exigencies of my life as a combatant, to allow ever longer and longer intervals to elapse between my letters to Rue Fontenelle, and thus by slow degrees the correspondence faded out and, together with the relationship that had occasioned it, was as good as dead by the time the Somme offensive was started. I was, however, the last to write, and when, week after week, I received no answer, I felt myself released from the embarrassing and time-wasting sequel which a year's self-indulgent folly at the base had cost me. I had been condignly punished for my vanity, and had by chance more than by design lighted upon a foolproof recipe for extricating myself from an awkward entanglement without the risk of a breach of promise action or other penalty. It is true that circumstances favoured me, for without the technicalities of gunnery it would have been difficult to find so rich a source of tiresome facts with which to exhaust a girl's patience. Many English girls, moreover, might display greater powers of resistance to the tedium of their young men's courting conversation than one could expect to find in their French sisters. Nevertheless, the recipe will surely always be worth a trial, and no man in a jam similar to that I was in can afford to scorn it altogether.

* * *

I should not like the reader to think that I feel at all proud of this episode in my career—on the contrary! But, as these are my *Confessions*, I could hardly leave it out, especially as, like all confessions, it has greatly relieved my mind.

Looking back on the five years I spent as a junior officer in the British army, I think I can truly say that on the whole it was, in addition to its educational value, an edifying and enjoyable experience. It is easy to disparage the military man, as de Quincey does, for instance, and during World War I it was customary to speak slightingly of the old brigadiers, colonels and majors whom everybody knew as 'dug-outs.' But I must confess that my close association with scores of these old officers, and with the younger men of the regular army, convinced me that in no other class of specialists in our modern world could one ever hope to meet with such a high percentage of men of good breeding, decent, chivalrous and honourable. Most of them impressed me with the soberness of their judgements, the general modesty of their pretensions and the marked self-discipline of their demeanour and carriage. They seemed to me to display much more composure and less awkwardness and self-consciousness than their contemporaries in other callings, and I often wondered whether perhaps their often irresistible charm and natural dignity — both of which qualities distinguished them sharply from the rest of the population, high and low — were not probably due chiefly to the years of unremitting discipline to which they had been subjected. In a world from which discipline has almost entirely vanished, it was exhilarating to become associated with a class of men habituated to self-control and whose whole life and temperament had undergone the salutary influence of constant discipline.

Ruskin evidently felt much the same as I do about this matter, for, referring to his association at Woolwich with a certain Major Matson, he says: 'Such calm type of truth, gentleness and simplicity, as I have myself found in soldiers and sailors only, and so admirable to me that I have never been able since these Woolwich times, to gather myself up against the national guilt of war, seeing that such men were made by the discipline of it.'[23]

Thus, even in his day, over a century ago, a shrewd observer of mankind was able to discern the charm and dignity of a class of men in England who, by virtue of their disciplined characters, stood prominently and advantageously to the fore, against

---

[23] *Praeterita*, 1885–1889, Volume II, Chapter 8. For a further eulogy of the soldier by Ruskin, see *Unto this Last*, 1862, Essay I.

the background of the more or less undisciplined multitude, high and low, composing the bulk of the population. What would he feel about the matter now?

One other question connected with the soldier's duties and character occurs to me as I write, and it relates to the precise value we are to attach to the virtue known as bravery. It is easy to be cynical about this and, by pointing to the prevalence of this virtue among the lower animals and even among farmyard hens, to show what a primitive commonplace quality it is. De Quincey, for instance, speaking of Henri Quatre, says: 'He had that sort of military courage which was and is more common than weeds.'[24]

Or, again, it is easy to recognise the prominent role vanity plays in making even a poltroon simulate courage, and to ascribe all bravery to this source. Thus Rousseau says of bravery: 'C'est la seule vanité qui nous rend téméraires; on ne l'est point quand on est vu de personne.'[25] Whilst Voltaire, in his *Siècle de Louis XIV*, says: 'Quiconque a beaucoup de témoins de sa mort meurt toujours avec courage.'[26]

I'm afraid I must confess that the part I had to play as a gunner officer in World War I taught me that my courage is precisely of this kind — a fact disclosed to me during the Somme offensive of 1916. Among the duties of an artillery subaltern on a static front, such as ours was for weeks at a time, was that of going forward to the front-line trenches accompanied by two signallers and, with the help of either a periscope or field glasses, to direct the fire from his battery in the rear upon targets which his proximity to the enemy lines enabled him to pick out. The routine orders prescribed the use of the periscope for this work, for, although we all wore steel helmets, the accuracy of the German sharpshooters in the opposite trenches was so good that to expose one's head above the front-

---

[24] *Posthumous Works*, XVI: Suspira Profundis.

[25] *Émile*, Book II. 'Foolhardiness is the result of vanity; we are not rash when no-one is looking.' — Ed.

[26] Chapter 27. 'Whoever has many witnesses of his death always dies with courage.' — Ed.

line trench often meant instant death.

All of us were well aware of this. Yet it was customary, if not *de rigueur*, at least in my brigade, to scorn the use of the periscope and to scan the German Front with field glasses. When, therefore, at intervals of a few days it came to my turn to perform this duty, I found myself standing on the duckboards of the front-line trench with my signallers crouching safely beside me, watching me closely so as to pick up quickly and transmit any message I might give them. But although on these occasions I was always stiff with fear, I found it impossible to prevail upon myself to use the periscope. Like my brother-officers, I invariably looked across at the enemy trenches through the battery field glasses. I longed to do otherwise, but with those four eyes observing me I couldn't. I was luckier than most, for I ultimately survived the war. Yet I was never for a moment deceived about the motives prompting me to behave in this apparently courageous manner. I knew it was due to pure vanity. I could not let my signallers think me less careless of my life than the subalterns they accompanied on other occasions.

As far as I was concerned, Rousseau and Voltaire were right, and when during World War II I read Captain Liddell Hart's *Thoughts on War*[27] I thought both Frenchmen abundantly confirmed, for in that book Liddell Hart, a recognised authority on military life and the science of warfare, says: 'Man does not dare to show himself a coward under the eyes of the comrades with whom he shares his duty and his recreation. . . . It is a constant admission from the lips of brave soldiers that they were urged on by the fear of showing fear, of being thought afraid.'

Nevertheless, my knowledge of a number of regular army men I came across during World War I has convinced me that the statements I have quoted from Rousseau, Voltaire and Liddell Hart do not contain the whole truth. The men I am thinking of possessed a kind of bravery completely divorced from all motives of vanity. They were congenitally fearless. Whether or not they were being observed, the thought of the dangers

---

[27] 1944, especially pp. 86 and 87.

they were running never entered into their calculations. I am far from suggesting that this kind of lion-hearted courage is more common than that which is prompted by self-esteem alone. But I am satisfied that martial valour is by no means always the contemptible, secondary and reactive virtue that Rousseau, Voltaire, de Quincey and Captain Liddell Hart declare it to be.

My Education III
(1916–1959)

When, after the Somme offensive in November 1916, I obtained leave and went to London, I put up at the Ivanhoe Hotel, Bloomsbury, where an excellent service was in operation for just such a miserable and vermin-ridden trench-rat as I was at the time. The management collected all my clothes and belongings, fumigated and cleaned them, and provided bathing arrangements for ridding men fresh from the Front of all lice and other vermin. Thus, to the great credit of the establishment, I very soon felt a new man. But not for long. Before forty-eight hours had elapsed I was running a high temperature and was taken to the officers' hospital at Milbank, where I stayed three weeks. My disorder was trench fever, and it left me very weak. After a brief convalescence, Mackenzie the heart specialist forbade my immediate return to the Front, and I was posted to the Ministry of Munitions in Northumberland Avenue. But not very much later, after I had faced three medical boards, I was told to report to the OC MI6 at the War Office, where my languages could be put to some use and where I contrived to make myself sufficiently useful to be retained. And after two years' work in intelligence, in 1919, as General Staff Officer, third grade, with the rank of Captain, I rose to be the head of my department (MI6 A).

I considered myself lucky. I had escaped the inferno and slaughter of the Somme offensive almost unscathed. It seemed little short of a miracle, for again and again I had left a spot in a trench, at the gun position or along the road to and from the wagon-line, only to see or hear a shell crash down on it a moment later. I often asked myself whether the prayers I knew my woman friends were offering up for me had anything to do with this extraordinary good fortune, but, although I used often to joke about these supplications and boast ironically about the immunity they procured me, secretly I suspected their efficacy.

The two years spent at the War Office gave me a good insight into the working of a large government department and, above all, into the mentality cultivated in the staff personnel by the duties they had to perform. It was interesting, too, to witness the complexity of the intrigues which preceded the King's birthday and the compilation of the honours list, which in the official mind was its principal feature. I was duly awarded the MBE, but, with no wish to slight my superiors who had recommended me for it, as soon as I got out of uniform I resigned from the Order. I could not help feeling that there was something degrading about accepting an honour which was an appeal to vanity alone, especially as the award placed me on a level with hundreds of typists, munition workers and clerks who, after all, had only done their duty in callings in which millions live and die without gaining any special distinction whatsoever. The light that genial writer, Miss E. M. Delafield, shed on the wartime worker, especially of the female sex, should suffice to temper anybody's raptures about war service at home performed by both civilians and *embusqués*[1] in uniform, and expose the sentimental stupidity of the politicians who in the post-war period thought that women's war service entitled them to be enfranchised.

When in World War II I was working under Colonel W. F. Stirling, he said I had made a mistake in resigning from the Order of the British Empire, because such awards are indications not merely of merit but also of capacity, and help subsequent employers to assess one's suitability for a particular job. But I do not regret my action. Owing to the vast number who nowadays are included in an Order of the kind in question, it ceases altogether from being a distinction. One's mind boggles at the thought that so many people, especially in the low-grade populations of the West, can have been capable of conduct so distinguished as to justify so wide a distribution of honours, and the esteem in which the award is held must suffer accordingly.

I was demobilised in the late autumn of 1919, and from that

---

[1] French soldiers who had a safe or easy posting. — Ed.

time to this have been engaged in literary work of all kinds, from freelance journalism, translation (from both French and German) and novel-writing to the compilation of treatises on such unpopular subjects as anti-feminism, conservative politics, sex psychology, health and even mythology. But of all this I shall speak in a later chapter. In 1920, however, my education was still far from finished. For not only did I marry in the March of that year, but in the course of the three ensuing decades I also had abundant opportunities, through lecturing and debating in public and by making and losing friendships, of learning yet more about what Fontenelle called 'the danger' of 'le commerce des hommes.'

It was during these thirty years, moreover, that I had three experiences of outstanding importance — my membership of the political society known as the English Mistery; my two visits to Hitler's Germany and the chance this gave me of seeing a good deal of the leaders of the National Socialist Party, including, above all, Hitler himself; and my eighteen years as a smallholder in Suffolk, during which I contrived to be self-supporting to the extent of growing all my own fruit and vegetables, most of the grain for my fowls and the hay for my goats, and supplying all my dairy needs, including our butter and cream.

I have already spoken of my membership of the English Mistery and how it introduced me to a particularly virulent form of the Anglo-Saxon infirmity, the lack of solidarity — a defect which may account for most of the less attractive features of the English way of life, from its multiplicity of religious sects to the absence of any public spirit in the general population. 'Chacun pour soi et Dieu pour tous'[2] would be the most appropriate motto to inscribe beneath the Lion and the Unicorn, and it should long ago have been adopted. For, at bottom, it is this spirit that makes it difficult for the Anglo-Saxon even to understand, let alone to practise, the principle of freedom. In no country is more empty verbiage expended on the desirability and blessedness of freedom than in England. Yet in his own,

---

[2] 'Everyone for himself and God for all.' — Ed.

and especially in his womenfolk's, social behaviour, an utter failure to grasp what freedom means is daily, if not hourly, displayed.

In their incurable habit of spreading litter wherever they choose to rest; in their reckless soiling of any pitch, whether on a beach or on field, which they temporarily occupy; in their fouling and disfigurement of public library books (in the Ipswich Public Library I have repeatedly found whole pages torn from dictionaries, railway timetables and even encyclopaedias); in the damage done by their offspring to public property in parks, on railways and in institutions (for their children are never trained in habits of public-spiritedness); and in the creation of distracting noise and clamour — to mention but a few of their asocial traits — the English manifest, quite unconsciously no doubt, their inability to grasp what is implied by freedom and the practices it enjoins. I say 'unconsciously,' and this, alas, is true, for unconscious activities being based on instinct are naturally more difficult than conscious ones to eradicate.

It is surely obvious that, if people are to be free to enjoy any natural or artificial amenity, those who precede them in enjoying these amenities must not behave as if they were the only people on earth. Yet in England the majority of the population, whether on the highway or elsewhere, whether they are young or old, behave precisely as if they were their Maker's unique creation, and it is probable that their lack of any capacity for solidarity and loyalty is also due to this failing. I shall return to this evil in due course; for the time being, it must suffice to point out that all the least pleasant consequences in both English politics and social intercourse are probably accounted for by this same defect. 'Après moi le déluge'[3] might thus be added as a supplement to the motto already suggested for the national coat of arms.

All this I had indelibly imprinted on my mind during the years in which I was a prominent member of the English Mistery, and, if I owe this society nothing else, I am at least indebted to it for having confirmed the lessons I had learned about 'le

---

[3] 'After me, the deluge.' — Ed.

commerce des hommes' when I was connected with the Nietzscheans and the *New Age* clique respectively.

Still, the English Mistery brought me some valued friendships. Many of these have of course by now been removed by death; but a few have endured until this day, and for this blessing I shall continue to feel grateful to the founders of the group.[4] To them I am also indebted for opportunities I had of becoming acquainted with the leading government personalities and the social conditions of Germany during the Hitler regime, for, had I not through the Mistery become known to the personnel of the German Embassy in London, I should never have enjoyed this unique experience.

The movement certainly attracted the attention of many of the foreign diplomats in London. Thus I met Signor Grandi, with whom I often had long talks. I cannot say that he impressed me very favourably; nor could I help being astonished to discover that Mussolini's chief emissary in England could hardly express himself coherently in English. Our dinners were also frequently attended by members of the German Embassy staff, as well as by the representatives of many political parties in France, Holland and Sweden, all of whom wished to learn something about our aims and outlook. We were, therefore, not altogether surprised when in the spring of 1936 the so-called Chancellor of our society, William Sanderson, received an invitation from the authorities in Germany to come to Berlin as a guest of the Nazi Party. The idea was that he should meet the leading members of the government and become acquainted with some of the reforms and innovations introduced by the National Socialists since Hitler's advent to power.

Sanderson accepted the invitation, and as I was the only German-speaking member of the Mistery, and was in other respects the best qualified to be his companion, it was arranged that I should go with him.

---

[4] In the 1970 typescript Ludovici names these friends as the Earl of Portsmouth (previously known as Lord Lymington), Major Fitzroy Fyers, Jack Burton, Charles Challen and Geoffrey Wilson, MP for Truro. — Ed.

We crossed over to the Hook of Holland on the night of 30th April, but neither of us was able to enjoy the luxury of our first-class deck cabins, for a dense fog enveloped us soon after we left Harwich and the constant hooting of the ship's fog signal throughout the journey prevented us from getting a wink of sleep. Owing to the slow pace at which our ship had been forced to travel, moreover, we reached the Hook too late for the boat train to Berlin, and when ultimately we reached the capital, shortly before midnight, instead of being in time for dinner, there was nobody to meet us, and it looked as if our hosts had given up all hope of seeing us that day. We were not too well impressed by this poor reception, especially when some time later we heard that no government official had heard about the heavy mist in the North Sea and the serious delay it had inevitably caused.

We were both famished and exhausted, and it was pelting with rain. However, I managed to find a taxi which drove us to the address I had been given by the embassy staff in London — i.e., at the Englischer Klubb near the Tiergarten[5] — and there we found a rather peeved and perplexed remnant of the company with whom we should have dined that evening, who, having given us up, were on the point of dispersing. We were astonished to hear that at the railway station they had heard nothing about the mist at sea, and that when the boat train had arrived they naturally inferred that we had not travelled on the night of April 30th as arranged. Incredibly bad management! For, even if the railway officials had been remiss in their duty, the party instructed to meet us at the station ought surely to have made exhaustive inquiries which would inevitably have elicited the facts.

They deplored our having missed the special dinner that had been prepared in our honour, ordered a snack supper which we found very welcome, and then drove us to the Hotel Splendide, a most luxurious hotel which was to be our headquarters throughout our stay.

As guests of the Nazi Party, who wished to introduce us to

---

[5] Zoo. — Ed.

every aspect of the new Germany they were creating, we were not allowed much peace. Having given us a kind and considerate young Foreign Office official as a bear-leader, we were taken to all important meetings and driven round the country to inspect the various camps, training centres and institutions which owed their existence to the new regime. As we had arrived just in time for the First of May celebrations, our first few days were pretty full.

In the course of our stay we were able to hear Hitler speak several times, and were always given such privileged seats at his meetings that we were able to get a close view of him and all his leading colleagues in the government. As Sanderson was partly blind and understood no German, I was compelled to be not only his visual aid but also his interpreter, and this compelled me to attend with particular care to all that was said and to all there was to see.

Of the whole bunch of men around Hitler, Blomberg—the C-in-C of that period—was by far the best and most distinguished-looking. The others—i.e., Goebbels, Himmler, Schirach, Hess, Funk, Ribbentrop and Goering—all struck me as commonplace, if not actually common. I disliked Hess and Ribbentrop, but little Goebbels, with whom I discussed Nietzsche, seemed to me rather attractive and the most intelligent of the lot. At a lunch Ribbentrop gave us at the English Club I tried repeatedly to convince him that the opposition to the Nazi regime, and above all to Hitler's often high-handed behaviour vis-à-vis of neighbouring states, was much stronger in England, especially among influential Englishwomen, than he and his colleagues seemed to think; and I pointed out that women of all classes in England were inclined to resent any movement which, like the Nazi regime, was predominantly masculine in spirit. Incidentally, the unanimity with which Englishwomen subsequently backed the war party in England, often against their menfolk's views, abundantly confirmed my opinion of their attitude in 1936.

I had, however, little success with Ribbentrop, who seemed quite unconvinced. Before the luncheon party dispersed, therefore, I button-holed his secretary and begged him to repeat my warning to his chief. But judging from the generally *protzig*[6] attitude of many of the Party officials at that time, I doubt whether even he listened very sympathetically to my appeal. Captain Fitzroy Fyers, as he was then, who happened also to be among the English guests at the 1936 Party Rally and who spent much time with me in Nürnberg, will remember that on the afternoon of the 12th of September, the last day of our stay, I told him that the greatest danger of all in my opinion was precisely this *Protzigkeit* of the leading officials of the Party. It was particularly marked in Himmler, with whom I spent some time that same afternoon together with the Duchess of Brunswick and her charming daughter. I thought him most objectionable, and much as I liked the two ladies I was glad to part company with him.

Later that evening, however, I had the good fortune to come across the two ladies again, for I sat between them at the dinner Himmler gave us at the Police HQ, and I vividly remember something Frederika—the Kaiser's granddaughter, now Queen of Greece—said to me. We were discussing English schools, and she told me that when she was at her English school (North Foreland Lodge, near Basingstoke) after World War I, and the whole school assembled for morning prayers, they often sang the *Ancient and Modern* hymn which has the same melody as *Deutschland, Deutschland über Alles*, and, as often as this happened, so she would have to cry. Ultimately, this was brought to the notice of the headmistress, who at once forbade the singing of that hymn as long as Frederika remained a pupil at the school.

My two most pleasant memories of Nazi Germany are my meeting with this young lady and her mother and my visit to the Duke of Saxe-Coburg in the previous May. His Grace was a most charming personality, and our talk during the tea he gave Sanderson and me at his house in or near Berlin was one of my most interesting experiences during that first visit to Nazi Germany.

I must have heard Hitler speak in public about a dozen

---

[6] Truculent or arrogant.—Ed.

times, but I met him to talk to only once, at the Englischer Hof Hotel in September 1936, where he gave the whole of the English visitors a tea. I was perhaps too much preoccupied in studying his features to do more than exchange a few words about Nietzsche with him, but I had time to have a good look at his hands and to observe his manner in private intercourse. He was extraordinarily self-possessed among us all and very gracious in the attention he paid to every one of his guests in turn. A moment later I heard him arguing animatedly with a man whom I believed to be Ward Price of the *Daily Mail*.[7] But it all ended in a good laugh, so I assumed that the argument had been friendly.

One was easily carried away by the amazing eloquence, sincerity and passion of his public utterances, and no-one who has heard him and who was capable of understanding what he said could fail to appreciate the reason of his irresistible appeal to all classes of the community. Many hostile critics, especially women, have led their English readers to believe that there was something hysterical and even pathological about his oratory and manner in public. But after watching him with particular care during many of his addresses, I saw no sign of anything of the sort. All about me in the audience were retired generals and field officers, professional men of all ages, and dignified sexagenarians who had had distinguished careers as judges, magistrates, university professors, etc., and I refuse to believe that they could have sat there, listening as reverently as they did, often with tears trickling down their cheeks, if they had been aware of any of the contemptible characteristics which hostile and bitterly biased English reporters imagined they saw in his public demeanour. Unfortunately, the falsehoods these people fabricated for the consumption of the ignorant newspaper-reader in England were only too readily accepted as facts, and of course enjoyed, by all those who were anxious to disparage the German leader. How distant seemed the days when even a Russian general could punish a subordinate for sneering at

---

[7] Author of *I Know These Dictators*, London, 1937; revised edition, 1938; and *Extra-Special Correspondent*, London, 1957. — Ed.

Napoleon, and that century BC when a Caesar could praise his enemies!

Nevertheless, I was always a little uneasy about some of Hitler's physical characteristics, for, believing as I do in the inseparability of body and mind, I could not help fearing lest in his character and actions these physical stigmata might eventually make their influence felt. There was, for instance, one feature at least of his face which indicated coarse, if not low, breeding. From above the bridge of his nose his mask was reminiscent of Bismarck and therefore most impressive, but his mouth revealed negative traits, and his eyes had an ominous outward cast. The lower part of his nose, moreover, owing to its recessive septum, presented a dark, ugly appearance as of a large inverted thimble.

In an article I wrote for the *English Review* in 1937 I discussed the Führer's morphology in some detail, and as this article was not accepted by the editors of the *Review* it may be worthwhile to quote certain essential passages from it:

> When I first met Adolf Hitler,[8] I had already had about a dozen opportunities of closely observing him and hearing him speak. On two of these twelve occasions, I had had the exceptional advantage of being able to watch him for hours at a stretch at comparatively close quarters—i.e., from a first-tier box at the Nürnberg Opera House. The first occasion was a gala performance of Wagner's *Meistersinger* (September 8th 1936), when he sat in the centre box in the same tier as mine; and on the second occasion, a day or two later, he stood well forward on an improvised platform built over the orchestra pit, to deliver an address on culture and the National Socialist state.
>
> He is middle-aged and of medium height. Stockily built and fairly muscular, he is a so-called 'dark-blond' with eyes that betray the blond strain in his ancestry. He moves with energy and decision, but never jerkily. The

---

[8] Which was on the occasion of my second visit to Nazi Germany.

general serenity of his person makes his occasional outbursts of passion all the more forcible. He has not the height that Symonds and Sheldon associate with leadership and aggressiveness; but he has the solidity, the deep manly voice, the commanding glance and gesture and the deliberation which inspire confidence. Nor should it be forgotten that although Confucius, Caesar, Edward I, de Gaulle etc. were all tall men, the first exceptionally so, Alexander the Great, Mahomet, Napoleon, Wellington and Frederick the Great were all either short or of only medium height. Frederick the Great was actually much below medium height.

The Führer has a fine intelligent brow and well-shaped ears in which every part is normally represented. Some morphologists attach much importance to this, because the stigmata of degeneration rarely occur singly, and malformations and irregularities in the ear, such as absence of the lobule [very common nowadays], or of the helix at the top of the pinna, or of the anti-helix, are therefore significant.

Against these good features are two less favourable physiognomic traits which however no-one who knew Hitler seems to have noticed. I refer to the outward cast of his eyes and an abnormally high nasal septum. The former, besides indicating a lack of stamina, often associated with a tendency to romanticism and vagueness . . . As to the latter, in which the wings of the nostrils fall below the level of the septum . . . this is a very unbecoming feature associated with random and low breeding. But no accurate morphological description should omit to mention it as it inevitably implies corresponding characterological traits. Even in a nobler mask than Hitler's it would still constitute a disquieting blemish. It is therefore important to bear it in mind when we speculate on the Führer's probable role in Europe's future.

Finally, I made a few remarks about his lack of sound bodily coordination which, I said, 'might occasion disquiet in the minds of all the true friends of the regime.'

This article was one of a series I was contributing to the *English Review* on the Third Reich, but to my surprise it was returned to me by the editors with the following note:

42 Upper Grosvenor St. W1
23.3.1937

Dear Ludovici,

Many thanks for sending along your article upon Hitler's morphology. I have read it through with the very greatest interest myself — but both Walker-Smith and myself agree that it is hardly suitable for the *English Review* ... I know you will understand when I say that, looked at broadly, we are rather doubtful about publishing it.

Yours sincerely,
Peter Brassey

Of course I understood! Thus, sugared as the pill was — for I had tried to give my warning as diplomatically as possible in order to avoid displeasing the German Embassy staff — the *English Review* editors nevertheless thought my deliberately temperate article too dangerous for publication in their magazine. Evidently they knew the political atmosphere in Europe at that time to be too thundery to allow of their printing the article with safety.

One last word about Hitler and I shall not need to discuss him further.

In this intellectually servile and sterile age, when both the high and the low in the land are equally sequacious and subservient, propaganda pays handsomely, whether in commercial advertising or in inculcating upon the population the opinions which the Establishment think it good for us to hold. Now, among these opinions none has been more diligently dinned into us than that the German people's acceptance of Hitler must indicate some morbid and unpleasant flaw in the German mentality. And as in modern England it suffices for such a view to be stated only once by some recognised member of the Establishment for it to be immediately taken up and re-echoed by thousands of lesser people, it follows that today one can hardly open a book or listen to a BBC broadcast in which it is not emphatically stated that, in accepting with almost complete unanimity a 'mental defective' such as Hitler, the German nation gave proof of its fundamental perversity.

A typical presentation of this view, which can now be found paraphrased in innumerable forms by prominent English people, from Mr Robert Birley, the Head of Eton, to the most ignorant female journalist, is that made by Colin Welch in his review of William L. Shirer's *The Rise and Fall of the Third Reich*, when he asked: 'Why on earth, for instance, did such a richly gifted people as the Germans prostitute themselves to become the tools of a maniac?'

Now, apart from the fact that the author of this rhetorical outburst, like all those who now obediently toe the Establishment's line, takes for granted that his readers, who in other contexts would pride themselves on demanding the evidence, will meekly accept the statement that Hitler was in fact a maniac, can the host of parrots who repeat this *rengaine*[9] about the German people's turpitude in accepting Hitler ever have asked themselves what Hitler meant to Germany in the decades following World War I?

The minute minority of Englishmen who happen to be well-informed do not need to be reminded of Germany's outstanding achievements in scholarship, science, music, philosophy and poetry, or to be told that a nation possessing the record of which she could justly boast in 1914 must necessarily have her pride, her consciousness of high endowments, entitling her to feel a worthy example of what European civilisation has so far produced. When, therefore, such a nation is humiliated, vilified and degraded as Germany was after World War I, the pain it undergoes is naturally proportionate to the honourable position it knew itself to have reached in the family of Western

---

[9] Same old story. — Ed.

peoples. The blow to its self-esteem must have been — could not help having been — staggering.

Let anyone, even outside this minute minority of well-informed Englishmen, imagine what England would have felt had she been similarly humiliated, or merely recall what England did feel after the retreat from Dunkirk, and the whole picture assumes a different aspect.

It was thus to a Germany still suffering acutely from the wounds of such a humiliation that suddenly someone appeared who contrived to restore the country's self-esteem and helped it to recover its self-respect and sense of worthiness. Naturally, inevitably, the response was one of rapturous gratitude and affection. Even if Hitler had really been the monster the Establishment wished us to believe he was, the enthusiastic response to his appeal would still be comprehensible.

Had not no less a person than Lord Lothian expressed his admiration for the conditions introduced by Hitler's regime? Nor, as we know, was he by any means the only Englishman who felt this way. In the *Times* of 1st February 1934, speaking of National Socialism, he had written that it has given 'Germany unity where it was terribly divided; it has produced a stable government, and restored to Germany national self-respect and international standing.'

These are the words of a sincere Liberal. Do they indicate that the charge of lunacy against Hitler and his administration was justified? Besides, we must remember that the German nation's humiliation after 1918 was not confined to the terms of the Versailles Treaty. There was also the degradation and deep injury inflicted on them by Allied troops, who occupied their country for years after the armistice. As a tourist it was not possible to learn the full magnitude of these injuries, but I remember when I visited friends in Düren in 1922 that the account I was given of the behaviour of the French black troops in the town appalled both my wife and myself.

'The Germans, a proud people,' says Mr Abel J. Jones, 'were reduced to such a state of humiliation as to welcome anyone, however unlikely or dangerous, promising to restore their confidence and pride.'¹⁰

The intelligence and understanding, not to mention the charity, revealed in this passage are admittedly quite exceptional in present-day 'fair-minded' England, and show a defiance of the Establishment reminiscent of more creditable eras in British history than that covered by the last thirty years. But the fact that at least one Englishman can have been found to express such a view suggests that, in any case, as recently as 1945 some good sense and psychological insight still existed in the nation.

For what F. L. Lucas so aptly remarks of the Age of Reason applies with even greater force to this age—namely, that it owes 'some of its most fatal mistakes to bad psychology.'¹¹

A notorious but by no means isolated example of the lengths to which blind prejudice against the German nation could go after the rise of Hitler is to be found in Lord Frederick Hamilton's *The Days before Yesterday*. Speaking of the word *Schadenfreude*, which means pleasure over another's troubles, the noble author says: 'How characteristic it is that there should be no equivalent in another language for this peculiarly Teutonic emotion!'¹²

But, apart from La Rochefoucauld's implicit claim regarding the prevalence of this emotion, when he wrote, 'Dans l'adversité de nos meilleurs amis nous trouvons toujours quelque chose qui nous ne déplait pas,'¹³ what would Lord Frederick Hamilton and his readers say or think if a German, calling attention to the word 'bully'—which means either using one's strength to hurt, injure or oppress one weaker than oneself, or else a person who is guilty of such behaviour—remarked: 'How characteristic it is that there should be no equivalent in another language for this peculiarly English weakness and type'?

Yet there is as much, if not more, justification for such a re-

---

¹⁰ *In Search of Truth*, 1945, Chapter 3, 2.
¹¹ *The Art of Living*, 1959, Chapter 1.
¹² 1920, Chapter 4.
¹³ *Maxims*, 99. 'In the misfortune of our best friends we always find something which is not displeasing to us.' —Ed.

mark as there is for Lord Frederick Hamilton's about *Schadenfreude*. Nor need the reader search very long for evidence of the prevalence of both the weakness itself or the type stricken with it.

Let him but read the following: T. Medwin's *Life of Percy Bysshe Shelley*,[14] *Poems of E. B. Browning*,[15] S. M. Ellis's *Wilkie Collins, Le Fanu and Others*,[16] Lady G. Cecil's *Life of Robert Marquis of Salisbury*,[17] A. L. Kennedy's *Salisbury*,[18] John Cowper Powys's *Autobiography*,[19] Sir Ian Hamilton's *When I Was a Boy*,[20] Viscount Mersey's *A Picture of Life*,[21] K. W. Jones's *The Maugham Enigma*,[22] L. S. Amery's *My Political Life*,[23] C. R. Sanders' *The Strachey Family*,[24] Kipling's *Something of Myself*[25] and Kenneth Robinson's *Wilkie Collins*.[26]

From these few books — and I could quote many more — the reader will be able to conclude not only that the vice of bullying and the bully type is widespread in England, but also that the type itself is by no means restricted to the least cultivated and most uncivilised strata of the population, for among the facts contained in the above-mentioned books he will find that two of the worst bullies ultimately became respected and famous Archbishops of Canterbury. I refer to Archbishops Temple and Benson.

As far as I know, no German has so far made the comment about the word 'bully' which would be the suitable retort to Lord Frederick's too hasty remark about *Schadenfreude*, but

---

[14] 1847, Volume I, Chapter 1.
[15] Preface to the 1887 edition.
[16] 1931, Chapter 5.
[17] 1921, Volume I, Chapter 1.
[18] 1953, Prologue.
[19] 1934, III, IV.
[20] 1939, III, IV and VII.
[21] 1941, Chapter 1.
[22] 1954, 112, Section 18.
[23] 1953, Volume I, Chapter 1.
[24] 1953, Chapter 15.
[25] 1937, Chapters 1 and 2.
[26] 1951, Chapter 2.

meanwhile I have attempted to repair the omission.

After having for two thousand years been exhorted not to behold the mote in your brother's eye before having first considered the beam in your own,[27] it is disappointing to find how frequently the admonition is ignored, especially in modern England.

* * *

I can speak only briefly about my experiences during World War II, for they were too galling to be comfortably related in detail. The spirit of witch-hunting which suddenly possessed the English people after their humiliation at Dunkirk, and which, fomented by the authorities and the press, prompted everybody with a secret grudge to practise delation and slander quite free of any risk, led to a state of affairs when malice, envy or merely the pleasure of twisting a neighbour's tail made life intolerable for anyone who had, however unwittingly, offended the sanity of those about him.

For after the unprecedented and wholesale defeat of the British army in northeastern France and Flanders in 1940, when 112,546 Allied and 224,585 British soldiers, most of whom had abandoned their arms and equipment, were evacuated from the beaches of Dunkirk, it proved an immense solace to the English people, and greatly helped to salve their wounded self-esteem, to be told that the Allied forces had not been beaten or outwitted by any superior military strength or genius, but had simply been let down. The inference being that, although militarily, everybody, including the politicians and the higher command, had been brilliantly efficient and that the advance into Belgium—an error subsequently exposed by all knowledgeable critics—had denoted no major deviation from modern scientific strategy, the whole disaster had been the outcome of quisling and fifth-column activities within the Allied ranks and populations.

The general public did not of course know, and were never

---

[27] Matthew 7.3.

told, that the debacle had been due, as Captain Liddell Hart subsequently pointed out, to 'the essential misunderstanding of modern warfare by the Allied leaders, political and military,' and that 'the French army paved the way for its own defeat because it failed to adopt or develop a defensive technique suited to modern conditions.'[28] The common people, therefore, especially in England, eagerly swallowed the canard about fifth-column activities as the major cause of the defeat. Their cruelly outraged self-esteem was thus salved and the authorities were able to conceal from the nation the enormity of the reverse and the culpability of those responsible for it.

The cry of 'quisling' and 'fifth columnist' had, however, the inevitable result of giving every knave, every failure, every fool envious of another's way of life or of his gifts, the opportunity to vent his venom. With his hand on his heart, everybody thenceforth had a patriotic excuse for injuring a fellow-citizen. Suspicion alone was enough.

I, for one, was soon made aware of the speed with which many of my dear neighbours in Upper Norwood who had resented my anti-Christian attitude or my hostile criticism of feminism and democracy, together with many of my former associates in the English Mistery, seized the chance of maligning and casting suspicion upon me, and by the 29th of May 1940 two detectives from Croydon Police HQ called to question me about my 'anti-Allied' opinions. I managed to appease their apprehensions, and they left.

A little later, at the office where I was engaged on intelligence work, however, I gathered that searching inquiries were being made concerning my ideological suitability for the post, and, despite emphatic protests and even apologies from my two chiefs, Colonel Stirling and Colonel Backhouse, these inquiries culminated in my being summarily dismissed on the 14th of August 1940.

From Colonel Backhouse I learned that the gravamen of the charges against me was my membership of the Right Club, a group professing political views of the extreme Right and di-

---

[28] *Dynamic Defence*, 1940.

rected especially against communism, to which, in view of my record, I naturally felt myself affiliated. But in expressing his regret for what had happened, Colonel Backhouse said: 'It all shows how careful we should be in choosing our associates.'

In vain did I retort both to him and the naval head of our branch of the intelligence service that among these very associates was none less than the Duke of Wellington, the president of the club, and that an ordinary commoner like myself might surely be excused if he thought that a group thus led must be above any suspicion of national disloyalty. I also pointed out that, as every fellow-officer in my department knew, I had openly displayed the badge of the Right Club, a silver spread-eagle, on my lapel and had explained to both Colonel Stirling and Colonel Backhouse what it stood for. Was this the sort of conduct that might be expected of a member of a seditious organisation? Both merely shrugged their shoulders and, whilst admitting the cogency of my pleas, professed themselves unable to alter the decision of the authorities. As I was then due for promotion in my department and had even had an interview with Colonel Backhouse about it (for by that time Stirling had left), it has often struck me that among those who may have had a share in maligning me there may have been one or two who aspired to the position I was due to fill.

Meanwhile, under Regulation 18B scores of people as innocent as I was myself of any seditious activities or intentions, including Captain Ramsay, MP, had been arrested and sent to prison without trial. What had happened to *habeas corpus*, which Dr Johnson said was the one feature of English life which made England superior to any Continental country?

But no sign of protest came from the nation at large, and even in Parliament the protests against arresting and imprisoning people on the grounds of suspicion alone and for holding views unsympathetic to the authorities were both feeble and unsupported. Historically, however, the dictatorial methods of the authorities acting on the strength of Regulation 18B were a complete innovation. Everybody knew perfectly well that at the end of the nineteenth century, when the Liberals, including Lloyd George, had, as Sir Sidney Low and Lloyd C. Sanders maintain, denounced the Boer War 'as a crime and a blunder committed not by the Boers, but by the imperial Cabinet at the instigation of the Rand financiers,' and had been dubbed 'Little Englanders,' no disaster had overtaken them, any more than it had overtaken the many prominent people who had opposed the war policy of the government in Napoleon's day. Again in 1914, we had seen men as distinguished as Lord Morley and John Burns oppose the Government of their day on the question of war with Germany, and they had done so with impunity. They were no more suspected of disloyalty to the nation than Lord Lansdowne was when in 1917 he had wisely but ineffectively pleaded in favour of making peace.

Thus, to all my friends and myself there appeared to be nothing calling for either secrecy or fear in our openly disagreeing with the government over the policy of war with Germany in 1939, and as the Right Club was particularly determined in this matter we were anxious to support it.

What was my surprise, therefore, when on the 14th of October 1940 I suddenly became aware of the fact that I must have more formidable enemies conspiring against me than some of my Norwood neighbours and my colleague at the office, for, on returning home in the evening of that day, I found my wife and Alice Cook (our faithful retainer) in a state of extreme agitation, and was told that three detectives from the Special Branch, Scotland Yard, had spent the whole day searching our house from top to bottom.

What they expected or hoped to find, I cannot imagine. But they must have felt confident of pouncing on some incriminating evidence, for their search had been prolonged and exhaustive. To say that, like Tolstoy, when his house, Yasnaya Polyana, was searched by the police, I was 'insane with rage,'[29] would be an understatement. For the outrage committed against me was not only quite gratuitous, but also completely and flatly contradicted by everything I had since my early childhood been led to believe about the English way of life, with its alleged freedom of opinion and judgement.

---

[29] Tikhon Polner, *Tolstoy and his Wife*, 1946, Chapter 4, 3.

Never could I have imagined that such a Terror could arise against any minority group in England of the twentieth century on the score of their opinions alone. Having as a young man read with agreement and conviction Buckle's *History of Civilization in England*,[30] where, much too hastily as it has now proved, he proudly drew the conclusion that henceforward no man in this country was ever again likely to be persecuted for his opinions, I was now faced with the disquieting truth that, after all, the whole of England's alleged respect for private judgement — the whole of the democratic boast, in fact — had never been more than a fair-weather policy. The much vaunted tolerance, by virtue of which England had for centuries been basking in the admiration and envy of the Continent, had proved no more than a pretence, and its greatest dupes, like Montesquieu and Voltaire, had unfortunately not lived to discover its hollowness.

'Yes,' says the defender of Regulation 18B, 'but do not war conditions create an emergency situation and justify a tightening of the attitude towards deviationists who in peacetime may be ignored?' Surely the reply to this is that a principle that is observed only when no claim is put upon it is nothing but a fair-weather expedient. It is like a sheet-anchor of papier-mâché, carried along to give a crew a factitious sense of security. Unfortunately, both Continentals and the more knowledgeable among English people had for centuries believed that this sheet-anchor could be put to the test.

But to recover the thread of my narrative, soon after breakfast on the morning following the search of my house, the Special Branch, Scotland Yard, telephoned to say that I must doubtless be anxious to know why my house had been ransacked and, as they wished to interview me, they would like to see me at the Yard as soon as possible.

It was five minutes past eleven am on Friday the 8th of October 1940 when I was invited to sit at a bare table in a bare room on one of the upper floors of the building, and found myself facing a dark young man who had in front of him what ap-

---

[30] Volume I, 1857, Chapter 7.

peared to be my dossier. In a gloomy corner of the room to my left sat another young man, fair and distinguished looking and about the same age as my vis-à-vis.

I felt pretty sure that these two fellows were not going to be my only listeners and that by some secret device all I said would be heard and weighed by a more senior officer in another room. Little purpose would be served by my attempting to give even a brief summary of all that passed between me and my examiners. I need only say that I was asked to give an account not only of my opinions on current affairs and of my political views, but also to describe the whole of my career as an adult.

I spoke almost uninterruptedly from 11.05 am to the close of the interview at 12.40 pm, and spent much of the time disentangling the political views I had held since writing my *Defence of Aristocracy* from the complex of Fascist and Nazi doctrine. For apart from the absurd identification made by most superficial English men and women at that time of Fascist and Nazi views with the traditional attitude of the English Right—a confusion largely engineered and encouraged by the communists who wished to discredit conservative politics—there prevailed at this period in the war much more popular sympathy (especially among influential women) with Leftish views than with opinions consistent with the English Right.

By referring to my own books, I was fortunately able to show that I had never once departed from the old Tory position, and I told my examiners that when I had been a member of the Mistery I had repeatedly warned my associates against confusing our attitude with that of the Continental Fascists. I was moreover able to tell the two young men before me something about the motives animating those whom I suspected of having informed against me. For during the interview one of my examiners had said: 'I think we ought to tell you that quite a number of important people have testified against you.' This led me to explain why I, together with such old associates as Lord Lymington (now the 9th Earl of Portsmouth), had seceded from the Mistery and to point out that, although we felt we could no longer support the movement, quite a number of important people not sympathising with our reasons for quitting it—or, what was more probable, never having been told what these reasons were—still belonged to it. And I added that, among these important people (one of whom I actually named), there must naturally be a few who, having accepted the hostile explanation of our defection, would imagine they were performing a patriotic duty in denouncing me.

I think this explanation, together with the fact that I had been able to name one of the VIPs who was already probably known to the Yard as having informed against me, rather impressed my examiners, but, at any rate, precisely at 12.40 pm I was told I could leave the building as a free man, and I was never again either questioned or importuned by any member of the Special Branch. Indeed, with the detective, Mr Mann, who was my examiner-in-chief at this deplorable interview, my relations subsequently became quite friendly.

Like the less fortunate of the examinees—I refer to those who were ultimately imprisoned without trial—I was asked about my attitude to the Jews. I could not readily see the relevance of this question in connection with any suspected disloyalty to England. For what had a man's private views about the Jews to do with his national loyalty? However, I replied by pointing out that I was no more anti-Semitic than I was anti-English. But, as I regarded both the English and the Jews as essentially particularists in Henri de Tourville's sense,[31] I feared they were both inclined to behave in an asocial manner and to abide too rigidly by the principle, *après moi le déluge*—the Jews owing to their nomadic, and the English owing to their Northern and Scandinavian, ancestry.

As I strongly suspected that Scotland Yard had been told of my anti-Semitic views by my old associates of the Mistery, who were well aware of how damaging in 1940 the charge could be, I took the opportunity, when later on Detective Mann paid me a friendly visit, to lay a strange document before him. It con-

---

[31] The point is explained in 'Transform society's values,' my contribution to *Gentile and Jew: A Symposium on the Future of the Jewish People,* edited by Chaim Newman, London, 1945, pp. 165-85.

sisted of a letter addressed to me in 1918 by the very man, the head of the English Mistery, whom in 1940 I suspected of having instigated the conspiracy against me, and it contained his severe rebuke to me for having depicted with too much fairness and favour the Jewish character of Dr Melhado in my first novel, *Mansel Fellowes*.[32]

Mann asked me why on earth I had not brought this letter to Scotland Yard in October 1940. I explained that I had only recently turned it up among my papers, otherwise I should certainly have done so. However, I think Mann must have reported the matter to his superiors, and the Mistery testimony must have suffered accordingly.

* * *

My education, though not yet finished, was nearing completion. I had yet a long, new and gruelling experience to undergo, and that was my life as a smallholder in the heart of rural Suffolk from April 1941 to June 1959. It was a valuable experience for a townsman born and bred like myself, and I do not regret it. For during those eighteen years, although the work was hard, the life was wholesome and it enabled my wife and me to enjoy the great luxury of eating fruit and vegetables fresh from the garden and of supplying all our needs in milk, butter, cream and eggs. By arranging our chicken runs so as to be able to keep our hens always on good fresh grass, the eggs we produced from our own birds certainly spoilt my taste for any I have had since.

I learnt to grow most of what we required, for, being largely vegetarians, we depended little on outside providers for our daily food. I even grew the maize I needed for my fowls and always gathered and stacked the hay I gave to my goats. On my two and a half acres I got little help from my neighbours, for, apart from the fact that it was very difficult throughout my stay at Rishangles to find anyone who was free to work for me even part-time, Suffolk yokels and their wives are so hope-

---

[32] London, 1918.

less—inarticulate and incapable of lucidly explaining anything they have been in the habit of doing for generations; they are, moreover, so unready to impart information to 'foreigners'—that I soon learnt the necessity of carrying on without appealing to them. Nor in the end did this prove such a serious drawback as I imagined, for their own methods are often so faulty that it is better not to emulate them. For the first year or two—that is, before I had acquired the scraps of knowledge and mastered the various procedures necessary for the successful performance of my work as a gardener and dairyman—I was therefore thrown on my own resources and, helped only by the study of the relevant textbooks, was obliged to learn most things in the hard school of trial and error.

It was very soon after my momentous interview at Scotland Yard that my wife and I decided to leave our London house and to move into the country. We expected rates, taxes and other living expenses to soar, as of course they very quickly did, and as we had only slender private means we thought the sooner we could become more or less self-supporting the better. In April 1941, therefore, we moved into a thatched cottage in Rishangles, near Eye in east Suffolk, which had once belonged to the local miller, and there, after many setbacks and losses (for I knew nothing whatsoever of either horticulture or agriculture), we contrived at last to become largely self-supporting and to save a good deal of money. It was, however, a hard grind, and without our devoted retainer, Alice Cook, who helped considerably in the garden, with the goats and fowls, and on the paddock in haymaking, we could scarcely have made good. But Alice's help outside meant that most of the domestic chores fell to my wife, who incidentally loathed every form of household work, so that I am afraid our eighteen years in rural Suffolk proved rather an unhappy period of her life. Unfortunately this could not be helped, for, although I was master of only two and a half acres and kept never more than three goats and eight hens, the work outside the house was as much as Alice and I could cope with.

Two jobs, however, I never mastered, and I always had to employ some local man or youth to do them for me. They were the mowing of my hay, for I suppose I was too old to learn the use of a scythe, and the thatching of my haystack.

During all these eighteen years the three of us had to take separate and very short holidays, and always in the winter months, as absences at other times of the year were out of the question. Indeed, had I not taught Alice to milk and to do the dairy work, I should never have been able to take a holiday at all.

Nevertheless, despite our total initial ignorance of all the techniques and skills required for the successful management of a smallholding, we actually contrived in the end to be able to give our much more experienced neighbours a number of valuable lessons, and in true Suffolk style they did not accept them too gracefully. We were the first in the whole area, for instance, to produce ripe maize-cobs — a feat which greatly astonished many of the local farmers. For, thanks to the kindness of the Earl of Portsmouth, who gave me my first supply of the special seed that was required for the growing of ripe maize-cobs in England, I was able to meet all my requirements in this essential commodity. But the novelty of my first crop was such that one of my farmer neighbours, after begging me for one of my ripe cobs, went about the district for days exhibiting it as a local wonder. We also gave the village folk a lesson or two in the hatching of chicks from our Rhode Island Reds. For, to my surprise, I found that it was customary among the local farm-labourers and their wives to regard a successful hatching from a clutch of thirteen eggs more as a matter of luck than of careful and knowledgeable management.

After long and bitter experience I had, by observing Nature and the conditions governing the hatching of eggs laid in the wild, discovered the only rational and foolproof method of securing regular and satisfactory results, and learned incidentally how mistaken even people of long experience may be when they blindly follow a faulty, although traditional, method, instead of exercising their wits and studying Nature's solution of their problems. For they had only to think what happened when one of their hens reared a family in the wild, and suddenly turned up proudly with a large brood of sound and vigorous chicks, all reared without human interference, in order to learn what was wrong with their own methods.

But all this, together with many other experiences of rural life is related in my book, *The English Countryside*,[33] so that I need not dwell any longer on our life at The Homestead, Rishangles, and on all we learned and did there. Suffice it to say that, although in those eighteen years of comparative exile I never obtained many lessons from my grandmother in the art of sucking eggs, I was certainly able in the end to give her one or two useful hints about the performance of the operation.

---

[33] Although Ludovici left money in his last will for *The English Countryside* to be published after his death, along with these *Confessions*, the book has never appeared in print. Typescripts of these two works are held by the Special Collections Division of Edinburgh University Library. See the Editor's Foreword. —Ed.

My Friends I

Only comparatively late in life was I made to understand that I am a bad friend and that, to some extent at least, this explained the many broken friendships that have marked my career. The fact was first brought home to me by Roland Berrill, who was good enough to state it quite plainly.[1] In December 1938 he had invited me for a week to his house in south Devon, and when at the end of my stay he drove me to the station he urged me with strange insistence to read a recently published American book on the art of making and keeping friends. Puzzled by the warmth of his appeal, I asked him to explain, and it was then that he kindly but emphatically informed me that I knew nothing whatsoever about friendship and that the sooner I learnt the better. As I was then approaching my fifty-seventh year the outlook seemed rather hopeless, for, although I ultimately recognised the justice of his criticism, I could see little chance of reform, no matter how many textbooks I studied.

Nevertheless, I have ever since felt grateful to Roland Berrill, for without his candid admonition I doubt whether I should ever have discovered my inaptitude for friendship. Looking back on that week in south Devon, I am to this day still uncertain of how I transgressed and failed to come up to Berrill's expectations. But his rebuke was so kindly, genuine and generously intended that I feel sure he must have had serious grounds for administering it.

When I ask myself why I am temperamentally ill-endowed for friendship, I often wonder whether perhaps the passionate and satisfying attachment I formed in my early years to my two closest relatives, my mother and my sister Lily, may not have made me indifferent to all other human ties; whether, in fact, the enjoyment of these immense riches may not have inclined me to scorn more meagre treasures. When I had digested Berrill's re-

---

[1] Presumably, the Roland Berrill who in the 1950s co-founded Mensa. — Ed.

buke I appreciated how careless I had often been of nursing the various friendships I had formed in the past, and, knowing myself to be a bad mixer and consequently ill-equipped for cordial relations with my fellow-men, I felt obliged to accept Berrill's view of my many failures. I saw, moreover, the obvious moral it implied. For friendship often means that influence is being exerted in one's favour. It means that, when the occasion arises, one is more likely to be praised than disparaged. In the end, therefore, a capacity for good friendship may mean not only social but also material success.

Another possible explanation of my failure as a friend is my inability to pay compliments and to flatter, even when I am genuinely prompted to admire. The philosopher F. H. Bradley says, and I think quite correctly, that 'if anyone is to remain pleased with you, he should be pleased with himself whenever he thinks of you.'[2] Thus, people tend to like those with whom they feel self-satisfied, and any behaviour or bearing that causes a stimulation of the deep-seated inferiority feelings latent in all of us moderns is incompatible with friendship. Nor need the sort of behaviour that is subconsciously resented be always deliberate. It may consist, as in myself, simply of a lack of zealous solicitude for a friend and his affairs. The faintest sign of this lack of interest is instantly felt as an affront, or as a reason for not loving him who displays it.

This may partly explain why my best, fastest and most loyal friends have all been women, because I am more prone to show genuine approval of a woman and to convince her of my interest in her and her affairs than I am to manifest the same feelings to a man, no matter how much I may respect his accomplishments.

Another important factor in the making of friends is the extent to which one can endure, or actually prefer, loneliness. If solitude is no hardship, as it never was to me, one is careless about making friends and especially about retaining them, and one is prone to lose them, as I am afraid I have often done, without a struggle.

Proust seems to have had much the same temperament as

---

[2] *Aphorisms*, 1930, 26.

mine, otherwise he could hardly have said of friendship: 'Elle est si peu de chose que j'ai peine à comprendre que les hommes de quelque génie, et par example un Nietzsche, aient eu la naïveté de lui attribuer une certaine valeur intellectuelle.'[3]

It seems probable to me that, apart from the social and material benefits friendship may bring and the good repute a circle of friends may create for you, the value of friendship and its sentimental beauties have been exaggerated. For even good mixers who break none of the rules like my friend Berrill evidently had in mind are, as far as my own worldly experience goes, extremely rare. As La Rochefoucauld maintained: 'Quelque rare que soit le véritable amour, il l'est encore moins que la véritable amitié.'[4]

Most close observers of humanity would, I think, concur, and when Samuel Johnson asked, 'Who eats a slice of plum pudding the less because a friend is hanged?,'[5] he was surely not merely cracking a joke.

When we reflect how prevalent morbidity of some kind or other is today, and how common must therefore be its sequel in the form of widespread inferiority feelings; when, moreover, we think of the solace that is subconsciously and momentarily derived from denigration—for every act of denigration is accompanied by a transient feeling of superiority—we appreciate the difficulty of accepting a too idealistic view of friendship. No-one can have lived very long in England without having been impressed with the habit of adverse criticism which is immediately indulged by friends and acquaintances the moment someone known and even dear to them has turned his back. The ominous opening, usually consisting of an expression of affection for the person to be run down, is quickly followed by open disparagement. And the people who have this habit display a good deal of naïveté, for they forget that the natural inference their listen-

---

[3] *Le coté de Guermantes*, Volume II. 'It is so small a matter that I find it hard to understand how men of some genius, such as Nietzsche, have the naïveté to give it a certain intellectual worth.' —Ed.

[4] *Réflexion morale*, 473. 'However rare true love is, it is less so than true friendship.' —Ed.

[5] James Boswell, *The Life of Samuel Johnson*.

er will draw is that he too will be similarly discussed when once he leaves them. Again and again at house-parties I have been shocked by this sort of behaviour, which has often made me feel rather doubtful about the alleged sacred bonds of friendship.

Three centuries ago Pascal wrote: 'Je mets en fait que si tous les hommes savaient ce qu'ils disent les uns des autres, il n'y aurait pas quatre amis dans le monde.'[6]

All those years ago, Pascal appears to have been aware of the fatal negativism which manifests itself in this form of backstairs denigration, and as it seems probable that our general morbidity has meanwhile increased, and that with it there has been a corresponding wider spread of inferiority feelings, it looks as if the present-day possibility of true friendship had diminished almost to nil.

My own experience is that when once you have gained their complete confidence, affection and devotion, women are much more loyal than men. But in order to enjoy such loyalty, it is essential to capture and retain their attachment on more than a material basis. They must be emotionally won and emotionally sustained in their friendship.

Whenever I have been able to establish such a relationship to women—as I was able to do with my mother, my elder sister, my present housekeeper and, above all, with my wife—I have always experienced a form of devotion and unswerving loyalty of which I believe few men capable. This has been denied. But those who deny it must, I suspect, not only have failed wholly to capture a woman's affection and trust, but also cannot have been aware of the extent of their failure or the reasons for it.

Prince Felix Youssoupoff, for instance says: 'Generally speaking, I have found among men that loyalty and disinterestedness which I think most women lack.'[7] Whilst Jacques Trêve, herself a woman, speaking of the role of women in the life of heroes, quotes with apparent approval Vigny as saying: 'Plus ou moins

---

[6] *Pensées*, 101. 'If all men knew what others say of them, there would not be four friends in the world.' —Ed.

[7] *Lost Splendour*, 1953, Chapter 9.

la femme est toujours Dalila.'⁸

I can only retort to Prince Youssoupoff that he seems never to have succeeded in wholly capturing a woman's devotion, and to Jacques Trêve that she could never have known what it is to have her affection and devotion thus captured. For naturally when the bond is not a fast one, a woman's affection, trust and devotion cannot have been completely enlisted, and it amounts to purely romantic idealism to expect loyalty and faithfulness from her. In other words, I do not believe Samson had ever really possessed Delilah in this way.

Be the truth of this as it may, I can only declare, speaking from my own experience, that I have found such loyalty and fidelity only in my woman friends, and above all in the four already mentioned. I have, I am proud to say, had many others. No male friends could have been more loyal, devoted and generous to me than, for instance, the late Frau Dr Marguerite Kottmann, of the well-known and wealthy family of Müller in Solothurn, Switzerland, whom I first met when I was a lad of nineteen and at whose delightful house in her native town I spent the whole of May 1957. The late Miss Agnes Birrell was equally devoted, and to her I owe all the inestimable benefits I derived from F. M. Alexander's teaching. The same is true of the two daughters of my old friend Guy Drew of Down Bros (surgical instrument makers), Dr Dorothy and Miss Jane Drew, the well-known architect. And there are many others, less outstanding but not less faithful. Among them I may mention Mrs Max Rink, to whom my debt, for all she taught me about diet, I can never repay. Her devotion, it is true, was ultimately shaken and loosened by her husband and second son, who never liked me and who detested my views. But in her case, the partial lack of constancy may be excused, for it is never easy for a woman to resist the influence of a beloved son and a husband whom she respects.

On the other hand, among the women who never met me and knew me only through my anti-feminist and other writ-

---

⁸ *Du rôle de la femme dans la vie des heros*, 1913. 'The woman is more or less always Delilah.' — Ed.

ings—I refer to Lady Rhonda, Mrs Belloc-Lowndes, Mrs Bertrand Russell, Mrs Pethwick Lawrence and Virginia Woolf, and others less well-known to the public—I certainly had my most formidable and damaging enemies. But this does not affect my claim about women's fidelity and loyalty.

* * *

Having said all there is to say about my mother and sister, I shall now confine myself to an account of my wife, née Elsie F. Buckley, whom I lost on 6th May 1959. It was Oscar Levy who in 1908 introduced me to her, and, no matter how bitter my ultimate relationship to him became, I shall always feel deeply grateful to him for having by this introduction procured me one of the greatest blessings of my life.

She was a very good-looking young woman, and at the age of 26, when she was still comparatively slim, her appearance was strikingly aristocratic. This she doubtless inherited from her mother's side, although all her relatives on her father's side, including her father himself, also had excellent features which, unlike those of the majority of even well-bred people today, seemed well-drawn, regular and symmetrical.

She had been at Girton, had a wide knowledge of classical and European literature, was an exceptionally good French scholar, and her outlook even before we met was singularly similar to mine. That is to say, she had long recognised the failings and dangers of democracy, was very dubious about the merits of Christianity and, whilst acknowledging the sins of most of the European aristocracies, favoured the aristocratic solution of government.

She had distinguished relatives, and her uncle, Henry Buckley, who was a judge of the High Court (Chancery Division) and became a Lord Justice of Appeal, was raised to the peerage as Lord Wrenbury in 1915.

The most conspicuous trait in her character was her inveterate nobility, and in this respect, as is more often the case than most moderns care to admit, her appearance did not belie her. She was noble in all her impulses and reactions, often refusing to accept even compelling evidence of meanness and turpitude in another, simply because she was incapable of them herself. Indeed, she here taught me a valuable psychological truth — namely, that people apt to harbour suspicions of all kinds should themselves be held suspect, for human beings do not usually suspect in others conduct of which they themselves are incapable.

This innate nobility of character may have contributed to her capacity for unswerving loyalty and faithfulness. For one of her most remarkable qualities, uncommon in the wives of materially unsuccessful men, was her total abstention from anything in the nature of a reproach or complaint. And this, despite the hardships and privations our relative poverty often imposed upon her. She appreciated to the full the unpopularity of my anti-feminist, anti-democratic and anti-Christian views, and knew what an obstacle they were, especially after World War I, to material success. Yet not once in all our thirty-nine years of married life was I ever depressed or discouraged by a reproach from her.

Writing to me a week after her death, her great friend Mrs Rowan Robinson, who had been with her at Girton, said: 'I think that she felt herself so strongly in sympathy with all your views that you need not feel any self-reproach for having brought it about that she had a harder and a less comfortable way of life than she would have had, had she not so wholeheartedly believed in the opinions which you hold; but when she was persuaded that they were right, they really did become a religion to her, and I did most sincerely admire her courage in upholding them.'[9]

This is all very true. But it does not diminish by one iota the respect one must feel for the nobility of character which led her unflinchingly, and above all without ever uttering one word of discouragement to me, to endure many trials and privations which, in view of the kind of life she had been used to before we married, must have been particularly painful. One thinks of the wife of the French painter François Millet in this connection, and

---

[9] Letter of 14th June 1959, written from 26 Meadway Court, Hampstead Garden Suburb.

also of a woman of quite the opposite kind, the wife of Bernard Palissier. But although such nobility in a woman whose attachment to her spouse is deep and ineradicable may not be as rare as many might suppose—for I believe, as I have argued in another chapter, that the female's instinctive orientation is primarily and principally to the male—a certain affinity between a pair composing a devoted couple seems to me an essential component of any bond that is to prove ideal and permanent. And it was this fundamental affinity between us which I think cemented our relationship.

She displayed her innate nobility also in another way. For, although throughout our married life she was the better off of the two, and without the financial help she and her family gave me we could not in the early years have paid our way, she never once took the slightest advantage of the situation in order to domineer over me or otherwise to assert that authority which might have seemed warranted to a less noble character. Not once did she either humiliate or cow me by reminding me of my relative dependence, as I have too often seen other wives do in similar circumstances. Indeed, among our friends, there was one very intelligent and widely travelled spinster who, so we heard, often expressed her astonishment that I should be 'so little under Elsie's thumb, seeing that she held the purse-strings.' And her listeners shared her perplexity. Thus, so unusual did my wife's behaviour appear in the first half of the twentieth century in the eyes of our contemporaries, especially the women among them, that one can but infer that the majority of the wives of the period usually did, and were actually expected to, behave quite differently from her when similarly situated.

She often used to report how old friends would openly chide her for being what they called 'a doormat,' as if her acceptance of my philosophy implied pusillanimous submission to male domination. But this was to overlook entirely her native strength of character, her considerable intellectual gifts and the independence of her spirit. Above all, it was to overlook the fact that, from her earliest days as a reasoning being, she was, as her attitude at her school debates had apparently often shown, singularly well-endowed to become the spouse of a man professing my views. Even on the question of feminism, she, who had witnessed female higher education from within, entirely agreed with me, and many of the disabilities from which I found her suffering when we first met, and of which I am glad to say I gradually helped to cure her without continuing any recourse to the medication to which she had become addicted, she always ascribed to the profound misunderstanding of female anatomy and physiology that marked the customary routine of the more fashionable girls' schools of her day. Nor do conditions in this respect seem to have changed much even as late as 1934, because, when in that year a symposium entitled *The Old School* appeared, E. Arnot Robinson, in her contribution about Sherborne, entirely bore out my wife's strictures.[10]

Nevertheless, even in resisting the foolish gibes so often directed by frustrated Englishwomen at a wife who is happy and contented to live in spiritual harmony with her husband, my wife again revealed her steadfast loyalty, and I was frequently baffled by its bulldog pertinacity. For to suffer gibes is to be subjected to a powerful challenge to one's vanity, and in never reacting in the expected way to such a challenge she displayed yet another facet of her aristocratic temperament. *Le qu'en dira-t-on*[11] never bothered her, and she could never understand why to most people it meant so much.

It is, I hope, no slight on her memory to say that the only parallel we have of such fidelity and attachment as she showed me is in our domestic animals, the dog and the cat. Indeed, these are the qualities that chiefly endear them to us, but with this important difference—that whilst in the animal they are undiscriminating and uncritical, in the human being, on the contrary, they are unremittingly associated with narrow and hourly critical observation, and this makes them all the more wonderful.

Fortunately my wife and I always agreed on the question of progeny. Neither of us wanted children, and we took steps to avoid them. Not that we necessarily held Proudhon's view that

---

[10] E. Arnot Robinson, 'Potting shed of the English rose,' in *The Old School*, edited by Graham Greene.

[11] What people will say.—Ed.

'à l'amour proprement dit la progéniture est odieuse,'[12] although I believe there is much to be said for this view; but at bottom, apart from wishing to escape the economic burden of a family, our feelings were averse from multiplying a species of animal for which neither of us felt very much respect, and in this matter would rather have sympathized, even if we did not altogether agree, with Alexander von Humboldt (1769-1859).

In his *Memoirs* there is this remarkable passage: 'I regard marriage as a sin and the procreation of children as a crime. Moreover, I am convinced that he who burdens himself with the yoke of matrimony is an evil-doer because he brings children into the world without being able to guarantee their happiness. I despise mankind in all classes. I foresee that posterity will be much more miserable than we are.[13] Should I not be a sinner if, despite this outlook for my offspring, I thought of having any?'

Years later, George Moore was even more emphatic: 'That I may die childless,' he said, 'that when my hour comes, I may turn my face to the wall, saying, I have not increased the great evil of human life—then, though I were a mundane, a fornicator, thief and liar, my sins shall melt even as a cloud. But he who dies with children about him, though his life were in all else an excellent deed, shall be accused by the truly wise, and the stain upon him shall endure for ever.'[14]

The satanic Aleister Crowley was even more bitterly misanthropic, for he exclaimed: 'Kill off mankind and give the earth a chance; Nature may find in her inheritance some seedlings of a race less infinitely base.'[15]

These may seem hardly tenable exaggerations, and as Humboldt's and Moore's were uttered a century ago they may sound unjustified. But to those youngsters who may think that for the septuagenarians and octogenarians of today to adopt an attitude

---

[12] *Amour et mariage*, 1860, deuxième étude, Chapter 2, ix. 'To love itself, progeny is hateful.' —Ed.

[13] How prophetic! And Heine made the very same prophecy in 1842. See his *Französische Zustände*, Part II, Chapter 42.

[14] *Confessions of a Young Man*, 1886, Chapter 13, iii.

[15] Quoted in Louis Marlow, *Seven Friends*, 1953, Chapter 3.

of negativism and hostility to the modern world and humanity is unwarranted, if not contemptible, let it be solemnly and emphatically stated that no young person of the present day can ever know what we old Victorians feel about the many staggering changes that have come over the world since we were adolescents like them. They who have been born in a world already loudly humming with the whirl of mechanical transport, punctuated with the deafening detonations of motorcycles; whose skies were already being crossed and criss-crossed by machines travelling faster than sound, and whose peace and enjoyment of life and its former amenities have become more and more and habitually limited and threatened by innovations of all kinds, even in the most rural recesses of the land; whose very freedom of movement and of other activities has become exasperatingly hampered by the teeming hordes of a redundant population, so that every want, from a postage-stamp to a seat in a bus, train, restaurant, theatre or park, can be satisfied, if at all, only after a harassing wait or a bitter contest with competing crowds, especially in towns where every inch of pavement has to be conquered before it can be occupied — they, I say, who have been born in such a world, with all its present political uncertainties, dangers and confusions, cannot imagine how enchanting was our world of 1890, and how desperately we deplore its evanescence. To remember the peace, the freedom of movement, the serenity, stability and, above all, the predictability of English life in the nineties of the nineteenth century; to have known the absence of the perpetual scrimmage which now rages along every street, in every railway station and at every holiday resort in the land; even to see what has happened to the South Downs since we first trod their resilient turf seventy years ago, is to appreciate what the young of today have lost and are doomed to lose ever more and more irretrievably.

The prevailing smell of London in those days may have been that of stale horse-dung. But was that as unpleasant and lethal as the fumes from internal-combustion engines? The speed of horse traffic may have been lamentably slow, but is any modern youth aware of the fact that in our old horse-buses we of the late Victorian era often reached the Mansion House from Marble Arch more quickly than he can now reach it in a motorbus?

But although I deplore the passing of the horse-bus, I do so more because of what its substitute has brought in its train than because of its actual disappearance from our streets. For as long as it lasted, I at least, from my earliest childhood, hardly ever remember going out in London without having my heart-strings torn by the sight of those willing beasts and all the cruel strains and stresses to which they were daily and constantly subjected. When I grew old enough to question the bus-drivers about the matter, they always told me that, owing to the exceptionally strenuous work their horses had to do, their lives were relatively short, and I often formed the impression that to some of these men the inhumanity that thus curtailed the lives of their animals was as painful as it was to me.

When one reflects that, no matter whether the bus was travelling up or down hill, whether it was full or comparatively empty, or whether it was wet or fine, at the ring of the conductor's bell the two willing horses had to be pulled up sharp and were doomed to have to restart their heavy load afresh after every stop, one can have some idea of what their life was. A signal from a pedestrian on the pavement, or the request of a passenger in the bus, was all that was needed to halt the bus along any part of the route, and I remember how, when travelling uphill on one of these old buses, I used always to dread hearing the ring of the conductor's bell, which meant that the poor panting brutes would have to be pulled up short to allow someone to alight or ascend, and how my heart used to sink whenever I heard it.

Strange to say, although I was born and bred in a nation that boasted, year in, year out, of its humanity, I met with exceedingly few people who shared these feelings with me, and I cannot recall a single occasion in all those far-off days when a man, or least of all a woman, preferred to walk to the top of a hill, or walk down it after alighting, rather than halt a full horse-bus mounting an incline.

Nor is it insignificant as an example of the disparity between precept and practice so often encountered in England that it was only when mechanised transport came in that the authorities concerned rigidly fixed definite stopping-places, between which buses were not expected to pull up and never in fact do. In short, more mercy was shown to the inanimate internal-combustion engine than to the living animal.

On this account alone, and in spite of all the horrors it brought with it, I welcomed the advent of the motorbus. It is the only feature of the modern world of which I approve, because it has brought me relief from what long ago was a daily source of distress. Those who are old enough to remember the conditions I have described will perhaps sympathise.

The vexatious problem of overpopulation, of having to live among human beings as rank as weeds, is no trifling matter. When modern people discuss this question, some benign wiseacre always intervenes to point out, in the words of old Gladstone, that 'the resources of civilisation are not yet exhausted,' and that it will always be possible to produce the food needed for our increasing billions.

Such optimists, however, constantly forget that the major inconveniences and dangers of overpopulation are not restricted to a possible shortage of foodstuffs, although even today millions are already suffering from undernourishment. The equally serious and inevitable consequences of a redundant population, such as we are beginning to feel the effects of in this country, are that not only does it destroy many of the amenities and pleasures of life, and with them the *joie de vivre* of millions, but also, owing to the increased and exacerbated rivalry for room, air, accommodation, services of all kinds and, above all, of peace and comfort, it actually turns all of us into angry and secret misanthropists and enemies of mankind. For how can we cultivate even a minimum of sociability when the numbers of our fellowmen give us a surfeit of them, and we struggle with resentment in our hearts for everything that makes life possible? Indeed, I should never be surprised if it were eventually discovered that the increasing incidence in recent years of suicide, crimes of violence and even of homicide has been due in large measure to the occult hatred and contempt for life and humanity which conditions in our overcrowded urban centres necessarily generate.

Now, nothing of this belonged to the world in which we Victorians were born, and for this reason we may perhaps be forgiven for the nausea we feel when we contemplate the changes that have taken place in our time.

But even before we married in 1920, my wife and I were already conscious of the ominous drift of world affairs and of home conditions. We sensed that the general trend pointed irrevocably to an aggravation, rather than to any attenuation, of the symptoms of world anarchy and chaos, and we may therefore perhaps not be judged too severely if we refrained from augmenting that chaos by multiplying our kind.

As things have turned out, we proved abundantly right, and we lived to marvel at the sanguine temper of those who, belonging to what might have been our children's generation, seemed unable to read the many signs which, especially after World War II, indicated the probable fulfilment of von Humboldt's and Heine's solemn warnings.

About five years before her death, my wife began to suffer from some difficulty in moving her lower limbs, and the gravity of this alarming symptom rapidly increased. Numerous specialists were consulted and many remedies tried but without success, and she gradually grew more and more incapacitated. It was only owing to the progressive deterioration of her powers of locomotion that we decided to have a car, for until then our dislike of this form of transport, and my own horror of handling the mechanisms connected with it, had always prevented us from wishing to be self-propelled. When, however, it seemed to have become an urgent necessity we eventually bought a second-hand Ford 8, and in my seventy-second year I began to take lessons in driving. My age made the acquisition of an instinctive use of the controls a long business, but as I believed that only such an instinctive use could ensure safety on the road I persevered. Then, to my own surprise and that of all those who had been watching my efforts with doubt and apprehension, on 8th December at Bury St Edmunds, when I was within a month of my seventy-second birthday, I contrived to pass the driving test at my first attempt, and was able, until 1957, when she entered a nursing home for good, to drive my wife about.

When ultimately it became no longer possible for Alice and me to take proper care of her, to attend to her wants and help her to get about — for she constantly fell when she moved without assistance — I was obliged to look for a suitable private establishment where she could receive the necessary care and attention. In the end I had to move her several times, and during the years 1957, 1958 and 1959 had ample opportunities of discovering the deplorable conditions prevailing in many of the nursing homes I visited and in those at which she stayed. It seemed to me that they were in much the same state as were many of the private schools and lunatic asylums before Dickens wrote his *Nicholas Nickleby* and Henry Cockton his *Valentine Vox*, and I came to the conclusion that no Ministry of Health action was more urgently needed than an investigation into the management, staff competence, exorbitant charges and general conditions prevailing at many of these private hospitals. Large numbers of them were shameless rackets run by brazen profiteers. But although most of the people I had occasion to meet at these places agreed with my criticism of the shocking conditions that paying patients had to put up with, few were prepared to make a fuss about them.

Strange to say, the above paragraph was only just written when I learned that a book entitled *Nursing Homes in England and Wales* had been published. It was the work of two sociologists, Mr Peter Townsend and Mrs Caroline Woodroffe, and in one of the reviews of it which I read the writer said: 'in their report they [i.e., the authors] call for Government action to ensure a closer scrutiny of the type of people running nursing homes. They also urge that there should be provision for more thorough and frequent inspection.'[16]

'There is something wrong,' writes Mr Townsend, 'about a system that practically allows any qualified nurse to set up a nursing home, charge patients what she likes, and give them what conditions and services she likes.'[17]

No-one familiar, as I ultimately became, with only a small selection of these establishments could quarrel with these sentiments. At last, at Scole I found a really well-run private hospital,

---

[16] *Daily Mail*, 2nd October 1961.
[17] *Ibid*.

owned and managed by a competent State Registered Nurse, Miss Ward, and it was there that my poor wife was finally released from her crippling infirmity. Her affliction was diagnosed as cerebral sclerosis and was apparently incurable. We buried her in the cemetery at Scole on 11th June 1959. She was the third of the three great woman friends who predeceased me, and her death deprived me not only of a precious and ever-interesting companion and help, but also of that citadel of refuge into which I felt I could always withdraw from the outside world with the certainty of finding peace, comfort, encouragement and appreciation.

* * *

This account of my greatest woman friends would be incomplete and fail in gratitude were I to omit all reference to my present housekeeper, Alice Cook. She was twenty-nine years old when she first came to us in 1920, but she had previously been a housemaid at my mother-in-law's in Clanricarde Gardens, London.

Of working-class parents living in Notting Dale, she is a true Cockney, but her character and features betray her un-English origins. For from her Irish mother she inherited her positive and genial mould of countenance, her gift for witty repartee, her sense of humour and her fiery temper; and from her father, who was strikingly Mongolian in appearance, she inherited the Mongolian fold on the inside corners of her eyes, her steadiness of purpose, her reliability and that capacity for plodding, devoted and conscientious industry which make her a most valuable retainer.

She has proved her disinterestedness and devotion in many ways, especially during our eighteen years at Rishangles, but they were never more conspicuously displayed than throughout my wife's illness and, subsequently, when I was falling more and more ill owing to the enlarged state of my prostate. Indeed, in the few weeks that preceded my operation—i.e., during the latter part of September and all of October 1960[18]—she frequent-

---

[18] The operation for prostatectomy, performed with great skill by

ly carried out duties for me which would not only have repelled most people, but which were compatible only with an exceptional sense of personal attachment and a rich fund of good nature. Indeed, for these services alone, which I could hardly have received from anyone else, I can never hope adequately to repay her. Even a paid trained nurse would hardly have done all she did, or have done it with the same good grace, skill and cheerfulness.

To compensate for certain irritating traits, such as a tendency to self-pity, to exercise dominion, to dwell at tedious length on her achievements, and to shine with much more lustre as a talker than a listener—a failing which often led to regrettable misunderstandings, but which seems to be typically Irish—she has many admirable qualities. Besides being very good-natured, generous and intelligent, she is upright, straightforward and honest, self-denying to those who have won her confidence and affection, and possesses enough dignity, independence and pride never to aspire to belonging to a social rank higher than that to which she knows she was born. Thus, in spite of forty years in our company, she never showed the slightest inclination to aspirate her h's or to acquire a 'ladylike' style of speech, as her cousins and those of her old school and rugby club friends did who in the course of time grew more prosperous. She never bothered to pretend to be more cultivated than her sister and parents, and when a rather benighted and pedantic local farmer who lived not far from Rishangles, and was somewhat proud of his education, occasionally ventured to correct her when she dropped her h's, or spoke of 'chimley' (meaning chimney), or the 'drivelling snow' (meaning driven snow), or said she was out of 'bref' (meaning breath), or wanted 'nothink' (meaning nothing), she always gave him a blistering dressing-down. He stubbornly persisted in what he mistakenly regarded as a charitable endeavour to improve her, but his kind services were not accepted, and finally they exasperated her so much that she gave up visiting the family. The more hypocritical farmhands in the

---

Mr Langley, FRCS, of the East Suffolk and Ipswich Hospital, took place on November the 14th of that year.

area were often embarrassed by her frankness, for although most of them, despite their regular attendance at chapel, habitually indulged in licentious talk when among themselves, in the presence of company or of their wives, Alice's insistence on calling a spade a spade shocked them enormously.

In physique she is a schizothyme and has preserved her schoolgirl figure and weight to this day. Very active, enamoured of domestic work and never happier than when she is doing some washing, ironing or cleaning a room, she has proved an ideal housekeeper for me in my widowerhood. Even cooking, which she dislikes, she now does very well, and in her seventy-first year shows little evidence of wear.

Her integrity, unquestioning loyalty and natural dignity compel respect; and, when I think of her early beginnings in Notting Dale, her complete illiteracy, and her lack of any training in manners and good taste, I often wonder whether the alleged advantages of a good education are not perhaps exaggerated today, and whether, after all, a sound heredity and good moral and physical endowments are not the secret of a desirable race of human beings. For Alice's father and mother, although poor and members of London's proletariat, were both honourable, industrious and well-disciplined people, and her father in particular was an able, resourceful, trustworthy and conscientious workman.[19]

---

[19] In the 1970 typescript Ludovici records that Alice Cook died on 5th September 1966 at the age of 75, making him for a while 'demented with grief.' — Ed.

My Friends II

The reader will already have gathered that my relations with men have not been as pleasant or as lasting as with women. For although I have enjoyed the friendship of many members of my own sex, and some of these friendships have endured unclouded for years and were of great value to me, most of them ended either in total estrangement or else in open hostility. The most disastrous from my point of view actually ended in acts of treachery of a kind so spiteful and implacable that ever since I have been at a loss to discover what I could have done or left undone to provoke such complete revulsions of feeling.

In a very revealing French horoscope of the people born under the sign of Capricorn, which contained many accurate statements about my physical constitution, my features and even the sort of ailments with which I might expect to be afflicted, I found the following warning: 'Méfiez vous de la traitrise de certains amis,'[1] and such was its appropriateness that it might have justified my conversion to astrology.

In some cases, the treachery coming at the end of a long and intimate friendship was so unexpected and inexplicable that it seemed to point to a fatal curse, the existence of which that French horoscope indicated, or else to an unwitting trespass on my part, the wounding nature of which had escaped me and had certainly not been intended.

Not all my friendships with men ended in this way, but, strange to say, one or two of the most valued among them did. As, however, in the foregoing chapter I have mentioned how my own carelessness may have contributed even to those broken friendships that ended only in estrangement, I need not dwell on this aspect of the matter again.

I have already alluded to the habit of denigration which, owing to its tendency to produce feelings of superiority, and

---

[1] 'Beware the treachery of certain friends.' — Ed.

therefore of relief in the denigrator, may become widespread in periods of general physical defectiveness. The fact that it may operate as a powerful destroyer of loyalty in personal relationships, however, hardly requires stressing. But where it is compounded with a lack of any instinct of solidarity, so that all human groups associated for what purpose soever are subjected to a centrifugal force dispersing rather than uniting them, it is not difficult to see that fast friendships must necessarily be rare.

Now, in modern England, as my experience at least has taught me, the habit of denigration appears to be endemic, and, as it is coupled with a lack of any capacity for solidarity, fast bonds of friendship and affection between men and groups of men are seldom possible.

In all groups, there are certain individual men who, owing to their relative 'harmlessness' and good mixing qualities, never become the target of malicious criticism. Their particular form of usefulness to the group, by being modest and unobtrusive, is seldom exposed to denigration. Such men remain popular and unassailed. Given, however, a group member distinguished by any conspicuous quality of function, and from the moment all eyes are focussed upon him he enters a danger zone from which his only escape is flight, either alone or accompanied by a fragment of the group as escort.

The only exception to this behaviour on the part of modern human groups occurs when the danger from outside is so acute as to bring about a closing of the ranks and therefore unity, and when the qualities of the conspicuous member or members are so essential for the group's success or victory as to silence criticism and denigration for a while.

Given, however, calm waters in which the group is aware of no grave menace from outside, and immediately denigration of the conspicuous member or members will start, hostile cliques will plan a revolt and the centrifugal processes splitting up the group will gather strength.

In private social circles composed of various families all professing to be friends, the same forces operate but are not necessarily exacerbated by private ambitions or by the pursuit of aims and objectives of a political or ideological nature.

In case this may sound exaggerated or imaginary, the reader may find a certain letter interesting as lending independent support to what I am contending. It was written by a founder-member of the English Mistery—H. E. S. Bryant Irvine, the present Member of Parliament for Rye, Sussex—to the so-called Chancellor of the Mistery on 26th March 1936. It will be seen that the writer was beginning to be disturbed by just those tendencies in our movement which I have been analysing in the above preamble, and although it constitutes but one documentary confirmation of these tendencies (and I need hardly say that I could produce many similar testimonies), it is trenchant and outspoken enough fully to illustrate my contention. The letter is as follows:

1, Essex Court, Temple, EC4
26th March 1936
To the Chancellor of the English Mistery

Sir,

In consequence of our recent conversations it is quite apparent to me that few members of the Mistery understand what you mean by the tradition which existed in the Red Rose Movement and is now lost. As I am one of these members, I can see no purpose in my attending the Council of Strength until you can assure me I am better able to understand what you do mean.

The energy which should effectively be used against our enemies has for many months, particularly in London, been wasted in contention among ourselves. This has led to a lack of balance in our outlook and, for example, blinded us to the importance of Ludovici's vital work for the movement. I hope the step which I am taking will at least make for some contribution to the unity of the Mistery and assist in increasing our determination to attack the many real dangers which exist.

Faithfully in the service of our sovereign lord the King,
H. E. S. Bryant Irvine
A founder of the English Mistery

It seems unnecessary to dwell too insistently on the fact that in a nation and an age with the shortcomings I have described, and are more than hinted at in this letter, fast friendships with men at least must be difficult to contract. For, as I have already maintained, these shortcomings are to all intents and purposes endemic in modern England. I have moreover made it plain that the very same obstacles to lasting friendly relations, and to the successful prosecution of corporate aims which I met with in the English Mistery, had previously become familiar to me both among the early Nietzscheans and the men and women of the *New Age* group. In the army alone I was conscious of a different and healthier atmosphere. Was this perhaps because, as already pointed out, military men, as a disciplined set in an undisciplined society, are more practised than the average civilian in habits of self-control? Or may it be due to the fact that, as members of a body selected according to certain standards of health and stamina, soldiers feel less compelled to seek relief for nagging inferiority feelings by the denigration of their fellows?

Be this as it may, it should now be obvious to the alert reader that in view of the obstacles to fast friendships met with in modern England I was singularly ill-fated for the enjoyment for such bonds, because my lack of the qualities of a good mixer, my contentment in solitude and my consequent neglect of those attentions and considerations which help to cement human ties only complicated the difficulties already created in England by the national character and the present inferior physical condition of the population.

The negative features of my character certainly hardened as I grew older, for my capacity for friendship at least with males was greater in my youth than in my maturity and old age. Thus, from my tenth to my thirtieth year I made many male friends, some of whom remained loyal for years. In the more passionate of these relationships, however, my attachment sprang more from an appreciation of qualities I greatly admired and even coveted in the object of my affection than from any affinity of temperament, tastes or disposition. Thus, there was always the danger that the moment my admiration insensibly weakened, as, for instance, if I found myself getting abreast of or surpassing a friend in the command of powers which had first drawn me to him, my attachment would suffer a corresponding decline. Yet while it endured my friendship was often passionate enough to strike onlookers, chiefly my relatives, as obsessive.

First of all, there was that beloved schoolmaster, Sidney H. Wright, who directed my early footsteps in philosophy, science and English literature, and did most towards moulding my destiny by adding the weight of his authority to my mother's strong literary influence. For fourteen years, from 1894 to 1908, we were the fastest friends. We were indeed inseparable, and he was the object of my complete devotion. I was prepared to perform any service for him and to make any sacrifice to prove my affection. After he married, for instance, and was trying to support his wife and family by writing, among the signal services I rendered him I cheerfully and unhesitatingly pawned the gold watch and chain my family had given me for my twenty-first birthday — a treasure never, by the by, to be seen again — in order to help him over a serious crisis in his affairs.

I mention this, as I hope the reader will believe, not to offer an example of my good nature, a quality to which I lay no claim, but only to indicate what his friendship meant to me as a young man. Besides, in assessing the apparent self-sacrifice displayed in the various services I rendered him after his marriage, it should not be forgotten that to a junior, and especially to one who had once been a humble and reverent pupil, these repeated calls on my help, which as a rule I could ill afford to give, were a source of immense satisfaction to my self-esteem. In addition to enabling me to play the *beau rôle*,[2] they gave me a rewarding sense of importance and power.

How this passionate relationship gradually cooled and de-

---

[2] The leading role. — Ed.

generated into open hostility would take too long to tell in detail. Wright was my senior by at least twenty years, so that it may be difficult for me to appreciate the extent to which the steady decline in my discipleship may have wounded him. I may even have been occasionally indelicate in my manner of showing this decline. For that he was once very fond of me — so fond as sometimes to have been guilty of excesses in displaying his feelings towards me; excesses which my schoolfellows could not help noticing and resenting — there can be no doubt whatsoever.

Indeed, I probably enjoy the rare distinction of being among the few octogenarians, if any such there be, who can recall having as a schoolboy had the harrowing experience of hearing his master rebuked before a whole classroom of boys for showing him favouritism. To this day I still squirm when I recall the deplorable scene. The boy who assumed the knight-errant role of pronouncing the charge was a fellow called Tozer. He was in no respect hostile to me, nor was he an unruly and mischievous lad. When, therefore, he suddenly stood up in the middle of a lesson and uttered his protest, declaring Wright to have for some time shown me undue leniency and tolerance, I froze in every limb. How poor Wright extricated himself from the acutely awkward situation, I cannot remember. Although I felt his embarrassment and to a great extent shared it, I was deeply stirred to notice precisely what was said and done after the accusation had been made. That it was probably entirely justified and marked the culmination of a long history of injudicious behaviour on Wright's part, I do not doubt, for, as we all knew Tozer's steady and stolid character, his intrepid action was otherwise inexplicable. Besides, Wright was a popular master with all the boys; he was, moreover, a good and stern disciplinarian. Thus, no-one present could have thought Tozer's action wholly gratuitous.

The first faint signs of any diminution in my respect for Wright began to appear after my twenty-second birthday, when a growing sense of his religious fervour, already incomprehensible to me at the time, shook my faith in the infallibility of his judgement. He was an ardent Catholic. His elder brother had, I believe, been a priest, and I have already referred to his failure to win me for the Holy Catholic Church. By this failure alone he must have become aware of my declining attachment to him.

Even in my early twenties I already knew enough about mankind neither to expect gratitude for what I had done for him, nor to feel hurt when it was withheld. As early as 1907-8 I did not need Lord Vansittart to tell me, as he told the world fifty years later, that 'gratitude is an unnatural virtue.'[3] So that I may truthfully claim that in the break-up of our great friendship resentment on my part had played no share whatsoever. The principal solvent on my side, as was to happen so frequently in later years, was the decline in my admiration; whilst on his side, I believe, it may have been mingled grief and disapproval over my steadily increasing independence of judgement and all the other evidence he had of my scorn of his philosophy. I think also that he was not a little hurt by my cool appreciation of his novel, *Chasma*. At all events, by little and little the ties of our fast friendship became hopelessly loosened, and in 1908, when I published my first book, *Who is to be Master of the World?*, the final break occurred with sudden and unexpected violence.

I was astonished by the fury with which he responded to my interest in Nietzsche. After he became aware of it, the temper of his letters grew ever less and less restrained, and in the end, when to satisfy his curiosity he resolved to obtain firsthand knowledge of the German thinker by reading one of his books, his abuse and disparagement of *Beyond Good and Evil*, which, as far as I know, was the only Nietzsche original he ever read, became distinctly coarse. Indeed the vehemence of his opposition suggested that, like a bereaved guru, his possessiveness rather than his philosophic convictions had suffered and that he was moved more by defection than by the hatred he felt for the teacher to whom I had deserted.

At all events, by the time he went to India to occupy some post in the editorial office of an English newspaper published

---

[3] *The Mist Procession*, 1958, Chapter 26.

there, shortly before the outbreak of World War I, we had already ceased to meet and communicate with each other, and when he died in France in 1915, whilst serving as an officer in a Pioneer Corps, I did not even know of his whereabouts. Only some years later, in 1922 or 1923, did I hear from his brother that he had died of diabetes whilst on active service.

I can never forget the deep affection and admiration he once inspired in me. Our friendship was certainly the fastest I have ever enjoyed with any man, and it was all the more significant to me for having constituted an indispensable stage in my development and an essential factor in determining my career.

It was real bliss for a boy of twelve to be conducted round the Natural History Museum in South Kensington by such a teacher and to listen to his informed comments on all the exhibits. I was well aware of the privilege I enjoyed when, at the Tower of London or at Westminster Abbey, he was my guide, and I was proud when, through Professor Hobday's influence, I was able to make some slight return by obtaining permission to show him over the Veterinary College and give him the opportunity of watching an operation on a horse.

He was an interesting companion, and when, after his marriage, he settled down in Whitstable, we used to take long and delightful walks into the surrounding country. I particularly remember visiting Canterbury with him and the magnificent view we had of the city as we approached it from the north. I don't know what this country is like now, but in those days the area between Faversham and the cathedral city was unspoilt and very beautiful.

My admiration for Wright was by no means confined to his intellect and erudition, for I thought him very attractive as a human figure. He was an Anglo-Saxon blond with deep-set, penetrating blue eyes, and was singularly good-looking. His rich baritone voice lent considerable charm to his discourse and his eloquence was persuasive. Even in those early days, however, I thought his pronounced and premature stoop was a blemish, though naturally I had then no idea of its gravity as a psychophysical handicap. Strangely enough, in his 1822 essay, 'On the Conduct of Life: Advice to a Schoolboy,' Hazlitt says:

'A stoop in the shoulders sinks a man in public and private estimation.' I now appreciate that this should be so, but I doubt very much whether Hazlitt's remark would be valid today, for it is my private impression that modern people would be most unlikely to pay very much attention to this postural defect and least of all draw any unfavourable inferences from it.

All in all, therefore, I look back on this first experience of a deep friendship with a male with feelings preponderantly grateful and pleasant, for I now more easily condone the sudden and violent revulsion of Wright's feelings towards me when I reflect that it was most probably but an indication of the strength of his original attachment.

* * *

Although my next warm friendship with a male cannot compare with that I have just described, or with the one which will follow, I should be guilty of a grave omission if I failed to give an account of my connection during three whole years with a lovable and highly gifted little man called Horace Wallich, who trained me as an engraver. He was a descendant of Dr Nathaniel Wallich (1786–1864), the famous botanist, who was by birth a Dane and who in 1829, after becoming vice-president of the Linnean Society, was elected a Fellow of the Royal Society.

Wallich was one of those interesting craftsmen who are above the work by which they earn their living, and constant association with him was an apprenticeship in many arts besides those of the use of the graver and roulette. The incarnation of sincerity and candour, he very rightly made a cult of accuracy in every concern of human life, for he believed that more than half of the world's troubles were due to mankind's general lack of this quality. He charged women above all with an inveterate inability to observe accuracy in any matter whatsoever, and I once saw him slap his wife pretty sharply for one of her grosser 'terminological inexactitudes.'

Wallich and I became very much attached to each other. He used to invite me for long spells to his pleasant little house in

Esher, and only the importunacies of his wife, a lively and very temperamental Austrian woman, made it in the end difficult for me to continue enjoy his hospitality. I asked Wright's advice about this, and he urged me very earnestly always to offer some plausible excuse for declining Wallich's further invitations. But this was only after the three of us had spent a very enjoyable holiday together at Étaples, the place where the slapping incident occurred.

At all events, Mrs Wallich's importunacies were not the ultimate cause of our estrangement. For Wallich's character had one flaw which I and others among his subordinates greatly resented. He was inordinately secretive about the mysteries of his craft. This is not uncommon among skilled technicians, and in his case, as I subsequently inferred, it probably arose from his dread of being superseded by one of us and therefore of losing his job. Be this as it may, the strict jealousy with which he guarded the secret of the precise composition of the iron perchloride solutions he used in etching his plates — one of the most essential processes in their production — always incensed us. For to discover it, as we were later compelled to do when we started production on our own, led to many difficulties and not a little expense. Strange to say, moreover, not one of the textbooks I was able to procure gave any description of the formula.

Thus, at bottom, it was his exasperating reticence rather than his wife's inconvenient behaviour that ultimately caused the breach between Wallich and me, for, rightly or wrongly, I felt his attitude was incompatible with the deep friendship he professed for me.

Nevertheless, I was sorry to part with him. There is something unique about every friendship, and in responding to the attachment of a fellow-being one tends to develop or discover facets of character in oneself which are peculiar to one's relationship to that particular fellow being alone. When the friendship ends, therefore, something in oneself is irrevocably lost, and one suffers what is in reality a shrinkage of one's personality. In Wallich's case, the loss was unusually severe as he was richly endowed and consequently stimulated a wealth of uncommon responses. Another reason which caused me to deplore his loss was that, both in him as in Wright, I undoubtedly sought a father-substitute, for what I now see I missed in my childhood and youth was precisely that most precious apprenticeship of all—the training and leadership a boy can obtain from his male parent.

Incidentally, it was after I and an assistant called Machen had been running an engraving business of our own for some time, producing plates for various London publishers, that a most unfortunate incident occurred which ultimately made us dissolve our partnership and give up our work as commercial engravers. And as it is an outstanding example of its kind and illustrates the eternal character of feminine passion, I feel I must relate it.

Machen, a most devoted, straightforward and generally likeable working-class man, about thirty years old, performed all the less skilful work in the production of our engravings, and ran all the necessary errands, whether for delivering our plates, collecting orders or fetching from the wholesalers the materials we required. Among his duties, moreover, he had to take our plates to a copperplate printer for the first pulls from which I was able to judge their state and decide what I had to do by hand to finish and prepare them for the publisher's use.

Now, this copperplate printer was an oldish man, certainly in his middle fifties, and his wife was about twenty-five years younger. I seldom saw the couple because, although he worked at home and had his own clientele in the trade, it was my assistant who always took him our plates.

For a long time the arrangement worked perfectly, and Machen and Mr B. became very good friends. Then suddenly one day my poor little assistant—who, I should mention, was by no means an Adonis—arrived unexpectedly at the house in St John's Wood where I lived with my parents, looking the picture of misery and told me the following story. Having taken some of our plates to Mr B. and found him out, he had decided to wait, and before taking a chair in the kitchen had asked Mrs B. whether she would kindly let him go to the sink to wash his hands—a request she immediately granted. Then, when after a minute or two, he returned to the kitchen, he had found her barring his way in a most wanton and challenging manner and heard her make a proposal which, as he said, made his blood run cold. Seeing his embarrassment and doubtless misinterpreting it, she had quickly added that, as her husband could not possibly be expected for at least an hour, there was no possible danger of their being discovered and in any case assured him that he need fear no untoward consequences of their adventure.

Machen, as honest and upright a working man as I have ever known, was naturally horrified. The printer was both a good friend of his and a tradesman who performed an essential service for us for a very moderate charge. He not only always did his best to make our less successful plates pass muster (because in hand-printing of this sort, much may depend on the wiping of the plate), but was also, apart from any question of loyalty, a man who on business grounds alone it would have been folly to offend.

My unfortunate assistant was therefore petrified with astonishment and confusion. He tried to stammer a few words of expostulation and protest, endeavoured to reason with her and point out the obvious moral objections to her proposal, and said enough to make her understand that he firmly refused to comply with it.

She listened to his homily with every sign of increasing coldness and vexation, became suddenly very uncivil, and then ceased to address a word to him until her husband returned. When at last Mr B. appeared she seized every opportunity of conveying to him by her manner the loathing and indignation Machen now inspired in her, and when Mr B. had made the pulls from our plates and Machen gathered them up to take his leave, she ostentatiously refrained from adding her good-bye to her husband's. It was evident that her spouse was intended to infer that something very serious had passed between them during his absence.

Judge, therefore, of my unfortunate assistant's shock when, on his next call at the printer's, he was met by an outraged and infuriated spouse who accused him of having, like the traitor and villain that he was, made the dastardly attempt to seduce a lonely and defenceless woman, and ordered him never to show his face in the house again. Our account was to be closed at once, and I was no longer to be served unless I severed all connection with Machen. Mr B. even threatened to inform the whole trade and instruct them to boycott my work if we attempted to carry on with any other printer whilst continuing our association.

It was useless for Machen to try to disabuse him of his blind faith in Mrs B.'s version of what had happened, for every attempt he made to exculpate himself he merely succeeded, by impugning Mrs B.'s veracity, in enraging Mr B. the more.

Having quickly grasped the situation, I did not for a moment hesitate to believe every detail of Machen's story. For, apart from the fact that I knew him to be incapable of inventing it, and above all unlikely to have been the guilty party, had he been only half as straightforward and truthful as I knew him to be I should have accepted his very circumstantial account of the incident as authentic.

The strangest feature of the whole affair was that neither Mr B. nor Machen had the faintest notion of what had actually happened. Neither seemed to possess that minimum of worldly knowledge which would have enabled him to piece together the various portions of the puzzle in order to form an accurate picture of the whole. Old B.'s substantial seniority over his wife, the probable recent waning of his reproductive powers, and Mrs B.'s exasperation over his neglect, not to mention the Potiphar legend—all these things meant nothing to them. What was to me no more than a routine recurrence of a classical sex-drama was to them something wholly unique, unprecedented and inexplicable, except in the light of man's notorious concupiscence.

Machen, for instance, firmly believed that Mrs B. must suddenly have gone off her head, and nothing I could say succeeded in shaking his belief in her insanity. As for old Mr B., as he never for a moment doubted his wife's words, and the popular morality in which he had been brought up inclined him in any case always to suspect the male party as the more likely sinner in an illicit sexual relationship —

Who is to blame if her head hangs in shame?
It's a man ev'ry time, it's a man!⁴

— he was resolved to make Machen pay the uttermost farthing for his crime, and never paused to reflect on the improbabilities of his wife's story.

The English of those days were not good psychologists. Above all, they knew nothing about sex psychology, and their working classes were in this respect even more defective than the rest of the nation. Nevertheless, I could not understand how two adult males, neither of whom was unduly benighted, could have been so simple as never to have harboured a suspicion of the truth.

As the incident occurred at a time when I was seriously thinking of giving up engraving in order to spare my eyes, and as Mr B.'s vindictiveness made my further association with Machen difficult, if not impossible, I was obliged very reluctantly to give up our small business and part with my much ill-used partner. And about a year later when I was working at Meudon as Rodin's secretary I heard that the poor little man, after deciding to migrate to America, had died of some affliction on the cattle boat on which he was working his passage. I never knew the nature of his last illness.

* * *

My next memorable friendship with a man was that which I contracted with Ferdinand Schmidt, the blind and highly gifted German musician who became my constant companion after I had settled down at Frau Nippel's in Cologne in 1907. He was an extraordinarily good-looking fellow about a year younger than me, and his amazing achievements despite the severe handicap he had suffered from childhood brought home to me the humble nature of my own unhampered progress since I

---

⁴ Chorus of a music-hall song popular in the first decade of the twentieth century.

had left school. In him I was confronted by one who, in spite of his disability caused by retinitis pigmentosa, had overcome every obstacle, and when I first knew him was performing the most impressive feats in musical composition and performance and the training of choirs. Even experts in his own profession looked on his achievements with admiration. How paltry did my own record seem in comparison! For his family had been relatively poor, and only his brilliance had secured his advancement.

Nor were his interests and accomplishments confined to music, for with the help of Braille he had obtained a wide knowledge of his native literature and, although quite unaided by vision, had acquired a surprisingly shrewd understanding of his fellow-men. He was able to draw many accurate inferences from the sound of their voices alone, and when, from such auditory criteria, he concluded that a man or woman was intolerable, he generally proved right. He once tried in vain to form some idea of my features by passing his fingers over my face. But he would have needed to be a sculptor to obtain any correct idea of my appearance from such tactile impressions.

His mastery of life was remarkable. He had developed a technique for dealing with every part of his daily routine, and except for actually walking in the street had minimised most of the difficulties caused by his infirmity. Hard as it must have been, for instance, for one so handicapped to meet the pressing needs of his young and vigorous manhood without causing any scandal or alienating such friends as Frau Nippel and the pastor of the church at which he played the organ, he had found the means sometime before I arrived of leading a normal sexual life and, at the same time, of receiving the help he needed in reading the music which, owing to his infirmity, he was obliged always to learn by heart in order to discharge his duties, whether as choirmaster or otherwise.

This twofold service was devotedly and lovingly performed for him by Alma Nippel, Frau Nippel's second daughter, a slim, intelligent brunette, by no means beautiful but efficient and good-natured. Yet it was only after I had been at the Nippels for two or three months that he told me Alma was his mistress. His choice of her rather than his sister-in-lawlessness, Hedwig, was an example of the discernment he was able to exercise with his ears alone. For Alma, although no Venus, was more attractive than Frau Nippel's third daughter, Hedwig, and more vivacious and intelligent. If in the end I learnt to prefer Hedwig, it was only because, being less preoccupied than Alma with Ferdinand and his wants, she was able to spare more time for me, which she did with unstinting generosity.

Whether Hedwig knew of her sister's relationship to Ferdinand, I never discovered. But in view of the rivalry that too often prevails between two spinster sisters, and of the bitterness it may provoke, I often marvelled at Hedwig's wholehearted admiration of Ferdinand and her constant readiness to pilot him about the streets or otherwise to help him if he happened to need any extra assistance.

In view of Frau Nippel's remarkable beauty, the unfortunate plainness of her two younger daughters was surprising. But when I was shown a photograph of their father I understood.

As Ferdinand knew no English whatsoever, I was bound to speak to him in German, and the progress I made in the language was consequently rapid. Feeling it my duty to try to make some return for the many kindnesses he and his adoring mother used to show me, I often spent some time of an evening reading aloud to him, especially translations of famous English authors with whose works he wished to be acquainted, and I was thus able to introduce him to many of the more reputable English novelists, as also to Spencer, Darwin and even Oscar Wilde.

He quickly detected the decadent features in Wilde's philosophy, and as he had long been aware of this author's immense popularity with the German reading public of the day, especially its *haute volée*,[5] he was correspondingly alarmed. With his stepbrother, Dr Otto Schmidt, he infected me with an enthusiasm for Nietzsche, for although this German thinker was one of the post-Kantian philosophers I had intended to study when I came to Germany, my ultimate concentration on

---

[5] High society. — Ed.

his writings and exhaustive study of them, most of which I had read aloud to Ferdinand before I returned to England, were due chiefly to the two Schmidt brothers.

Today, I look with mixed feelings on Nietzsche's contribution to modern thought. After discovering what he borrowed from Schopenhauer and especially from Heine, not to mention his indebtedness to Dostoyevsky and Stendhal, I appreciate his limitations more than I did during my stay in Cologne. Nevertheless, there remain certain unique features in his teaching, without which I doubt whether much headway can be made by any modern thinker. I refer more particularly to his doctrine of morals. Thus, although my admiration for his life work may have suffered some diminution, I can never be grateful enough to Ferdinand and his stepbrother for having induced me to make a thorough study of his writings.

I left Germany in 1908, therefore, well-grounded in the thought of her latest philosopher, and inasmuch as this ultimately led to my meeting Dr Oscar Levy and being introduced by him to the young woman who was to become my wife, there seems to have been the finger of destiny in Ferdinand's influence over me in Cologne, and Mrs Dufresne's remarkable prophecy, if not a mere fluke, had been magically fulfilled.

In order to spare Ferdinand one of the least tolerable of the many humiliations that the blind have to put up with, I took with me to England not merely a knowledge of Braille but also a Braille typewriter, so that he could hear from me without having to have my letters read to him and could write to me without the help of his mother or brothers.

As my train drew out of the *Hauptbahnhof* of Cologne and gradually gathered speed, I saw him aimlessly turning his head from side to side as if, moved by some old instinct long useless to him, he was running his eyes over the length of the train to try to catch a glimpse of me, and I was again reminded of his terrible disability and the wonderful mastery of life by which he led one to forget it.

I felt the wrench of our parting as deeply as he did, and from its severity I knew that another decisive stage in my career had closed. Nor could I feel much hope of recapturing the spell that had been upon me ever since I first met him, for that year in Cologne had certainly been the happiest in my life so far.

He had been more than a friend to me. Quite unwittingly, he had grown to be a source of constant stimulation, almost my second conscience. His noble fight against his affliction, the gaiety and courage with which he waged it, and the complete lack of self-pity and broody melancholy with which he confronted every problem of his daily life compelled respect.

We remained the fastest friends until his death, which occurred soon after the end of World War II. During the years 1909 to 1938, whenever I had occasion to go to Germany I always enjoyed his hospitality, and in 1925 my wife and I spent a delightful month with him at a pleasant inn at Nideggen in the Eiffel district. After he married and bought a house in Düren I visited him again and was more than ever impressed by his mastery of his problems, for it was here that he brought up two sons and was able to give them an excellent education.

In view of the long and unclouded duration of our friendship and the exception it provided to my customary fate, I have sometimes wondered whether the distance that separated us and the relative rareness of our meetings after 1908 may not have contributed to the unbroken harmony of our relationship. It will be remembered that Dr Thomas Fuller, in his *Introductio ad prudentiam*, says 'to keep a friend, be not with him too long at a time,' and counsels us to visit our relatives, but adds significantly, 'I advise you not to live too near them,'[6] a sentiment shared by the Rev. R. S. Hawker.[7]

Even Norman Angel, the ardent pacifist, held the same view, for in 1951 he wrote: 'Can any passion equal that of village hatreds? That is why I have always been a little sceptical of the view that enmity between nations can be ended by frequent contacts, "by getting to know each other better."'[8] So much erroneous psychology is current today, especially among the sen-

---

[6] 1727, Maxim 1131 and Volume I, 529.
[7] See his *Life and Letters* by C. E. Byles, 1908.
[8] *After All*, p. 289.

timental mob, high and low, that these views are certainly not popular. But I cannot help feeling that they are well-founded, and I often deplore the enormous amount of treasure and effort that are wasted by the relatively novel custom of shipping hordes of schoolchildren to Europe in the belief that this may cement the 'natural love of men for one another.'

Be this as it may, Ferdinand Schmidt is among the few great male friends from whom I was not ultimately estranged, and I feel the less inclined to assume that this lends colour to the popular adage, 'Distance lends enchantment,' because, although during my year in Cologne we met daily and often spent hours in each other's company, we never experienced any cooling-off in our affection or in our desire to be together.

* * *

My return to England in the summer of 1908 opened a period in my life, during which I formed many friendships with men, for in the few years that preceded the outbreak of the First World War, I became a member of the Nietzsche and the *New Age* groups. Of these friendships, by far the most delightful and profitable were those I enjoyed with Drs Oscar Levy and G. T. Wrench, both brilliant men whose companionship was a constant source of interest and pleasure.

Levy was a man of peculiar charm. Like his personal appearance, his mind was elegant and polished. It harboured no dowdy theories or ideals, rejected all the sordid details of life and was tastefully furnished with the best products of European culture. Witty, always genial and good-tempered, and ever-eager to show his appreciation of any enlightening remark one might contribute to the conversation, he was a stimulating companion. Although he had a lot to say, he was a good listener and, if presented with a personal problem, his advice was always helpful.

Like Wrench, he belonged to that breed of medical men who are above their calling, turn to literature as a release from its drudgery, and, like Montaigne, never cease from betraying their secret contempt of it. Both men were abreast of the latest discoveries in psychology, but whereas Levy, anticipating much of what Adler subsequently claimed, found Freud's work unsatisfying, Wrench was more inclined to accept the Freudian psychology as valid.

The three of us became much attached to one another, always enjoyed meeting and lost no opportunity of doing so. As already pointed out, Levy repeatedly invited me to join him when he took a short holiday on the South Coast, and I have no doubt that these favours shown to me by the head of the group were instrumental in fomenting much of the ill-feeling which ultimately turned the Nietzsche fraternity into a hotbed of denigration and deliberate slander. Nor did Levy's final and most generous invitation to me in 1910 to join him on his tour of Italy, Greece, Syria, Palestine and Egypt tend to mend matters in this respect.

The fact that we enjoyed being together must have been plain to all our associates, and as Levy's natural nobility prevented him from ever making me feel my many obligations to him, the relationship, as far as I was concerned, was ideal. I have since observed this particular form of nobility in rich Jews and have come to the conclusion that it is probably an inheritance from ancestors accustomed to affluent circumstances and to the patronage of dependants. It is certainly less noticeable in Gentile upstarts, no matter how rich they may be.

What chiefly drew Levy and me together was the similarity of our tastes. My French realism matched his own Jewish aversion from romanticism and all forms of cloud-cuckoo dreams, whilst his preference for a bachelor's life was rooted in a belief, common to us both, that by and large modern women, as he constantly declared, had become 'too impudent.' He ultimately married the mistress with whom he was living at his flat in Museum Street, where I first met him. But he did so under the pressure of the peculiar circumstances created for aliens, especially Germans, by the outbreak of World War I, and even after his marriage, when he left England to settle down in Wiesbaden, he led the life of a married bachelor rather than that of the average spouse.

Until late in the second decade after World War I only one

discordant note marred the harmony of our relationship, and that was his total inability to understand my taste for the kind of humour to be found in books like *Through the Looking-Glass* and *Alice in Wonderland,* and I well remember strolling with him one Sunday morning along the Bois de Boulogne, trying in vain to make him see the rich fun and irony of some of the best passages in these two books.

I had always thought Carroll's two masterpieces untranslatable. But after all Levy was a good English scholar and did not need to have the text translated. He was, however, by no means the only German I met who was inaccessible to Carroll's humour, although the superb translation of the 'Jabberwocky' in the German version of *Through the Looking-Glass* proves that Carroll's works have been well understood by at least one German, and in a manner that leaves the French translation far behind.

It was only later on, in the middle thirties, that a further and more serious cause of disagreement arose between us, and that was over Mussolini, whom Levy had visited in Italy. Like Wrench, Levy greatly admired the man, disliked my repeated criticisms of him and rejected my view that at bottom he was a mountebank. Ultimately, Levy admitted his mistaken judgement in the matter, but for a time our correspondence about it was considerably embittered, and although I never actually crossed swords with Wrench about Mussolini I gathered that he sided with Levy.

It has since struck me that even in those far-off days, with his keen powers of observation and acute sensitiveness, Levy was probably well aware of my failings as a friend. Although he himself seemed ready to overlook these shortcomings, he was evidently not blind to their untoward effect on other people. Thus, whenever I told him of any difference that had occurred between me and another member of our set, he always exclaimed: 'Flatter him, Ludo! Flatter him!' He never explained exactly what he meant by this, but I feel sure he intended me to understand not that I should try toadying or fawning to the person in question, but that I should employ all those little arts of attention and consideration which make a man feel that you regard him as important and worthy. This was precisely the kind of behaviour I was least capable of, and the fact that Levy had perceived this, and whilst remaining my friend constantly warned me about it, shows that, although he himself was prepared to overlook my defect, he was anxious to spare me the consequences of it in my dealings with other people.

It is now, however, idle to wish that I might more diligently have followed his advice, for one cannot alter one's character, and, if such behaviour as Levy recommended did not come naturally and spontaneously to me, had I tried to put it into practice I should only have betrayed its deliberateness by either bungling or overdoing it.

Levy and I remained the fastest friends until about 1936–37, when two unfortunate developments suddenly brought our disagreements to a head and finally wrecked our long friendship.

I must first explain that for some time — ever since 1915, in fact, when I had published my *Defence of Aristocracy* — Levy had disapproved of my policy of presenting the Nietzschean values in books and articles not professedly concerned with Nietzsche's own writings. He thought there was far too little about Nietzsche in much that I wrote, especially in the book in question. I, on the contrary, believed that the best and subtlest way of illustrating and advocating the Nietzschean *Weltanschauung* was to employ an indirect approach and to show through history and current events how the application of Nietzschean values would prove salutary.

However, my disagreement with Levy on this matter, although a cause of some friction, never threatened to lead to any breach between us. But when once the National Socialist Party under Hitler came into prominence, and claims began to be made about the Nietzschean source of some of the Party's tenets, Levy expected from me a course of action I was conscientiously unwilling to adopt.

Knowing as I did the development of Nietzsche's thought from his early pro-Wagnerian days to his ultimate breakdown, I took the view that the essential Nietzsche, the doctrines recognised by all authoritative Nietzschean scholars as most characteristic of his thought, were to be found in the works published after 1882, including his world-famous *Thus Spake Zarathustra*. And as I saw in many aspects of these later works ideas which might well have inspired some of the more important features of the Nazi teaching, I did not mind saying so and actually supporting my contention in a series of articles published in the *English Review*.[9]

Meanwhile, however, I had learnt to my surprise that Levy was taking the view that Nietzsche's most important and characteristic works, those that most truly represented the core of his teaching, consisted of those published before 1882. Furthermore, at an important stage in the controversy a book appeared in France, written by M. P. Nicolas, entitled *De Nietzsche à Hitler*,[10] in which by means of staggering feats of *legerdemain* the author contrived, to his own satisfaction at least, to prove what Levy was anxious to establish—namely, that the essential and genuine Nietzsche was the author of only those books that had appeared before 1882. At Levy's suggestion, Nicolas presented me with a copy of his book, the impudence and disingenuousness of which so greatly shocked me that I immediately wrote to the author pointing out the palpable weakness and speciousness of his case. I quoted Dr Mügge's claim to the effect that it is the Nietzsche of the period 1882 to the end that is the Nietzsche 'as usually meant by that name,' and that it is in that period that 'occurs the greatest display of originality.'[11]

Before 1882, Nietzsche is either deeply under the influence of his scholastic training or else under that of other men. At all events, I stood firmly by the view that the works of Nietzsche's last period contained the essential principles of his teaching, and seeing that in my various prefaces to the translations I had made, in my own three monographs on Nietzsche and in my commentaries I had adopted this point of view with Levy's

---

[9] 'Hitler and the Third Reich,' *English Review* 63, 1936, pp. 35–41, 147–53, 231–9; 'Hitler and Nietzsche,' *English Review* 64, 1937, pp. 44–52, 192–202. — Ed.

[10] Paris, 1936.

[11] *Nietzsche: His Life and Works*, 1909, Part III, Chapter 1.

complete approval, it seemed to me extraordinary that he should suddenly assume the position taken up by Nicolas, more especially as Nietzsche himself, in a letter of 21st June 1888 to Professor Karl Knortz of Evansville, Indiana, advising him which of his own books he should read first, said: 'I should be almost inclined to advise you to start by reading the latest of my books which are the most far-reaching and the most important (*Beyond Good and Evil* and *Genealogy of Morals*).'[12]

Surely this should have been conclusive. When, however, we bear in mind that it is easier to light on at least rough analogies between many of his doctrines of this last period and those professed by the National Socialists of Germany in the thirties of this century than it is to find corresponding similarities in the works published before 1882, Levy's *volte-face* and the thesis championed by Nicolas immediately acquire a new complexion. And we are left with the suspicion that, after the ascendancy of the Nazis in Germany, Levy must have felt it not only politic, but also actually enjoined by his loyalty to his hero and master, to try to prove that the Nietzsche to whose doctrines the Nazis claimed adherence was not the true Nietzsche at all. Consequently, all the books published after 1882, in which the majority of the similarities between Nietzscheanism and some of the National Socialist beliefs are to be found — I referred to only a few of these in my *English Review* articles — were, if not actually negligible, not to be regarded as representative of genuine Nietzschean thought. Only thus in Levy's view, or so it appeared, could Nietzsche be exculpated from the charge of having inspired the hated Nazis.

Without in the least wishing either to defend National Socialism or to discredit Nietzsche, I refused to subscribe to this point of view, which I thought both gratuitous and purely opportunist; and Nicolas's book, besides being a poor production in itself, seemed to me calculated only to mislead the ill-

---

[12] See the *Selected Letters of Friedrich Nietzsche*, 1927, p. 323. His actual words were: 'Fast möchte ich rathen mit den letzten Werke anzufangen, die die weitgreifendsten und wichtigsten sind (*Jenseits von Gut und Böse* und *Genealogie der Moral*).'

informed. Even Nicolas's running criticism of Julien Benda's many references to Nietzsche in *La trahison des clercs*,[13] most of which are drawn from the books of the last period, struck me as disingenuous and unfair.

Levy was very angry — so angry that, quite unjustifiably, he began telling everybody that I had gone over to the Nazis, was therefore an anti-Semite and had deserted both him and Nietzsche. Later on, he even wrote to one of my most devoted readers in America, William Simpson, accusing both him and me of infidelity to the 'true' Nietzsche and of having adopted what he called 'the Wagnerian heresy,' by which he meant anti-Semitism.[14] Simpson sent me these letters, and in that of the earlier date Levy, referring to the Nietzschean movement, said of my attitude: 'Nothing of course would have hurt Nietzsche more in the long run. But our present position would have been compromised if I had not counteracted Ludovici's Wagnerian heresy. I did so very early, and already in 1936 I encouraged a French friend [Nicolas is meant] to write a book against the German and English Nazi interpretation of Nietzsche . . . when Ludovici received a copy of this book he wrote back to the author, "Your book is a catastrophe."'

I certainly felt entitled to tell Nicolas that his book was a catastrophe, because I repudiated Levy's view that what he called the 'German and English Nazi interpretation of Nietzsche' was wholly spurious. The implication was that, because it was based on the books published after 1882, therefore it was to be rejected as representative of Nietzsche's thought. When I wrote to Nicolas I explained that I disapproved wholly of his attitude because I believed, as I still do, that if we overlook Nietzsche's own open avowal and the traditional view of his teaching held by all competent Nietzsche scholars, and proclaim his pre-1882 writings as more essentially authentic than the later ones, we not only lose most of the more valuable, characteristic and innovatory aspects of his teaching, but also do both him and the ill-informed public a serious injury.

---

[13] Paris, 1927.
[14] Letters of 1st December 1945 and 11th July 1946.

Grave as was this difference from Levy, it might in other and less agitated times still have failed to wreck our friendship and blot out the memory of all we had been to each other. But those readers who can recall the atmosphere in western Europe and especially in England at the time when this controversy arose and who are able to appreciate what it meant to a man, particularly a publicist like myself, to be openly charged with Nazi sympathies and above all with anti-Semitism — all such readers will perhaps understand how deep were the wounds Levy's angry propaganda inflicted on me. Much later on, in 1945, he wrote to me from Oxford seeking a reconciliation. But as I felt that I could not then respond with any sincerity to his appeal, I replied that I felt no wish to renew our relationship.

It was all most deplorable. I had been very fond of Levy and owed him countless favours and generous services. No-one could remain long in company without feeling the fascination of his personality, the charm of his manners, the versatility of his mind and the ever-compelling but subtle persuasion of his handsome Jewish features. Only the fierce animosities and fanatical ideological prejudices of the late thirties could, I felt, have blinded him to the fundamental unsoundness of his own and Nicolas's pleas in favour of the pre-1882 Nietzsche, and to this day I remain convinced that, but for the association of some of Nietzsche's doctrines with the policy and practice of the Nazis, we should never have heard of this relatively belated and heterodox exaltation of the books of Nietzsche's early period.

So ended another great friendship, in bitterness and open war. Yet I still do not see how I could conscientiously have adopted a different attitude.

He died on 10th August 1946 at Oxford. He was in his eightieth year, and I never knew the nature of his last illness. Philip Mairet asked me to write the obituary for *The New English Weekly*. I did so and in it tried to do full justice to him as a man and a thinker.[15] But my best and most sympathetic description

---

[15] 'Dr. Oscar Levy,' *The New English Weekly*, 14th November 1946, pp. 49–50.

of him is undoubtedly enshrined in my novel, *Mansel Fellowes*,[16] where as 'Dr Melhado' he plays the leading role. As he was delighted with this portrait of himself, and many of his closest friends acknowledged the fidelity of the likeness, I have no hesitation in recommending it to all those who may wish to obtain a close view of this lovable and, in many respects, remarkable man.

* * *

Before turning to my great friend, Dr G. T. Wrench, I must speak of my friendship with another interesting and highly-gifted Jew, Leonard Magnus, the second son of Sir Philip Magnus who in the decade before World War I was Member of Parliament for the University of London. Leonard Magnus had neither Levy's good looks nor his impressive serenity and poise. He was, on the contrary, a neurotic personality of slender build, with a permanently strained and haunted expression, who as a comparatively young man was already afflicted with a stoop. He also had a bad stammer. But he was an interesting and witty talker and could be irresistibly funny in his criticisms of Nietzsche. He lived in chambers in Gray's Inn, and I often used to lunch or dine with him there. He could make a delicious omelette, and the meals he provided were always enlivened by the most entertaining talk. I often thought of him as a possible reincarnation of Heine, for he had the same good nature, biting wit and debilitated physique.

It was at his chambers that I used to meet and dine with G. K. Chesterton, and we three had many a lively debate in which Magnus always took and vigorously expressed a Leftish point of view. Often Chesterton and I would have to wait half a minute or more before his stammer allowed us to hear what he wished to say. But we had no cause to repine, for our host's remarks were usually pungent and illuminating.

I painted his portrait and gave it to him, but what became of it I do not know. Sometime after the War of Belgian Independ-

---

[16] London, 1918.

ence he became so deeply enamoured of Bolshevism and the aims of the Russian communists that he went to the pains of learning Russian, and in 1920 or thereabouts, to my regret and deep alarm, he actually went to Russia with the object of helping the struggling Bolsheviks to solve their manifold problems. I wished him good-bye in a Putney bus in Piccadilly and never saw him again.

Subsequently we heard that, owing to an infection in his right arm, he was no longer able to write home, and finally he was reported to have died of some unspecified illness. I understood that Sir Philip and his son Laurie Magnus did their best through the Foreign Office to obtain particulars about his end, but that all their efforts had failed.

Knowing Leonard's extreme independence of mind, his rigorous sense of justice, his Leftish convictions and his capacity for ardent cooperation in any cause in which he believed, I formed the impression that, when once he had sought contact with the ruling minority in Russia and tried to be of service to them, he had probably seen so much that shocked him and outraged his sense of charity and justice that, unable to withhold his criticisms and censure, he had become a nuisance to his superiors and had been quietly liquidated.[17]

Despite his extreme Leftish prejudices and his innocent acceptance of Bolshevik professions, he had an acute intellect and was a dear good fellow. I owed him many happy hours and much generous hospitality. If I had to thank him for nothing else, it was at least through him that I had the privilege of seeing a good deal of one of the most celebrated journalists of that day, G. K. Chesterton. My repeated meetings with this popular Fleet Street figure at Magnus's chambers and the opportunity they afforded of a close study of his personality have left me with a vivid recollection of his character and outlook.

Chesterton was my antipodes. Very fat and anything but polished in his appearance and manners, he and I revealed our

---

[17] According to Frank Foden's *Philip Magnus: Victorian Educational Pioneer*, London, 1970, p. 96, Leonard Magnus probably died of typhus. — Ed.

fundamental disparities by our looks alone. He was a pyknic; I was a schizothyme. He was massive and ponderous; I was slight and wiry. He appeared to be wholly unaware of the handicap his extreme obesity imposed on his activities. Indeed, owing to the unaccountable and inveterate predilection English men and women, especially the latter, are wont to show for fat men — hence the ease with which people of the Horatio Bottomley type become trade union leaders, Members of Parliament, successful commercial touts and prosperous racecourse tipsters — Chesterton's experience had no doubt taught him that, far from being a drawback, his bulk had always been one of his greatest assets.

He usually wore a frock-coat, the lapels of which, owing to his habit of constantly fingering them when speaking, shone with grease; nor did his fingers ever strike me as too clean. There was a look about his heavy moustache as of a beer-drinker and heavy smoker, and I sometimes suspected that he rather liked to be thought of as a modern Dr Samuel Johnson. His huge head with its mane of long hair made his shoulders seem narrower than they actually were, and when he sat down his great bow-front kept him so far from the table that there was always something pompous and magisterial in his appearance at a meal.

He spoke with that curious fluctuation of two keys so often heard in the voices of fat men. Thus the noises would rise and fall from bass into falsetto and back again, with an undeniably pleasing effect which often lent persuasiveness to a remark.

But he was a most difficult opponent in debate, and to come to grips with him was usually impossible. As I soon found, however, the greater part of this difficulty was due more to the behaviour of the rest of the company than to him, for, no matter what he said, they insisted on thinking it funny, and as in England to raise a laugh in debate amounts to proving your point, no matter how far-fetched, Chesterton was an easy winner in all our arguments.

Once, for instance, I was trying to argue that the sense of sin might be merely the inability to digest or forget a reprehensible action, and that people endowed with smoothly functioning bodies which quickly disposed of their waste or harmful products would be less likely than the costive and congested to harbour feelings of guilt. 'That's all very well, young man,' he exclaimed, 'but when you stand before your Maker with your knapsack of sins across your shoulders, you won't cut much ice with that sort of argument.'

Everyone laughed, and the discussion closed with G. K. the acknowledged victor.

When one evening I tried to explain that it was quite impossible, even if you believed in Him, to imagine what the Almighty was like, as none of us could possibly grasp what a being looked like who could create something out of nothing, Chesterton objected most violently. 'Not a bit of it!' he said. 'Think of the kind of thing you find most lovable and seductive on earth. I can easily imagine God as a beautiful glossy Newfoundland dog [loud laughter]. I can honestly, and I like to think of Him as that.'

On yet another occasion we were discussing aristocracy. He had been saying that all aristocracies had abused their power, and I rejoined that not only was this untrue historically, but that there were also many reasons for believing that under an aristocracy people might be much more free than in a democracy.

'Oh, get along with you,' he retorted. 'You are the sort of romantic who wants the joy of fireworks at midday.'

Whenever at public dinners I heard him speak I noticed without fail that, as soon as his name was called, all present began to laugh just as audiences used to do, but with much greater justification, at the old Tivoli and Oxford music halls the moment Dan Leno's number appeared on the front of the stage. And when he actually began to speak, and offered us one of his many variations on his elephantine figure, the company would rock with laughter. Often one could not help admiring the resolute good will with which, in Chesterton's case, the crowd responded to the sheer power of a reputation for 'humour.'

I do not know what modern readers think of him. But when I look again at his essays and stories I find them quite unreadable, and it seems to me most likely that quite soon — unless this has occurred already — he will be regarded by most people as among those celebrities of the twentieth century who were consistently and grossly overrated by their age.

* * *

I now turn to the last of my particularly great friends, Dr G. T. Wrench. He had done brilliantly in medicine. A gold-medallist MD of London and a late Assistant Master at the Rotunda Hospital, Dublin, he had specialised in gynaecology and had subsequently been engaged in cancer research at the Middlesex Hospital. But medicine did not satisfy him, and when I first came across him he was at work on a book about European culture which was ultimately published under the title of *The Mastery of Life*.[18]

In the early autumn of 1908 I began to notice a tall, fair, youthful-looking man who constantly occupied the seat next to mine in the British Museum reading-room. Although he appeared to be only in his early thirties, he was already going slightly bald *à la diplomate*,[19] and this made the fine dome of his brow all the more conspicuous.

He seemed not uninterested in what I was doing. But I did not at first respond to his many attempted approaches, chiefly because my first impression of him had been unfavourable. His nose struck me as too small for a man, his brow too smooth and vertical — that is to say, not retreating enough to be typically masculine — whilst the rosy tint of his skin added to the effect of femininity and softness in his appearance. Altogether, his features seemed too immature to harmonise with his tall, well-proportioned and manly build.

In the frontispiece of his *Mastery of Life* there is a none too flattering photograph of him, from which, in addition to his looks, one or two other of his traits may be gathered. It will be seen, for instance, that although tidy and conventional there was no straining after smartness in his attire. His tie is careless-

---

[18] London, 1911.

[19] In the style of a diplomat. — Ed.

ly knotted and no attempt has been made to look well-groomed. He looks out into the world without perplexity, revolt, anger or disapproval; above all, without any trace of that truculence which is barely concealed in the portraits we have of men like Bishop Gore, John Bright, Gladstone, Thomas Henry Huxley or Carlyle.

He contemplated life and his fellow-men more or less dispassionately because—and this was the secret of his failing self-confidence and sense of inadequacy—he was lacking in passion. Objective enough to recognise this lack, and intellectually honest enough not to interpret it as some form of superiority, his knowledge that passion was necessary for any sort of creative work often caused him moments of acute melancholy and pessimism, whilst in his occasional outbursts of strong feeling and ardent conviction there was always a noticeable strain of artificiality and improvisation.

But his very failing made him an ideal scientist—hence, perhaps, his success in medicine. Nevertheless, he was capable of some singularly false deductions from his study of mankind. For instance, he never tired of exalting the Chinese above the Christian attitude to man, and always argued that man was born good and not, as Christianity more accurately maintained, a creature of evil propensities requiring an act of Grace to fit him for society. It never dawned on him that, no matter how absurd the rest of the Christian credo might be, at least in this respect it was more penetrating and psychologically tenable than Chinese philosophy and the doctrine championed above all by a romantic like Rousseau. Even in medicine, despite his manifold heterodoxies and the independence of his judgement, he often seemed to me too much inclined to be overruled by his early hospital schooling; and when ultimately he died of cancer I could not help thinking that he had perhaps been too prone to scorn all lay and unprofessional contributions to the sciences of hygiene and diet because of his inability to shake off completely the effects of the rigid disciplines he had undergone as a student.

When at last we came to know each other, and to exchange our views on life, I found him much more interesting and original than his rather typically GP appearance had led me to expect. He had a deep melodious baritone voice; in conversation he was witty and full of pungent comments on men and affairs, whilst his wide travels supplied him with an endless store of examples and similes which enriched his discourse. For the first year or two the hours I spent in his company amounted to a finishing education, especially in science, for he soon discovered my ignorance of human anatomy and physiology and constantly instructed me in both, including above all those of the sexual functions.

He was five years my senior and seemed particularly concerned to protect me against the pitfalls of what is called 'getting a girl into trouble.' Levy showed the same solicitude about my sexual life, but whereas he always advised me strongly to cultivate the affections of some accommodating married woman—Levy's word for this was 'hospitality'—which he considered the safest form of sexual adaptation for a bachelor, Wrench, being English and therefore more moral, was content to teach me the essentials of birth control and to show me how and why the best methods secured contraception.

We saw a great deal of each other and became the fastest friends. In many respects we were each other's complement. My mother, like most women, thought him delightful and he was the means of affording her great comfort when, suspecting that she might be threatened with mammary cancer, she asked him to examine her, and he quickly dispelled her fears.

In our close relationship Wrench and I always maintained an attitude of the strictest candour towards each other. But although we never spared each other's feelings if mutual criticism was called for, because we accepted and practised Nietzsche's doctrine that one should be 'a hard bed to one's friend,'[20] we never took or gave offence. Mistakenly suspecting, for instance, that I cherished illusions about my good looks—a form of vanity, of which as a good and experienced draughtsman I was never guilty—he would on occasion, especially if I appeared too exhilarated after a successful encounter with a girl, remind

---

[20] *Thus Spake Zarathustra*, Part II, iii: Of the Compassionate.

me of my ill-shaped nose or of my 'humble and deprecating stoop.' For, at that time, owing probably to my early unconscious emulation of my beloved master Wright's villainous bodily coordination, I had long been developing a stoop, and it was only seventeen years later that, in Alexander's hands, I learnt not only how to get rid of it, but also how much more serious it was than a mere postural blemish.

I, on the other hand, would chaff him about his temperamental shortcomings and would sometimes crow over him for catching him out on a question of logic when he was reasoning about some medical data. I also always insisted on the fact that people drawn to Nietzsche might be unwittingly influenced by their inferiority feelings and that, just as in my case early awareness of physical subnormality (for instance, muscular asthenia) might be the cause — for I believe Adler to have been perfectly correct in his analysis of this matter — so, in Levy's case, his early experience as a Jew in a German school and at the university might have been the determining factor, whilst Wrench himself might have suffered the same sort of consequence from his consciousness of his temperamental deficiencies.

Although Levy always denied that inferiority feelings had had anything to do with his Nietzscheanism, least of all his experiences as a Jew in Germany, Wrench acknowledged the possible truth of my contention but maintained that there was a flaw in it somewhere, because as a rule inferiority feelings tended to drive people in a Leftish direction, whereas we Nietzscheans all upheld aristocratic values. Other factors, he argued, must therefore be involved.

My connection with Wrench lasted beyond the period when I first began my course of training under Alexander, yet, strange to say, I was never able to make him understand the Alexander method, its object and importance, and could therefore never get him to acknowledge its necessity. This was probably to a great extent my own fault. It is, however, by no means an easy matter to explain. Owing to the fact that it is a sensory experience, the understanding of the Alexander method and of the use of the self acquired by practising it are largely unamenable to verbal expression. Nevertheless, Wrench should have known me well enough to feel certain that I could never be the dupe of pure charlatanry, and it was here, I think, that his early disciplines in medicine again led him astray.

Still, he had a tremendous faith in his visual judgements of men and, with the object of satisfying himself about the soundness and value of Alexander's teaching, he called on him one day simply with the object of obtaining an interview and therefore the chance of scrutinising the man himself. He evidently counted on being able to infer from Alexander's appearance and bearing the significance to be attached to his teaching.

Old F. M. Alexander was, however, both too busy and much too wily to waste time over anyone moved by curiosity alone, so that after ascertaining from his vigilant and formidable buffer-secretary Miss Webb that all Dr Wrench required was an interview, and that he was not asking for lessons, he instructed her to turn him away unsatisfied.

This made a very bad impression on Wrench, but he was mistaken in the conclusion he drew from it. At all events, from that day he ceased from wishing to hear any more about the Alexander technique and would sometimes openly deride it. Not that he was among the many millions of modern people who are in urgent need of it, for his was on the whole a well-coordinated body, upright and unstrained. It seemed to me a pity, however, that his acute brain and medical knowledge were never put to the service of Alexander's teaching, for I felt sure that he would have been able to strengthen the scientific arguments in its favour.

Women were much attracted by him. But I could not help noticing that those who found his personality most 'bewildering,' as I sometimes heard them describe it, were chiefly of the type that make good social workers, missionaries and heads of institutions. He, on the other hand, aware of his temperamental defects and objective as usual, knew that the kind of woman he needed was one with enough fire for two. He believed that his family line had been physically impoverished by generations of middle-class puritanism, and, as he once put it to me, he felt he had to find a mate capable of supplying 'a vigorous gust of fresh vitality to lift his drooping family pennant.' His brother was unmarried and likely to remain so, whilst his sister, although married, was not overflowing with life.

Thus, I should have felt little surprise when one day he told me that he had fallen in love with and proposed to marry an attractive and intelligent young Jewess, Annetta Schebsmann, about fifteen years his junior, with whom I had for some time been carrying on an ardent flirtation, and whose intense vitality was magnetic.

From every point of view, except perhaps that of his family tradition, his choice was a wise one, and a further proof of the objectivity of his judgements. For Annetta certainly had enough fire for two and resembled more the furnace of a centrally-heated mansion than the open grate of a Kensington drawing-room.

I spent their wedding-day with them, and, although already at that time I saw signs of possible difficulties likely to arise from their temperamental disparity, I felt that on the whole he had by his choice at least served the best interests of his family line. Whether, from the standpoint of her future contentment, the match was equally commendable seemed both to Levy and me more doubtful. For although Annetta's devotion to her husband never abated, the ardour of her sensibilities can hardly have met with adequate response from the fading embers of his passion, and this may have caused her some hardship.

The gradual and steady estrangement that came over our friendship had a variety of causes, and I have no doubt that among them was my besetting aim of neglect and carelessness in all those little attentions which maintain the warmth of a friendship. Without, however, wishing to give the impression that to me the duration of amicable relations is wholly contingent on their utility and the advantages they provide, I cannot help feeling that at bottom all friendship must have some utilitarian foundation. This may not always be obvious, but I always listen with profound scepticism when anyone claims that a certain lasting attachment was wholly disinterested, or what is popularly called 'unselfish.'

The degree of realism in one's character may on this account be an important factor in determining the duration of a friendship, and people of French origin like myself, owing to their realistic habit of mind, are more likely than romantics to experience short friendships. Be this as it may, I have always been aware of an approaching menace to all my friendships the moment their profitableness began to decline, and it is probable that simultaneously with this awareness I have invariably been guilty of neglect and carelessness.

Is there such a thing as disinterested love? I would reply that, when it appears to be operating, the interest motive has either been forgotten or remained hidden to the parties concerned. At all events, I think it fair to claim that in all friendships there is a moment of complete saturation when both parties cease to be able to absorb or to give any more, or when one of the parties reaches this stage. In the first case, the coolness and indifference that supervene may be mutual; in the second, they may prove such a shock to him who is still unsaturated that it may occasion him great grief.

Another cause of my ultimate estrangement from Wrench was the divergence of our interests. He was much less convinced than I was about the evils of heterogeneity in a population. He thought my untiring assaults on feminism and my reiterated attacks on random mating and miscegenation excessive, and sided with Levy in countenancing and even favouring the unrestricted miscegenation that was beginning to be passionately championed in all the democracies after World War I.

I accused them both of subjectivity in this matter. For, whilst Wrench had gone out of his class and race by marrying a Jewess, Levy, in his marriage with Frieda, had also chosen an alien in the person of a goy. But my charge, at least as far as Wrench was concerned, was probably unfair, for he had many other motives, besides his belief in random mating, for his marriage with Annetta.

Wrench continued to show an interest in my writings, and in Karachi, where he had settled with his wife, he introduced every one of my books as they appeared to the local sahibs' club. Occasionally, when he was more than usually struck by the vehemence of my hostility to feminism, he would write asking me whether I could have forgotten my mother, whom, as we have seen, he greatly admired. But by the time World War II broke out we had ceased to feel the need of each other's thoughts and presence, and when, rightly or wrongly, I felt I had reasons to suspect that he had got in touch with some of my old enemies in the English Mistery and had taken to deriding much of what I stood for, including the Alexander teaching, the final breach occurred.

I probably deserved a good deal of this treatment, for I got a letter from him, written in Karachi in the early fifties, in which he deplored the loss of my friendship and from between the lines of which I discerned a note of reproach. But I could do nothing to repair the damage. For, when once the spell of a deep and affectionate relationship has been broken, I have always found it futile to try to recapture it. I even look on the attempt to do so as a tasteless undertaking. For the attempt to repeat a passionate experience, however well-meant it may be, is surely an artistic blunder. Nevertheless, much pleasure can be obtained from recalling the highlights of a great friendship, and to indulge in such recollections is more rewarding than to try to reproduce the conditions which made them a reality.

As Proust so well says: 'Si cette grande marée de l'amour s'est retirée à jamais, pourtant, quand nous nous promenons en nous-mêmes nous pouvons ramasser des coquillages étranges et charmants, et, en les portant à l'oreille, entendre avec un plaisir mélancholique et sans plus en souffrir, la vaste rumeur d'autrefois.'[21]

Wrench died in Karachi on my seventy-second birthday, 8th January 1954, and my friendship with him remains one of my happiest memories. It was certainly one of the most profitable relationships of my life, and one the richness of which I was

---

[21] *Les plaisirs et les jours* [*Pleasures and Days*], p. 221. 'If that great tide of love has ebbed forever, nevertheless, when we stroll through ourselves we can gather strange and charming seashells, and, in lifting them to our ear, hear with a melancholy pleasure and without suffering, the immense murmur of the past.' — Ed.

never again destined to enjoy.

At the height of our friendship, about the year 1918, I tried in my novel, *Too Old for Dolls*,[22] to depict him in the person of Lord Henry Highbarn, and went to great pains to make it a good likeness. But both Levy and I agreed that, although it brings to life many of those aspects of Wrench's character which made him an outstanding personality, the portrait was not as successful as the one I had previously drawn of Levy himself in my novel, *Mansel Fellowes*.

Incidentally, it was in this same novel that I also attempted to portray Mrs Dufresne, the lady friend who had made that remarkable prophecy about my forthcoming visit to Germany in 1907. In 'Mrs Delarayne' I think I drew a fairly good likeness of her, especially of her valiant struggle against the ravages of age. But to my regret she never lived to recognise herself in my portrait, and the fidelity of the delineation remained unappreciated by her who had sat for it.

* * *

I propose to leave to the next chapter, which deals with my life work, a discussion of my attitude towards the Jews. For, as I have often been charged with anti-Semitism and as the part played by Jews and Jewesses in my life has been of capital importance, I owe my readers an explanation of my true position in regard to these people.

To return now to the history of my male friends, the broken friendships with men which proved most disastrous to me and to my career all belong to the period after the publication of my *Defence of Aristocracy*. This book proved the means of introducing me to a number of peers and wealthy landowners, all of whom belonged to a level of society completely strange to me, in which I always felt I was an unnaturalised foreigner, and naturally, owing to the greater influence these people were in a position to exercise, quarrels with them had more serious consequences than those with ordinary commoners.

---

[22] London, 1920; New York, 1921.

In all social hierarchies, a man's title to admission into a higher rank is subjected to a narrow scrutiny, and if it seems insufficient he is suspected of venal motives for his intrusion. He is made to feel he that must produce a valid passport, and if he is sensitive, and of an independent nature, he may find this an affront. Rousseau, who had this experience, speaks of 'l'inconvénient de fréquenter des gens d'un autre état que le sien.'[23] For a man's dignity requires that he should not press himself into circles where he does not stand on his own native footing, *proprio jure*.[24] If he appears merely anxious to climb, it is assumed that he is doing so to serve his own ends and he is accordingly scorned. If, on the other hand, he wishes to establish his right to be accepted, at least *pro tem.*,[25] he has, as it were, to work his passage by performing some recognisable service for those above him.

This service may consist of giving information, advice, instruction or even entertainment alone. But the essential thing is that the interloper should prove useful. Naturally this involves the danger that, the moment his usefulness ceases, he is likely to be politely ushered to the door.

In my case the situation was aggravated by the fact that in my *Defence of Aristocracy* I was advocating a policy in which noone, least of all the aristocrats themselves, any longer believed. This disadvantage laid me under the suspicion of trying to pay my way in by a piece of gratuitous political and class toadyism. Those peers who had long ceased to believe in aristocracy — and they constituted the majority — thus regarded my work not only with profound scepticism, but also with secret disapproval, rather as if I had set out to write a defence of piracy or arson. Whilst the few who thought my work might perhaps add a welcome strut to the decaying structure of English conservatism and the political philosophy of the Right granted me their condescending attention.

---

[23] *Confessions*, Part II, Book 10. 'The disadvantage of associating with people from a different class than one's own.' — Ed.

[24] His own right. — Ed.

[25] For a time. — Ed.

None of them, however, had an inkling of the strong case that it is still possible to make out for an aristocratic revival — that this case has recently been argued by liberals themselves[26] shows how justified my thesis was — and I often had evidence of the fact that peers who had bought my book, and pretended to study it, believed so little in the feasibility of my proposals that they had been content after reading the title-page to take the rest of the book for granted. One peer in particular, for instance, quoted a certain passage to me from a book published long after my *Defence*, as if it offered fresh support to my argument, and was surprised when I pointed out that the passage in question had been lifted without acknowledgement from my book. The passage related to the interplay of the three fundamental instincts of man — the self-preservative, the reproductive and the social. If the peer in question ever lives to read this (and he is still alive as I write), he will remember the incident. It betrayed the fact that, like most of his class, he believed so little in the possibility of defending aristocracy that he had not troubled to read my treatise.

The greater part of the trouble arose from the fact that these men and their womenfolk, with typical English illogicality, confused my defence of aristocracy as a political regime with a defence of the class composing the so-called 'aristocracy' of the land — a misunderstanding which, owing to their laudable sense of their own unworthiness, made them dismiss my thesis as almost laughable.

Nevertheless, a few members of the nobility and one or two wealthy landowners became my friends. The peer abovementioned, who by accident had revealed that he had never troubled to open the covers of *A Defence of Aristocracy*, remained my friend from the early thirties to late in the forties. He gave me much hospitality, was unfailingly kind, and I think would have been friendly to this day had it not been for his womenfolk, who for various reasons became openly hostile and, owing to their great personal wealth or expectations of it, commanded respectful attention.

---

[26] See my *Quest of Human Quality*, Chapter 3.

It would serve no purpose to mention names. Yet there are a few I could name who, before their ultimate and, as far as I could discover, unaccountable revulsion of feeling towards me, became even closer friends than the peer above-mentioned.

One wealthy landowner, with whom I was on truly *Brüderschaft*[27] terms from about 1918 to 1936, and at whose country house I often enjoyed long spells of hospitality, was for a while my *alter ego*. We kept no secrets from each other and shared all each other's pleasures and problems. Owing to the evil influence I was supposed to exert over him, his womenfolk detested me. With their customary precision in measuring the exact balance of power in their homes and circles, they became aware of a definite hardening of his attitude to them whenever he had been in contact with me, and this coincidence, whether imagined or real, inevitably antagonised them. Often, however, the knowledge of their resentment only strengthened his attachment to me, and this state of affairs lasted over a long period. He was my junior by about ten years and, being an Englishman, could not at first feel the same horror as I did at the feminine domination which, whether covertly or unashamedly, is habitually exercised in all English circles, high and low.

Then, quite suddenly, the whole picture changed, and I became aware of his increasing coolness towards me, and even of signs of open hostility. Soon I heard that wholly unfounded slanders were being circulated about me and that they emanated from him, and I was at a loss to understand their cause. Only gradually, and by putting two and two together, I got on the track of some of the sources of the trouble. The first was the deliberate action of a mischief-making cousin of his, who disapproved of me so much that she treated me with the utmost rudeness; and the other was similar behaviour on the part of a working-class protégé of his, extremely jealous of my ascendancy over two of his patrons, did his best to wreck our relationship. Added to these influences, and away in the background, was the steady denigration of me and my work by a popular scientist of the day (exposed, incidentally, by no less

---

[27] Fraternal. — Ed.

an authority than Veblen) whose views carried great weight in the opinion of my friend.

It is, however, important to mention two factors which were common to both of these powerful friends — the peer already referred to and the wealthy landowner just described — and these were, first, that there was insanity in both of their families, a possible cause of some instability in their characters; and, secondly and probably more important still, that both men, like myself, were authors.

I do not wish to suggest that common interests and aspirations necessarily impair friendships, but in both men I certainly noticed comparatively early in our relationship ominous signs of incipient rivalry. They might at first be no more than modest criticisms, tactfully expressed. Subsequently, however, gratuitous fault-finding should have warned me of currents of deeper hostility, and if I failed to be alarmed by them it was only because outwardly, at least for a time, our relationship appeared unchanged.

Voltaire maintained that 'tout homme est jaloux de la prosperité de ceux qui sont de son état, ou de l'état desquels il croit être,'[28] and in *The Way of My World* Ivor Brown says: 'The primal curse of all professional life is jealousy.'[29] There is much truth in these remarks. Whether in the case of the friends in question this curse played a major role in bringing about our estrangement, it is difficult to say. Most probably it acted merely as a last straw which, once other factors had already sapped the position, tipped the scales in favour of a breach.

At all events, I can hardly doubt that the gravity to me of these two broken friendships was proportionate to the influence each of the two men was capable of exercising. For the denigration that inevitably followed our estrangement only helped to swell the volume of detraction let loose by my defection from the English Mistery. It is true that a few stalwart

---

[28] *Supplément au siècle de Louis XIV*, 2me Partie. 'Every man is jealous of the prosperity of those who belong to his class, or the class he thinks he belongs to.' — Ed.

[29] 1954, Chapter 12.

sympathisers joined me when I withdrew from this body and that they remained loyal. I refer particularly to one who is now a Member of Parliament. But in modern life, with all its fierce rivalries, a handful of loyal friends can do little against the determined hostility of influential former friends; and when, at the outbreak of World War II, I had to face an investigation by the Special Branch, Scotland Yard, it was only by my own unaided efforts, unsupported by any pressure from powerful friends, that I contrived to escape the ordeal of becoming a detainee under that odious Regulation 18B.

It would be inaccurate to pretend that in all this sad history I was guiltless of conduct calculated to alienate close associates, for I have already sufficiently emphasised my poor endowments for friendship. In the case of the wealthy landowner in question, for instance, I can recall many an incident which revealed me as self-centred, inconsiderate and too easily reconciled to solitude to be on my guard against behaviour that might appear unfriendly. In regard to both friends, moreover, I was inclined, as a man of foreign descent, to underrate the effects of the immense power exerted by women in England. Although I was aware of this power I never hesitated to defy it if I felt justified in doing so, because I foolishly reckoned on the support and loyalty of these women's menfolk. But in this I always proved mistaken, for in England the average man of all classes tends to wilt when opposed by his wife or by any determined female in his circle.

Be this as it may, I can hardly do better than conclude this account of my more unfortunate friendships with men by quoting Rousseau's admirable advice to his readers concerning friends with whom one has quarrelled. 'N'écoutez ni le P. de Tournemine,' he said, 'ni moi, parlant l'un de l'autre, car nous avons cessé d'être amis.'[30]

* * *

---

[30] *Confessions*, Part II, Book X. 'Listen neither to Father Tournemine nor myself when we speak of each other, for we are no longer friends.' — Ed.

The friendships we contract late in life are undoubtedly weaker than those we make at an early age. But, before closing this account of my male friends, I cannot omit all reference to one who has done most to impart a midsummer radiance to my declining years, and whose loyalty and devotion, though often sorely tried by many an inconsiderate action on my part, has remained unshaken.

I refer to my friendship with Captain Aubrey Trevor Oswald Lees, RA, a man of distinguished attainments and great natural gifts whom I met soon after my wife and I had moved into Suffolk in 1941.

Lees, my junior by seventeen years, had been educated at Repton, where he was a classical scholar, and underwent his military training at the Royal Military Academy, Woolwich. First commissioned in the Royal Field Artillery in 1919, he saw active service in various parts of the world. Ultimately, however, he applied for secondment to the Colonial Office. In 1926, after completing only half the course for candidates for the Colonial Administrative Service, he had already been selected to fill the post of Assistant District Commissioner in the Zanzibar Protectorate and later filled many appointments under the Colonial Office, finally serving in Jerusalem, Galilee, Jaffa, Gaza, Hebron, etc., variously as Assistant District Commissioner, Magistrate, Land Judge and in the Secretariat.

Owing to his sharp disagreement with the authorities over conditions in Palestine, and particularly over the situation of the Arabs, he ultimately fell under a cloud, was most unjustly treated and, finally, improperly and illegally retired on pension.

His stern sense of justice, clarity of vision, independence of judgement, and the fact that he never allowed himself to be intimidated by the risk of losing favour with the authorities constituted him the ideal public servant and the sort of high government official Nevil Shute so ably describes and commends as essential to any efficient government service.[31] But popularity in

---

[31] See *The Autobiography of an Engineer*, 1956, Chapter 7, and particularly my comments on it in 'The specious origins of Liberalism,' Part XVII, *The South African Observer*, October 1962, pp. 11–12.

official circles, certainly after World War I and during and after World War II, was not to be gained by the sort of officer who was not a yes-man, and Lees no doubt sacrificed his future on the altar of his courage and integrity.

Owing to his wide experience of conditions in both the Near East and Africa, he was always an interesting and illuminating talker, whilst his superior command of English, his general cultivation, the soundness of his judgement and his intimate knowledge of government service make friendly intercourse with him a constant source of entertainment and instruction.

He has the typical composure, serenity and balance of the trained soldier, and such is the general soundness of his judgement that I always found it worthwhile to consult him on any problem. I have no doubt that, thanks to that same patience and endurance with which military men uncomplainingly survive the hardships and perils of active service, he successfully weathered many of the more difficult passages in his friendship with me, and the kindness and loyalty he has continued to show me have long inspired my admiration and gratitude.

This again leads me to reflect on the enormous advantage of a strictly disciplined upbringing, and I am reminded that the men I have most liked and respected have all been soldiers. Whether in the person of the commissionaire who opens your tailor's or your bootmaker's door for you, or in that of the officer who has passed through Sandhurst or Woolwich, the military man, as the product of a discipline which the ordinary civilian never undergoes, possesses a distinction and displays personal attributes which are denied to men in all other walks of life.

It is therefore with the utmost pleasure that I here record that my most unclouded friendships have been with men of the old regular army. From my Battery Commander in 1916, Major Leonard Warren, and my OC Prisoners of War at Le Hâvre, Captain W. C. Hunter (son of Sir William Hunter of the *Gazetteer of India*) who remained my friend until his death, down to Captain A. T. O. Lees, I have only had to congratulate myself on any close association I have had with army men.

The reader may feel inclined to ask, 'But do not doctors, surgeons and engineers also have to undergo severe discipline?'

Yes, but with this importance difference—that, whereas in soldiering the discipline constantly extends, often with gruelling results, to man's management and control of his whole body as well as his mind, so that from the very inception of his training he is subjected to a regimentation which is psychophysical and embraces the government of his nerves and sensory reactions, the training of the recruit to other professions is much more exclusively mental. Hence, I believe, the superiority of the soldier. Because mind and body are best given approximately equal attention, and to confine training chiefly to the intellect or to the intellect alone amounts to disregarding the intimate interaction of the physical and psychical components of the organism.

In this recording my happy and unclouded relationship with Captain A. T. O. Lees, which has proved one of the most pleasant experiences of my declining years, I have no wish to detract from my grateful appreciation of the enduring loyalty and kindness of such other old friends as Jack H. Burton, R. Lester Williams, FRCS, Cyril A. Guild, Major Fitzroy Fyers, G. W. L. Wynne, Colonel H. Holderness, DSO, Hugh Lowder, and above all William Simpson of Prattsville, New York, USA, to all of whom I owe not only much friendly interest and entertainment, but also constant encouragement and sympathetic understanding.

To conclude these two chapters on friendship, a word should be said about affection in general, for it must strike most fairly observant students of humanity that, without affection, friendship, like a marriage of convenience, is merely a formality, a euphemism for a relationship which may have become necessary only through business or other interests, or even by the accident of birth, as in the heart of a family.

Now, in looking at the world of men, we must be inordinately obtuse if we cannot see that an enormous amount of the supposed close friendships and goodfellowships that appear to give society cohesion and stability are based on nothing more than conventional affection. And this is true even of relationships between members of the same family. Many people who pass through life more or less unaware of the deeper waters remain permanently ignorant of the many brothers and sisters in their circle—aye, and of the many fathers and sons—whose affection for one another is and always has been purely conventional; so much so, that no sense of loss ever follows any sudden and permanent separation. And if this applies to close relatives, how much more true is it of many alleged friends.

There are, however, some people—and I confess I am one of them—to whom this conventional affection makes no appeal; who from the start are aware of its trivial and bogus character, and who chafe under the perfunctory formalities it enjoins. Such people feel no compulsion to remain attached to either friend, brother or sister if or when such conventional affection is the only reason for doing so. But before charging such people with heartlessness and negativity, it would be well to make sure that the countless millions in every civilised country who are content to endure the bondage of conventional affection in various relations are necessarily less heartless and negative than they who prefer isolation before trumpery sentiment.

MY LIFE WORK

In his *Essais*, Montaigne, comparing authorship with parenthood, says: 'Je ne sais si je n'aimerais pas mieux beaucoup avoir produit un [i.e., a piece of writing], parfaitment bien formé, de l'accointance des muses, que de l'accointance de ma femme.'[1] And here he expresses feelings which must have been shared by many an author since his day.

Of the two forms of authorship—the procreation of another human being and a literary production—the latter has by some odd caprice of the popular mind generally been regarded as the more conceited and arrogant. Yet the plain truth is obviously the other way round. For it is difficult to conceive of any act that needs more self-assurance, self-complacency and self-approval than that of unhesitatingly foisting on the world a second edition of oneself, or of oneself plus the contributions made by the mate of one's choice.

Indeed, the resolute self-confidence with which the average father of no matter what class, what rank in the scale of physical desirability and character will parade his offspring before a public, which, particularly in this age, is surfeited with the sight of its teeming fellow-beings, is one of the most perplexing phenomena of civilised society. If it were not so common as to be taken for granted; if the average person could be induced for only one brief moment to think of the colossal vanity that the act of procreation presupposes, more especially when performed by couples whose perpetuation is the very last thing which a national plebiscite would be likely to authorise, a very different status would be granted to parenthood and fewer flags would fly when a birth was announced.

At least the author, before he can go into a second edition, re-

---

[1] *Essais*, Book II, Chapter 8: 'Of the Affections of Fathers to their Children.' 'I am not sure if I prefer making something well-formed by the acquaintance of the Muses than by the acquaintance of my wife.' — Ed.

quires the suffrages of the public. He has to await a mandate from his potential readers. Even his first edition has to survive the soured scrutiny of a succession of experts at every stage of its passage to the press. As Porson used to say when anyone told him that he intended to publish a book: 'Remember that two parties must agree on that point—you and the reader.'[2]

Let us therefore not too hastily charge Montaigne with conceit for preferring authorship before parenthood.

On the other hand, as every reader knows, there are two principal kinds of literary authorship—that which follows the urgent craving of a pen for paper, and that which results from the brain-racking study of a sheet of paper by a pen. And when the paper instead of the pen is the beggar, the literary production generally lacks power. As the outcome of an impatient impetuous overflow, a powerful literary composition runs a headlong irresistible course. 'Cela coule de source,'[3] as the French say, and dodges or overrides every obstacle.

Goethe's *Hermann und Dorothea* is a supreme example of this ideal form of literary production, and the fact that it was the poet's favourite work testifies to the easy, spontaneous nature of its birth. Other examples, taken at random, are, I suggest, Balzac's *Peau de chagrin* and *Mémoires de deux jeunes mariées*,[4] Emily Brontë's *Wuthering Heights*, Kipling's *Captains Courageous*, l'Abbé Prévost's *Manon Lescaut*, Thackeray's *Vanity Fair* and Wordsworth's 'Intimations of Immortality.'

Examples of the other and inferior kind of literary production are, in my opinion, all Henry James's and George Meredith's works, Bourget's *L'Étape*,[5] Bernard Shaw's *Back to Methuselah*, Balzac's *Les paysans*,[6] Kipling's *Puck of Pook's Hill* and Wordsworth's *The Excursion*.

Of Meredith, Levy once remarked: 'He expresses in a Gothic

---

[2] *Recollections of the Table-Talk of Samuel Rogers and Porsoniana*, 1856, p. 218.

[3] 'It flows from the spring.' —Ed.

[4] *The Wild Ass's Skin* and *Memories of Two Brides*. —Ed.

[5] *The Stage*. —Ed.

[6] *The Peasants*. —Ed.

style the fact that he has nothing to say.'

It is this 'having something to say' that drives men to authorship, for no other medium can serve. That is why some doctors turn from their medicine, some engineers from their workshop and some painters from their easel, in order to engage in literary authorship.

Explaining why he found the study of art wearisome, George Moore remarks very significantly: 'I was beginning to regard the delineation of a nymph or youth bathing as a very narrow channel to carry off the strong tide of a man's thought.'[7] This exactly expresses what I felt about pursuing the calling for which, owing to my heritage from my paternal grandfather and my father, I was undoubtedly gifted. For, powerful though my mother's influence may have been in weaning me from the graphic arts, it would have proved less effective had I not felt cramped by the narrow 'channel' that art offered for carrying off the 'full tide' of my thought.

And this leads me to reflect on the character of the artists I have known. Did they usually feel cramped by the 'narrow channel' their art offered them? If not, did this indicate the poverty of their thought, and did they remain simply painters because of this poverty?

Degas, who should have known what he was talking about, tells us that painters are usually stupid. 'Le peintre,' he said, 'en général, est bête.'[8]

After a lifetime spent in the company of artists, I rather incline to Degas' point of view, and have long suspected that painters abide contentedly by their palette and brushes not because their passion for painting, like a de Neuville's, overrides all else — 'Je voudrais peindre des kilometres avec un balai'[9] — but because they do not feel the 'channel' they have chosen too narrow to carry off the full tide of their thought.

This, of course, does not apply to a versatile genius like Leo-

---

[7] *Confessions of a Young Man*, 1886, iii.

[8] Clive Bell, *Old Friends*, 1956, Chapter 2. 'Painters in general are stupid.' — Ed.

[9] 'I would like to paint kilometres with a broom.' — Ed.

nardo, who took painting in his stride. But it is true of most of the artists I have known.

Be this as it may, when I claim that I am among those who, though gifted for the pursuit of the graphic arts, preferred literary authorship, I do not wish to be understood as implying that 'the full tide of my thought' found the channel of painting too narrow because it was pregnant with works of outstanding creative value. For, let it be well appreciated by posterity that by far the greater part of nineteenth- and twentieth-century authorship was less spontaneous and creative than reactive. It was less a response to inner riches than to external and exasperating stimuli.

The works of Shaw are a typical example of this class of second-rate literature and, unlike *Manon Lescaut*, would never have been written had they not been provoked by the harassing circumstances of the times. I say 'harassing,' because for all sensitive natures, the social conditions of the period in question allowed of no rest, no change of equanimity, until they had reacted with criticism and suggested reforms to provocative features of their age.

Even Dickens, like Henry Cockton and Besant, was not guiltless of this mainly reactive kind of literary production. But at least in Dickens there was enough natural poetry and artistic improvisation to enable him to clothe his works in a dress which often brought them within deceptive proximity to the kind of authorship which springs from inner riches alone.

I happened to be one of those caught up in this fiat of social disorder and whose 'tide of thought' therefore found the graphic arts an unsuitable channel for its expression. I claim no more. And it may perhaps be regarded as one of the great plagues of our age that 'having something to say' should in so many cases find itself diverted, if not forced, into the channels of political, social and economic reform.

* * *

I have already dealt at sufficient length with my work on Nietzsche, and, if it is still possible to catch in my books and prefaces about his 'philosophy' the note of youthful enthusiasm that animated them, their lack of any critical approach to his doctrines will perhaps be condoned. For I wrote with the zeal of an advocate and a propagandist. Only in private did I sometimes voice the doubts I felt about certain aspects of his teaching.

At all events, there was one major feature of Nietzsche's work which seemed to me essential for estimating its value, and that was that he too was chiefly a reactive thinker. What is more, his reactions—say, to his sister's marriage to Förster and to the later works of Wagner—although couched in intellectual terms, were fundamentally emotional. As a gifted poet, he was able to impart a compelling beauty and authority to his utterances, especially in *Thus Spake Zarathustra*. But except for such masterpieces as his fine poem 'Aus hohen Bergen,' I can think of few of his productions which bear no trace of reactive inspiration.

He certainly owed much to his great predecessors, Schopenhauer, Stendhal, Dostoyevsky and Heine, and when his borrowing from these four penetrating thinkers (especially in psychology) is eliminated, his work is appreciably denuded. Nevertheless, his original contributions to the problem of morality and his masterly analysis of modern nihilism are likely to ensure his fame for all time, and they probably account for the fact that a profound thinker like Albert Camus could regard him as 'the greatest European writer.'[10]

I do not now feel able to endorse this view of him, for in recent years I have grown more and more inclined to agree with Tolstoy, who, writing to his friend Fet in 1869, said: 'I am convinced that Schopenhauer is the greatest genius ever produced by the human race.'[11]

Nietzsche influenced me chiefly by his consistent advocacy of aristocratic values in art and politics, and in my first independent works it was to art and politics that I confined my attention.

In discussing art, I wrote as one who from his earliest childhood had listened to the talk of painters, sculptors and gravers in their studios, and at the age of twenty-five was beginning to feel deeply shocked by the anarchy that prevailed in these circles. No canon decided the value of a work of art. No authority, no tribu-

---

[10] Leader on Albert Camus, *The Times*, 5th January 1960.
[11] Tikhon Polner, *Tolstoy and his Wife*, 1946, Chapter 6.

nal existed before which a young aspiring artist could take his 'masterpiece,' in the sense of the old craft gilds, just as a doctor can take his thesis to those of his seniors who are in a position to grant him his doctorate. On the contrary, everything was at sixes and sevens. No two artists agreed on any principle of artistic production. All was chaos and uncertainty. I could think of nothing more discouraging to a young artist than the state of darkness and confusion that prevailed.

The critics were bad enough, for, as Professor C. M. Joad truly observed, 'Art criticism is a battle of ipse-dixitisms.'[12] But among artists themselves there was even less clarity and definition. Destitute of standards and of any criteria for assessing the value of their work, their chance of popular acclaim depended on their own self-advertising efforts and their capacity for gaining enough journalistic support to herd a sufficiently impressive number of fans into their fold, all bleating their name.

When, therefore, I began to study aesthetics and tried to discover principles which, even if they fell short of a canon, would at least lend a certain consistency to my judgements, I naturally disregarded all contemporary art criticisms, especially those of the leading critics in the *Times*, the *Telegraph*, the *Morning Post* and the *Standard*, the weeklies and the foremost Parisian journals, as quite useless, and tried to frame out of all I had heard at home, at Rodin's and in the studios of friends a sound basis for aesthetic judgements.

Above, all, what I was most eager to combat and refute, because it struck me as wholly perverse, was the teaching of James McNeill Whistler, whom I had known ever since I was a child, to whose conversation I often listened, and who repelled both my mother and me as a man, and me in particular as a teacher. Early in my acquaintance with him I had grown doubtful about his integrity, and suspected that his art principles were prompted to a great extent by his own deficiencies. Even more significant, in my view, was the striking similarity between his sophistries and those to be found in a certain famous philosophical treatise, which I felt

---

[12] *Return to Philosophy*, 1935, Chapter 5. 'Dogmatic pronouncements.' — Ed.

sure he knew nothing about and which, when I first read it, seemed to me thoroughly specious.

Even those who first wisely resisted the initial steps of the movement that has culminated in all the extravagances, abuses and charlatanry of our latest forms of art appear to have been unaware of the philosophical doctrines to which all ultra-modern artists might appeal for a vindication of their practices.

In view of his intellectual gifts, Ruskin would certainly have been able to fight with greater authority and success the precursors of the latest school of so-called painters, if only he had known the philosophical treatise which, when he was at his zenith, was already one hundred years old. For, in spite of the genius of its author and the intimidating grandeur of his achievements, Ruskin might well have detected the flaws in the great German's aesthetic theories and forestalled by three or four generations the need of demonstrating their heretical character.

But neither Ruskin himself, nor any one of his sympathisers or opponents seems to have had any knowledge of the Teutonic arsenal of revolutionary aesthetic doctrine from which, at any time after 1790, the secessionists from the Academy and the Beaux Arts might have drawn their munitions of war. Thus, when Manet and Whistler propounded the fundamental principles which in the remote future were to bear fruit in the form of 'abstract art,' no-one had any inkling of the aesthetic war that lay ahead, or of the formidable artillery of German manufacture that might have been used by the innovators for their assault and by their adversaries for spiking the opposing guns.

Passing over Manet's contribution to the secessionist credo of the middle of the last century as neither as pernicious as Whistler's, nor as strangely identical with those of the famous German thinker, it will suffice for my present purpose to show the extraordinary agreement of these two men—one an American painter, and the other a Teutonic thinker who had probably never held either a palette or a paintbrush in his hand—and to reveal how much was missed by both sides in the aesthetic controversy which shook the art world of the late nineteenth century, and how much still appears to remain unknown to the moderns who continue to take sides in the conflict.

Nor should I like it to be thought that in indicting Whistler, as I have always done, I had any wish to assail the teaching of the early French Impressionists, many of whose innovations and reforms were at once salutary and opportune.

It will be remembered that, both in his *Ten O'Clock*[13] and especially in his letter to *The World*,[14] Whistler made it plain that what he held to be the important, if not the chief, concern of an artist in painting a picture was not the subject depicted, nor that aspect of Nature that had inspired him with a wish to perpetuate it for himself and his fellow-men — that did not matter; but the picture's composition, its harmony, its colour scheme. Hence his insistence on such titles for his paintings as 'Symphonies,' 'Arrangements' and, with a deliberate allusion to such musical compositions as we associate with Amedée de Beauplan, Plantade and Chopin, 'Nocturnes.'

In his letter to *The World* he actually embarked on the dangerous undertaking, pregnant with mischief for the future of the graphic arts, of assimilating pictorial art to music. 'As music is the poetry of sound,' he said, 'so is painting the poetry of sight, and the subject-matter has nothing to do with harmony of sound or colour.' Then, most recklessly for a graphic artist, he added: 'The great musicians knew this. Beethoven and the rest wrote music — simply music, symphony in this key, concerto or sonata in that,' the implication being that the painter also could completely fulfil his function by producing 'simply' harmonies, symphonies and arrangements — of course, in colour.

The breathtaking novelty and seductive plausibility of this idea concealed from Whistler's ill-informed and standardless public its utter speciousness. Because the graphic artist has a task so different from the musician's that what the great musicians knew and practised can have no relevance whatsoever for him.

The musician is in no respect preoccupied with what Zola aptly described as 'un coin de la création' which, 'vu à travers un tempérament,'[15] becomes the graphic artist's *œuvre*. Indeed, the

---

[13] 1885.
[14] 22nd May 1878.
[15] 'A part of creation . . . seen through a temperament.' — Ed.

more the musician strives to interpret through his temperament 'a corner of creation,' the more descriptive he makes his music, the less value it usually has. Thus, Englefield Hull quite properly speaks of music's 'freedom from the necessity to represent things, its non-representative character, its qualities of abstraction.'[16]

The graphic artist, on the other hand, by tradition, almost by definition and by the nature of his function, has always been engaged in works of a representative character; had his attention turned to some corner of creation, and has always eschewed abstraction. The sparking-plug to the whole process which terminates in a work of pictorial art has always been an aspect of creation inspiring enough to induce him to perpetuate it for himself and others, and by his genial version of it to uplift us more than could our own unaided contemplation of it.

But—and here is the whole crux of the matter—the essential factor in the graphic artist's inspiration is the corner of creation which, by moving him to perform his skilled office, gives us that corner of life enhanced by the power of his genius.

If, however, in emulation of the musician, he merely extemporises in shades and tones and seeks only harmonies, compositions and arrangements, he insensibly descends to a more humble craft, an inferior aesthetic performance. Even if he does not wholly usurp, he certainly draws confusingly close to, the craft of the wallpaper, carpet or chintz designer. Now, the musician runs no such risk when he eschews a corner of creation as the basis of his expression. On the contrary, by the very exigencies of his art his highest manner is the production of works which are exclusively harmonies, arrangements and variations of a subjective mood, unrelated to and not attempting to portray any particular corner of creation. His genius produces an abstract theme independent of life's forms and in terms far from explicit, and our judgement concerning whether his work is well or indifferently done bears no relation to its representational character. His art is thus *de rigueur* 'abstract art.' He steps up by doing what the graphic artist steps down to do. And when the graphic artist steps down in this way, we, as the recipients of his impression, are left with the standards

---

[16] *Music: Classical, Romantic and Modern*, 1927, Chapter 1.

proper only to the judgement of a tartan, a Fair Isle pattern or a patchwork quilt.

For as Dr Ananda Coomaraswamy so pertinently remarked in 1945: 'The fundamental judgement [of a work of graphic art] is the degree of the artist's success in giving clear expression to the theme of his work. In order to answer the question, has the thing been well said?, it will evidently be necessary for us to know what it was that was to be said. It is for this reason that in every discussion on works of art we must begin with the subject-matter.'[17]

This flat refutation of Whistler's frivolous dismissal of the subject from the painter's legitimate concern indicates how seriously we err when, like Whistler, we confuse the painter's with the musician's task.

Dr P. R. Ballard also offers a shrewd criticism of Whistler's shallow heresy. Commenting on the hackneyed tag, 'Verisimilitude is not art,' which is often adduced in defence of Whistler's foolish dictum on the subject (for a picture having a subject—i.e., a corner of creation—as its basis need by no means necessarily be photographic), Dr Ballard says: 'Yet verisimilitude cannot be wholly ignored. For art is not merely expression, it is also communication; and communication is only possible through a series of symbols which have virtually the same meaning to the parties concerned, the communicator and communicatee. Appearances are the words of his [the painter's] language.'[18]

Certainly let the harmony of colours and the composition of a picture be among the concerns of the artist. But to make them his principal, let alone his only, concern is nonconformist bigotry with all the lower-middle-class narrowness that this implies. That way leads inevitably to all the flagrant abuses of modern abstract art and the charlatanry that it promotes and even suggests. It opens the ranks of graphic artists to every house-painter who may have the effrontery to display his subjective splashes of paint as a masterpiece. And the fact that the Royal Academy, in ultimate submission to the aesthetically illiterate clamour of the press and

---

[17] *Why Exhibit Works of Art?*, Chapter 1.
[18] *Educating for Democracy*, edited by J. T. Cohen and R. M. W. Travers, 1939, Chapter 13.

certain sections of the public, should at last have bowed its head before this anarchical teaching, and opened its doors to the hawkers of this spurious form of art, is but one proof the more of the derelict condition of the art world. No greater *trahison des clercs*[19] has ever occurred in the history of culture than the support given by most of the leading national newspapers, including above all the *Times*, to those so-called artists who have desecrated their calling and sometimes made great fortunes by so doing.

I am not forgetting the nefarious role played by the speculative picture-dealers of the period, especially in Paris, who, after investing relatively small sums in the early products of these abstract painters, created an artificial fame for them in order to reap handsome profits on their purchases. As for the public, all those who are inclined to be haunted by the dread of appearing reactionary or behind the times, or prefer being robbed to being suspected of defective connoisseurship, hastily swallowed the bait held out to them by those whom they imagined authorities, and the consequence was that a wholly factitious vogue was created for what we may hope will be regarded merely as so much junk in a hundred years' time.

In the Summer Exhibition of, I believe, the year 1961, I saw on the line at Burlington House a huge picture purporting to represent the advent of spring. It consisted merely of parallel lines of yellow, green and purple rectangles running from the top to the bottom of the canvas, the execution of which was well within the powers of any junior schoolboy, let alone of any house-painter, and as I examined it I could not help for the thousandth time deploring Whistler's baneful influence and his impudent assumption of authority in art matters.

Unfortunately, he lived in an age when to be much talked about was to be accepted as an authority on anything. The crowd and the national press, confusing mere notoriety with omniscience, could not doubt that one who enjoyed so much publicity must be an expert in every branch of knowledge.

It was a thousand pities that George Moore's sensible attitude to Whistler and his teaching was not shared by a larger number of

---

[19] Treason of the intellectuals. — Ed.

his contemporaries. For, evidently referring to the American artist's *Ten O'Clock* and similar effusions, he once observed to the great painter, J. E. Blanche: 'Il ferait mieux de faire de la peinture et de laisser ses blagues à Oscar Wilde et Cie.'[20]

The word *blagues* is well-chosen. But it was precisely Whistler's *blagues* that the press, the public and many of his fellow-artists, including my own father, took most seriously; and all for the want of an attack on his position more enlightened and more formidable than that launched by Ruskin in 1877. But Moore was, in any case, never convinced of Whistler's *bona fides*, and even believed that the American painter declared Story's mediocre figurines — Story was a sculptor — to be similar 'if not equal to the Elgin marbles,' merely because Story 'had given evidence favourable to Whistler in the Whistler–Ruskin action for libel.'[21]

Turning now to the aesthetic doctrines which as long ago as 1790 forestalled the Whistlerian heresies, the relevant treatise is Kant's *Kritik der Urteilskraft*.[22] Following the Bruno Erdmann edition, we read: 'We must not feel the least concern about the existence of the subject, but in this respect be quite indifferent, in order to act as judge in matters of taste.'[23] Again, Kant observes: 'Taste is the ability to judge an object or a mode of representation by feelings of wholly disinterested pleasure or displeasure. The object of such pleasure is called *beautiful*.'[24]

Then Kant concludes: 'The beautiful is what causes a general feeling of pleasure, independently of any idea it may suggest.'[25]

---

[20] Joseph Hone, *The Life of George Moore*, 1936, Chapter 3. 'He'd be better off painting and leaving the jokes to Oscar Wilde and Co.' — Ed.

[21] *Avowals*, 1936, Chapter 16.

[22] *Critique of the Power of Judgement.* — Ed.

[23] 1880, p. 39: 'Man muss nicht in mindesten fur die Existenz der Sache eingenommen, sondern in diesem Betracht ganz gleichgültig sein, um in Sachen des Geschmacks den Richter zu spielen.'

[24] *Op. cit.*, p. 45: 'Geschmack ist das Beurteilungsvermögen eines Gegenstandes oder einer Vorstellungsart durch ein Wohlgefallen oder Missfallen ohne alles Interesse. Der Gegenstand eines solchen Wohlgefallen heisst schön.'

[25] *Op. cit.*, p. 46: 'Das Schöne ist das was ohne Begriffe als Object eines allgemeine Wohlgefallen vorgestellt wird.'

Although, as we see, Kant confines his remarks to the judgement and not the production of a work of art, his insistence on the view that the beautiful is the object of entirely disinterested pleasure, and that the subject has no importance in this respect, can at once be seen as having closer affinities with the appreciation of music than with that of any picture or sculpture. For, essential to the judgement whether the graphic artist has competently fulfilled his function, and displayed any genius in perpetuating for us a corner of creation, is not only the subject he represents, but also our gladness at having it perpetuated for us in terms transcending our own unaided contemplation of it. Indeed, the deeper our interest in the particular corner of creation represented, the greater will be our pleasure at seeing its beauties enhanced by his inspired vision of it.

When, therefore, Kant argues that 'in painting and in all the plastic and graphic arts—in architecture and gardening—in so far as they are beautiful arts, the *design* is the essential factor,'[26] and adds, 'and here it is not what pleases our sensibilities, but what gives pleasure *through its form* that is essential for taste,'[27] the likeness to Whistler is more than ever pronounced, for the passage might be a paraphrase of Whistler's insistence on composition, arrangement and colour scheme as the fundamental, if not the only, concern of the artist.

Two pages earlier, Kant states even more explicitly a principle which, had it been lifted and used by Whistler, would have caused no surprise.[28] Indeed, it is difficult to read this part of Kant's *Kritik der Urteilskraft* without being constantly reminded of the *Ten O'Clock* and, above all, of Whistler's practical application of his own doctrines in some of the pictures he painted.

The justification which Kant's aesthetic principles proffer by anticipation to the worst excesses of modern art remained concealed for close on a century, and it was left to Whistler, who, as

---

[26] *Op. cit.*, p. 61.

[27] The italics are mine; the German reads: 'In der Malerei, Bildhauerkunst, ja, in allen bildenden Künsten—in der Baukunst, Gartenkunst—sofern die schöne Künste sind,' etc.

[28] *Op. cit.*, p. 59.

far as I am aware, knew nothing about them, to give them independent expression and thus to start the artistic trend that has culminated in abstract art. For this act of corruption it is to be hoped that an enlightened posterity will not forgive him. But such is the hypnotic influence exercised by fame alone, irrespective of merit, that it is doubtful whether the art world's emancipation from the thraldom of his dogmas is likely to occur before many generations have passed on. For at the present time abstract art has become a vested interest. Millions of pounds have been invested in the hardly sane products of the school, and the museums and public and private galleries that have become its dupes are hardly likely to acknowledge their error.

There remains one interesting question. Assuming that Whistler knew nothing of Kant's *Kritik der Urteilskraft*, what affinity between the two men could possibly have led them independently to propound much the same aesthetic heresies?

Strange to say, they were in one important respect related. For whereas Whistler, through his mother, could trace his ancestry to the McNeills of Skye, Immanuel Kant was the grandson of an immigrant from the north of Scotland whose name was Cant. So that it may well be that their common provenance bore some relation to the similarity of their teaching.

When we consider the couple's insistence on the design, the composition, the arrangement of a graphic artwork, their denial of the interest of the subject, and their common tendency to luxuriate in greys, half-tones, blacks and sombre shades,[29] it is difficult not to recognise their common negativity, their readiness to turn away from the world of the flesh, to regard the 'corners of creation' as more or less negligible. And here perhaps we light at least on one of their major temperamental affinities—the unconscious negativism deriving from their ascetic Scottish ancestry.

Be this as it may, my work as an art critic and as a writer on aesthetics was directed from the start chiefly by my pronounced aversion from Whistler's teaching—an attitude that naturally

---

[29] For Kant's claim that colour adds nothing to the beauty of the form but rather distracts the mind from it, see Part I, Division I, Paragraph 14 of the *Kritik*.

made me unpopular. For even if I feel constrained to acknowledge that in some of his best works he departed sufficiently from his own doctrines to produce paintings whose quality accounts for Moore's lamentation quoted above, his *blagues* have caused too much havoc for his memory to remain wholly unsullied.

* * *

In politics, whether owing to a temperamental bias in favour of aristocracy, or to the many influences I underwent from boyhood onwards at the hands of men I liked, all of whom upheld the principles of the Right, I cannot remember any period in my life when I was not aware of the grave objections to a democratic regime. In later life I set out these objections in my *Quest of Human Quality*,[30] but at no time in my career have I regarded democracy as a desirable or even workable form of government. Sooner or later, it always seemed to me, in all those countries where no steps were taken to mitigate its worst effects it must lead to anarchy, chaos and national decline.

I reached this conclusion not merely on historical grounds and not solely on account of self-observation, or what is called introspection, but also as the result of watching my fellow-men, including the wisest among them, and the fact that I reached it sometime before female suffrage was granted absolves me of the charge of having been influenced by anti-feminism in my politics.

Aware, as I soon became, of the fact that success for democracy must depend on the widest possible distribution throughout a nation of public-spirited people, above all of men and women who, in choosing any measure, policy or representative, are prompted at least by sound healthy instincts—for to wish them prompted by knowledge and wisdom was, I knew, romantic—it seemed to me that the theory of democracy was founded on entirely fantastic presuppositions about human nature. Indeed, I decided quite early that in order to be a convinced democrat a man must be either intellectually dishonest enough to make a false estimate of himself, or else so incompetent in psychology as to mis-

---

[30] London, 1952.

read, misunderstand and misinterpret what he saw when he looked into his own character and that of his fellow-men.

Rousseau put his finger on the key to the whole problem of popular government when he said: 'Quand un homme feint de préférer mon intérêt au sien propre, de quelque démonstration qu'il colore ce mensonge, je suis sûr qu'il en fait un.'[31]

This is realism emerging willy-nilly from the broodings of a thinker who was in the main impulsive, sentimental and romantic; and the logic that prompted it crops up again in his *Social Contract*, where he remarks: 'Were there a people of gods, their government would be democratic. So perfect a government is not for men.'[32]

Some 150 years later, Santayana echoed these sentiments when he said: 'If a noble and civilised democracy is to subsist, the common citizen must be something of a saint and something of a hero.'[33]

One has but to stroll along the main thoroughfare of any one of our English towns and to observe the throngs of men and women that encumber the pavements in order to see innumerable signs of their faulty judgement, untrustworthy instincts, shocking taste and defective self-control. Scrutinise them more narrowly and the evidence of their inability to choose what will ensure even their own welfare, and prove an advantage to themselves and their dependants, becomes overwhelming. The close observation of any modern populace consequently leads to the conclusion that, even if we could postulate of every one of them the saintliness and heroism that Santayana would have them possess, and the public spirit and disinterestedness Rousseau had in mind when describing the *Social Contract*, it would still be doubtful whether any political judgement they could pronounce would be either wise or nationally beneficial.

To think otherwise, to be able to assert without misgiving and without abandoning the democratic position, as Asquith once did,

---

[31] *Émile*, Volume III, Book 5. 'When a man professes to put my interests before his own, I detect the falsehood, however disguised.' —Ed.

[32] 1792; G. D. H. Cole's translation, Chapter 4.

[33] *The Life of Reason*, Book II: *Reason in Society*, 1905, Chapter 5.

that the essence of democratic government is 'that the will of the people shall, both in legislation and policy, prevail,'[34] presupposes in an intelligent man so much deliberate blindness and resolute fidelity to a fond ideal that, where such opinions can be solemnly expressed, we feel ourselves in fairyland.

The reader may retort: 'But cannot the same be said about the advocacy of aristocratic government? What superior guarantee does aristocracy offer of wise, disinterested and public-spirited government? Have the aristocracies of the past, have individual aristocrats, shown a greater proneness to conduct themselves and control the lives of others wisely and benevolently than the governments of the democracies?'

To this reasonable objection, I have replied in great detail in my various works on politics, but most comprehensively in my *Quest of Human Quality*.

No-one can accuse me of having concealed or minimised the pitfalls and snags of an aristocratic regime, or of having understated the vices and errors of most of the European aristocracies of the past. Indeed, as one friendly critic said of my *Defence of Aristocracy*, 'Your book should more accurately have borne the title, *Aristocracy: An Indictment.*'

If, in spite of all that history records against aristocratic government and all we know about human nature and its inveterate frailties, I still clung to my belief in the superiority of an aristocratic over a democratic regime, it was because, except in one or two cases, no aristocratic regime had ever been given a fair trial. And I mean by a fair trial that opportunity of displaying its advantages under conditions allowing for the correction and control of human error.

The reader who for a moment will ponder the difference between an aristocratic regime and one like the present democracy of England, with its universal suffrage, its periodical general elections, the freedom of its electors to vote as they like, and above all the secret ballot—such a reader will hardly fail to be struck by one fundamental distinction, which is that, whilst in an aristocracy control over the rulers is practically possible and has indeed been

---

[34] Nigel Nicolson, *People and Parliament*, 1958, Chapter 1.

found a workable method of securing good government, it is quite impossible by any means whatsoever to control millions of voters to the same end.

Wherever the necessary machinery has existed for the effective control of the rulers, we have had conspicuous examples of good aristocratic government lasting over centuries. But in no democracy hitherto has it ever been found possible to control the political behaviour and influence of the voting masses. For how can we discover a particular voter's attitude or wisdom, when the ballot does not allow us even to guess for what policies he or she may have voted? Suppose the issue to be 'Shall England survive or perish?' Under our present system, millions might treacherously vote for the second alternative without running the slightest risk of having their villainy discovered. No aristocrat could, however, act in a like manner without immediately becoming the object of popular indignation and loathing.

For although an extreme issue like the one quoted may never actually arise in practice, we should not forget that, among the ill-informed and easily misled masses, high and low, there may be hundreds of thousands who, although never wishing to bring about England's ruin, would yet unwittingly, owing to their lack of wisdom, information and insight, be able with a clean conscience to support a policy which insensibly over the years might amount to a sentence of death to the nation, or at least to a decline in its prosperity.

So that, to begin with, the most fundamental superiority of an aristocracy over a democracy is that the aristocrat in his political behaviour may be controlled and if necessary brought to book, whereas the democrat cannot be.

And it is most significant that the only examples European history gives us of successful aristocratic government—that is to say, of an efficient aristocratic administration that has secured the public welfare over a long period—relate to those regimes in which suitable machinery existed for the effective control of the rulers.

It is strange that throughout the Middle Ages, in spite of the example set to the various bodies of European rulers by such institutions as the craft gilds, for instance, in which strict control was maintained over the competence of candidates for admission, and over the quality of the work done by them after admission, it never occurred to any of the European aristocracies (except in one or two cases) that, if the quality of their administration and the competence of the members of their class were to be maintained, they must improvise methods by which the members of their order could be disciplined and controlled and their competence for rulership severely tested.

In recent times, the wisdom of such methods for maintaining efficiency, competence and worthiness among the members of a body performing an essential public service, so that they could continue to deserve the trust and approval of the population, has been convincingly illustrated by the medical profession and the two branches of the law, the solicitors and barristers. For we cannot doubt that if the prestige of these bodies has been maintained and public belief in their trustworthiness and indispensability has remained unshaken, it is because they were prudent enough to establish within their order a central controlling board before which incompetent, disreputable or otherwise unworthy members could be arraigned and summarily punished, sometimes by expulsion from the order. And this is not to mention that in all three cases high standards of competence are set, which candidates for admission must be able to reach before being passed as qualified to practise.

The public know of the gruelling tests applied by the medical board of examiners before an aspirant to medical practice is allowed to exercise his skill on the public, and how doctors arraigned before the disciplinary committee of the General Medical Council for 'infamous conduct in a professional respect' may be struck off the register of their order and thus deprived of the means of earning their living. The people also know how solicitors guilty of conduct unfitting a member of their profession may be struck off the roll of solicitors by the disciplinary committee of the Law Society.

Can anyone doubt that if the professions in question had failed to institute such methods of controls they would long ago have lost their standards of quality and forfeited the confidence of the public?

Satisfied that he is posing a question that will baffle and silence all champions of aristocracy forever and prove an unanswerable objection to the necessity of an elite in society, that ardent liberal and democrat Dr David Spitz asks: 'What if the aristocrat does wrong . . . but refuses to arrest, imprison or execute himself? We cannot look to another aristocrat for the remedy, not merely because the other aristocrat may also have done wrong, but because by the logic of this construction, only the aristocrat himself can judge himself.'[35]

From the wording of this astonishingly shallow observation, one suspects that Dr Spitz must often have found it a successful debating point on public platforms and, knowing the value of creating a laugh, especially in an English audience, thought it good policy to repeat it even in an ostensibly serious political treatise.

Yet it seems hardly credible that he could have been so ignorant of the historical and other relevant facts to assume that it was in any sense a statement worth making except before a wholly ill-informed gallery. For, had he but looked about him and seen how today vast orders of skilled technicians contrive decade after decade to maintain standards of efficiency, quality and reliable public service; if only he had remembered his European history and had seen that there was nothing in 'the logic of the construction' of the learned corporations in question to prevent a doctor from judging another doctor, or a lawyer from judging another lawyer—if, I say, he had but recognised such facts, he might, provided that he was given the time, possibly have come to understand why so many aristocracies of the past had foundered and why that of Venice, which happened to have had a board of control, endured with success for centuries. Above all, what we hope he might in the end have grasped was the fact that the failure of any particular aristocracy presents no rational ground for dismissing aristocracy as a regime, if it can be shown that the aristocracy in question had adopted no measures of internal control to maintain its efficiency, competence and credit.

All this argument, together with the relevant supporting documentation, will be found set out in detail in my *Quest of Human Quality*, but it is adumbrated in books I published as early as 1915.

---

[35] *Patterns of Anti-Democratic Thought*, 1949, Chapter 5, ii.

Although an important plea in favour of aristocracy, it represents only one aspect of the defence that may be made for the regime.

Political philosophers often forget that one of the primary needs of a society, civilised or savage, is a body of leaders who, besides administering the defensive, economic and social affairs of the community, also sets its tone — i.e., establishes its norms of acceptable behaviour, its taste, its concepts of honour, civility and good tone, and provides it with a model of the standards to which it should aspire. Without such tone-setters, composed of an elite able by its worthiness and prestige to give common people guidance in a sound way of life and in the choice of their goals, a society is a derelict mob given over to anarchy and chaos. It becomes the sort of riotous rabble, high and low, which we see about us today.

It is therefore most significant that the indispensability of such an elite should at last have been recognised and argued with particular emphasis by the very political philosophers who only yesterday were denying the need of an aristocracy and refusing to see any sense in a leisured class whose principal function was leadership in every branch of the national life. Indeed, I do not remember ever having seen a more cogent plea for the revival of such a class in England than that recently advanced by such fervent democrats as Middleton Murry, Professors Alfred Weber, Wilhelm Röpke, Karl Mannheim and above all Sir Fred Clarke.

'The vast bulk of the higher cultural achievements of mankind,' says Sir Fred Clarke, 'have come from the presence in society of a minority so placed that, either through its own energies, or through its discerning patronage of genius, it will concern itself with the higher refinements of living.' And he proceeds: 'It would be a grave and disastrous mistake to assume that the free society of the future will dispense with such a minority as being contrary to the principle of democratic equality. . . . A free society of common men is possible and safe only if it can ensure that the right sort of uncommon man will continue to emerge and be so placed that he can discharge adequately all his essential functions.'[36]

Professor Weber, discussing the urgent necessity of a class that

---

[36] *Freedom in the Educative Society*, 1948, Chapter 2.

is best qualified for political and practical leadership, pleads for the revival of an elite 'composed of persons spiritually, intellectually and characterologically pre-eminent' who can 'act as models.'[37] Whilst Professor Wilhelm Röpke, insisting on the need of such an elite to establish the tone, taste and ideals of decency and honour among the majority, thinks, like the able Englishman Nevil Shute, that the elite in question must in any case be composed of men of property, if only in order that they may have the independence to oppose, if necessary, officialdom and the state in the public interest.

Speaking of the families composing the elite, he says: 'At the risk of shocking democratic sentiment, it must be confessed that it lies in the interest of society that a certain number of the rooted families should exceed the average in the amount of property they possess and also in the virtues which would alone justify their doing so,' in order 'to be of service to the community.' For, again like Nevil Shute, he sees the need of a class of what he calls 'secularised clerks' — i.e., 'independent men' who could act as 'counterweights to the state' and be the champions of truth, justice and honour in the interest of the majority.[38]

Eight years later, that English engineer of exceptional talent, Nevil Shute, made a similar and even more powerful plea for the existence of a class independent enough to resist if necessary the power of officialdom and all serious flaws in government administration, and illustrated his argument with such startling facts drawn from his own experience as an English state servant that the attack which his disclosures enabled him to make on death duties, for instance, is unique in the literature of economics and is among the most intelligent and enlightening I have so far read.[39] Yet I came across this valuable book only by chance and cannot recall having had my attention directed to it by the sort of publicity it deserved. To this extent does an unseen hand now exercise a literary censorship to conceal from public notice facts and views considered prejudicial to the opinions which an ignorant and vul-

---

[37] *Farewell to European History*, 1948, Chapter 6.
[38] *Civitas Humana*, 1948, Chapter 2.
[39] See his *Autobiography of an Engineer*, 1956, especially Chapter 7.

gar Establishment think it good for us to hold.

Even an ardent democrat like Dr Karl Mannheim acknowledges that 'the lack of leadership in late liberal mass society can be diagnosed as the result of the change for the worse in selecting the elite.'[40]

Yet all these pleas, well-founded and cogent as they are, and the more impressive for hailing from convinced democrats (except Nevil Shute), are advanced by thinkers whose schemes for the aristocratic revival they advocate break down utterly when they outline the measures which they propose to regenerate a national elite. For without exception, all of them except Dr Karl Mannheim see in education the only means whereby a new aristocratic class can be brought into being. But what hope can we entertain of creating a body of men worthy of becoming a national elite by taking specimens of the disharmonious, unbalanced, unstable, heterogeneous and largely sick rabble, high and low, composing the populations of the Western democracies and 'educating' them? How can we expect to rear out of such mobs recruits for an elite who are to restore order, harmony, dignity and health to society and provide it with models of decency, honour, discipline and sound taste?

Broadcasting on 30th December 1951, Lord Beveridge, another convinced democrat, exclaimed with ill-concealed despair: 'The question now is, where will leadership come from in our economically flattened society? That is the most interesting problem facing us today. Just from where in our classless collection of men and women, the leaders will come to make us a society with a sense of unity in service to one another and to the world, I do not know.'[41]

To reply that only by educating recruits drawn from this 'classless collection of men and women' can we achieve the end desired is so romantic that one is tempted to suspect those who advocate this solution of our difficulty of having their tongue in their cheek. No, the fundamental and only hopeful solution happens to be the very last modern democrats are likely to think of or to adopt, and

---

[40] *Man and Society*, 1940, Part II, IV.
[41] *Daily Mail*, 31st December 1951.

that is selective breeding from specially chosen desirable stocks.

Yet, of all the avowed democrats who have recently admitted the necessity of a presiding elite if society is to be maintained in a sound and wholesome state, the only one I have so far been able to discover who has had the candour to recognise that nothing short of a rebirth, a new breed of superior men, will serve is Dr Karl Mannheim, who has at least seen that the problem amounts to 'transforming man.' This introduces a refreshing note of realism into the controversy and suggests that Dr Mannheim would not shrink from recommending those measures, so unpalatable to English liberals and democrats, which the psychophysical regeneration of a human group would inevitably involve.

It was of course very gratifying to me to find that policies I, as a champion of the Right, was rather pessimistically advocating as early as 1915 should in the middle of the twentieth century be unexpectedly meeting with support from my political opponents. For, among my pleas for a revival of aristocracy, none had been more emphatically and lucidly stated than that relating to the indispensability in a healthy society of tone-setters who can act as models for the populace.

It is true that these converted democrats who were veering in my direction still clung to means and remedies which even in 1915 I had rejected as worthless. For what hope was there of being able to recruit the nucleus of a national elite by merely educating a section of the degenerate mob, high and low, composing our existing population? Professor Mannheim alone seemed to see that the problem went deeper than that. He at least recognised that nothing short of 'transforming man' would serve.

Here again, this did but confirm policies I had been advocating ever since the publication of my *Defence of Aristocracy* in 1915, for I have never ceased to stress the need of regenerative breeding if we are to hope for any improvement in our national human stocks and, above all, in the elite that is to lead and serve them as models in their way of life.

Thus, in all my political works — A *Defence of Aristocracy*,[42] *The*

---

[42] London and Boston, 1915; 2nd edition, London, 1933.

False Assumptions of 'Democracy,'[43] *Man: An Indictment,*[44] *A Defence of Conservatism,*[45] and above all in *The Quest of Human Quality*[46] — I dealt either directly or indirectly with the importance of good breeding if 'good' men and good aristocrats are to be expected, whilst in my book, *The Choice of a Mate,*[47] the whole question of human breeding is discussed with comprehensive thoroughness.

In my *Sanctity of Private Property*[48] I confined the issue to the aristocratic attitude to private ownership, and in so doing forestalled to some extent both Professor Wilhelm Röpke and Nevil Shute in insisting on the dependence of the sanctity of private ownership upon the appropriateness of the owner. Whilst in the brochure, *Violence, Sacrifice and War,*[49] I dealt with the problem created by the inevitability of violence in this world, and the wisest method of effecting the sacrifices it entails. It is a short treatise, but one which lays bare a state of affairs which liberals and democrats are always loath to face and which, when they do face it, they never treat realistically.

The extreme unpopularity of my political attitude, especially in regard to the prerequisites for the regeneration of an elite, is to be explained by the wholly emotional and deeply-rooted bias with which all Westerners, and particularly Anglo-Saxons, are afflicted in connection with human breeding. Convinced though they may be, whether as animal or plant breeders, of the necessity of good stock and selective mating if good results are to be expected, they invariably fight shy of even considering sound rules of breeding for human beings. Throughout my various works I have tried, even as late as 1961 in my *Religion for Infidels*, to show the specious roots of this bias. But I am now inclining more and more to the conclusion that it will prove ineradicable. For the influences against the spread of any enlightenment in this matter, at least in

---

[43] London, 1921.
[44] London and New York, 1927.
[45] London, 1927.
[46] London, 1952.
[47] London, 1935.
[48] London, 1932.
[49] London, 1933.

the West, are so powerful that it looks as if the people of the Western democracies will prefer to perish altogether before they will recognise that sooner or later the principles of what they derisively call 'the stud-farm' must be applied to humanity, if survival is really desired.

For, as W. C. D. and C. Whetham stated as long ago as 1909, 'The essential factor in the rise and fall of nations is the quality of the people.'[50]

It happens to be the curse of Western civilisation that 'the quality of the people' will continue to be understood by the majority and its blind leaders only in a spiritual, intellectual or soul sense, and that the importance for the creation of a new elite of superiority also in the physical and animal aspects of man — an importance that Disraeli, for one, always emphasised — is unlikely ever to be appreciated.

* * *

In a previous chapter I undertook to explain my attitude to the Jews, and, as this seems an opportune moment for doing so, I shall now discuss my alleged anti-Semitism.

When the average man or woman of our post-Hitlerian world speaks of anti-Semitism, he or she has in mind the sort of bullying nitwit who, whilst calmly taking for granted the desirability of his own survival and that of all like him, would gladly see an end to the Jewish race. This typical Jew-baiter knows nothing of the priceless contributions the Jews have made to European civilisation, its science, art and philosophy, and would probably never have heard of any prominent Semites beyond those learnt in a scripture lesson.

Such is the sense in which the charge of anti-Semitism is usually made, and, although the Jews themselves know perfectly well that in this sense it is inaccurately applied to men like myself, it serves their purpose not to draw any too fine distinctions which might temper the fury roused in all humanitarians at the slightest sign of 'racial discrimination.'

---

[50] *The Family and the Nation*, London, 1909.

Yet no-one like myself, who has never concealed his admiration for such great sages of the past as Montaigne, Heine, Freud and Adler, to mention only a few; who has acknowledged the valuable help and understanding he has received from Jews and among whose friends, from Dr Oscar Levy to Max Rink, the greatest and most lasting have been mostly Jews — no-one, I say, who can claim such a record can fairly be classed as an anti-Semite. I don't suppose many who are alive today know anything of my first novel, *Mansel Fellowes*,[51] in which the hero is really the Jew, Dr Oscar Levy. But no-one who has read this novel could believe it was written by an anti-Semite.

I have suffered at the hands of certain Jews. Their extreme and unreasoning sensitiveness (probably the consequence of their history), which often makes them react with exaggerated rancour to a supposed slight, led, as I have shown in Chapter 7, to the sculptor Epstein doing me a serious injustice. But against the many substantial benefits I have derived from my connection with Jews, this one unfortunate incident sinks into insignificance.

No-one, moreover, with as many Jewish friends as I have had can ever reckon the sum of enjoyment and interest he owes to their usually unfailing wit, wisdom and native shrewdness. Nor can anyone who has frequented educated Jews fail to have noticed the ease and spontaneity of their powers of expression, their facility in lighting on the aptest terms in which to couch an ordinary remark, even when they are not using their native language. In this connection I think of Levy's 'women listen with their eyes,' of a young Spanish Jew's definition of a swan as 'a neck with a body attached,' and the remark of an old German Jew (in his early eighties, like myself) whom I meet at the Ipswich Public Library occasionally, and who, after facing me for a minute or two on the opposite side of the road, waiting for a chance to cross, exclaimed as we ultimately passed each other: 'We don't want to be cut off in our youth!' I could mention many more instances of the kind, especially some of a more *scabreux*[52] kind I remember having heard while dining with the Wertheimers in Connaught Place, for all

---

[51] London, 1918.
[52] Indecent. — Ed.

Wertheimer's daughters were naturally witty. But no-one with any knowledge of Jewish society can fail to have noticed the trait to which I refer.

In the instances quoted above, it would be difficult to light on a better choice of words for what the speaker wished to say, and, reflecting on the possible reason for this natural felicity of expression in even quite ordinary Jews, I have sometimes wondered whether Semites perhaps have the gift of pithy concentrated speech and of that economy of words which are the peculiar charm of good poetry. When we remember that Tennyson and Browning have been suspected by some of having had Jewish blood, and that many of the more enchanting passages in our seventeenth-century Bible owe their power to the original Hebrew text, it seems not unlikely that there is in the best Jews (obviously not in Philo!) a gift for brevity of expression which, besides being the soul of wit, is also an essential of good poetry.

It is strange that, despite their many acquisitive traits, the Jews I have known intimately have always shown themselves remarkably generous. Nor have I ever had to complain of any reluctance on their part to share with less knowledgeable people their peculiar expertise in finance. My wife and I certainly owed all our most successful Stock Exchange deals to the advice we were kindly given by an Austrian Jew named Max Rink (husband of the Mrs Rink mentioned in Chapter 6). And if in subsequent years we found our prosperity greatly enhanced, it was solely due to his counsels.

Two investments he recommended proved failures — one in an Argentine railway and another in a South American tobacco company. But in neither case were the sums involved considerable, and we were abundantly compensated by the profits made in other undertakings. He displayed with singular virtuosity the flair and sound judgement in money matters for which his race is famous, and succeeded in accumulating a handsome fortune. When I last saw him as a man of over ninety in Zurich in 1957 he told me that the directors of the Swiss Bank that had charge of his affairs had often had to thank him for advice which they had found it profitable to follow.

In forming a judgement on the Jewish question, an objective observer of mankind cannot lightly dismiss the matter with a summary nod of approval or disapproval. For essentially it is the problem of aristocracy over again, and he who once maintained that in Western civilisation the Jews composed an 'aristocracy of brains' was on the track of the truth. Not that it would ever be desirable or prudent to create an aristocracy of brains, because good rulership is as much a matter of character and psychophysical constitution as it is of intellect. But if we are at all justified in attributing to the Jews of the last 150 years increasing and very far-reaching political and social power, it is clear that they owed this ruling position to the fabulous riches they had contrived to acquire, and that we are entitled to describe their dominion as that of an 'aristocracy of wealth.'

This being so, Western Jews must be susceptible to the same kind of criticism to which all other aristocracies have been subjected, and one is entitled to ask the same questions about them as were asked about the old aristocracies of history.

What sort of tone did they spread in the communities over which their power extended? How, as leaders, did they discharge their function of establishing notions of becoming behaviour, good taste and decency? What standards of honour, civility and worthiness has their influence popularised and exalted?

For, as Aristotle aptly observed over two thousand years ago, 'What those who have the chief power regard as honourable will necessarily be the object the citizens in general will aim at.'[53]

If, therefore, the influence of the Jews in our Western world, at least during the last century and a half, can be shown to have been at all deleterious, they are as much open to censure as were other ruling minorities of the past who proved similarly defective.

And it is here, I suggest, that a man like myself—as, indeed, I explained to my examiners at Scotland Yard on that memorable October morning in 1940—runs the risk of passing as an anti-Semite. For if, whilst remaining a champion of aristocracy, I have never refrained from dwelling on the manifold sins of which successive generations of aristocrats have been guilty, I could hardly be expected to assume a different attitude towards the aristocracy of wealth gradually established through the financial power of the

---

[53] *Politics*, II, Chapter 11, 1273a–1273b.

Jews from the end of the seventeenth century to the present day.

Critics may question the justice of identifying the increasing social and political power wielded by the Jews with the power once wielded by the old aristocracies. But if the justice of the identification is conceded, it is clear that I had no choice but to put the same questions concerning the effects of Jewish power, as I had put about the effect of other forms of power, and that I could do this without any more incurring the charge of anti-Semitism than I incurred that of anti-aristocratism when I attacked the aristocratic rulers of Europe in the various political treatises I published from 1915 onwards.

When, therefore, we consider the increasing domination of our society by the Jews during the last century and a half at least—a domination they achieved by their control of most channels of publicity and propaganda; when, moreover, we bear in mind that as ostentatious and conspicuous spenders of wealth they set an example to the masses, high and low, of what should, in the words of Aristotle, be regarded as 'honourable,' we may, I suggest, with complete justice measure their rulership according to the same rigid standards as those applied to the rule of former aristocracies.

Nor is this alleged domination of the Jews a mere myth, for as early as 1888 we find the Jewish writer Simon Wolf saying of his coreligionists: 'We all know that the first bankers of the world—Rothschilds—are Jews; we know they control not only the money market, but also the political destiny of the European world. The press of Europe is mostly controlled by Jews; the leading editors are Jews.'[54]

Moreover, no-one aware of what has happened since the day in 1888 when Simon Wolf made this revelatory statement would for a moment doubt that the control of which he speaks has immensely increased. And if we wish to sum up in one sentence what has been the essential nature of this control, and what sort of influence it has exercised over the masses of the West, we cannot do better than quote the testimony of another prominent Jew, the

---

[54] *The Influence of the Jews on the Progress of the World*, Washington, D.C., pp. 37–39.

Right Honourable Sir Henry Slesser, PC, who, writing in 1944, said: 'It is true to say that they [the Jews] stimulated the worship of money.'[55]

This exaltation of affluence to the highest ideal of Western civilisation has had many deplorable consequences, none of which has more seriously vulgarised and debauched the popular taste than the desire publicly and unremittingly to display the power of lavish expenditure. And this has so steadily invaded all classes of society that what the French call 'paraître,' and what we may conveniently translate as 'keeping up with the Jones's,' has become the ruling passion throughout all Western peoples.

Almost sixty years ago, Paul Adam pronounced the noble sentiment that 'l'honneur n'est pas d'être envié mais d'être respecté.'[56]

But no candid chronicler of the period that has elapsed since those words were written could claim that there is now the slightest sign anywhere in our civilisation of honour among ordinary people earned by anything else than the power of exciting envy.

Envy has in fact become the ruling passion of our day, and the means of exciting it are pursued with an ardour that excludes most other interests. It is particularly prominent among the factors accounting for trade disputes, and one writer to the *Times*,[57] G. Rossiter, commenting on the repeated demands made by workers for higher pay, said quite truly: 'All the exhortations of governments, trade unions and economists cannot touch the workers' minds, because they are blinded by envy of those earning more. Thus the spiral can never be halted.'[58]

As there is some evidence of the existence of this kind of vulgarity, at least in England, long before the Jews acquired enough influence to foster it, it would be inaccurate to ascribe it wholly to their influence during the period of their dominion. Indeed, in my

---

[55] *A History of the Liberal Party*, London, 1944, Chapter 8.

[56] *La morale de l'amour*, 1907, Chapter 18. 'Honour is not to be envied but to be respected.' — Ed.

[57] 10th February 1962.

[58] See also my article, 'Work in Western civilisation' in the *Hibbert Journal* 55, 1956–57, pp. 30–34.

most personal account of my attitude to the Jews, in the symposium, *Gentile and Jew*,[59] and above all in my *Quest of Human Quality*,[60] I give many data indicating that, years before the Jews could have acquired any social influence, this trend towards the vulgarisation of honour had already gathered some strength, and by the close of the sixteenth century pecuniary prestige had become a highly coveted form of distinction.

On the other hand, no-one familiar with the development of national sentiment during the last century and a half could claim that anything was attempted or done by the Jews during the period of their dominion to oppose this vulgarising trend and to spread a nobler attitude throughout the nation. In the total absence of any endeavour on the part of the Gentile leaders of England to arrest the national drift into ever greater and more shameless vulgarity, not once did the Jews in their recently acquired ascendancy initiate any movement to bring the masses, high and low, back to the conditions 'of the old order,' in which, to quote Dr J. A. Williamson, 'Labour did not envy property.'[61] Generous as they were in their charity, they never used their powerful influence to chasten and elevate the taste of the people.

When, therefore, we see, as we do today, the desire to excite envy rather than respect, the mainspring of all individual striving, and when we contemplate the havoc this has wrought in the character and economic life of the nation; when, moreover, we find the vulgarity that prompts only a means test for estimating the worthiness of our fellows, extending even to popular judgements of scientific competence, so that 'a medical specialist buys a large car, because a small car might embarrass the GP who asked him to visit a private patient'[62] — when, I say, we find such indubitable signs of vulgarity in the population, it is impossible wholly to exculpate the Jews, whose uncontested dominion during the relevant period of England's history is acknowledged even by Jewish

---

[59] London, 1945.
[60] Chapter 8.
[61] *The Evolution of England*, 1951, Chapter 8.
[62] *British Medical Journal*, 14th March 1959: review of T. H. Pear, *Personality, Appearance and Speech*, Chapter 1, p. 22.

historians themselves.

If, therefore, the aristocrats of the past are to be condemned for having in most cases failed as tone-setters to the nation, we can hardly absolve the Jews of a precisely similar failing—nay, in view of their much higher average intelligence, the sin of the Jews in this matter is proportionately greater than that of the ancient aristocrats—and if such a judgement constitutes anti-Semitism, then on that ground I am an anti-Semite.

I have published two treatises dealing exclusively with the Jews—*The Jews, and the Jews in England*, published in 1938 under the pseudonym of 'Cobbett,' and the contribution to the symposium, *Gentile and Jew*, already mentioned, published in 1945.

The first I wrote at the suggestion of the Earl of Portsmouth, who as Lord Lymington was the leader of the English Array, a party formed by all those who had seceded from the English Mistery. He wished me to write for the guidance of his party a short history of the Jews in England, and it was he who proposed that I should use the pseudonym 'Cobbett.'

The second I wrote in response to the request of the editor, Chaim Newman, and, as already indicated, it is the more personal of the two essays. Apparently, Chaim Newman had been struck by my allusions to the ancient Israelites and the Jews in the seventh chapter of my *Defence of Aristocracy*, and, on the score of the understanding he thought I there displayed, considered me a suitable contributor to his symposium.

* * *

Although I dealt exclusively with health and its importance in only one or two books, none of my writings, not even my novels, fail to call attention to the subject. For, from the moment when I first began to think for myself, I knew Montaigne must be right in placing health at the top of all human desiderata. I also grew more and more convinced that the most disquieting feature of modern Western life is not merely the wide prevalence of ill health, but also and above all the shamelessness with which it is admitted and endured by all classes of the community.

Certain as I was from the start about a fact that science has abundantly confirmed—namely, that body and mind cannot be separated and regarded as independent of each other—I have always distrusted those wishful thinkers who believe that the present quality and future of our civilisation cannot be adversely affected by the inferior stamina and general morbidity of the population, and who would certainly deny that even the prevailing lack of comeliness and of fine physiques everywhere noticeable today is a matter to feel any concern about.

At all events, no-one can believe in aristocratic values and appreciate the importance of quality in all its aspects without placing health among the first prerequisites of any self-respecting society. Indeed, wherever morbidity and physical defect are seen coupled with self-respect, it should be impossible not to sense a certain depravity of taste among a people, or else their corruption by the Socratic elements in Christianity. Certainly, no man who presumes to be able to lead his generations, in what field soever, should think himself qualified to do so unless he is sound in mind and body.

As Professor G. Catlin so aptly remarks: 'It may be that science will show that only the man in health, of a good stock and nature, nurtured on a good diet, physical and emotional, free from anxiety and with his natural confidence unbroken—the natural aristocrat—is capable of the highest excellence, mental and spiritual, and of raising the level of civilisation itself.'[63]

This most significant admission, so alien to all popular and even cultivated prejudice, has unfortunately come very late in the day—so late that, owing to its very uniqueness and the unpalatableness of its sentiments, it can hardly be expected to do much good. For our world has already travelled too far in the opposite direction into the cloud-cuckoo land of sickly romanticism, where the supreme importance of health and personal comeliness is frivolously disregarded, and where it is in fact felt to be rather a sign of superiority so to disregard it.

Nor should it be forgotten that, if it is to mean anything of value, health should not imply, as it usually does to the crowd, a person's chance momentary freedom from any contact with a hospi-

---

[63] *A History of the Political Philosophers*, 1950, Chapter 3, 5.

tal or medical or dental attendant, but nothing less than the fact that he or she has never required such contact and is unlikely to do so in the future.

But to assume, as we do today, that anything desirable can possibly emanate from the physical shoddy we have now become; to believe that anything of value can possibly come from a sick degenerate like D. H. Lawrence, for instance, or that we may confidently expect beauty from the forbidding ugliness of many of our modern artists and poets, is so fantastic that unless, against all existing evidence, we still cling fanatically to the belief that body and mind are utterly separate, we should at once recognise the absurdity of our attitude.

How this sickroom attitude has become general is explained in many of my books, but in none more clearly than in *Religion for Infidels*. In any case, in most of my writings I argue persistently against it, and much of the unpopularity of my works has doubtless been due to this leitmotif which runs through all of them.

My first long treatise on health was *Man's Descent from the Gods*, published in 1921. Its theme arose from a new reading of the Prometheus myth, the novelty of which I probably owed to my freedom from any of those hard-and-fast notions concerning classical mythology that are acquired through the usual school and university training. For I saw in the myth the first occult intimation of the peril that may attend any drastic departure by humanity from traditional and old-established dietetic customs. And my argument was apparently sufficiently cogent to lead at least one reviewer of my book to acknowledge in the *Journal of Hellenic Studies* that it constituted a genuine contribution to Greek mythology.

I recognised in the myth one of the earliest records we possess of a setback or fall in human affairs, a more or less universal state of distress due to a sudden injudicious change in the dietetic habits of mankind in a certain area. But except for the handsome tribute paid to me by the journal above-mentioned, and the flattering reference to my book in Dr G. T. Wrench's *The Wheel of Health*,[64] the work attracted little attention. This was probably because

---

[64] London, 1938, p. 104.

most people, especially scholars, hate to see any traditional hero such as Prometheus divested of his glory. The fulsome laudations of a Shelley and a Byron are more to their taste. The general public, too, who have been taught by their leaders in culture grossly to overrate Shelley, disliked very much my curt dismissal of his so-called interpretation of the Prometheus myth in his preface to *Prometheus Unbound*.

During the early researches I had to make in order to substantiate my reading of the myth, an extraordinary incident occurred which, while it ultimately confirmed my faith in my theory, was a strange example of the correction of a faulty English translation of a Greek text by one who knew no Greek, simply owing to the fact that the mistranslated passage did not happen to fit a preconceived idea regarding what had most probably happened.

In the Loeb translation of Hesiod I was much shocked to find a passage the sense of which conflicted with my interpretation of the Prometheus myth, and for a while I was naturally filled with the gravest anxiety, particularly as I thought it unlikely that the passage in question could possibly be a mistranslation. However, so deeply was I convinced of the probable validity of my theory that I thought it might at least be worthwhile to question the translation.

I was working in Folkestone at the time, spending most of my day reading and writing in the reference room of the excellent municipal library there. So, with a sinking heart, I summoned the courage to write to Miss Elsie Buckley, who was then the secretary of the Loeb Classical Library at Heinemann's. I explained my difficulty and asked whether she could possibly check the translation of the passage which threatened to invalidate my thesis.

She immediately sent my inquiry on to Dr Page, one of the English editors of the series, and begged him to be so kind as to look into the matter. A few days of cruel suspense followed. Then, at last, to my unspeakable astonishment and joy, I heard that the passage to which I had called attention was indeed wrongly translated and that Dr Page had undertaken to see that in subsequent editions it would be corrected to give exactly the sense my theory required! Thus it was that, without any knowledge of Greek worth speaking about, I was able through my heterodox interpretation of the Prometheus myth to be instrumental in correcting an error in one of the Loeb translations. This success so much encouraged me that I there and then proceeded with the fullest confidence to develop my thesis, and in 1921 Heinemann published my work under the title of *Man's Descent from the Gods*.

It may interest scholars to learn that in Hugh G. Evelyn-White's original translation of Hesiod's *Theogony* for the Loeb Classical Library I found at line 535 the Greek word ἐκρίνοντο translated as 'were divided.' As this did not suit my theory, I acted as I relate above. When, therefore, Dr Page decided that a better translation would have been 'were contending,' or 'had a dispute,' I was naturally delighted, because the amended version gave exactly the sense my theory required.

In two later books, *Health and Education through Self-Mastery*[65] and *The Four Pillars of Health*,[66] I returned to the question of health, although I had discussed some aspects of it in *Man: An Indictment* and *The Truth about Childbirth*.[67] But in neither of these last-mentioned books was health the main subject.

In the first-mentioned book, published in 1933, I undertook the difficult task of explaining the supreme importance of F. M. Alexander's method of conscious control in the use of our bodies. I tried to make it clear that if there was to be no injurious interference with our functions, including breathing, some such conscious control of our bodies in activity, and even at rest, had now to be learnt. In a later publication, *Religion for Infidels*, I described how I had come across Alexander's teaching and the benefit I derived from it.

At the time, in 1933, apart from Alexander's own books, which, as friend and foe agreed, were unfortunately obscure, involved and incompetently written, there was hardly any literature on the subject, and my little book was thus a pioneer effort. As a treatise on the Alexander method it was, however, far from satisfactory, and for the simple reason that I was never allowed a free hand in my exposition of the principles involved. It had been my idea to

---

[65] London, 1933.
[66] London, 1945.
[67] London, 1937; New York, 1938.

try to condense in a few brief and lucid rules the essentials of the teaching. But Alexander would have none of it, and at the time I could not help feeling that his attitude rather indicated a reluctance to acknowledge that the method was a little more simple than he made it out to be. Naturally, the critics complained that, although my book was propaganda for Alexander, it gave the reader a very inadequate grasp of what the technique of conscious control actually was. But this was hardly my fault, and the task of summarising in a few brief rules what the teaching of conscious control amounts to still remains to be done—at least in this country. For I gather that in South Africa and certain places elsewhere it has already been accomplished.

Twenty-four years after the publication of this book, when I was in Scotland, I happened one day to be taking a walk with a young woman related to my hostess whose perfect bodily coordination I could not help noticing. It was something so exceptional that my curiosity was aroused. On questioning her about it, I learned to my surprise that she had been attending a female physiotherapist in Zurich who had evidently acquired some knowledge of Alexander's teaching, for, when I asked her to describe the method followed by this Zurich specialist, she recited, almost in the very terms I should have chosen to summarise the essentials of Alexander's technique, the main features of her expert's teaching. How her physiotherapist had come across Alexander, she could not tell me. But later on she informed me that the lady had indeed mentioned Alexander on occasion. One fact, however, which seemed to me significant was that her physiotherapist insisted on her pupils keeping the muscles of their neck 'locker' (i.e., loose, relaxed) in all their bodily activities, a rule which might be regarded as the crux of Alexander's teaching.

In my *Four Pillars of Health* I again stressed the importance of the Alexander technique if perfect bodily coordination in activity is to be maintained. But, unlike the former book published in 1933, this book dealt with other aspects of health maintenance and contained a severe criticism of all those writers on health, including my old friend Dr G. T. Wrench, who argued as if correct diet alone were the panacea for all ills. Wrench had published his *Wheel of Health* some years before, and I could not forgive him this grave exaggeration of the importance of one single factor in the basic requirements of a healthy life.

* * *

Apart from portraying people whose personalities had struck me as interesting, what I chiefly tried to do in my novels was to convey through the situations arising out of the story the influence of the aristocratic values I stood for. And when I speak of aristocratic values in this respect I do not mean only or even chiefly their influence in politics, but their control of every action and relation of life.

I have already spoken of two novels in which my leading figures were Dr Oscar Levy, Dr G. T. Wrench and Mrs Dufresne respectively: the first-named in *Mansel Fellowes* and the two others in *Too Old for Dolls*.

In *Catherine Doyle*, published in 1919 between the appearance of the other two, I depicted a young working-class woman who had greatly attracted me during my first two or three years as a reader at the British Museum. Like the heroine of this novel, she was a waitress in the tea-room that used to stand on the south side of the Egyptian Gallery. But I idealised her in the book, for, after I had ventured to acquaint her with my interest in her person, had been out with her a few times, dined with her and taken her to the theatre, I discovered that, in spite of her good looks and great charm, her working-class upbringing and education set such a formidable barrier to our mutual understanding that a harmonious relationship was out of the question. I believe she must have felt this too, for soon we began to see each other less frequently, and gradually, without any note of drama or mutual recrimination, our meetings ceased altogether.

Dr Wrench watched the development and decline of this romance with friendly anxiety and was, I believe, genuinely relieved when he knew it was all over.

Kathleen—for that was her name—was too charming, confiding and ingenuous to inspire anything but respect. Had I really made up my mind to play a part in order to win her, had I been determined to possess her, I suppose that by making an effort constantly to meet her on her own plane, and to entertain her with the sort of small talk to which she was accustomed and herself mastered with some brilliance, I might have succeeded in throwing down the barriers that separated us. But I was too well-aware of the fact that this would have amounted to wanton desecration, to the sort of sensual vandalism not uncommon in the relation of the sexes, and I held back while secretly hoping that someday she would meet the man of her own class who was worthy of her. My fears lest she might not do so, and that her pathetic docility in the presence of one she liked would expose her to exploitation at the hands of some coarse creature unable to recognise her rare qualities, are brought out in Books II and III of the novel and given their most pessimistic expression. I can only trust that she experienced nothing of the kind.

In *What Woman Wishes*[68] I depicted for the first time another young working-class woman's character, which I was to use again in a much later novel. This was the young person called 'Jimper,' who in real life was more superior to her upbringing and education than was poor Kathleen. She was in fact the woman mentioned last in my list of female friends, and in my picture I included many an incident drawn from her life. As to the other characters, especially the men, they were all more or less accurate portraits of various members of the so-called upper classes whose acquaintance I owed to the minor vogue my *Defence of Aristocracy* had enjoyed. The 'Acorn,' for instance, gives the reader an unmistakable likeness of a young man I came to know very well in the exalted circles in question during the years 1919 and 1920, as does the figure of his father, Lord Lewes. The women too, particularly 'the Hon. Mrs Price-Pruen,' are all based on real people, 'pris sur le vif,'[69] as the French say, whilst in 'Constance' I attempted to draw a rough sketch of my wife, and repeated almost verbatim a few of her verbal tussles with the women who resented what they called her 'doormat' attitude to her husband. Strange to say, although I know that the original of the 'Acorn' read the book, I understood that he was more amused than offended by it.

---

[68] London, 1921.
[69] 'Taken from life.' — Ed.

As an instance of daringly faithful portraiture remaining unrecognised by the model who sat for it, no case is more extraordinary than that of the man whom I depicted as 'Oliver,' the father-hero of my next novel, *The Goddess that Grew Up*.[70] For although in this book I had not refrained from giving very thinly disguised descriptions of actual happenings in his house, he never showed the slightest sign of having seen his own reflection in the mirror I had held up to him. Such was the deep unconsciousness of his whole course of action during the years of our friendship that he appears never once to have seen an allusion to himself in the story his personality had inspired me to write. Indeed, he complimented me warmly on the book, but I was never able to discover what his wife thought about it, and was so frightened to awaken her suspicions that I never dared to ask her whether she had read it. Whether or not the fact is revealed in the story, the figure of 'Oliver' nevertheless represents a superior officer whose acquaintance I made in World War I and whom I very much admired and respected. His complete lack of self-consciousness was, however, a trait I never found exceptional in the English military man.

The development and final unravelment of the story represent of course a very fanciful and highly coloured picture of the end his character might conceivably and logically have brought about, and it may be that these dramatic features of the story seemed so unlike the realities of his life as to deepen rather than stir to wakefulness the unconsciousness of his behaviour. Be this as it may, however, until his death shortly before World War II we remained sufficiently friendly for me to be able to make sure that 'Oliver' had remained in his mind a wholly fictional character.

The object of my next novel, *French Beans*,[71] was to show by a description of one of the most extreme aspirations of feminists — their hope of ultimately dispensing altogether with the male, at least as a life-partner in the breeding of the race — that feminism is, as a rule, a reaction to defective masculinity in the men of the countries where it occurs. And by the lack of masculinity I meant not merely physical, but also characterological, shortcomings. It

---

[70] London, 1922.
[71] London, 1923.

was the only one of my novels to reach a second edition. Some of the reviews objected strongly to the role I allotted to the young French hero, André de Loudun, but not one appeared to have grasped the main theme of the novel, which was an analysis of the deeper causes of the feminist movement.

In my next novel, *The Taming of Don Juan*,[72] the setting of which was a Dorset village I knew well, I tried, besides giving a picture of rural life in that county, to offer a criticism of the methods of milk-production and distribution and to suggest an alternative to the system then prevailing of purifying the milk by pasteurisation. In describing some of the hero's adventures in World War I, I drew upon my own experiences as a gunner officer on the Western Front, and everything I relate in this respect is based on fact.

'Dr Hale' is an idealised portrait of an old doctor with whom I became friendly on one of my summer holidays on the East Coast after the war, but the powder I speak of as his discovery was really a discovery of my own. Nor have I ceased to regret that, after many determined trials, I found it impossible to produce it in amounts large enough to enable my wife, our faithful retainer, Alice Cook, and me to have a constant supply of it. The labour of producing it was so exhausting that, after I had failed to persuade a man much wealthier than I was to commission a competent engineer to construct in accordance with my directions a small hand-machine for the production of the powder, I gave up all attempts at making it.

For weeks, my poor wife, Alice Cook and I used to take it in turns to work at the processes required for the making of the powder, for we found its effect so invigorating that we tried our utmost to continue its production. But in the end we had to give it up. The quantities we were able to produce were so small compared with the time and labour they cost us that we saw ourselves robbed of its benefits owing to the extreme extenuation the labour entailed.

My wife expressed exactly the effect the powder had when she said that after taking it she felt she was 'walking on air.' We were all middle-aged at the time, and the feeling the powder gave us

---

[72] London, 1924.

was one of sudden and complete well-being, coupled with all the effects of rejuvenation. I had long suspected that there were more forms of chronic food deficiency than avitaminosis, and that most people today suffered from the obscure effects of a lack of some essential minerals in their diet. I therefore lighted on a method of supplying these essential minerals in minute quantities daily by the use of this powder, and my theory seemed to be so abundantly verified by the effect the powder had that my own and my wife's confidence in my discovery never wavered from that moment. It is a thousand pities that the production of the powder proved beyond our strength, because I feel sure that all three of us — my wife, Alice Cook and myself — would have enjoyed a much happier old age had we been able to keep ourselves supplied with it.

The constituents of the powder were calcium phosphate (90 per cent), calcium carbonate and magnesium phosphate (10 per cent). As I understood that calcium phosphate is highly insoluble and that its assimilation might consequently prove difficult, I was afraid lest this might destroy the value of my powder. When, however, I remembered that all the carnivora crunch and eat the bones of their prey — dogs and cats certainly do — and by this means doubtless keep themselves adequately supplied with the accessory mineral substances essential to health, I took heart and determined to carry out my experiment. For it struck me that if the carnivora could assimilate the allegedly insoluble calcium phosphate of their prey's bones, although in the form of more or less large splinters, how much more easily could this mineral substance be assimilated if it formed a component in a powder. When finally, therefore, I produced my first ounce or two of the powder in question and its favourable effects on my wife, Alice Cook and myself surpassed even my most sanguine expectations, I was immensely relieved and, incidentally, not unpleased at finding the reasoning which had led to my theory so abundantly confirmed.

For a long while after this last novel I wrote no more fiction. But I had the feeling, supported by the opinion of a few friends, that, owing probably to the many heterodox views expressed in my novels and above all in various of my other publications, I had never been fairly treated by the reviewers on the leading national newspapers. And as I would never descend to any sort of literary log-rolling, and had not the means to offer any impressive hospitality to newspaper men, I felt that the reading public had never been made properly aware of my existence and my work.

On this account, about fourteen years after the publication of *The Taming of Don Juan* I thought I might try to publish a novel under a pseudonym that would conceal my identity from the journalists. I knew how difficult this might prove, as publishers like to know all they can about any author they include on their list. However, the experiment seemed worth attempting, and on finishing a novel I called *General Schools* I sent it under the name of 'David Valentine' to Macmillan's. They returned it in a week, but with such an encouraging letter that there and then I took the book to a literary agent with Macmillan's letter and he agreed to try to place it for me. A friend in Stockholm had undertaken to forward all correspondence to me, so I gave an address in Sweden. In the end, however, having found this roundabout way of getting my letters too irksome, I imprudently had my letters directed to an accommodation address near my home in London, and I believe that ultimately, as far at least as one newspaper was concerned, this leaked out and proved my undoing. The principal reviewer on this newspaper had long been my enemy, and it is possible that, having recognised certain familiar features of my style, he had prosecuted inquiries and had inferred from the locality of the cover-address that his suspicions about the real authorship of the book were correct.

This, however, is to anticipate, for in every other respect the ruse was a great success. Only a few weeks after my literary agent had been given the novel he wrote me an enthusiastic letter saying that Jonathan Cape had accepted the book, was enamoured of it and was prepared to publish it immediately if I would agree to make certain alterations. He wished me to suggest another title and to introduce more details about the background of the heroine, Mary.

Now, 'Mary' in this novel was merely another portrait of the young woman I had already depicted as 'Jimper' in *What Woman Wishes*, so that I found it easy to comply with Cape's request regarding her, and from among the new titles I suggested he accepted *Poet's Trumpeter*.

The book was published on 6th January 1939 and was the first of my novels to be 'Recommended by the Book Society.' It was also the first of any of my books to be reviewed in the *Times*, and from the mostly laudatory tone of the reviews in other newspapers it was clear that my disguise had answered and had borne out my suspicions concerning the treatment hitherto given me by the press.

The *Sunday Times* was the only paper that published an adverse criticism, and it was so unfair and gratuitously censorious that I felt no doubt whatsoever about the writer of it. It was signed by a woman, but I felt sure she had acted merely as the ghost of my old enemy, the reviewer-in-chief of the paper. He had once been a friend but had turned against me after my quarrel with Levy.

This proved my last novel, but its reception confirmed my belief that my unfair treatment at the hands of the press had been due more to the prejudice my views had created than by any fair estimate of the merits of my work. This was true more particularly of *The Times Literary Supplement*, for a friend in close touch with the editorial staff of this publication assured me that Mrs Belloc-Lowndes and her satellites had long been busy blanketing my work.

* * *

Before discussing the various books I wrote on feminism — works which, owing to the universal raptures of the public and the press from 1918 onwards over the triumphant progress of the woman's movement, no doubt greatly increased my unpopularity — I must first speak of two odd works which, like my *Personal Reminiscences of Auguste Rodin*, have no place in any classified list of the subjects I dealt with. The works in question are *The Secret of Laughter*[73] and *The Child: An Adult's Problem*.[74]

By 1932 I had become so much inured to unfair treatment by

---

[73] London, 1932; New York, 1933.
[74] London, 1948.

the national press that I failed to be as shocked as I should have been by the literary world's surprising neglect of the first-named work. For, in the theory of laughter, its nature and cause which it presents, the reading public were given a treatise which had so many new features, and explained so many of the facts overlooked by other and widely acclaimed theories of laughter, that, as any well-informed reader can now discover for himself, my book was at the time and still remains the most comprehensive explanation of laughter so far published. He who reads it with attention cannot help seeing that, compared with the theory of laughter advanced in this book, that of Kant, Spencer or Bergson is palpably inadequate and incomprehensive, selecting only one or at most two aspects of laughter and building thereon a theory of the whole phenomenon which is anything but all-embracing.

Knowing the literature of the subject as I did, I was therefore not a little puzzled when I found both the public and the press responding so coldly to my work that it might have been no more than an amateur performance hardly reaching the standard of such pedestrian efforts as Professor Kimmins's *The Springs of Laughter* or Eastman's *The Sense of Humour*.

What was the secret of this most unfair, not to say unintelligent, reception given to my book?

I ascribe the gross neglect it encountered to two facts, both of which would suffice to this very day to make a book on laughter unpopular with the majority and, above all, unpalatable to the Establishment that sets the tone in England.

In the first place, at a time when everybody was thoughtlessly repeating the parrot-cry that a sense of humour was among the most creditable qualities anyone could possess; when it was impossible to open a newspaper or a book (certainly not a biography) without coming across some fulsome praise of a sense of humour, so much so that it had come to be regarded as the *sine qua non* of a decent character, and its absence as a sufficient ground for condemning him who lacked it—at such a time, I had dared openly to question whether, after all, a sense of humour was such a desirable gift as was generally supposed.

When we remember that I did this at a time and to a society in which five notabilities in succession—Charles Kingsley,[75] Chesterton,[76] Hugh Walpole,[77] The Right Rev. J. E. Mercer, DD, Bishop of Tasmania[78] and Dean Inge[79]—had all felt moved to the absurd extreme of granting God himself and Jesus a sense of humour, thinking they could pay them no greater honour, the enormity of my heresy will be imagined.

And as the general public habitually assume that any parrot sentiment or slogan they have the docility to repeat is a child of their own brain, and forget the steady inculcation by which their daily reading and the hearsay of their world have forced it on them, they resented just as bitterly my attempt to question it as if I had impugned the charm and beauty of their own offspring.

Had they not heard every day, almost every hour, from people as parrot-like as themselves, that a sense of humour was a quality that redeemed any iniquity?[80] How dare anybody question its supreme desirability? Was the Kaiser not sufficiently disposed of when his sense of humour was questioned? And later on, was not Stalin's possession of a sense of humour made to depend on his particular conduct towards the West at various conjunctures in world affairs?

Thus, a sense of humour had acquired a sanctity that placed all those said to possess it above reproach, *hors concours*.[81]

The irreverent doubts I had dared to cast on this national faith affronted public sentiment and seemed as gratuitous as insulting the flag. And as the less original and native an idea may be, the more fanatically people tend to hold it, all those who fancied they had by their own unaided cogitations reached the profound thought that a sense of humour was the most precious of gifts

---

[75] Stephen Winstin, *Salt and his Circle*, 1951, Chapter 1.
[76] *Orthodoxy*, 1908, Chapter 9.
[77] *Jeremy at Crale*, 1927, Chapter 11.
[78] *Hibbert Journal*, January 1911.
[79] Count Keyserling, *Europe*, 1928, Chapter 6.
[80] In Earl Winterton's *Orders of the Day*, 1953, it is mentioned eighteen times and always in commendation of the person alleged to possess it.
[81] Beyond judgement.—Ed.

writhed in anger when they saw a sign of interrogation set against their cherished belief. It amounted almost to treason, for, after all, was not the belief essentially British?

If they ever knew it, they had forgotten that there was hardly a great rogue in history, from Talleyrand to Horatio Bottomley, who had not had a keen sense of humour. Nor had it ever occurred to them that three of the greatest books in the world—*Robinson Crusoe*, Rousseau's *Confessions* and *Wuthering Heights*—were destitute of anything that could make their readers laugh. George Moore and Edmund Gosse both argued that J.-J. Rousseau had 'attained a unique reality in literature by abstention from humour,' and that 'very little humour would have turned a great and beautiful book into a vulgarity.'[82]

Yet in the last eighty years the maniacal exaltation of a sense of humour has reached such a pitch that to deny anybody the possession of it has become a traditional form of excommunication. As Max Beerbohm with exceptional sanity perceived, although the suspicion of its lack 'is always false,' it is 'useful in the form of an accusation.' For 'to convict a man of that lack is to strike him with one blow to a level of the beasts of the field, and to kick him outside the human pale.'[83]

Historically, this monomania of the English people is something relatively modern, and it ultimately occurred to me to ask whether it might not perhaps be connected with developments in the nation which were, at least, disquieting. In the ridiculous exaggerations to which it led, and in its universal prevalence, I therefore suspected morbid features.

Mine was not the only dissentient voice. Others were conscious of certain abnormal aspects of the nationwide standardisation of the craze.

John Cowper Powys, for instance, observed in his *Autobiography* that 'of all human traditions by far the most insidious is the commonplace sense of humour.'[84] And he says: 'what is this sense of humour of the average human animal? It is a premature explo-

---

[82] *Avowals*, 1936, Chapter 2.
[83] *Yet Again*, 1909, 20.
[84] 1934, Chapter 5.

sion of the sadistic desire to hurt and to torment that which is queer and out-of-the-way.'[85]

This brings me to the second of the two facts about my *Secret of Laughter* which made the book unpalatable to both the Establishment and the mob, high and low. It was the principal factor, I believed, to be responsible for Mrs Belloc-Lowndes's indignation over the book, for, as the voice of the Establishment, she not unexpectedly treated my book as negligible in *The Times Literary Supplement*.

This second fact was my ruthless analysis of the phenomenon of laughter and my conclusion that it was by no means the innocent and enchanting expression of emotion that both the masses, high and low, and many psychological 'authorities' wished to think it was.

By means of numerous examples I showed that there was in every laugh an element anything but harmless, and having divided my authorities into two classes — those who thought it harmless and those who took the opposite view — I proceeded to vindicate the second group. By connecting the countless methods of provoking laughter with the nature of the phenomenon as a physical expression, and with the probable evolution of that expression, I exposed the sinister, if not harmful, element in every laugh, no matter how rarefied and 'spiritual' the provocation to it might be.

This done, I showed, I think satisfactorily, that in every laugh there is an unconscious claim to, or assertion of, 'a sense of superior adaptation'; and, knowing how slipshod and slapdash most reading is nowadays, even on the part of the educated, I emphasised the fact that by a sense of superior adaptation I did not mean a feeling of personal superiority, but merely a temporary recognition of being superiorly adapted. For instance, when a crowd laughs at a man groping in the street after the hat of which the wind has deprived him, it does not necessarily mean that they all feel personally superior to the hatless man, but merely that, not having themselves lost their hats in the wind, they are for the moment in a position of superior adaptation to him. That this

---

[85] 1934, Chapter 6.

warning was not superfluous is shown by the fact that a university lecturer, Dr D. H. Monro of the University of Otago, New Zealand, made the mistake of confusing my term 'superior adaptation' with the expression of superiority in general.[86]

In the many possible manifestations of this sense of superior adaptation I hinted at the occasions in which a genuine element of cruelty may lurk among the promptings culminating in every laugh, and I indicated that even in the most abstract and rarefied refinement of the motive for laughter there is always a strain of this sinister feature.

Twenty-three years after the publication of my book, Geoffrey Gorer wrote: 'A careful analysis of the most popular BBC radio and television comedy and variety programmes will show to what a remarkable extent humour for mass English audiences is based on insult and humiliation, either of one character to another or even to the self. Real or supposed physical defects or weaknesses — age, baldness, fatness, impediments of speech, even skin colour — or conceit are the continuous small coin of these comedy shows, and apparently always good enough for a laugh with the mass of listeners and viewers.'[87]

This pleasure culminating in laughter, which is felt by the witness of another person's humiliation, discomfiture or inferiority (however momentary), must, it seemed to me, indicate a constant readiness, if not eagerness, in modern humanity to enjoy the feeling of superior adaptation when contemplating other people in an awkward, or at least an inferior, situation.

Yet when I published my *Secret of Laughter*, in which I showed conclusively that laughter is the expression of superior adaptation, every humourist in England and America howled with fury.

The very noise the laugher makes suggests his subconscious desire to call attention to his momentary exaltation. It is all so obvious that only an intelligentsia as *moutonnier*[88] as that of England,

---

[86] See his *Argument of Laughter*, 1951, Chapter 2. He does, however, pay me the compliment of devoting a whole chapter of his book to my theory of laughter.

[87] *Exploring English Character*, 1955, Chapter 15.

[88] Mutton-headed. — Ed.

determined at all costs to look on a sense of humour as highly commendable, could remain blind to it.

The next problem that faced me was to explain why precisely in the last century or so there should have arisen an ever-increasing idolisation of a sense of humour and a correspondingly growing demand for the occasions provoking laughter.

And here, in my solution of this problem, I again offended the self-esteem of the age and fell foul of the self-complacency of my contemporaries. For what I said was that in an age of increasing morbidity, defect and physical inferiority of all kinds, an age when the wearing of artificial dentures by children still at school is a commonplace — and I need not repeat here the mass of data collected in my other books about the prevalence of the nation's morbidity — it was but natural that the mob, high and low, should display a boundless desire to experience the sense of superior adaptation which provocations to laughter can, however transiently, induce.

On the basis of Adler's psychology alone this was sound reasoning, for if, as he maintains, inferiority feelings are the natural outcome of physical shortcomings, it follows that in a period of widespread and increasing physical morbidity there should arise a corresponding desire in the whole population to experience the relief to be derived from the feeling of superior adaptation which momentarily gives rise to and accompanies every laugh.

Hence my implied charge in *The Secret of Laughter* that the present fierce exaltation of a sense of humour, and its accompanying exaggerated worship of laughter, are sinister manifestations of the age.

The indignation this charge aroused completely blinded people to the importance of my theory of laughter. Forgotten was Lloyd George's declaration that 'the result of the physical examination of the manhood of Great Britain demonstrated that the physical condition of the British people is lower than that of any other civilised country.'[89]

Nor was there any consciousness in the country of the state of affairs which Dr Ffrangcon Roberts was to describe twenty-five

---

[89] *British Medical Journal*, 17th February 1934.

years later when he said: 'Are we in fact becoming a healthier nation as the politicians never weary of assuring us? Judging by mortality, we are. But morbidity tells a different tale.'[90]

I had dared to tell the British public and their leaders that their worship of a sense of humour was not the beautiful, spotless passion they imagined, and my work suffered accordingly.

The most Compton Mackenzie could find to say about it in the *Daily Mail* was that it was controversial. J. B. Priestley gave the book a long but most unfair review in the *Evening Standard*, by which, incidentally, he revealed that he had not read my argument with care. I wrote a private letter to him pointing out his mistake and hoping he would take an early opportunity of correcting it, but I obtained no response.

The Saturday Review acknowledged the brilliance of the book and urged 'every thoughtful person' to read it, as did also *John O'London's Weekly*, but the latter journal warned its readers that 'many people may drop the book in horror' — a significant confirmation of much I have claimed above. *The New Statesman* was the only journal to declare the book 'important,' and only one fellow-publicist, Aldous Huxley, congratulated me on my achievement. 'A first-rate piece of work,' he wrote; 'the completely satisfying hypothesis.'

Two books published in 1951 — *The Origins of Wit and Humour* by Albert Rapp and *Argument of Laughter* by D. H. Monro — acknowledge the value of my solution of the problem of laughter, the second most handsomely.[91] But I succeeded only in infuriating Max Eastman in America, who was never able realistically to grasp the seamy side of humour and laughter.

***

In my book, *The Child: An Adult's Problem*,[92] I tried — in vain, I fear — to call England to her senses concerning at least the absurd exaltation of immature humanity, which I suggested was rooted

---

[90] *British Medical Journal*, 15th September 1957.
[91] See his *Argument of Laughter*, p. 177.
[92] London, 1948.

in Jesus's palpably false view of children as recorded in Matthew 19.14.

Believing, as I still do, that Dr Fritz Wittels was right when he declared our 'present-day excessive preoccupation with children is a decadent ideal,'[93] and convinced, as I still am, that the staggering rise in juvenile delinquency has been due chiefly to three factors: 1) the ascendancy of women in our society; 2) the self-indulgence which causes mothers to prefer spoiling rather than disciplining their children; and 3) women's general subconscious and deep hostility to discipline of any kind, as being to their minds (from early girlhood to maturity) peculiar to a masculine and oppressive order of being, I attempted a realistic revaluation of childhood in the light of modern psychology. In doing so I outlined a system of discipline for the young which would inculcate upon them at least a minimum of public spirit — the virtue chiefly lacking in modern children — and at the same time help parents in the admittedly difficult task of leading their children out of the dominion of the pleasure principle into that of the reality principle which fits them for social life.

I tried to show that the root of the alarming prevalence of juvenile crime was due to the fact that the vast majority of modern children never effect this transfer and are consequently never really made fit for civilised life in society.

I described with care the role played by women in bringing about this state of affairs and the reasons for their share in its production. But, as this will be exhaustively discussed when I deal with my books on feminism, I need not explain it here. Suffice it only to emphasise the fact that, as both in this country and America the increase of juvenile crime has kept pace with the growing influence of the female sex over our society, we are concerned with a problem that is not nearly as obscure as many of our psychological 'experts' would have us believe, and all the solemn wiseacres who nowadays attend learned conferences and committees on the subject merely display their failure to see the wood for the trees.

Among the matters of moment discussed in my book on the

---

[93] *Die sexuelle Not*, 1909, Chapter 3.

child to which, however, I shall not again have the opportunity to refer is the question of sex-instruction in schools, to which I devoted the whole of Chapter 12.

Now, it is precisely in the recent advocacy and realisation of the policy of giving sex-instruction to school children that we see the utter incompetence and futility of the wiseacres above-mentioned, who assemble in solemn conclave to devise remedies for evils they do not understand. For, of all the gaffes ever perpetrated by 'experts,' none has been more egregious and disastrous than that which culminated in the bright idea of providing sex-instruction in schools.

Among the juvenile crimes recorded early in the century, only a small proportion were sexual. It was, however, imagined—and here I cannot help suspecting the cerebrations of one woman or several—that if only little girls and little boys could be taught the 'facts of life' this knowledge would protect them from all the untoward consequences of submitting to, or committing, sexual offences.

It all seemed most plausible, not to say self-evident. Nor should the reader conclude from my suspecting the female brain behind the innovation that I am unaware of the gallant support women received from male collaborators. On the contrary, I am only too painfully aware of the important part masculine 'authorities' played in introducing sex-instruction in schools. Indeed, the hostility my opposition provoked among them led to much bitter comment.

Yet, when we look at the results of the innovation; when we see how immensely that variety of juvenile crime classed as sexual has multiplied in recent years—i.e., ever since the introduction of sex-instruction—are we not entitled to ask how and in what respect this alleged remedy or preventative of juvenile sexual delinquency is supposed to have succeeded?

Promiscuous juvenile sexual intercourse has now reached such alarming proportions that the authorities are at their wits' end to know how to abate its frequency. For four or five years now a growing volume of protests has been coming from all quarters of the nation, and by no means from churchmen alone, demanding immediate measures for the arrest of this comparatively novel and disquieting trend and effective means of spreading a more decent moral tone among our adolescent girls and boys.

In the *Times* of 18th July 1961 we read that 'the increase in venereal disease among adolescents and the need for energetic measures to counter it, was debated here [in Sheffield] today by doctors attending the spring session of the British Medical Association's annual representative meeting'; and five months later, Dr C. E. Godber, in his first annual report as Chief Medical Officer of the Ministry of Health, wrote: 'More and more girls under 17 are bearing illegitimate children or contracting venereal disease . . . This shows a change in the sexual behaviour of the young which could have disturbing consequences for family life.'[94]

Reports from local authorities all over the country tell the same tale. The Medical Officer of Health for Surrey, for instance, Dr K. A. Soufar, stated that 'there was a disturbing increase in venereal disease in Surrey last year. This and the fact that the proportion of illegitimate births is the highest for ten years, is indicative that there may be a sickness in the community which is more moral than medical.'[95]

Such statements hailing from Medical Officers of Health and other authorities all over the kingdom could be multiplied indefinitely. Everywhere, in fact, alarm is felt concerning this comparatively recent and deplorable development in our society. Yet, in spite of the many conferences and committees convened to find measures to combat it, nowhere is there any sign of some understanding of its principal cause. Anne Scott James, for instance, announced that 38,161 illegitimate babies were born in 1959, and informed us that 'the number of illegitimate births is steadily climbing.'[96] But no passage in her article gives any evidence of her having the slightest inkling of the root of the trouble. Yet the fact that, *pari passu* with the increase in illegitimate births, there has occurred a corresponding increase among adolescents in the use of contraceptives of various kinds might surely have served

---

[94] *Daily Mail*, 4th December 1961.
[95] *Daily Mail*, 26th October 1961.
[96] *Daily Mail*, 22nd May 1961.

as a pointer to the fundamental source of what we cannot but regard as a blot on our civilisation.[97]

Nor, when I speak of this recent and alarming phenomenon as 'a blot on our civilisation' do I wish to imply that I regard it with all the traditional horror of a puritan. On the contrary, aware as I now am of the latest scientific findings about sexual development in man and woman, I know that, because the peak of sexual potency and readiness for sexual functioning in both male and female occurs much earlier than was supposed fifty years ago, it was only to be expected that, given the knowledge, the implicit sanction of society and the opportunity for the relief of the ardent impulses of adolescence, full use would naturally be made of them.

I remember perfectly as a child of ten, my father, in conformity with the ignorant beliefs of the time, telling me on his fortieth birthday (10th July 1892) that he had, as he put it, reached 'the prime of life.' Had he been told, as he would have been by any knowledgeable authority of the present day, that if he meant by this that he was at the zenith of his reproductive powers, his statement was quite untrue, and that, on the contrary, he had in this respect long been in a state of decline, he would have been both shocked and incredulous.

But let us not forget that his mistaken belief formed an essential component of the culture and social habits of the age. It was but one of the many accepted ideas concerning the stage in human life when sexual maturity was supposed to be reached, and, far from adult men and women in their early thirties or even late twenties being regarded as having already travelled some way along the road to reproductive decline, it was a commonplace for them to be looked on as having just reached the age when their reproductive functions could be normally exercised. If anyone younger than twenty-two or twenty-three was known to be eager for the prompt exercise of his or her reproductive functions, it was assumed that he or she could not be quite normal or 'nice' or 'pure.'

---

[97] For evidence of contraceptives found in possession of schoolgirls, see the *Daily Mail*, 12th March 1962.

Our whole social structure was built on these erroneous assumptions, and, as the customs and regulations evolving from them acquired an odour of sanctity from the sexphobia and sexual taboos of Christianity, so-called sexual precocity, which meant active reproductive behaviour before the falsely assumed age of 'maturity' had been reached, was not only frowned upon but also systematically suppressed by every convention of the age. The youth of both sexes, and certainly all adolescents, far from being encouraged to make any claim to freedom in sexual expression, were all brought up to believe that that side of life was not for them and that they must await marriageable age before they could hope to receive the freedom of Venus's city. Thus, until an age now recognised as reproductively late, the whole of 'that side of life' was kept a close secret, and adolescents, even among themselves, spoke about it only in shamefast whispers.

That this attitude lingered on even as late as 1937 is shown by the fact that when I tried in my *Truth about Childbirth* to show what havoc the belated exercise of the female reproductive functions was causing, and in anticipation of Dr Kinsey's discoveries advocated a much earlier age than custom then allowed for the first childbirth, a howl of indignant protests was raised in all quarters of the nation, and among women in particular I succeeded only in provoking greater hostility than ever.

That the state of affairs described led to much secret autoeroticism among both male and female teenagers we know to be a fact. But in view of Western society's total failure to make any accepted provision for the exercise of the reproductive functions of adolescents—i.e., at a time when, as we now know, their readiness for this exercise is at its peak—and in view of society's belief, explained above, that no such provision could be regarded as at all necessary, the whole of youth grew up under the impression that any indulgence of their sexual impulses was something not merely reprehensible but also actually 'unnatural.' Thus, guilty feelings were the universal sequel to any breach of this convention which undoubtedly acted as a brake on all youthful desires and impulses connected with sex.

Now, no-one like myself who has lived throughout the period during which this convention prevailed would today dream of defending it. But, no matter how utterly we may condemn and reject it, we have to acknowledge that at least it dovetailed admirably into the whole fabric of our social life. In the absence of any acceptable provision being made for the normal expression of the sexual impulses of adolescents when, as we now know, sexual potency is at its peak, the solution offered by the so-called Victorians was after all the only possible one. It may have been stupid, ill-informed, unnatural and oppressive, but, given the ignorant beliefs of the time, it was at least comprehensible and consistent.

To alter this state of affairs by selecting one aspect alone of our culture and recasting it, without considering the effect of the modification on the rest of our social pattern and, above all, without so remoulding our lives as to make some provision for the normal expression of adolescent sexuality an accepted, workable and harmless part of it, was so foolish, so unlikely to effect anything but untoward developments, that to anyone aware of the essential interdependence of every part of a social pattern upon the whole it could only spell disaster.

Yet such was the step advocated and taken by the champions of sex-instruction in schools. I am well aware that many of these champions were supposed to be men of science. But this only makes their error more heinous. Thus, ready as we may be to forgive the many women who were active supporters, if not the instigators, of the innovation—for, after all, it is not altogether their own fault that women are now expected and allowed to express their views on all matters and to have these views seriously considered—it is difficult to condone grave errors of judgement on the part of men who are supposed by their training to have been made competent examiners of all proposed reforms.

The Victorian culture may have been indefensible, but at least it formed a consistent whole in keeping with the knowledge and beliefs of the age. It could therefore be safely dismantled only if the substituted structure was also a consistent whole. But to select as the object of our reformatory zeal only one feature of its structure and to put in exchange a 'bright' improvisation of our own, regardless of how it would fit into the old edifice, was an act which, however plausibly it may have been and indeed was defended, could only be described as one of the utmost folly.

Let us then see how the promoters of sex-instruction in schools proved themselves guilty of all the oversights and errors of judgement I have enumerated. For, although these are dealt with in my book on the child, they may be briefly summarised here, if only to show how unfair was the reception accorded to this book in 1948 and how deeply it must have incensed the male and female feminists who, like St Peter at the Gates of Heaven, stand guard at the portals of English and American publicity.

In the first place, the adult world's very act of giving instruction on matters which had for generations been held a close secret—this very act constituted such an abrupt volte-face, so sudden a reversal of the former attitude, that the youth of the nation could be excused if they interpreted it as a gratuitous and unsolicited distribution of forbidden fruit. Even if this inference involved an exaggeration, it was hardly avoidable. For, to release *pro bono publico* a body of information which from time immemorial had been regarded as accessible only to a privileged class—the adults of the nation—and which in unprivileged hands had traditionally been regarded as shameful, inevitably gave the impression that a ban had been lifted and that henceforth all were free to possess and discuss it and had society's highest authority for so doing.

So much for the effects of the first severe clash with accepted custom caused by the policy of giving sex-instruction in schools.

The second but in every respect most far-reaching effect of the innovation, which, however, was also not foreseen by the beclouded vision of the reformers, resulted from the implications which naturally inhere in the very notion of instruction. For to instruct presupposes some practical purpose—i.e., an end which the imparted knowledge is intended to serve. Men are instructed in the use of small firearms at the Musketry School at Hythe, Kent, in order to become competent marksmen. Medical students are instructed in the science of medicine in order to practise it, and art and languages are taught with a similar object in view. The apprentice or learner expects one day to become a graphic or plastic artist or else a linguist, as the case may be. Instruction is thus seen to be an activity envisaging use as its object. To give instruction in any subjects necessarily suggests, even to the uneducated and simple-minded, that the knowledge to be imparted is intended for use. There is no sense in instruction without this ultimate purpose, tacitly or openly acknowledged.

What, then, could have been more easily foreseen and foretold than that instruction in sex would necessarily suggest, even if it did not enjoin, some use of the knowledge in the form of exercising the reproductive functions? Even if it could be cogently argued that all instruction need not necessarily imply use, how could this obvious inference be prevented from striking the minds of the children and adolescents receiving sex-instruction, especially in view of the pressure exerted upon them by the urgent promptings of their reproductive impulses?

To have overlooked this inevitable consequence of sex-instruction surely constitutes the gravest charge that can be brought against the bright so-called leaders of society who, from the early years of the twentieth century onwards, began to advocate and ultimately introduced sex instruction in our schools. And when we see, as we do today, a terrifying proportion of our modern youth riotously and anarchically—that is to say, without either law or order—engaging in sexual activities, we only make ourselves more ridiculous than ever when we imagine that by appointing learned bodies to sit in solemn conclave to investigate the matter we shall discover the 'obscure' cause of the scandal. Does not the main cause stand out a mile?

The third but by no means the least important cause of the moral disorder of our adolescents, male and female, is the result of one of the more superficial and short-sighted demands made by the champions of feminine emancipation. This was to grant to all girls and young women complete freedom of movement, even after dark, without the company or chaperonage of some responsible escort—a form of licence which staked on the assumption that all the young men they were likely to meet and with whom they might spend their time would be either utter congenital neuters or else sufficiently high-minded and chivalrous to take no improper advantage of the opportunities this freedom offered. This form of licence also assumed that the girls themselves would always be sufficiently self-respecting and well-disciplined to deprecate and discourage all improper liberties.

As I pointed out in 1954, the young female's ignorance of male sex psychology, by often allowing her 'boy' to take liberties which, while leaving her more or less cool and calm, tended to inflame his ardour to a pitch when control was no longer practicable (for recklessly exacerbated tumescence in the young vigorous male easily induces violent if not ruthless behaviour), produces a situation in which either seduction without coercion, or else rape attended by violence and often injury to the girl, can be the only sequel.[98]

Nor in such cases is it altogether fair for the judge to address and sentence the young man in question as if he were always a deliberate thug. For if society by its levity and insensate feminist blindness places young nubile females in a position to excite and provoke an ordinary young man's ardour to a point when he loses control, a considerable share of the blame surely rests with those who have stupidly misjudged the effects of the licence they have granted.

If wise people like the Hindus and the modern French and Japanese can be so deeply conscious of the inflammability of youthful ardour as to ensure that the situations in which it may be ignited shall be rigorously prevented; if by means of vigilant supervision and chaperonage they make sure that their girls and young women are preserved from the dangers of any unprotected dalliance with young men, it is nothing less than idiocy to suppose that we in England and America are so highly civilised and schooled in decency and self-discipline as to be able to let our young folk a freedom that could safely be granted only to a generation of castrated saints.

As I point out in my article, however, most of the absurd assumptions on which the claims of feminism rested owe their bloodless and unrealistic character to the fact that, as the leading feminists hailed from the effete and most passionless ranks of our middle classes, and were accustomed to the society of men as effete and passionless as themselves — men in whose company they knew perfectly well their daughters might travel round the world

---

[98] 'Criminal assaults on young women in England and Wales,' *The International Journal of Sexology*, Volume 8.2, 1954, pp. 83–88.

in perfect sexual safety—they very foolishly demanded reforms which were in keeping with their own and their menfolk's temperamental anaemia and, forgetting that in the more vigorous and primitive strata of the population young men were not quite the constitutional nincompoops their own middle-class males were, they promoted a state of licence which not unnaturally spelt sexual depravity for a class of people with more stamina and native ardour than themselves.

Thus, no brief summary of the major causes of present-day sexual anarchy among our teenagers should fail to include the factor of female emancipation, for to the two first-mentioned major causes arising out of giving sex-instruction in our schools it added that of unlimited opportunity.

It may seem astonishing enough that all three of these major causes of the present deplorable condition of our young folk should have been overlooked by the wiseacres who represent authority in our society. But what is even more astonishing is the fact that it should not have been seen that the innovation which ushered in this state of affairs could only have been justified and tolerated if simultaneously with it some orderly and decent provision had also been made, as it is made in many primitive communities, for a properly controlled method of permitting the normal expression of adolescent reproductive impulses.

This hardly credible omission on the part of the powers that be is, however, little less than typical, and reminds me of a similar although less serious oversight which characterised their action during World War II. I refer to the reckless way in which they allowed the English countryside to be overrun with black troops of the US army without also providing some means of relief for the pressing sexual needs of all these young and vigorous men. The consequence of course was that everywhere, at least in my area of rural Suffolk, young women and girls (often while still of school age) were assaulted and raped without the local police being able to do anything to abate the outrages. Our own faithful retainer, although over fifty at the time, was one of the victims, and when I addressed my protest to one of the leading local magistrates I did not hesitate to point out to her that the action of the authorities in letting loose this horde of blacks without at the same time providing them, as our wiser and more realistic ancestors of the Middle Ages would have done, with a suitable supply of black whores was an act of criminal folly.

But to return to the shocking oversight of the authorities, which allowed them to give to our adolescents a form of instruction which at least suggested the use, if not the abuse, of their reproductive functions, without at the same time providing for the decent and orderly expression of their sexual impulses, it may be objected that any such unprecedented provision would have meant a total and formidable reconstruction of our social pattern, a complete reorganisation of our communal life. This is, of course, absolutely true. But the obvious justice of this objection merely confirms what I was careful to emphasise above—namely, that we cannot arbitrarily select only one feature of our culture and drastically reform it without radically interfering with the whole of the remaining portions. Similarly, therefore, we might have foreseen that we could not safely introduce so novel and revolutionary a feature as sex-instruction in schools without modifying the rest of our social system so as to provide the means of meeting the inevitable and indeed logical consequences of the innovation. To have proceeded with the innovation without thinking of such a provision—especially now, in view of the findings of the Kinsey Reports—is only a further proof, if such were needed, of the fundamental incompetence and stupidity of our epicene Establishment and of the unsoundness of its authority.

If it seemed impossible or impracticable to make proper provision for the orderly expression of adolescent reproductive impulses, the 'bright' idea of sex-instruction in schools should have been dropped.

Many other and minor objections to the innovation will be found discussed in my *Child: An Adult's Problem*, among them the acute embarrassment so often felt by both teachers and pupils during the progress of the instruction in the classroom. But such is the pertinacity of even the most benighted reformers, enamoured of their 'intuitions,' that it is unlikely that any serious notice will be taken of the sort of criticisms of the innovation that I have advanced. Nor is it at all likely that they will ever be brought to see the connection between their bright idea and the calamitous state of affairs it has helped to bring about.

At all events, my book was given but very limited publicity, and it certainly procured me one implacable enemy among the more prominent champions of sex-instruction.

* * *

It was my great misfortune to have been one of the few and the most vociferous of those who from the very beginning saw the many perils which were certain to overtake any nation that wholly accepted and instituted the reforms demanded by the movement known as feminism in the late nineteenth and early twentieth century. I was hardly likely to be forgiven for publishing radical attacks upon it, including the most pessimistic prophecies concerning its consequences (prophecies which, by the by, have been abundantly fulfilled), at the very time when the whole bias of the public and the press was in favour of the changes that promised to establish feminine influence over every department of our national life.

It was above all my misfortune that in every one of my anti-feminist books I dealt blows at the feminist position which were unanswerable and could therefore be safely met only by silence. Thus, whilst the resolute feminists composing the editorial staff of *The Times Literary Supplement* (to mention but one example) always gave long laudatory reviews to all the publications written by my opponents, all my books were systematically disparaged or left unnoticed.

The reader will remember my having mentioned in a previous chapter that my old friend Dr G. T. Wrench used often to chide me for being so ardent an anti-feminist in spite of my well-known devotion to my mother.

The question always struck me as pointless. For, apart from the fact on which I repeatedly insisted, that an anti-feminist need not necessarily be anti-feminine and therefore that there was no essential incongruity in my attitude, I might well have replied to Wrench in the words of Alexandre Dumas *fils*: 'L'homme qui méprise le plus les femmes ne méprise-t-il jamais sa mère . . . Sa mère n'a pas de sexe dans la pensée de l'Homme; elle est d'ordre divin.'[99] And even this defence would have been irrelevant, because to despise feminism is not synonymous with despising women.

It has always struck me as odd that, to the Anglo-Saxon of both England and America, the anti-feminist could never be regarded as a philogynist, for, owing to the deep understanding of women of which only the philogynist is capable, he cannot have failed to have observed, whether as son, brother or husband during his association with the opposite sex, all their natural virtues and corresponding foibles. For the understanding of a human being means precisely that. We cannot understand one another if, like adolescents, we are despotically driven into the arms of a member of the opposite sex by the overpowering hurry with which our vigorous reproductive impulses seek expression. That is why love in its objective sense, as based on a full knowledge of the loved object, cannot be experienced by the young as it is by the middle-aged. Only in his relation to his mother — and, according to Freud, even this is not always true — can the adolescent male obtain a precursory knowledge of that love for the opposite sex which comes late in life and is based on understanding.

As I pointed out in an article on free love written for *The International Journal of Sexology*,[100] the young are no more free or self-determined in their love than are the steel filings that fly to the surface of a magnet, and to speak of their attachment as love, in the sense of deep understanding, is about as sensible as to maintain that the Flying Scotsman leaves King's Cross and dashes towards Edinburgh owing to its deep appreciation of that city's compelling qualities.

That is why I believe Anatole France for once argued quite correctly when he said: 'L'amour est comme la dévotion; il vient tard. On n'est guère amoureux ni devotée à vingt ans.'[101]

---

[99] Preface to *L'ami des femmes*, 1869. 'The man who despises women the most never despises his mother ... His mother doesn't have a sex in the man's thinking; she belongs to a sacred category.' — Ed.

[100] Perhaps unpublished. — Ed.

[101] 'Love is like devoutness; it comes late. One is hardly loving or devout at twenty years old.' — Ed. Heine would have agreed with this

Madame du Deffand held much the same view, for in one of her letters she wrote: 'Toutes les liaisons qu'on peut former avec la jeunesse ne tiennent qu'aux sens, et c'est peut-être tout ce qu'il y a de réel pour bien des gens';[102] whilst Marcel Aymé, doubtless aware of the compulsory nature of 'love' in early and late adolescence and thinking of the free love to which I am now referring, observes that 'On ne devient amoureux, passé vingt-cinq ans, que lorsque on le veut bien.'[103]

Nor is it necessary, in order to feel this love for a person of the opposite sex, to be blind to their faults and weaknesses or unaware of them. In her diary, Madame Tolstoy wrote: 'You can't really love someone who knows you intimately with all your weaknesses . . . That's why married people drift apart in their old age.'[104]

I think this quite untrue. The rare understanding which always accompanies genuine free love is never possible without a recognition of the loved object's shortcomings. But I venture to doubt whether this kind of love can ever be experienced while the urgency of the reproductive impulses is at its height. That is why I speak of it as 'free.'

Thus, there appears to me to no necessary incongruity in the position of an anti-feminist who is also a philogynist, and all those who think there must be—and they constitute the great majority—are evidently labouring under the delusion that to feel genuine love one must cherish the romantic illusion that the loved object is flawless and destitute of any blemish.

I have therefore no hesitation in claiming to be a philogynist whilst professing strong anti-feminist views, and I shall now proceed to explain how I reconcile the two attitudes.

In order to be an anti-feminist one must recognise in woman

---

wholeheartedly. See his *Gedanken und Einfälle*, V.

[102] 'All the relationships that one can have in youth stay only in the mind, and it is perhaps all there is of reality for many people.' —Ed.

[103] *La belle image*, 1941, Chapter 6. 'After twenty-five years old, one only becomes amorous when one is willing.' —Ed.

[104] *The Diary of Tolstoy's Wife*, 1928 edition, entry for 11th December 1890.

certain inveterate defects and natural weaknesses that render the demands and aspirations of feminism either invalid or unrealisable, or both.

In his *Study of Sociology*, Herbert Spencer says: 'That men and women are mentally alike is as untrue as that they are alike bodily. Just as certainly as they have physical differences which are related to the respective parts they play in the maintenance of the race, so certainly have they psychical differences, similarly related to their respective shares in the rearing and protection of offspring. To suppose that, along with unlikenesses between their parental activities, there do not go unlikenesses of mental faculties, is to suppose that here alone in all Nature there is no adjustment of special powers to special functions.'[105]

This is very good and marks a great improvement on his previous discussion of the subject, written some thirty years earlier, in which he speaks of 'the moral sense, by virtue of which the masculine mind responds to the law of equal freedom, [and which] exists in the feminine mind as well.'[106]

This, bad and inaccurate as it is, is in keeping with the whole of the rest of the book, which throughout discusses human beings in every possible relation as if they were no more than disembodied spirits. But, although the previously quoted passage is very good, it still falls short of an adequate statement of the case, and this is to be ascribed to the fact that Spencer, though deeply versed in the science of biology, was still very much the child of his period and had not yet fully assimilated the now established truth that body and mind cannot be separated.

If, then, despite the strange difficulty that even today most of us moderns feel about regarding body and mind as inseparable, we try calmly and objectively to contemplate woman in order, on the strength of her bodily characteristics, to determine what are likely to be the ruling principles of her nature, what is it that first strikes us most forcibly?

I say 'strikes us most forcibly,' but am I likely to be believed when I assert that although the characteristic I am about to de-

---

[105] 1880, p. 373.
[106] *Social Statics*, 1951, Chapter 16.

scribe, together with its accompanying inevitable consequences, strike us most forcibly, no sexologist—in fact, no writer on the subject of the sexes from Schopenhauer to Mill and Havelock Ellis, except myself—has ever confessed himself struck by it in the sense that I mean—i.e., together with an appreciation of its inevitable consequences?

And what is this obvious, palpable, unmistakable bodily characteristic of woman that should, along with its inevitable implications, be the first to strike us?

Surely it is woman's marked resemblance to the child. In her contours, her late retention of the softness, suppleness, immature appearance and freshness of the child, and in the relative absence of any rigidity in her muscles and ligaments. These may all be characteristics which facilitate her athletic feats during parturition, but that they are typical of her long after reaching adulthood cannot be questioned. Indeed, consciously or subconsciously, adult men feel that much of her charm resides precisely in the protracted immaturity of her physique, in her prolongation of the freshness and pristine flexibility of childhood into adulthood, and the very message this projects as an appeal to the masculine desire to protect and fondle.

This late retention of infantile features by the human female has not of course escaped the notice of scientists, and all modern sexologists, from Havelock Ellis to Dr A. Heilborn, refer to it. The latter, for instance, speaks of the 'infant type more nearly approached by woman than by man.'[107] Dr Bernard A. Bauer refers to the 'rounded contours of the female body' being due to 'a less-developed musculature,' and he speaks of the 'comparative softness of the female.'[108] Havelock Ellis says: 'in woman there is an earlier arrest of development . . . as a result, the proportions of women tend to approach those of children. This greater youthfulness of physical type in women is a very radical characteristic.' He also tells us that 'the adult man diverges to a greater extent from the child type than the adult woman.'[109]

---

[107] *The Opposite Sexes*, 1927, Chapter 1.
[108] *Woman*, 1927, Book IV, Chapter 5.
[109] *Man and Woman*, 1926, Chapters 3 and 18.

Dr Oskar Schültze is emphatic on the point. 'In appearance,' he says, 'woman's musculature is more akin to the child's than is the more rigid musculature of man . . . In woman the layers of fat, like those of the child, are much more copiously developed. In all these respects woman more nearly resembles the child than does man . . . Thus, as we have seen above, woman remains more like the child, not only in her build and constitution, but also in her bodily proportions . . . and reaches maturity sooner than man.'

He refers to the infantile characteristics of the female cranium, and in conclusion says: 'Woman in the whole of her bodily nature remains more a child than man does.'[110]

Many similar testimonies could be quoted.[111] Indeed, the facts are a commonplace of sexology. But, strange to say, the necessary inference they suggest is never drawn. It still seems alien to European thought to be able to abandon the dualism which for over two millenniums has crippled mankind's reasoning and perverted its psychological insight, and when F. L. Lucas declares that the 'Age of Reason . . . owed some of its most fatal mistakes to bad psychology'[112] he really understates an important truth. For the fact is that most of our worst modern errors in social legislation and in the judgement of our fellows, of children and of women have all been due simply and solely to our inability to shake ourselves free from the Socratic teaching that body and soul—body and mind—are unrelated.

In the estimate of women's nature which we find in the relevant treatises, and in all the discussions about the role of the female in our society and the influence of women, we look in vain for any appreciation or recognition of the inevitable consequences that are likely to result from the fact that woman's bodily characteristics more closely resemble those of the child than do those of man.

---

[110] 'Das Weib bleibt in seinem ganzen Körper mehr Kind als der Mann.' *Das Weib in anthropologischer und sozialer Betrachtung*, 1920, I, II and III.

[111] See, for instance, Lipschütz, *The Internal Secretions of the Sex Glands*, 1914, p. 19.

[112] *The Art of Living*, 1959, Chapter 1.

Yet, unless we are to return at this late hour to the dualistic superstitions of our forefathers, how can we believe that, along with the physical characteristics of the child, woman can be free from many of childhood's mental characteristics?

Indeed, to attempt to understand the female character without taking into account the many resemblances of her physique to that of the child is to revert to the very errors that vitiated much of mid-Victorian thought and led even a biologist like Herbert Spencer to discuss human beings (especially in his *Social Statics*) as if they were disembodied spirits.

If, however, on the contrary, we recognise the inevitable implications of woman's physical affinities to the child, and thereby obtain some idea of the qualities she is likely to possess which differentiate her from man, our problem is immediately clarified, and the blind speculations of such ardent male feminists as John Stuart Mill, Benjamin Kidd, Lyon Blease, Henry Sidgwick and Ruskin will seem hardly to rise above the guesses of savages about the nature of the Moon.

Now, among the more salient attributes of the child are, first of all, its bland, cool assumption of its prescriptive right to appropriate anything it can lay its hands on; to enjoy every small present gratification even at the cost of some prospective greater one; to be unable to look on its actions in the light of their public effect — in fact, to lack any public spirit; to be quite unable to understand the need or purpose of discipline, and to accept corrections of its behaviour only as tiresome obstacles to be circumvented and bearing no relation to its future conduct; and, finally, to have no sense of truth — that is to say, to use speech only as expediency requires, without any thought of accuracy or exactitude.

Its behaviour is marked by complete unscrupulousness. Its conception of the role of morality is merely that of a meaningless interference with its freedom, like a sudden heavy downpour of rain, or a violent gust of wind, having no bearing on its subsequent action. In short, to condense in one sentence the sum of its mental characteristics, we cannot improve on Freud's statement that the child is ruled exclusively by the pleasure principle.

Young humanity arrives in this world, fresh and inexperienced, knowing nothing of the function of rules and restrictions in the regulation of our social life, and ready to remain more or less indefinitely profoundly dubious about their necessity. If nothing is done gradually to release it from the dominion of the pleasure principle and bend its nature to the requirements of the reality principle, it is never likely to abandon its scepticism about the necessity in question. Properly trained and intelligently and vigilantly disciplined, however, the male child, as it slowly progresses towards adulthood and sheds the physical characteristics of its unripe years, will succeed in ultimately submitting to the demands of the reality principle and in cheerfully accepting the limitations it imposes on personal freedom. But nowadays, as we know from innumerable signs, the subjection of our boys to the discipline of the reality principle is becoming an ever more exceptional occurrence, and good, in fact excellent, human material is thus often lost to society, because of this failure to mould and cultivate character in our young folk. We moderns, who are witnessing a steadily increasing incidence of crime of all kinds perpetrated by the youngsters in our population, turn in bewilderment from the homes to the schools of the nation to seek the true cause of the trouble. But we look in vain if we fail to grasp that, at bottom, the cause is the complete breakdown of all discipline in our society, with the inevitable sequel that extremely few of our young folk are ever trained to accept as a second nature the dominion of the reality principle.

Now, one of the most significant aspects of this increasing volume of juvenile delinquency in recent years is the fact that it has run almost parallel with the growth of feminine influence over our national life. As we shall see in a moment, a few exceptionally perspicacious moderns have recognised this — but, alas, much too belatedly to serve any useful purpose! Whilst recognising their insight, we can hardly absolve them of the charge of having been wise after the event. Yet the warnings about the dire consequences of feminine dominion have been plentiful. From the past history of Europe and Asia alone, moderns might have inferred what would be the inevitable fate of those who surrendered the direction of the community to women.

At all events, I can truthfully claim that I was among the few who early and vociferously in the history of the movement denounced the aims of feminism, as I suffered many rebuffs and earned much unpopularity by so doing.

What, then, were the important considerations that both the male and female feminists overlooked when, in the latter half of the nineteenth and the first two decades of the twentieth century, they championed the cause which led to the domination of our society by women?

First and foremost was the frivolous and hardly sane disregard of the fact that woman's bodily and mental nature must be related. Late-born creatures of an era during which everyone had been taught to believe that body and soul (body and mind) were unrelated, they failed altogether to see any significance in the fact that woman's physical characteristics closely resemble those of the child. And from this failure of vision there necessarily followed the inability to suspect the probable mental consequences of the resemblances.

Yet from its earliest days mankind had felt that danger lurked behind any paramount feminine influence over society. The very story of the Fall hints at the antiquity of man's awareness of woman's anarchical tendencies, whilst the whole of the Eastern world, unlike the West, still clings resolutely to the policy of resisting feminine influence over human life.

Following Heine, as he so often did (and without acknowledgement), Nietzsche tells us that no man of any depth can fail to think of women as Orientals do.[113] But even among Europeans there has been no lack of men and even of women who have warned their generation against woman's influence over society.

Aristotle was the first eminent European to do so when he showed how much Sparta's fall had been due to the Spartans having conceded too much power and independence (through the right of inheritance) to their womenfolk.[114] The fate of Athens and Rome was, however, no better than that of Sparta, for both fell into complete decay after they surrendered to their women the leadership in the customs and manners of their society.

At all events, from Rabelais to Montesquieu, Madame de Ré-

---

[113] *Beyond Good and Evil*, Book VII, Paragraph 238.
[114] *Politics* II, Book II, Chapter 9.

musat, Balzac and Alexandre Dumas *fils*, anti-feminist sentiments, although never widely accepted, have been repeatedly expressed. It is true that these sentiments have hailed chiefly from the French, who have always been singularly gifted as psychologists and have never been so wholly enamoured of feminine domination as have the Anglo-Saxons. But similar sentiments are also found, as we have seen, in Heine and Nietzsche, whilst in Schopenhauer they received peculiar emphasis. Among Anglo-Saxons they are much less common, and it seems to have been a characteristic of these people to be unable to regard women, as my friend Dr Wrench put it, except as 'a sort of queer man.'[115]

Already in the sixteenth century, Rabelais revealed his knowledge of woman's true nature when he made Rondibilis speak of her influence on society as nefarious. 'Quand je di femme,' says Rondibilis, 'je di un sex tant fragile, tant variable, tant inconstant et imparfaict, que nature me semble (parlant en tout honneur et révérence) s'être égarée de ce bon sens, par lequel elle avait crée et formé toutes choses, quand'elle ha basti la femme.'[116] Nature, he adds, thought more of perpetuating the race than of creating a perfect creature when it produced woman.

Montesquieu declares flatly that 'une nation où les femmes dominent le ton est une nation perdue.'[117] Whilst Madame de Rémusat, in her *Essai sur l'éducation de la femme*, acknowledges that 'Dans ce qui concerne les intérêts essentiels de la société dès que nous prétendons donner le mouvement, tout dégénère.'[118] That gifted psychologist, Balzac, was no less emphatic. Heine reports

---

[115] *The Mastery of Life*, 1911, p. 247.

[116] *Pantagruel*, Book III, Chapter 32. 'When I speak of woman, I speak of a sex so frail, so variable, so changeable and imperfect that Nature seems to me (speaking with due honour and reverence) to have strayed from the good sense by which she created and formed all other things when she had woman built.' — Ed.

[117] *Pensées diverses*, 1858 edition. 'A nation where women set the tone is a ruined nation.' — Ed.

[118] *Essay on the Education of Woman*, 1824, Chapter 1. 'As far as the essential interests of the society are concerned, from the time we lay claim to have change everything degenerates.' — Ed.

that Balzac once assured him with a sigh that 'la femme est un être dangereux.'[119]

Fifteen years later, Alexandre Dumas *fils*, in his preface to *L'ami des femmes*, addressing women, wrote: 'Toute société où vous dominez, que vous vous appelez Laïs, Poppée, ou Dubarry, est une société qui va s'écrouler et faire place à une autre. Dès que vous débordez sur les choses et sur les hommes, c'est le signe que les choses se détraquent et que ces hommes s'avilissent. Vous êtes le dernier culte de l'homme dégénéré . . . Après vous il n'y a plus que l'invasion des barbares!'[120]

Such warnings were less frequently given in Germany, but perhaps Schopenhauer, in the fervour and depth of his diatribes against feminism, makes up for this dearth of cautionary appeals in his country. At all events, in his essay 'Über die Weiber' in *Parerga und Paralipomena* he clearly states that, owing to the fundamental and incurable shortcomings of women, which he enumerates, their increasing dominance and growing share in setting the tone in modern society is corrupting it wholly.[121] His claim that woman is an 'inveterate philistine' is echoed by Baudelaire, who, in the very year when *Parerga und Paralipomena* was published, expressed the view that 'la femme est-elle toujours vulgaire.'[122] An explanation of the biological reasons for woman's natural vulgarity will be found in Chapter 10 of my *Woman: A Vindication*.

Now, oddly enough, none of these warnings concerning the evil influence of woman on society trace it to her physical affinities to the child, and one only—Schopenhauer's—without specifically referring to these affinities, goes so far as to call attention to woman's childlike nature. 'In short,' he says, 'women remain

---

[119] *Geständnisse*, 1853-54. 'Woman is a dangerous being.' —Ed.

[120] 1878 edition, p. 51. 'Every society where you rule, whether you call yourself Lais, Poppaea or Dubarry, is a society which is going to collapse and be replaced by another. As soon as you encroach on the things and the men, it is the sign that the things break down and that the men degrade themselves. You are the last cult of degenerate man . . . After you, there is nothing but the invasion of the barbarians!' —Ed.

[121] 1851, Chapter 27, Paragraph 369: 'ist ihr Vorherrschen und Tonangeben der Verderb der modernen Gesellschaft.'

[122] *Mon cœur mis à nu*, V 6. 'Woman is essentially vulgar.' —Ed.

great children all their lives; a sort of halfway stage between child and man.'[123]

Yet, whether explicitly stated or not by those who have recognised the danger of any feminine domination of society, the experience of the wiser among mankind who have learnt the lessons of history points to the conclusion that they must always have sensed, however dimly, that woman's nature became a menace when allowed to become reflected in the population as a whole. Thus, whether they connected this effect of woman's domination with her physical peculiarities or not, we who have now given up all belief in dualism must ascribe the unanimity of their warnings to their recognition, however vague, of some such connection.

And the inevitable implication of recognising this connection is that the most important truth about woman is that, through her childlike body, she carries into adulthood the characteristics of the child.

Hence, wherever she becomes the dominant influence there necessarily occurs a steady breakdown of all order, all discipline, all public spirit, all sense of responsibility and all morality. Anarchy prevails, and crime inevitably increases at every level of society and among people of all ages, because the population as a whole is bred to obey only the dictates of the pleasure principle.

Inured and consequently blinded as we may be by sheer habit to the prevalence of lawlessness in every aspect of our national life, we need but to glance cursorily at our present world in order to become aware of the fact that anarchy is everywhere increasing. No-one thinks of observing any rule, any public-spirited measure, any social duty, if it can be flouted without fuss or bother. Every owner-driver of a car knows that he cannot travel half a mile from his home without witnessing the deliberate breach of some highway regulation or local bylaw by some other user of the road. Far from everybody now possessing a conditioned sense of social duty, the only compelling motive for tolerable behaviour is the dread of having to pay for its converse. Make the risk of discovery negligible, and everybody today acts as if everything is allowed.

---

[123] Paragraph 364. 'Mit einem Worte [Frauen] Zeit Lebens grosse Kinder sind: eine Art Mittelstufe zwischen dem Kinde und dem Mann.'

The average citizen need only resort to some rural beauty spot for a picnic, or try to secure a pleasant pitch on some seaside beach, in order to find that his own and his family's freedom to enjoy the amenities expected has been thwarted by a predecessor who, in this 'land of the free,' with no understanding of freedom in a civilised community and destitute of any instruction in its essential limitations, has left the area disfigured, soiled, polluted and infected by the decomposing debris of a meal, garbage of all kinds, broken glass and other forms of offensive litter.

Let him stand in a queue, whether in a shop or at a bus-stop, and if he does not find that someone is trying to jump it, or has actually done so, he will be singularly lucky. Some of the angriest scenes I have ever taken part in, especially with women in shop-queues, have been due to the vigilance with which I always watch and finally pounce on anyone making sly manoeuvres to steal a march on other shoppers. Yet it has too often been my experience to find that the rest of the queue would give me no support in my protests, nor themselves manifest any resentment over the abuse. Such is the deplorable familiarity of the crowd with lawlessness that it ceases to be noticed.

Often, in that part of the town in which I now live, I am obstructed and even endangered on the pavement by teenagers who, with all the brazen effrontery of modern youth to whom everything is permitted, ride their bicycles straight at me, taking for granted that respect for the pedestrian is now *vieux jeu*.[124] On the same pavements, however narrow, and even on busy days, groups of gossipers will gather who, oblivious of the convenience of other pedestrians, will completely bar one's passage, with the result that one must either step into the roadway at the risk of life and limb, or wait patiently for the group to disperse. I know of one young woman who, some years ago in Lewes, was forced in this way to step into the road in order to proceed on her errand, and received a foot injury from a passing car which crippled her for life.

If, to change the scene, we look into the homes of the masses, high and low, in order to see what is happening there, we behold

---

[124] Old hat. — Ed.

conditions more disquieting still. For here, in this gynocratic milieu, we have the diverting spectacle of the pleasure principle presiding over the reality principle, with all that this means in completely haphazard and opportunistic regulation.

Inconsistency in reprimand; inconstancy in the fulfilment of threats; the measure of rightness and wrongness reduced to what happens momentarily to suit the convenience, mood or caprice of the female parent; and the repeated improvisation of rules, on the spur of the moment, which the children know from experience possess no validity for the future—these are some of the more salient behaviour-features of the average home today. Discipline under such conditions necessarily becomes a farce, and the young grow up without any sense of self-restraint; with a secret contempt for all authority; with a profound disbelief in the necessity or even reality of either rules or order; with a bias in favour of snap judgements on every possible subject; and in complete ignorance of those obligations to the rest of the community which constitute what is called public spirit.

Rarely, if ever, does any trace of masculine authority make itself felt in the domestic circle—not because a few men here and there do not occasionally try to introduce some order or method into the chaos, but because the number who do not do so, or have given up trying to do so, is so great that masculine interference is completely out of fashion. It is no longer done. Where and when it is attempted it only provokes indignant surprise. Even the BBC finds it perfectly safe, if not *de rigueur*, to present plays in which paternal endeavours to introduce a minimum of law and order in the home are held up to ridicule and obloquy. On Sunday evening,[125] for instance, I witnessed a shocking play of this kind on BBC TV. It was entitled *My Flesh and Blood*, and depicted an exemplary father's vain efforts to inculcate upon his teenage and adult children some of that sense of decency and propriety with which their earliest education, at the hands of their mother, had failed to equip them. But, supported by their 'Mum,' the children showed only resentment at this socially heterodox intrusion of masculine conceptions of order into their lives, and in the end not only was

---

[125] 24th July 1960.

his interference shown to have been mistaken, but he himself was also represented as a monster.

This surrender of all male authority in the home has been no sudden occurrence. It has taken two or three generations to become firmly established. But it would be both foolish and unfair to accuse women of having been alone responsible for it. Without the factor of male degeneracy in modern Europe and particularly in England, and without the cooperation of man's progressive weakness and loss of mastery, it would have been impossible.

Among certain superficial research-workers into the causes of juvenile delinquency, it became fashionable to ascribe the loss of paternal authority to the two World Wars. But the influences which led to this loss were already in active operation long before World War I. For, in the clash and incessant war, though predominantly Cold War, of the sexes, the will to power inherent in all human beings is the determining factor, and, irrespective of any international conflicts, conditions were bound to tip the balance against the sex which showed any tendency to wilt, soften and weaken — or, if not to weaken, to suffer, as the majority of Anglo-Saxon males did and still do, from the illusion that masculine ascendancy can safely be relinquished, at least in part, in favour of the female who, after all, was only 'a sort of queer man.'

The part was of course speedily extended to the whole, and by 1914, on the eve of World War I, there was already every sign of the advent of that feminine hegemony of society which we now see fully realised.

Speaking of the decline of masculine authority in the home, Dr Joseph V. Walker says: 'in this virtual dethronement of the head of the household, women have to some extent been the allies of their children.'[126] What he does not point out is the great interest the children have in supporting their mother in this matter, for it enables them to do more or less as they like. In the *Housewife* there is an interesting comment on the same phenomenon. Writing on 'Dominating wives on the increase,' Dr David Mace says: '[Owing to the fact that in our modern world] the power is much more equally distributed between husband and wife, there is a much

---

[126] *Health and the Citizen*, 1951, Chapter 5.

greater chance that the balance may tip in the wife's favour. There is some evidence [what an understatement!] that this is happening in some areas on a widespread basis. Some years ago a team of Australian social psychologists found in a study of husband–wife relationships, that in urban families more of the vital decisions were being made by the wife than the husband . . . I don't believe that as yet we have a similar situation in this country. But there are evidences of the kind in the same direction, a trend that we ought to be watching carefully.'[127]

This manifestly too moderate statement, with its much too sanguine conclusion, indicates that even the blind are now beginning to see light. But how little light may be inferred by anyone familiar with the actual condition of affairs. For it is not, as Dr Mace says, merely a matter of 'more of the vital decisions being made by the wife than the husband.' The present rule is that the principal, if not the only influence to which the average child is now subjected is that of the mother. It is her character, her behaviour, her conception of right and wrong, her attitude to law and order, that is constantly held up before his eyes, so that it amounts simply to this — that the child is given as an example and standard merely a life-size adult model of its own immature being.

More recently, a London clergyman has given his impression concerning the eclipse of the male in the regulation of the home in our society. 'I have noted over the year,' says the Rev. W. Bulman, vicar of St Gabriel's Church, Cricklewood, 'a distinct change in the social attitudes of our own people, and I do not think for the better. The most noticeable is the abdication of man and the decline of dad. From the time the banns are put up it is the girl who makes all the decisions.'[128]

But this reduction of the modern male to a mere cipher in his own home cannot have escaped the notice of any alert observer of our present world. Only the universality of the phenomenon can account for the general unconcern with which it is regarded.

C. W. Valentine says: 'It is, I think, very probable that the frequent appearance of "problem" children in "broken" homes is

---

[127] August 1961.
[128] *Daily Mail*, 6th April 1962.

partly due to the fact that in such homes the discipline is likely to be inadequate, inconsistent and erratic, and especially too lax, either because there is only the mother in the house, or if there is only a father, because he is unable to exercise proper supervision through being out most of the day.'[129]

But the complacent view that 'problem' children and juvenile delinquents come only or chiefly from 'problem' homes is quite inaccurate and was flatly denied by the Commissioners of Prisons in their Report for 1954. They said, in fact, that it had little to do with it. 'Lack of parental control,' they maintained, 'is obvious among the causes, and still more lack of parental example.'[130] Besides, C. W. Valentine forgets that, in any case, it is not only in 'broken' homes that 'there is only the mother in the home' to control and run it, but that, owing to the present feminine domination of our society, she is in the majority of homes today the only source of authority. And, to judge from the results, there seems to be abundant justification for Robert T. Lewis's conclusion that 'the hand that rocks the cradle can wreck the world.'[131]

This now seems to be fairly well understood by most of those now engaged in investigating the causes of the spectacular rise in juvenile and adult crime all over the country. For, from the Home Secretary, Mr R. A. Butler, to the Chief Constables and Commissioners of Police throughout the nation, all agree that the source of this unruliness and crime in teenagers, children and adults who were children at the time of World War II is the treatment to which they were subjected in their own homes during the crucial years of infancy and early childhood. And, condensed into a few brief and pungent sentences, the views of the authorities in question would find support in the conclusions of Madeline Kerr, a lady who undertook to study conditions in a typical area of present-day England.

'Mothers,' she says, 'tend to accept the word of their children and do what the child wants . . . On the whole children are trained by a mixture of indulgence, shouting and threats . . . Discipline

---

[129] *The Difficult Child and the Problem of Discipline*, 1947, p. 53.
[130] *Times* and *Daily Mail*, 20th August 1955.
[131] *Romulus*, 1929, p. 21.

seems generally to take the form of an attempt to get peace for the moment rather than any long-term policy.'[132]

K. G. Collier, speaking of life in poor homes, says: 'Discipline ... is like everything else inconsistent. Behaviour which is at one time smiled at indulgently and perhaps proudly, is at other times greeted with a shout or a hard blow, it depends on the mood of the mother. Also, mothers are continually issuing orders and prohibitions, making threats, which are not carried out. In everyday life the child is essentially undisciplined. Because of this, children at first see the demands imposed on them by the school, or any other authorities as meaningless, and they are ignored just as demands made by the mother are ignored, and then fiercely resented when it becomes clear that the outside authorities mean the demands to be met.'[133]

All this is so typical also of homes not necessarily poor that we cannot be surprised if such conditions lead to an unruly and lawless generation. And when we see deeds of hardly credible cruelty to animals increasing among young people; when we hear almost daily of the wanton destruction of public property in parks, on our railways or in public buildings and streets — according to the parish councillors of Derbyshire alone, 'the wilful damage to street lamps in one scattered parish was said to 'be "absolutely fantastic"'[134] — not to mention all those other crimes which point to the lack in modern youth of any habits of self-restraint, of any notion of social morality or the limits of personal freedom, of respect for authority, of discipline, or of a conditioned suppression of their primitive aggressive impulses, we must be blind to the first principles of a sound education if we fail to recognise that the source of this ruffianism and violence is the failure of the present-day presiding genius of the people's homes to inculcate upon the growing generation a sense of decency, law and order, and self-control in the crucial period of their childhood.

I say again, it would be both inaccurate and unfair to hold women responsible for this state of affairs. It is not their fault that,

---

[132] *The People of Ship Street*, 1958, Chapter 5.
[133] *The Social Purposes of Education*, 1959, Part IV, Chapter 11.
[134] *Times*, 12th October 1959.

in keeping with their physical constitution, they carry into adulthood the characteristics of the child and are therefore incapable of leading childhood out of the dominion of the pleasure principle into that of the reality principle. It is not their fault that, owing to the emasculation of the men of the nation and/or that basic misunderstanding of women of which even the best of them are guilty, male authority in the home has been abandoned. Nor is it women's fault that, even if adult males now old enough to be the fathers of families were to try to introduce some discipline into their homes, they would be incapable of doing so owing to the fact that, as they belong to a generation born after the establishment of feminine dominion in England, they too are all afflicted with the same ignorance of discipline and self-control which characterises the majority of their juniors.

'The social world of contemporary Britain,' says Dr Joseph V. Walker, 'is indubitably of feminine type. . . by this we mean that the community is feminine in its outlook and under the fundamental control of women's opinion.' As to discipline, he adds, our society 'hardly understands the word.'[135]

The result is the state of anarchy we see everywhere about us today, and I have explained why this must be so.

Other people have recognised the necessity of widespread anarchy wherever and whenever women's influence prevails in a society, but have ascribed it to reasons which seem to me less fundamental than those I have outlined. This does not mean, however, that much may not be said in favour of their arguments, though if they are valid they merely strengthen the case of the anti-feminist.

Two independent investigators, an Englishman named James Corin and an Austrian, Dr Fritz Wittels, neither of whom, as far as I am aware, knew the other's work, both suggest that women are fundamentally inclined to anarchy—i.e., opposed to the law and order of civilised society—because this society denies them the primitive right of 'free-mating,' which throughout the course of evolution has been (among most animals) as much a female as a male privilege.

---

[135] *Health and the Citizen*, 1951, Chapter 2.

In *Mating, Marriage and the Status of Women*,[136] Corin speaks of this loss of the right of free-mating as a conscious grievance in all women. Dr Wittels, on the other hand, with whom I feel inclined to agree, argues in *Die sexuelle Not*[137] that the sense of this loss, though acute in the civilised female, is largely unconscious.

At all events, both men argue cogently that the resentment felt by women, whether consciously or unconsciously, over the loss of the right of free-mating suffered through civilisation makes them instinctive enemies of society, contemptuous of its rules and regulations, and consequently predisposed to promote anarchy and to welcome any national upheaval, such as a great war or revolution, which suspends for a while the irksome restrictions on free sexual intercourse.

There is so much to be said for this Corin–Wittels thesis that it cannot be dismissed out of hand. Nevertheless, even if only partially valid, it suggests many weighty reasons for suspecting feminine influence of having disruptive and asocial effects. In my *Woman: A Vindication* of 1923 I dealt with the question of the female's natural unscrupulosity. But I explained it along lines which I knew at the time would be more acceptable than those given above. This explanation may be, like Corin's and Wittels's, less fundamental than that I have presented in this section but it may still be part of the truth. For, incredible as it may seem, as recently as 1923 the grip dualism held over the English world, high and low, was still so strong that, had I argued that there was a connection between woman's physical characteristics and her tendency to lawlessness and anarchy, my case would have been regarded as self-refuted.

Indeed, such is the time-lag before any obvious inference is likely to be drawn from passing events by even educated and enlightened members of the English public that it is only quite recently that one or two exceptionally bright people have begun to see a possible connection between the spectacular increase in lawlessness and anarchy in our day and the growing influence of women over our society. And, as we shall see, even if we allow

---

[136] London, 1910.
[137] Vienna, 1909.

that the inferences in question indicate unusual insight, we cannot help also recognising how limited is the vision that prompted them.

Thus, Colonel O. G. Body, in a letter to the *Times*, said: 'The decline in moral standards during the past 50 years has been coincident with the gradual emancipation of our women. Is it not time we asked ourselves how far it is consequent upon it?'[138] Two days later, to my surprise, a lady, Elizabeth Scott Daniell, wrote, saying, 'Obviously Colonel Body's theory in today's issue of the *Times* should be looked into very closely.'[139] But the Duchess of Bedford, whilst evidently perceiving the same connection that Colonel Body sees between the ascendancy of women and the recent staggering increase of lawlessness and crime in the nation, wishes to ascribe it to the success of the women's suffrage movement. 'What would the Suffragettes have thought today?,' she asks. 'Would they be sorry? That the emancipation of women has led to our present problems I have no doubt... Thank you Suffragettes!'[140]

But such shafts of light thrown on the perplexities of our modern world, although laudable, are both too belated and too narrow in their grasp of the problem to serve any useful purpose today. It is too late. In any case, moreover, it is too simplistic to assume, as her Grace does, that the triumph of the female suffrage movement is chiefly responsible for the present state of affairs. For this movement, with all its extravagances and ridiculous exaggeration of the importance and wisdom of the parliamentary vote, was only one symptom of a national disease that had been incubating for decades before the first benighted suffragette dreamt of waving a banner in a London street.

I was never deceived by the ostensible motives of the female suffrage movement. From the beginning I suspected it of being prompted by subconscious forces bearing little relationship to politics, and as I stood in the crowds that used to gather about a speaker advocating votes for women I often used to marvel at the

---

[138] 27th September 1961.

[139] *Times*, 29th September 1961. A more or less similar letter from David Garnett appeared in the *Times*, 3rd October 1961.

[140] *Sunday Telegraph*, 19th November 1961.

naïveté of the men standing about me who could not see the naked truth beneath the elaborate political camouflage that concealed it.

Nevertheless, although I clearly recognised the real nature of the Anglo-Saxon female's passionate demand for the futile vote, I was never so deluded as to suppose that it represented the whole of feminism, or even that it constituted the core of the feminist movement and consequently the main cause of the increasing disorder and anarchy of modern life. For I was never in any doubt that the basic cause of the decline in the quality of our civilisation was the degeneracy of the civilised male. Throughout my attacks on feminism, therefore, as any reader can discover for himself, there was always a plain allusion to the emasculated male of the nation as the principal cause of the abnormal ascendancy of the female. It was he who, typical of the majority of males in the country, had abdicated his position as leader and tone-setter of the domestic and social circles of the community. On this account, feminism, far from being a spontaneous and wholesome uprising of ebullient and flourishing womanhood, was merely a morbid reaction to the general inadequacy, supineness and feebleness of the male, complicated unfortunately by the fact that, owing to the Englishman's total lack of psychological flair, even the best and most masculine men that remained in the nation were stricken with such inconceivable credulity as to be able to swallow all the ostensible and allegedly logical reasons which feminists, male and female, advanced for the realisation of their aims.

I hope I have made it clear that my anti-feminism of the early twenties and later was both justified and even prophetic, for anyone who reads the prognostications I made in my *Woman: A Vindication*[141] will be unable to deny that they have been abundantly realised during the four decades that have meanwhile elapsed.

Surprising as it may seem, moreover, in a book recently come to hand—Robert Ardrey's admirable *African Genesis*[142]—there is remarkable and quite unexpected confirmation of what I repeatedly allege in my anti-feminist treatises regarding the effect of the

---

[141] In the latter part of Chapters 10 and 11, particularly pp. 363-4.
[142] London, 1961, Chapter 5, 4.

decline of masculine influence. For, if Mr Ardrey is right, it would appear that the tendency for feminine influence to culminate in anarchy, and for masculine ascendancy to be the only means of checking it and of establishing order, is a phenomenon noticeable even among animals in the wild.[143]

* * *

I must now briefly refer to three books not already mentioned — *The Night Hoers*,[144] *The Truth about Childbirth*[145] and *Religion for Infidels*.[146]

The first two relate only incidentally to feminism. In the first I said all that I thought there is to say against birth control, and in the second I advanced my reasons, supported by massive evidence, for claiming that if childbirth casualties are to be reduced and the process of parturition made easier, especially for primiparae, popular beliefs about the proper age of marriage and for the first childbirth must be radically revised, so that it may be made customary for the first child of a marriage to be born, if possible, not later than a woman's eighteenth, nineteenth or twentieth year.

When I wrote this book, however, I did not know certain facts which have meanwhile come to light and have added considerable weight to my thesis, and these facts relate to the optimal years for successful and adequate lactation by the young mother.

Thus, in an article on 'Clinical and chemical studies in human lactation,' Dr F. E. Hytten says that there is 'a steady increase in the incidence of artificial feeding with increasing age. . . In primiparae the incidence of poor lactation rose from 4 per cent under the age of 20, to 37.5 per cent over the age of 34 . . . The relationship between the incidence of poor lactation and maternal age was highly significant . . . Poor lactation will continue to be a dominant disability, especially in primiparae, so long as a large number of women delay childbirth until their late twenties and

---

[143] See particularly pp. 133–34.
[144] London, 1928.
[145] London, 1937; New York, 1938.
[146] London, 1961.

thirties.'[147] In a leader in the same issue we read that Dr F. E. Hytten finds that 'about one third of mothers have inadequate capacity for lactation, the quantity of milk falling off quite steeply with age of mother.' More data confirming Dr Hytten's findings have been published since and can be seen in the various medical publications.

Thus, from the standpoint of normal parturition and of the capacity for adequate lactation, my thesis concerning the optimal age for the first childbirth is overwhelmingly supported by medical findings. Yet my book was met not only with angry misunderstanding and misrepresentation,[148] but one scientist, J. B. S. Haldane, was also sufficiently incensed, or else sufficiently incited by his lady friends, to denounce me publicly as a liar for claiming that normal, spontaneous childbirth in a healthy young woman under twenty-three could be relatively painless.[149]

Such are the rewards of vision when it is out of season. With much greater justification than ever Voltaire had, therefore, and in respect of many more years of work, I may truthfully exclaim: 'Qu'ai je gagné par vingt ans de travail? Rien que des ennemis.'[150]

In conclusion, it seems necessary to repeat what I stated in no equivocal terms above—namely, that there is no essential incongruity in being wholly philogynic and yet frankly recognising the inevitable consequences of women's physical affinities with children. Although we may know that women carry into their adult life the characteristics of the child, and may take steps to protect society and our children's education against the consequences of this inevitable feminine peculiarity, this need not in the least prevent us from recognising woman's compensating qualities and admiring and ardently devoting ourselves to her sex. Although I eventually became aware of many of my mother's and sister's basically immature characteristics and could see the latter in the female characters, whether fictional or real, I most greatly ad-

---

[147] *British Medical Journal*, 18th December 1954.
[148] See, for instance, Appendix III to my *Enemies of Women*.
[149] *John Bull*, 29th November 1937.
[150] Letter to Mlle Quinault. 'What have I gained by twenty years' work? Nothing but enemies.' —Ed.

mired—Emily Brontë's elder Catherine, above all—this never diminished by one iota my wholehearted devotion to them, nor can I understand why it ever should do so. For, unless we are romantic enough to insist on the total whiteness of those we approve of and to condemn as wholly black those whom we favour, we only betray our lack of realism by ceasing to feel attached to a loved object after we have recognised its inevitable shortcomings. We do not reject a piece of china because, unlike a pewter, silver or golden vessel, it will smash if dropped on the floor. We do not despise a dog because it lacks the cat's prehensile claws, any more than we love a cat less because it cannot bark.

On the same principle, there can be no essential incompatibility between continuing to love and admire women whilst recognising their inevitable shortcomings, and he who, like my friend Dr Wrench, sees a contradiction between anti-feminism and philogyny, and cannot therefore reconcile my condemnation of feminine domination of our society with my devotion to my mother, confesses himself a romantic.

* * *

In my *Religion for Infidels* I broke entirely fresh ground by trying to show that the whole of the religious practices of mankind—above all, prayer—could be linked up with spiritual factors that have played a part in organic evolution and the origin of species, and have their root and counterpart in those blind and unconscious strivings on the part of creatures lower than man to overcome the difficulties and dangers of their environment.

Thus, I assembled into a comprehensive whole many hitherto unrelated biological data, and in so doing offered a solution of many features both of religion and evolution which were still obscure and unexplained

In the course of my argument I was naturally obliged to deal with the question of Christianity and the validity of its interpretation of life and the universe, and I was compelled to demonstrate that both its teaching and its dogmata were utterly untenable. In this part of my argument, too, I broke fresh ground, for, although I took for granted all the usual objections to Christianity raised by the rationalists, I confined my own attack on the old religion to the exposure of the psychological heresies of its teaching, and showed that, as the source of the more important of these psychological errors was the Christian deity himself, it was impossible to regard such a deity as the supernatural, omniscient and omnipotent Being whom Christians claimed him to be. If, therefore, there was a power behind phenomena, I concluded that it could not possibly be the Christian god.

In my search for evidence pointing to the probable nature, or rather operating method, of the power behind phenomena, I therefore examined how life in our part of the universe—this earth—was conducted, how it worked, under what principles it appeared to be operating. Only thus, I maintained, could we hope to obtain even a vague idea of the character of the hidden forces behind it, and how we could make it possible to secure some sort of contact with these hidden forces.

In this way, I lighted on the possible link between religious practices—above all, prayer—with those factors in organic evolution that have probably been concerned with specific variation in the plant and animal world, and I concluded my argument by a few autobiographical notes indicating how I had used prayer in my own life and how I thought it had served me.

The book was received with almost complete silence by the press, and, among those of my friends and acquaintances who read it, it induced a few to go over to the side of my enemies. Much of the book, especially that part of it in which I discuss Christianity, consists of an array of facts and arguments that are quite unanswerable, and it is my belief that it is this quality of apodicticity which characterises so many of my works, especially those on feminism, that has accounted for much of my unpopularity and for the greater part of the silence with which my works have been met.

People do not mind being entertained with light attacks on their most cherished beliefs, provided always that such attacks remain in the nature of badinage, chaff or feeble and unsustainable criticism. But attack their outfit of prejudices, convictions and traditional loyalties with arguments they see no way of refuting, and they will be unforgiving and henceforth regard you as a bitter opponent.

Unfortunately, the logical mind I inherited from my French ancestors has always enabled me to light on the weakest links in the chain of reasoning supporting most modern superstitions and ideals, and whether these have related to democracy, feminism or religion I have always been able to demonstrate their fundamental untenability. In a country notorious for the congenital illogicality of its inhabitants, this faculty has not endeared me to the population, least of all its female readers who, in the sphere of thought as in everything else, now rule public opinion.

But, at bottom, I do not really deplore this outcome of my life's work. For I prefer to be known by posterity as a writer of accurate and prophetic vision, rather than as a time-server and stooge of philistinism who acquired ephemeral fame by toeing the conventional line marked out by his least enlightened contemporaries.

Final Reflections

I am not sorry to have reached the end of my eightieth year in 1962. Looking about me with all the impartiality I find it possible to summon, I see no reason for envying the young, least of all the growing children of the present day. As Heine so well remarked 120 years ago, they would be well-advised 'to come into the world with thick hides.'[1]

Having known Europe, and England above all, in the halcyon days before the advent of the internal-combustion engine, before our last remaining peaceful vista was disfigured, scored and raked by roaring aeroplanes and before all the perils and hazards of the primitive jungle had been reinstalled on our highways to account for an annual death-roll probably surpassing that which was ever caused by wild beasts — in short, having known Europe when one could travel north to south and east to west all over it, feeling sure of meeting everywhere with respect and cordiality and, more important still, without having to wrestle with hordes of creatures roughly and generally rudely contesting every inch of space one tries to occupy, whether on a train, a ship or a city pavement, I see little reason for assuming that the present and future hold out any promise of times happier than those I enjoyed as a late Victorian. Least of all do I see any prospect of a life of greater security, predictability and safety for posterity. There is now so little chance of discipline and good order being restored in our Western world, which grows daily, if not hourly, ever more lawless and anarchical, that we who shall not see the twenty-first century are hardly likely to miss an apotheosis of bliss on earth.

Civilised society seems to have become inured and indifferent to our tasteless policy of multiplying without any regard for quality or psychophysical desirability. Nor does it look as if, with soft sentimental humanitarianism everywhere paramount, any improvement in the human stocks of the West is at all like-

---

[1] *Französische Zustände*, II, Chapter 42.

ly. On the contrary, we can expect only a general deterioration of human health, stamina and intelligence. Only the great wars for food and living space now looming on the distant horizon—wars which will be fought with unprecedented bitterness, brutality and determination—may possibly offer a remedy for this state of affairs. Because if, in the extremity of its suffering during these wars, overcrowded mankind recovers some of its pristine wisdom regarding human rubbish, it may cease to cherish and maintain the diseased and defective at the cost of the sound and healthy, and a eugenic outlook may at last be forced willy-nilly upon Western peoples demented by centuries of the romanticism and false doctrine inculcated by Christianity and liberalism.

So that, by and large, whether socially, politically or domestically, I see no single feature of the present civilised world which I can honestly declare a blessing, an example of progress, or an improvement on the past.

But stay! There is one exception, and it was mentioned in an earlier chapter. Loathe the motor-car as I may—and as an owner-driver I can speak with some experience of the many reasons for hating it even as a driver in a line of traffic—I still feel grateful to its inventors for having been the means of sparing me the harrowing spectacle with which my boyhood and early manhood were daily confronted. I refer to the inhuman treatment of horses on our streets, a form of brutality in which the general public participated without ever seeming to be aware of the heartlessness of their behaviour. I do not mean that exceptional kind of ill-usage consisting of the flogging of an exhausted animal by an exasperated carman, which would provoke the wrath of the passing crowd. I mean that consistent, habitual and routine inhumanity, largely unconscious because a commonplace of the urban scene, by which thousands of horses on our streets were daily subjected to trials of strength and endurance which only their pathetic docility made possible. In France and Italy I have seen donkeys rebel against similar treatment and refuse to move when subjected to it.

Montaigne assures us that 'Si j'avais à revivre, je revivrais comme j'ai vécu,'[2] and he said this although during his later middle age he was racked with incessant pain by the stone in his bladder. Wisdom alone, however, precludes any other conclusion. For we know only the life we have led and the native resources with which we have met the slings and arrows of outrageous fortune. We cannot guess how we should have behaved in different circumstances.

Similarly, I think it bootless to regret or repent anything I may have done or omitted to do, however deplorable it may have seemed at the time. For it is impossible to know what worse calamities might have overtaken me, or what graver errors I might have committed, had my way of life been different.

Least of all do I regret my determination never to push a perambulator or to hear myself addressed as 'Father' by a junior whose critical attitude towards me would at best remain secret only through fear or good manners. 'Considering the general run of sons,' says Lord Chesterfield, 'it is seldom a misfortune to be childless.'[3] The truth in this remark rarely deters the average man from wishing to enjoy the ephemeral satisfaction of having demonstrated his potency to the world; nor does the customary unhappy relationship of children to their fathers seem to be a wholly recent development, for Montaigne in the sixteenth century was already complaining that 'nous vivons en un monde où la loyauté des propres enfants est inconnue,'[4] whilst Vauvenargues, some 200 years later, observed, that 'l'ingratitude la plus odieuse, mais la plus commune et la plus ancienne est celle des enfants envers leurs pères.'[5]

It has long been my belief that the civilised convention concerning the human male's relation to his offspring tends to put

---

[2] *Essais*, Book III, Chapter 2: 'Of Repentance.' 'Were I to live my life over again, I should live it just as I have lived it.' —Ed.

[3] *The Letters of Philip Dormer Stanhope, Earl of Chesterfield*, edited by John Bradshaw, 1892, p. 471 (15th July 1751).

[4] *Essais*, Book III, Chapter 9: 'Of Vanity.' 'We live in a world where the loyalty of one's own children is unknown.' —Ed.

[5] *Réflexions et maximes*, 1746, 174. 'The most odious ingratitude, although the most common and the most ancient, is that of children towards their fathers.' —Ed.

a strain on the feelings of both father and child. Because of its slender foundations in the evolution of the species, the whole situation created by an adult male remaining in the home after his progeny have grown beyond early adolescence is both artificial and therefore bound to be difficult. The conditions of our society may have made it necessary from the economic point of view, but nothing can make it either natural or desirable. And since the male parent's authority and influence in the home, especially his role as the disciplinarian, have, by the dominance of women, become, if not obsolete, at least uncommon, his continued presence among the brood he has sired merely exposes him to the contempt and contumely which all superfluous objects inevitably suffer. Consequently, when his children reach adolescence either they or he should quit — preferably, they. For, as all his family cannot reach their teens simultaneously, and as furthermore the relationship to his spouse, if still ideal, would make parting an intolerable wrench, the difficulties usually connected with his continued presence in the home would best be met and overcome by the departure seriatim of every child as it reached its third or fourth year of puberty. For, in any perfect relationship of the sexes, as I have already explained in another chapter, it is only as the reproductive urge wanes and loses its peremptoriness that love really becomes free, and none but the middle-aged and the senile can therefore hope to enjoy the bliss of this free love between the sexes.[6]

I think these remarks cover most of the difficulties of the father-child relationship, for, after all the centuries during which we have tried to adapt ourselves to the present anomalous arrangement, we still fail to do so, because the situation the civilised family has created is an essentially false one. Provided the contact of father and child endures long enough for the father to be able to mould his children's characters in the crucial years of their formation, that is all that civilisation can reasonably demand.

---

[6] In the 1970 typescript Ludovici refers to his *Truth about Marriage*, an unpublished work whose current whereabouts are unknown. — Ed.

Still, we know of many cases in which the present arrangement has proved eminently successful. Both Montaigne and Pascal, for instance, were devoted to their fathers. When girls and boys possess sufficient fine feeling and generosity, there is no doubt that the role of a worthy father may remain both pleasant and rewarding long after his children reach adulthood. Unfortunately, humanity does not produce a high proportion of such people. The average child feels and shows little gratitude for a good male parent's solicitude, sacrifices and care. Too much is taken for granted, and too little esteemed a favour. Gratitude, when it is not merely the anticipation of further benefits to come, is rarely found except in noble natures, and as the vast majority are anything but noble it cannot surprise us that filial piety is seldom met with.

It must be understood, however, that in this matter of gratitude we are concerned only with the worthy father, for it would be ridiculous and exorbitant to expect even a child of noble disposition to feel grateful for his father's procreative act alone. Generally speaking, therefore, the wise man will be well-advised to follow the course suggested by Lord Chesterfield's remark, and leave to the less wise the task of carrying on the race, for, as Shakespeare has so graphically hinted, there is nothing so unkind as ingratitude, and when it is displayed by one for whom we may have performed repeated feats of self-denial and self-sacrifice it is particularly heartbreaking.

Another step I have never regretted was that of having deliberately cast aside my undoubted gifts as a graphic artist. For, accurate and unhesitating as my draughtsmanship became, although I never underwent any training in art — and good draughtsmanship has always seemed to me the first prerequisite of an artist's accomplishments — I found in the act of graphic representation so little scope for the expression of my thoughts that, although I could doubtless have become a competent portrait-painter, for instance, and achieved greater material success had I chosen such a career than I have done by adopting the only profession in which thought can be adequately expressed, I do not think I should ever have been able to escape a sense of deep frustration had I remained loyal to my palette and brushes.

When one feels so powerful an urge to unburden one's mind as to make silence a source of anguish; when one has things to say that have not already been said — when, in short, one is not driven to pen and paper merely by the wish to call attention to oneself, one only courts disaster by bottling all one's mental energies and confining one's expression to pictorial representation.

One may have so many things to say that have not already been said that one's writings may range over a large number of apparently unrelated subjects, and this alone is certain to make one unpopular, because the English, above all, hate versatility. As Cyril Bibby has truly remarked, 'Nothing as surely damns a man as daring to work in several fields.'[7]

But any versatility I may have displayed was never laboriously sought or cultivated. The variety of subjects I have treated occurred naturally and spontaneously to my mind, because I felt I had something personal and new to say about them. It is, however, probable that it went a long way towards damaging my reputation, for such is the Anglo-Saxon bias against any attempt to show ability in many fields that the British public have been known to ruin their artists by insisting on their abiding by the manner and style that first made them famous. Thus, actors who as characters could not be immediately recognised as their old familiar selves in a play aroused disappointment rather than admiration in their matinée fans, and even musicians and painters were sometimes spoiled by similar insistent expectations on the part of a public they had once captured by a particular facet of their talent. In short, no matter what a man's potentialities in other forms of acting might be, the rule was: 'Once a clown, always a clown.'

Finally, I must confess that, in spite of all my unhappy relations with my fellow-men, my Fontenelleian sense of danger whenever I have attempted to mix with them and my awareness of my poor temperamental fitness for friendship, I feel no regret for having at least tried to meet and establish contact

---

[7] The London *Observer*, 27th November 1960.

with those members of my own sex to whom by chance I have felt drawn. For although I picked up little of value from most of them—least of all from those above the rank of commoner—it would be difficult to say how much I owe to those of my closest friends who belonged to the medical profession. Indeed, when I think of what I should have lost had I not enjoyed years of intimate friendship with doctors, I appreciate the risk a man runs who shuts himself off completely from his fellows. When we review the contributions recluses have made to thought—men like Thoreau and Nietzsche, for instance—although we may admire the depth and vividness of the discoveries their introspection, or self-vivisection, may have yielded, we cannot but notice the many illusions and errors friendly intercourse with men of their own intellectual rank might have corrected.

In the world of today it is difficult enough to find congenial companions capable of stimulating and usefully criticising our thought. But at least in the members of the medical profession one is fairly sure of meeting men whose studies have helped them to acquire some degree of realism, and, as this is the quality most conspicuously lacking in the average man, doctors are the class of men whose acquaintance today may most profitably be cultivated.

I have said enough in praise of military men to leave the reader in no doubt about my admiration of them as a class. But they have one fatal and besetting shortcoming which, besides making them the easy prey of their womenfolk, renders them incapable of perceiving or understanding the dangers of feminine domination. And this shortcoming, as all should know who have frequented them, is that they have not an elementary understanding of women. Too chivalrous to be masterful, too mystified by women to attempt to penetrate their wiles, and too credulous to put any other than its dictionary meaning to every word their womenfolk utter, they are easily hoaxed by their wives, their sisters, their cousins and their aunts, and this may explain how it comes about that, in nations largely military-minded, women contrive to rise to power. As Aristotle has pointed out, the influence of women in Sparta was largely attributable to the military pursuits of the country's menfolk; and

Kipling, in the photographic accuracy of his portraiture of soldiers, gives us evidence of a similar kind regarding the unconscious backing military men tend to give to feminism.[8]

Of all my associations with men I cherish none more wholeheartedly than those in which it was I who initiated the friendly approaches. And such is the pleasure I derived from these 'conquests' that I am more than ever persuaded that, on their account alone, if I had a second lease of life I should wish to live it exactly as I have lived the first one.

In their perfection as a source of gratification, I therefore set my friendships with men in the following order: first, that with my old schoolmaster, S. H. Wright; second, that with Ferdinand Schmidt; third, that with Wrench; fourth, that with Oscar Levy; and fifth, sixth and seventh, those with my military superiors Colonel L. E. Warren (Royal Artillery), Colonel W. C. Hunter (Oxford and Bucks Light Infantry) and Major J. Evans (Royal Inniskilling Fusiliers), all three of which were the outcome of World War I.

Outdistancing them all was my attachment to my old schoolmaster, Wright, for, to have been so attracted by his personality and the quality of his mind as to lay a determined siege to his attention and favour, and to have secured his ultimate capitulation despite the fierce rivalry of twenty-five other boys, most of whom were as attracted by him as I was, was at once such a singular and stirring victory, and its outcome in the form of about fifteen years of delightful friendship was such a rich reward, that for that blessing alone I should consider my life as worth living again just as I have lived it, down to the smallest details, including even its many miseries.

For a class of boys, headed by a master who is liked and admired, is a sort of royal court. To aspire to becoming his best-beloved, his favourite *en titre*,[9] is therefore not only natural but also inevitable and, apart from the joys it may subsequently bring, to succeed in such an endeavour constitutes an unforgettably blissful experience.

---

[8] See particularly *The Story of the Gadsbys*.
[9] Titular. — Ed.

Incidentally, in view of what I have said about doctors, it is interesting to note that Wright, too, was, if not exactly a doctor, at least a *médecin manqué*[10] or a *médecin malgré lui*,[11] for, although he never qualified, the studies which brought him three times within sight of qualification had left him with a rich store of medical information.

When the boy in me developed into the man, my determination to gain the friendship of men who attracted me was of the same order as that by which I obtained Wright's special favour. But no subsequent friendship could vie with that first one in the intensity of the pleasure I derived from it. Together with my most happy relationships with my mother and elder sister, such experiences make a life well-worthy of being lived again, alike in every respect to that already lived, and for these reasons I heartily endorse Montaigne's final estimate of his own life-span.

---

[10] A would-be doctor. — Ed.
[11] A doctor in spite of himself. — Ed.

APPENDIX

Looking now at Volume 16—*The Twilight of the Idols; The Antichrist; Notes to Zarathustra,* and *Eternal Recurrence*—I find that there must have been twenty-six discrepancies in my original English version, covering 233 pages of print. But, on examining these errors, it at once becomes plain that seven of them, at least, may be dismissed as obvious oversights—i.e., they consist of typing or printer's errors overlooked at one or both of the two stages of production. On page 6, for instance, 'humour' should read 'honour'—a simple but undetected typist's mistake. On page 26 'mongers' should read 'monsters,' and again on page 33 'one' should read 'our.' On page 90 'as' should read 'or,' on page 111 'Pessimism' should read 'Feminism,' on page 189 'away' should read 'astray,' and on page 195 'become' should read 'becomes.' As no-one could, in view of the rest of the translation, suppose me ignorant of the meaning of the German words 'Ehebegriff,' 'Unthier,' 'unter uns,' or of the difference between 'as' and 'or,' or capable of thinking that 'Feminismus' meant 'Pessimismus,' or that 'irreführen lassen' means 'led away' and not 'led astray,' such discrepancies are clearly examples, not of mistranslation, but of careless proof-reading.

An example of mistranslation is certainly to be found on page 41, where 'Sanktionen' is rendered by 'customs,' but this may also be an example of the failure of a colleague's check, to which I have already referred; whilst on page 52 the word 'suburban,' although hardly a translation of the German 'Bierbank,' is bolder I think than, say, 'public-house' or 'cafe' to describe the 'gospel' in question.

On page 69 (line 3): the word 'related' should be followed by 'and at bottom one'—an obvious oversight, because there can have been no difficulty about rendering the German 'an sich Eins.'

On page 79 (line 14): 'the greatest forgery' should read 'the greatest psychological forgery.'

On page 80 (line 10 from foot of page): 'He must communicate' should read 'He must communicate it.'

On page 96 (line 2): 'it' should read 'strength.'

On page 113 (line 15): for 'something popular' read 'something too popular.'

On page 114 (line 6 from foot of page): 'principe' should read 'Principe.'

On page 121: the words 'diamond' and 'charcoal' should be transposed. This is admittedly a bad error, obviously left undetected through careless reading of typescript or proofs, or both.

On page 136 (line 9 from foot of page): for 'squeaky' read 'unsteady.'

On page 138 (line 13): for 'argument' read 'arguments.'

On page 140 (line 14 from foot of page): for 'furthest' read 'most dangerously.'

On page 147 (last line): for 'beneath' read 'behind.'

On page 149 (line 14 from foot of page): for 'made a morality' read 'elevated to a moral principle.'

On page 187 (lines 4 and 5): for 'every St Peter and St Paul' read 'every Peter and Paul.'

On page 193 (line 6 from foot of page): for 'my *Genealogy of Morals*' read 'Essay I of my *Genealogy of Morals*.'

On page 194 (lines 2 and 3): for 'almost defiles one' read 'almost compels one to do so.'

On page 204 (line 8 from foot of page): for 'and beautiful' read 'and above all beautiful.'

Thus, in the original translation of *Götzendämmerung* and *Der Antichrist*, which cover 233 pages, there are at most seventeen discrepancies, only a few of which are actually mistranslations, and, as the revision of this book for the purpose of this chapter of my autobiography constitutes the first attempt made to check the accuracy of the version, these two books provide a fair sample of the fidelity of my translations of Nietzsche. In the two volumes of *The Will to Power*, on the other hand, which I revised before the third issue of the work in 1924, and which cover 814 pages, I found only eight discrepancies — chiefly oversights that had occurred in the typescript or proof stage of the production.

The only serious error — the rendering of 'Arbeiter' by 'noblemen'[1] — is a complete mystery, for in the first edition of the English translation the word 'Arbeiter' stands correctly rendered as 'workmen,' and, as I can hardly be suspected of having myself, in the process of revision, substituted 'noblemen' for the correct word, I can only conclude that the error must have been that of the printers who were responsible for the third edition. As I never had page proofs of this edition before it went to press, this major discrepancy remained undetected.

---

[1] Volume II, p. 209.

Select Bibiliography

Non-Fiction Books

Who is to be Master of the World? An Introduction to the Philosophy of Friedrich Nietzsche. Edinburgh: T. N. Foulis, 1909.

Nietzsche: His Life and Works (Philosophies Ancient and Modern). London: Constable, 1910; New York: Dodge, 1910.

Nietzsche and Art. London: Constable, 1911; Boston: J. W. Luce, 1912; New York: Haskell House, 1971.

A Defence of Aristocracy: A Text-Book for Tories. London: Constable, 1915; second edition, 1933; Boston: Phillips, 1915.

Man's Descent from the Gods: Or, The Complete Case Against Prohibition. London: William Heinemann, 1921; New York: A. A. Knopf, 1921.

The False Assumptions of 'Democracy'. London: Heath Cranton, 1921.

Woman: A Vindication. London: Constable, 1923; second edition 1929; New York: A. A. Knopf, 1923.

Lysistrata: Or, Woman's Future and Future Woman (To-day and To-morrow). London: Kegan Paul, Trench, Trubner, 1924; second edition, 1927; New York: E. P. Dutton, 1925.

Personal Reminiscences of Auguste Rodin. London: John Murray, 1926; Philadelphia: J. B. Lippincott, 1926.

A Defence of Conservatism: A Further Text-Book for Tories. London: Faber and Gwyer, 1927.

Man: An Indictment. London: Constable, 1927; New York: E. P. Dutton, 1927.

The Night-Hoers: Or, The Case Against Birth Control and an Alternative. London: Herbert Jenkins, 1928.

The Sanctity of Private Property. London: Heath Cranton, 1932.

The Secret of Laughter. London: Constable, 1932; New York: Viking Press, 1933; Folcroft: Folcroft Library Editions, 1974.

Violence, Sacrifice and War. London: The St. James's Kin of the English Mistery, 1933.

Health and Education through Self-Mastery. London: Watts, 1933.

Creation or Recreation. London: The First or St. James's Kin of the English Mistery, 1934.

The Choice of a Mate (The International Library of Sexology and Psychology). London: John Lane, The Bodley Head, 1935.

Abortion (with F. W. Stella Browne and Harry Roberts). London: Allen and Unwin, 1935.

Recovery: The Quest of Regenerate National Values. London: St. James's Kin, 1935.

The Truth about Childbirth: Lay Light on Maternal Morbidity and Mortality. London: Kegan Paul, Trench, Trubner, 1937; New York: E. P. Dutton, 1938.

English Liberalism (A 'New Pioneer' Pamphlet). London: The English Array, 1939.

The Four Pillars of Health: A Contribution to Post-War Planning. London: Heath Cranton, 1945.

Enemies of Women: The Origins in Outline of Anglo-Saxon Feminism. London: Carroll and Nicholson, 1948.

The Child: An Adult's Problem; First Aid to Parents. London: Carroll and Nicholson, 1948.

The Quest of Human Quality: How to Rear Leaders. London: Rider, 1952.

Religion for Infidels. London: Holborn, 1961.

The Specious Origins of Liberalism: The Genesis of a Delusion. London: Britons, 1967.

The Lost Philosopher: The Best of Anthony M. Ludovici. Ed. John V. Day.

Berkeley, California: Educational Translation and Scholarship Foundation, 2003.

Novels

Mansel Fellowes. London: Grant Richards, 1918.

Catherine Doyle: The Romance of a Thrice-Married Lady. London: Hutchinson, 1919.

Too Old for Dolls. London: Hutchinson, 1920; New York: G. P. Putnam's Sons, 1921.

What Woman Wishes. London: Hutchinson, 1921.

The Goddess that Grew Up. London: Hutchinson, 1922.

French Beans. London: Hutchinson, 1923.

The Taming of Don Juan. London: Hutchinson, 1924.

Poet's Trumpeter (written under the pen-name of David Valentine). London: J. Cape, 1939.

Short Stories

What the east wind brought. In *Thrills, Crimes and Mysteries: A Specially Selected Collection of Sixty-Three Complete Stories by Well-Known Writers*, with a foreword by John Gawsworth. London: Associated Newspapers, 1935, pp. 274–93.

A modern Delilah. In *Thrills: Twenty Specially Selected New Stories of Crime, Mystery and Horror*. London: Associated Newspapers, no date [circa 1936], pp. 133–45.

Essays & Reviews

Notes on 'Thus Spake Zarathustra'. In *Thus Spake Zarathustra: A Book for All and None* (The Complete Works of Friedrich Nietzsche, 11), by Friedrich Nietzsche, translated by Thomas Common. Edinburgh: T. N. Foulis, 1909; New York: Macmillan, 1911, pp. 405–58.

Introductory essay on Van Gogh and his art. In *The Letters of a Post-Impressionist: Being the Familiar Correspondence of Vincent Van Gogh*, translated by Anthony M. Ludovici. London: Constable, 1912; Boston: Houghton Mifflin, 1913, pp. v–xlvii.

The British war-horse on the Somme. *The Nineteenth Century and After* 89, 1921, pp. 727–39.

The return of the veteran. *The Nineteenth Century and After* 91, 1922, pp. 349–64.

The Conservative programme—a suggestion. *The Fortnightly Review* 111 (new series), 1922, pp. 948–62.

The Conservative programme: a further suggestion. *The Fortnightly Review* 113 (new series), 1923, pp. 600–14.

The fad of feminism. In *Fads and Fallacies*, by Joshua Brookes, with Anthony Ludovici and Ellis Barker. London: Brentano's, 1929, pp. 227–37.

Eugenics and consanguineous marriages. *The Eugenics Review* 25, 1933–34, pp. 147–55.

The importance to women of a youthful marriage. *Marriage Hygiene* 1 (1st series), 1934–35, pp. 393–407.

Efficiency and liberty—Great Britain. *The Listener* 19, 1938, pp. 497–8, 530–1 (in discussion with E. M. Forster, chaired by Wilson Harris).

What do we mean by 'class'? *The Listener* 20, 1938, pp. 765–6 (in discussion with G. A. Isaacs and Tom Harrisson, chaired by T. H. Marshall).

Welcome light on Proust. *The New English Weekly* 18, 1940–41, pp. 195–6.

Army officers and saluting. *The New English Weekly* 18, 1940–41, pp. 241–2.

A new interpretation of Jesus. *The New English Weekly* 19, 1941, pp. 177–8.

A Newton of health. *The New English Weekly* 26, 1944-45, pp. 104-5, 94-5 [sic].

Rilke's Rodin. *London Forum* 1.1, 1946, pp. 41-50.

Dr. Oscar Levy. *The New English Weekly* 30, 1946-47, pp. 49-50.

Rodin as I knew him. *The Listener* 37, 1947, pp. 97-8, 113.

The martyrdom of man in sex. *Marriage Hygiene* 1 (2nd series), 1947-48, pp. 21-7.

Nietzsche once again. *The New English Weekly* 33, 1948, pp. 45-6.

Sex in the writings of Bernard Shaw. *The International Journal of Sexology* 2, 1948-49, pp. 93-102 (with a reply by Bernard Shaw).

Sexual jealousy and civilization. *The International Journal of Sexology* 3, 1949-50, pp. 76-84, 154-62 (with summaries in French and German).

George Bernard Shaw: 1856-1950. *The International Journal of Sexology* 4, 1950-51, pp. 163-6.

Sex education and its advocates. *The International Journal of Sexology* 4, 1950-51, pp. 202-6.

Homosexuality, the law and public sentiment. *The International Journal of Sexology* 5, 1951-52, pp. 143-8.

Woman as the 'second sex'. *The International Journal of Sexology* 6, 1952-53, pp. 172-7.

The alimony racket. *The International Journal of Sexology* 6, 1952-53, pp. 236-9.

Divorce and the psycho-physical disparity of spouses. *The International Journal of Sexology* 7, 1953-54, pp. 1-11.

Sexual behaviour in the human female: a critical study. *The International Journal of Sexology* 7, 1953-54, pp. 150-8.

Criminal assaults on young women in England and Wales. *The*

International Journal of Sexology 8, 1954–55, pp. 83–8.

Woman: man's equal. *The International Journal of Sexology* 8, 1954–55, pp. 230–3.

Work in Western civilisation. *The Hibbert Journal* 55, 1956–57, pp. 30–4.

Confusion in the arts. *The Contemporary Review* 192, 1957, pp. 106–10.

Poems

The heart of an Englishman. *The New Age* 10, 1911–12, p. 253.

The heart of an English maid. *The New Age* 10, 1911–12, p. 421.

The South Downs. *The Saturday Review*, 27 January 1917.

Reflections of my patron saint. *The New Age* 23, 1918, p. 48.

The English flapper. *The New Age* 26, 1919–20, p. 84.

Visitors by night. *The New Age* 25, 1919, p. 432.

An artist's farewell to his mistress. *The New Age* 29, 1921, p. 144.

Ce que femme veut Dieu le veut. *The New Age* 29, 1921, p. 204.

A post-war maiden. *The Northern Review* 1, 1924, p. 170.

Creeping back to the cross. *The New English Weekly* 2, 1932–33, p. 90.

My testament. *The New English Weekly* 5, 1934, p. 323.

To the hedonists of intellect. *The New English Weekly* 6, 1934–35, p. 221.

Illustrations

Nothing But Nonsense, by Mary Kernahan, illustrated by Tony Ludovici. London: James Bowden, 1898.

The Duke of Berwick: A Nonsense Rhyme, by The Belgian Hare [Lord Alfred Douglas], illustrated by Tony Ludovici. London: Leonard Smithers, 1899.

Ludovici on the Internet

http://www.anthonymludovici.com

Works about Anthony M. Ludovici

British subscriber. 'Anthony Ludovici — conservative from another world.' *Instauration* 14.11, 1989, pp. 6-9.

Day, John V. 'What is best will rule: Anthony Ludovici on aristocracy and democracy,' *The Occidental Quarterly* 3.4, 2003, pp. 55-68.

_____. 'Writers of the Right: Anthony M Ludovici, 1882-1971.' *Right Now!* 45, 2004, pp. 14-16.

Gayre of Gayre, R. 'The late A. M. Ludovici's bequest to the University of Edinburgh.' *The Mankind Quarterly* 8, 1972-73, pp. 191-4.

Kerr, R. B. 'Anthony M. Ludovici: the prophet of anti-feminism.' In *Our Prophets*. Croydon: R. B. Kerr, 1932, pp. 84-99.

Knödgen, Marita. 'Anthony Mario Ludovici: die Verteidigung der Aristokratie.' In *Die frühe politische Nietzsche-Rezeption in Großbritannien, 1895-1914: Eine Studie zur deutsch-britischen Kulturgeschichte*. Dissertation, Fachbereich III, Universität Trier, 1997, pp. 60-7.

Simpson, William Gayley. 'One man's striving [excerpts].' *National Vanguard* 101, 1984, pp. 11-17.

Stone, Dan. 'Anthony Mario Ludovici: a "light-weight superman".' In *Breeding Superman: Nietzsche, Race and Eugenics in Edwardian and Interwar Britain* (Studies in Social and Political Thought). Liverpool: Liverpool University Press, 2002, pp. 33-61.

_____. 'The extremes of Englishness: the "exceptional" ideology of Anthony Mario Ludovici.' *Journal of Political Ideologies* 4, 1999, pp. 191-218.

INDEX

A
Adam, Paul, 254
Adler, Alfred, 12, 195, 209, 250, 274
Adventures of a Bookseller, The, 112 n15
African Genesis, 308
After All, 193 n8
Alexander, F. M., 108–9, 162, 209–10, 260–61
Alexander the Great, 141
Alexander technique, 209–10, 260–61
Alexandra, Queen, 4
Alice's Adventures in Wonderland, 6–9, 196
Allingham, William, 68
Amery, L. S., 146
Ami des femmes, L', 288 n99, 297
Amour et mariage, 167 n12
Angel, Norman, 193
Aphorisms (F. H. Bradley), 159 n2
Ardrey, Robert, 308
Argument of Laughter, 273 n86, 275
Aristophanes, 69
Aristotle, 252–53, 295, 320
Arlésienne, L', 123
Art of Living, The, 145 n11, 292 n112
Asquith, Herbert, 239
Athens, ancient, 295
Athens, modern, 91–94
'Aus hohen Bergen,' 228
Aus meinem Leben, 79
Autobiography (by John Cowper Powys), 146, 271
Autobiography of an Engineer, The, 221 n31, 245 n39
Avowals, 235 n21, 271 n82
Aymé, Marcel, 289
Ayrton, Major, 115–16

B
Back to Methuselah, 225
Backhouse, Colonel, 148–49
Baker, Mr, 114
Ballard, Dr P. R., 233
Balzac, Honoré de, 43, 74, 225, 296–97
Baudelaire, Charles, 68 n6, 297
Bauer, Dr Bernard A., 291
Beauplan, Amédée de, 231
Bedford, Duchess of, 307
Beerbohm, Max, 271
Beethoven, Ludwig van, 231
'Belgian Hare, The,' 26 n32, 332
Bell, Clive, 226 n8
Belle image, La, 289 n103
Belloc-Lowndes, Mrs, 163, 268, 272
Benda, Julien, 200
Benson, Archbishop, 146
Bergson, Henri, 269
Bernard of Cluny, 92
Berrill, Roland, 158–60
Besant, Walter, 227
Beveridge, Lord, 246
Beyond Good and Evil, 182, 199, 295 n113; see also *Jenseits von Gut und Böse*
Beyond the Pleasure Principle, 42 n1
Bibby, Cyril, 319
Biographical Dictionary, 2
Birley, Robert, 143
Birrell, Agnes, 162
Bismarck, Otto von, 140
Bizet, Georges, 123
Blackmore, R. D., 50, 77
Blanche, J. E., 235
Blease, Lyon, 293
Blomberg, Werner von, 137
Body, Colonel O. G., 307
Boswell, James, 160 n5
Bottomley, Horatio, 271
Bouillet, Marie-Nicolas, 2
Bourdelle, Antoine, 82
Bourget, Paul, 255

Boutet de Monvel, Louis Maurice, 43
Bowlby, Mr, 114
Bradley, F. H., 159
Bradshaw, John, 316 n3
Brassey, Peter, 142
Bright, John, 207
Bristol, Dean of, 16
Brontë, Charlotte, 68
Brontë, Emily, 65–66, 73–74, 77, 311
Brontës, the, 50
Brown, Ivor, 218
Browning, Robert, 251
Brunswick, Duchess of, 138
Bryce, Dr James, 46, 114
Buckle, Henry Thomas, 150
Buckley, Elsie F. (AML's wife), appearance of, 163; cerebral sclerosis of, 173; death of, 163, 173; does not want children, 166, 170–71; engaged to AML, 119; enters a nursing home permanently, 171–72; an exceptional French scholar, 163; family of, 163; introduced to AML by Dr Oscar Levy, 163, 192; invigorated by AML's mineral supplement, 265–66; knows classical and European literature, 163; loathes domestic chores, 155; loyalty and devotion of, 164–66; marries AML, 171; personality of, 163–64, 165; political and social outlook of, 163–64; portrayed in a novel by AML, 263; secretary of the Loeb Classical Library, 259; works with AML on their smallholding, 154–56
Buckley, Henry (later Lord Wrenbury), 163
Bulman, Rev. W., 302
Bunyan, John, 65
Burney, Fanny, 50, 60
Burns, John, 150
Burton, Jack H., friendship with AML of, 135 n4, 222
Butler, R. A., 303
Byles, C. E., 193 n7
Byron, Lord, 50, 259

C

Caesar, 140, 141
Cain, 68
Challen, Charles, friendship with AML of, 135 n4
Cals, Antoine Mario (AML's maternal grandfather), 2, 4–5
Cambis, Madame de, 18
Campe, J., 45
Camus, Albert, 228
Captains Courageous, 66, 225
Carlyle, Thomas, 207
Carpentier, Georges, 60
Carroll, Lewis, 6–9, 196
Catlin, George, 257
Causeries de lundi, 81 n27
Cecil, Lady G., 146
Chamberlain, Joseph, 19
Charles V, Emperor, 11
Charreau, Fernande, 117–22, 124–26
Charreau, Madame, 124–26
Chasma, 63, 182
Chaucer, Geoffrey, 65, 80
Chavasse, Dr C. M., Bishop of Rochester, 16
Chesterfield, Lord, 316, 318
Chesterton, G. K., 202–5
Chopin, Frédéric, 231
Christina of Sweden, 11
Cinna, 5
Civitas Humana, 245 n38
Clarke, Sir Fred, 244
'Cobbett,' ix, 256
Cockton, Henry, 172, 227
Cohen, J. T., 233 n18
Coleridge, Samuel Taylor, 50
Collier, K. G., 304
Commissioners of Prisons, 303
Common, Thomas, 89–90, 329
Comte de Monte Cristo, Le, 29
Conan Doyle, Arthur, 87

Confessions, Les (by Jean-Jacques Rousseau), 51, 215 n23, 219, 271
Confessions of a Young Man, 51, 167 n14, 226 n7
Confucius, 141
'Consolation à M. du Périer,' 34
Constable, the publisher, 90
Contemporary Review, The, 99
Cook, Alice (AML's housekeeper), appearance of, 173, 175; cares for AML's wife, 171; death of, 175 n19; devoted to AML, 173, 175; family of, 173, 175; first works for AML, 173; personality of, 173, 175; portrayed in two novels by AML, 263, 267; works on AML's smallholding, 155–56
Coomaraswamy, Dr Ananda, 100, 233
Cooper, Colonel, 116
Corin, James, 75, 305–6
Corneille, Pierre, 5, 43
Cosways, the, 101
Côté de Guermantes, Le, 160 n3
Cowper, William, 50,
Creasey, Ron, iv
Crowley, Aleister, 167

D

Dagens Nyheter, 17
Daily Mail, The, 139, 275
Dame aux camélias, La, 21
Dames de croix-mort, Les, 78
Daniell, Elizabeth Scott, 307
Darwin, Charles, 77, 191
Daudet, Alphonse, 43
David, Dr, 52–57
Days before Yesterday, The, 145
de Gaulle, Charles, 141
de Neuville, Alphonse, 226
de Quincey, Thomas, 127, 128, 130
'Dead, The,' 74 n13
Deffand, Madame du, 289
Degas, Edgar, 226
Delafield, E. M., 132
Deutschland über Alles, 138

Dewey, John, 8
Diana of the Crossways, 51
Diaries and Letters (by Friedrich Hebbel), 1
Diary of Tolstoy's Wife, The, 289 n104
Dickens, Charles, 50, 65, 77, 172, 227
Difficult Child and the Problem of Discipline, The, 303 n129
Disraeli, Benjamin, 249
Do What You Will, 68 n6
Dostoyevsky, Fyodor, 68, 192, 228
Douglas, C. H., 104
Douglas, Lord Alfred, 26, 26 n1
Douglas, Norman, 111
Drew, Dr Dorothy, 162
Drew, Guy, 162
Drew, Jane, 162
Dryden, John, 80
Du rôle de la femme dans la vie des heros, 162 n8
Dufresne, Mrs, 82–83, 85, 192, 214, 262
Duke of Berwick: A Nonsense Rhyme, The, 26 n32
Dumas *fils*, Alexandre, 287, 296, 297
Dumas *père*, Alexandre, 29, 43
Dynamic Defence, 148 n28

E

Eastman, Max, 275
Educating for Democracy, 233 n18
Edward I, King, 141
Edward VII, King, 4, 18, 19
Egypt, 94, 96, 195
Eisenhower, Dwight D., 18
Eliot, George, 50
Eliot, T. S., 51
Ellis, Havelock, 291
Ellis, S. M., 146
Émile, 128 n25, 239 n31
English Array, 256
English Mistery, 100, 101, 103, 133, 135, 148, 154, 178–79, 213, 219, 256, 328

Englischer Klubb, 136
English Review, 40, 142, 198, 198 n9, 199
Enoch Arden, 6
Epstein, Jacob, 109–11, 250
Essai sur l'éducation de la femme, 296
Essais (by Michel de Montaigne), 12 n14, 12 n15, 17 n26, 46 n9, 59 n19, 224, 224 n1, 316 n2, 316 n4
Essais de moral et de critique, 17 n26
Étape, L', 225
Evalina, 60
Evans, Major J., friendship with AML of, 321
Evelyn-White, Hugh G., 260
Evening Standard, The, 275
Evolution of England, The, 255 n61
Excursion, The, 225
Exploring English Character, 273 n87
Extra-Special Correspondent, 139 n7

F
Fabian Society, 104
Faerie Queene, The, 80
Family and the Nation, The, 249 n50
Farewell to European History, 245 n37
Faust, 5, 79
Fet, Afanasy Afanasevich, 228
Fielding, Henry, 50, 65
Fifty Years a Veterinary Surgeon, 29 n33
Foden, Frank, 203 n17
Fontenelle, Bernard le Bovier, 101, 133, 319
Förster, Bernhard, 228
Foulis, the publisher, 90
France, Anatole, 288, 146 n1, 272 n1
Französische Zustände, 314 n1
Frederick the Great, 141
Frederika, Princess of Hanover (later Queen of Greece), 138
Freedom in the Educative Society, 244 n36
Freud, Sigmund, admired by Dr G. T. Wrench, 195; finds children ruled by the pleasure principle, 293; a great psychologist, 249; identifies the death wish or death instinct, 41–42; often anticipated by Schopenhauer, 77; rejected by Dr Oscar Levy, 195; on the relationship of adolescent males with their mothers, 42, 288; some failings of, 16 n18
Fuller, Dr Thomas, 193
Funk, Walther, 137
Fyers, Captain (later Major) Fitzroy, 138; friendship with AML of, 135 n4, 138, 222

G
Gaitskell, Hugh, 18
Garnett, David, 307 n2
Gayre of Gayre, R., iv n3
Gazetteer of India, The, 116, 222
Gedanken und Einfälle, 289 n1
Genealogie der Moral, 199 n12; see also *The Genealogy of Morals*
Genealogy of Morals, The, 199, 324; see also *Genealogie der Moral*
Genlis, Madame de, 18, 19
Gent, Ellen
George V, King, 19
George, David Lloyd, 112, 149, 274
Geständnisse (by Heinrich Heine), 297 n111
Gillet, Louis, x
Gladstone, William Ewart, 19, 207
Godber, Dr C. E., 278
Goebbels, Joseph, 137
Goering, Hermann, 137
Goethe, Johann Wolfgang von, 5, 11, 51, 64, 58, 79, 80, 100, 225
Gore, Bishop, 207
Gorer, Geoffrey, 273
Gosse, Edmund, 271
Grandi, Dino, 135
Great Swindlers, The, 17
Greene, Graham, 166 n10
Grenier, Antoine Sebastian (AML's great-grandfather), 3
Grenier, Madame Louis (AML's great-great-grandmother), 3

Grenier, Marie Caroline (AML's paternal grandmother), 2, 3, 4
Griffin, Nick, iv, v
Guild, Cyril A., friendship with AML of, 222
Gurdjieff, George, 105-7
Gyp (Comtesse de Martel de Janville), 43

H
Haeckel, Ernst, 77
Haldane, J. B. S., 310
Hamilton, Lord Frederick, 145-46
Hamilton, Sir Ian, 146
Hardy, Thomas, 50, 77
Hatry, Clarence, 36, 36 n41
Hawker, Rev. R. S., 193
Haym, A. W., 78
Hazlitt, William, 51, 183, 184
Health and the Citizen, 301 n126, 305 n135
Hebbel, Friedrich, vii, viii
Hegel, Georg Wilhelm Friedrich, 100
Heilborn, Dr A., 291
Heine, Dr, 64-65
Heine, Heinrich, admired by AML's schoolteacher, 64; an anti-feminist, 296; influenced Nietzsche, 192, 228, 295; one of the great sages, 249; pinpoints the greatest evil as sickness, 45-46, 59; predicts a bleak future for mankind, 167 n13, 171, 314; thinks that true love comes in later life, 289 n1; told by Balzac that women are dangerous, 297
Henri Quatre (King Henry IV of France), 128
Henry V, 65
Henry VI, 65
Hermann und Dorothea, 51, 225
Hesiod, 259, 260
Hess, Rudolf, 137
Himmler, Heinrich, 137, 138
History of Civilization in England, 150
History of the Liberal Party, A, 254 n55
History of the Political Philosophers, A, 257 n63
Hitler, Adolf, 85, 133, 137, 198; appeal to Germany of, 142-44; character of, 140-42
Hobday, Sir Frederick, 23-25, 28, 29 n33, 183
Holderness, Colonel H., friendship with AML of, 222
Hone, Joseph, 235 n20
Hopkins, Frank, 25
Horneffer, Ernst, 84
Housewife, The, 301
Hugo, Victor, 4, 21, 43, 45, 61
Hull, Englefield, 232
Hulme, T. E., 110-11, 110 n13
Humboldt, Alexander von, 167, 171
Hunter, Captain (later Colonel) W. C., 116, 120, 121; friendship with AML of, 221-22, 321
Hunter, Sir William, 116, 222
Hunts, the, 101
Huxley, Aldous, 68, 77, 275
Huxley, T. H., 207
Hygiene Committee of the Woman's Group in Public Welfare, The, 16 n22
Hymns Ancient and Modern, 92
Hyrst, H. W. G., 63 n1
Hytten, Dr F. E., 309-10

I
I Know These Dictators, 139 n7
Impressionists, French, 231
In Search of Truth, 144 n10
Influence of the Jews on the Progress of the World, The, 253 n54
Inge, Dean, 270
Inquiry into the Nature of the Peace, An, 14
Internal Secretions of the Sex Glands, The, 292 n3
International Journal of Sexology, 284

n98, 288
'Intimations of Immortality,' 79, 225
Introductio ad prudentiam, 193
Irvine, H. E. S. Bryant, 178–79
Irving, Henry, 19
It's Never Too Late to Mend, 78

J
James Shoolbred's, 39
James, Anne Scott, 278
James, Henry, 51, 225
Jenseits des Lustprinzips, 42
Jenseits von Gut und Böse, 199 n12; see also *Beyond Good and Evil*
Jeremy at Crale, 270 n77
Jerusalem, 91, 93–94, 96, 220
Jesus, 270, 275
Joad, Professor C. M., 229
John Casimir, King of Poland, 11
John O'London's Weekly, 275
Johnson, Dr Samuel, 50, 119, 149, 160, 160 n5, 204
Jones, Abel J., 144
Jones, K.W., 146
Journal of Hellenic Studies, The, 258
Joyce, James, 74 n13

K
Kant, Immanuel, 64, 237, 269; aesthetic doctrines of, 235–37, 237 n29
Kennard, Lieutenant W., 125
Kennedy, A. L., 146
Kerr, Madeline, 303
Keyserling, Count, 270 n79
Kidd, Benjamin, 293
Kimmins, Professor Charles W., 269
Kingsley, Charles, 269
Kinsey, Dr Alfred, 280
Kinsey Reports, 286
Kipling, Rudyard, 19, 50, 117, 146, 225, 321
Knortz, Professor Karl, 199
Kock, Paul de, 43
Kölnische Zeitung, 83

Kottmann, Dr Marguerite, 162
Kritik der Urteilskraft, 235–37

L
La Rochefoucauld, Duc de, 145, 160
La Fontaine, Jean de, 43
Lamotte, Louis, 25
Lang, Andrew, 65
Lang, Matheson, 60
Langley, Mr, 174 n18
Lansdowne, Lord, 150
Lawrence, D. H., 74 n13,
Lawrence, Mrs Pethwick, 163
Lees, Captain A. T. O., friendship with AML of, 220–22
Légende des siècles, La, 45 n6
Leno, Dan, 205
Leonardo da Vinci, 52
Lessing, Gotthold Ephraim, 64
Let There be Sculpture, 111
Letters of Philip Dormer Stanhope, Earl of Chesterfield, The, 316 n3
Levy, Dr Oscar, admires Mussolini, 196; appearance of, 194, 201, 202; bored by his work as a doctor, 88, 194; death of, 201; denies his Nietzscheanism stems from inferiority feelings, 209; eloquence of, 194, 250; enjoys his portrayal in a novel by AML, 214, 250; first meets AML, 87; friendship with AML of, 90, 197, 321; generosity of, 90, 91, 195; gives AML works by Nietzsche to translate, 87, 88; his low opinion of Meredith, 225–26; holidays with AML, 91, 92–97; introduces AML to his future wife, 163, 192; likes AML's translations of Nietzsche, 88, 90; married to a Gentile, 212; personality of, 87, 88, 89, 194, 195, 201; quarrel with AML, 197–98, 200, 201; realism of, 195; rejects Freud, 195; suggests AML take a mar-

ried woman for a lover, 208
Lewis, Robert T., 303
Liddell Hart, Captain Basil, 129, 130, 147
Life and Letters (by Rev. R. S. Hawker), 193 n7
Life of George Moore, The, 235 n20
Life of Percy Bysshe Shelley, The (by T. Medwin), 145-46
Life of Robert Marquis of Salisbury, 146
Life of Reason, The, 239 n33
Life of Samuel Johnson, The, 160 n5
Lost Splendour, 161 n7
Lothian, Lord, 144
Lowder, Hugh, friendship with AML of, 222
Low, Sir Sidney, 149
Lucas, F. L., 8, 51, 145, 292
Ludovici, origins of surname, 2-3
Ludovici, Albert (AML's father), ancestry of, 2-3; appearance of, 10, 11, 11 n12; artistic gifts, 9, 30; death of, 11; his portraiture indifferent, 9; never wholly respected or loved by AML, 51; personality of, 30; siblings of, 3
Ludovici, Albert *or* Bert (AML's brother), 3, 12, 13, 14
Ludovici, Albert Johann (AML's paternal grandfather), 1, 3, 4, 9, 64

LUDOVICI, ANTHONY MARIO

CHARACTERISTICS
ancestry of, 1-2, 15, 30
androgynous characteristics of, 11 n13
anti-Semitism of, 153, 200-1, 214, 249, 253, 256
appearance of, 11, 11 n13, 12
artistic talents of, 5, 20, 49, 51, 226
belief in prayer of, 131, 311
has no regrets about the course of his life, 132, 154, 313, 316, 319
has no regrets about giving up
graphic arts, 227, 318-19
horoscope of, 176
inferiority feelings of, 12, 159, 209
loneliness of since his mother died, 113
love for his mother of, 39, 40, 41-42, 42 n2, 43, 45, 47-48, 58, 60, 61-62, 158
misunderstood and misrepresented consistently, vii-viii, 111, 268, 269, 310
needed a father-substitute, 186
no desire of to have children, 166-67, 316
Oedipal complex of, 11 n12
poorly equipped for friendship, 61, 158, 159, 176, 179, 196-97, 211, 213, 219, 319
pseudonyms of, ix, 63, 256, 267
relationships with women, viii n1, 159, 161-62
sensitivity of, 11
sincerity of, ix
suicidal thoughts of, 40, 42
works about AML, 333

LIFE OF
birth, 12
enjoys works of Lewis Carroll, 6-9
dislikes sweetmeats, 12 n13
very close to his sister Lily, 13, 33, 45, 158, 161
Lily suffers from consumption and dies, 23, 25, 26, 28
an omen apparently portends Lily's death, 27-28
illustrates Lord Alfred Douglas's *The Duke of Berwick*, 26, 26 n32
sister Dolly dies after swallowing a toy, 31-34
religious upbringing, 44, 63-64
teaches schoolchildren French, 49
studies English classics, 50, 180
tends his mother in Paris during an illness, 53, 55-57
mother's ill health attenuates his compassion, 58-59

first lectures on Nietzsche, 60, 90
mother dies, 60–1
attends local school, 49, 63
studies German, 78
reads and greatly impressed by *Wuthering Heights*, 66–75, 225
reads widely in science, philosophy and psychology, 77
influenced especially by Schopenhauer, 77, 78, 79
reads Schiller, Goethe and English classics, 77, 79
works in London as engraver, 184, 186
works as Rodin's private secretary, 81–82
spends a year in Germany studying German and philosophy, 83–85, 192
studies Nietzsche, 84, 85, 86, 191–92
a palm-reading apparently forecasts his interest in Nietzsche, 82–83, 85
translates several of Nietzsche's works, 87–90
introduced to his future wife, 192
goes on a grand tour with Dr Oscar Levy of southern Europe and the Near East, 91–97, 195
visits Jerusalem, 91–96
visits Athens, 91–94
visits Egypt, 94–96
visits a Turkish brothel, 94–95
the miracle of toilet paper in the desert, 95–96
depressed by eye disease in Syria and Egypt, 96
works as an art critic for *The New Age*, 90, 98, 100, 104
listens to Gurdjieff and Ouspensky, 105–6
public argument with Jacob Epstein, 109–11
talks with G. K. Chesterton, 202, 203, 204, 205
enrols in the British army in World War I, 114
takes French and German examinations as an interpreter, 114
serves with the Interpreter Corps, 115–17
observes thefts from dead soldiers, 117
relationship with a French girl, 118–22, 124, 126
fights at the Somme, 125, 128–29
diagnosed with trench fever, 131
serves in intelligence, 131
awarded the MBE but soon returns the award, 132
demobilised from the army, 132
marries Elsie F. Buckley, 133
subsequent literary career, 132–33
trained in the Alexander technique, 108, 109, 162, 209, 210, 260–1
membership of the English Mistery, 100–3, 133, 135, 148, 152–54, 178–79, 213, 219
membership of the English Array, 256
talks with the Italian ambassador in London, 101
tours National Socialist Germany, 118–23 133, 135–37, 138, 139
talks with Ribbentrop and Goebbels, 120
meets Adolf Hitler, 133, 138–41
membership of the Right Club, 148, 149, 150
works briefly in intelligence during World War II, 131–32, 148
investigated by the police in 1940 for 'Anti-Allied' opinions, 148–49, 150–54
leaves London to work as a smallholder, 133, 154–57
creates a mineral supplement, 266
learns to drive at the age of 71, 171
wife Elsie enters a nursing home permanently, 171

Index 343

Elsie dies, 173
stock market deals, 251
works generally ignored, vii-ix, 258, 268-69
works about him, 333
bequest for Edinburgh University to study miscegenation, iv
books to be published posthumously, iii-iv

OPINIONS
abstract art, originated in false doctrines of Whistler and Kant, 50, 100, 229-37
aristocracy, the case for, 101, 152, 215-16, 247
artists, often cannot express ideas properly in the medium, 226, 227, 318-19; should be placed in a hierarchy, 110; role of, 99, 100
body and mind, should not be regarded as independent, 140, 256, 258, 290, 292, 295
bullying, widespread in England, 145-46
cars, dislike of, 171, 314, 315
childbirth, should be started at a young age, 279-80, 309-10
children, currently venerated, 79, 275-76; poorly disciplined, 134, 276, 300-4; sired out of conceit, 224; relationships with fathers often problematic, 224 n1, 316-18, 316 n5
Christianity, correctly describes man as bad, 207; not the best religion, 311-12; sexphobia of, 280
crime, rising in the West, 104, 170, 276, 277, 294, 298, 303-4, 307
democracy, objections to, 163, 238-39, 240
dishonesty, nowadays widespread, 8, 16-17
English people, usually individualists, 102-4, 134, 153; habitually denigrate others, 102, 147, 160, 177, 273; illogical and mentally lazy, 7, 8, 9, 67, 216, 239, 313; mistrust versatile people, 319; misunderstand women, 166, 292-93, 296, 320
eugenics, need for, 85, 247-49
feminism, attack on, 287, 295, 308; condemnation of is not being anti-feminine, 287-88, 311; fills the vacuum created by emasculated males, 264, 301-2, 308; in history, 294-97; leads to anarchy, 75, 298-99, 303-5, 307, 309; a middle-class movement, 284; resisted more in France, 296; succumbed to more in England, 217; triumphant since 1918, 268
friendship, utilitarian nature of, 160, 211-12; need for, 159, 160; usually lasts a short time, 176, 212
great literature, spontaneous character of, 225
Hitler, Adolf, character of, 139-41
horses, cruelty to in Victorian times, 169, 315
illegitimate births, increasing, 278
Jews, generosity of, 91, 195, 251; intelligence of, 250, 252, 256; promote individualism, 153; realism of, 195; their contributions to European civilisation, 249-50, 253-55; wield great political and social power, 252, 253-55
love between the sexes, nature of, 80, 288-89, 317
modern life, ruined by noise and constant change, 168, 170, 171, 299; ruined by overpopulation, 167-68, 170, 315
morality, always used as a weapon, 85, 86, 87
National Socialist Germany, fea-

tures of, 136–38, 143–44, 152; drew on Nietzschean doctrines, 197, 198, 199–201

Nietzsche, Friedrich, analysed morality, 85, 86, 87, 192; analysed modern nihilism, 228; an anti-feminist, 256; appeals to people who have inferiority feelings, 209; chiefly a reactive thinker, 198, 228; described by Camus as the greatest European writer, 228; his advocacy of the aristocratic values in art and politics, 228; his doctrine of being 'a hard bed to one's friend,' 208; his quintessential ideas published after 1882, 198–99, 200; indebted to Dostoyevsky and Stendhal,192, 228; indebted to Heine, 228, 295, 296; indebted to Schopenhauer, 77, 78, 228; limitations of, 192; much maligned in England, 85; not AML's favourite philosopher, 192; overrated friendship, according to Proust, 159–60, 160 n3; a recluse, 320; see also Friedrich Nietzsche in the main body of the index

physical courage, source of, 128–30

political parties, struggle for power in, 90

poor health, common nowadays, 1, 256–57, 258, 274; leads to a certain callousness in others, 45, 59–60

random breeding, disapproved of, 1, 12, 15, 16, 141, 212

Schadenfreude, not peculiar to Germans, 145–46

school-leaving age, too low, 21–22

sense of humour, overvalued, 17, 269–71, 273–75

sex education, faulted, 285–87

sexually transmitted diseases, increasing, 278

soldiers, often a superior type, 127–28, 179, 221–22, 264; tend to side with feminists, 320–21

women, anarchy of, 305–7, 308; cruelty of, 80; dominant in the home, 300–4, 308; immaturity of, 290–91; indifference to truth of, 17; lack of taste of, 297; loyalty of, 161–63; main orientation towards males and not children, 76

WORKS (NON-FICTION)
Child: An Adult's Problem, The, 268, 275, 286
Choice of a Mate, The, 42 n2, 81, 248
Confessions of an Anti-Feminist, The, to be published posthumously, iii–iv
Defence of Aristocracy, A, 101, 152, 197, 214, 215, 216, 247, 256, 263
Defence of Conservatism, A, 101, 247–48
English Countryside, The, to be published posthumously, iii–iv, 157, 157 n33
Enemies of Women, 310 n148
False Assumptions of 'Democracy,' The, 101, 247
Four Pillars of Health, The, ix, x n2, 1, 260, 261
(contributor to) *Gentile and Jew: A Symposium on the Future of the Jewish People*, ix, 153 n31, 254, 256
Health and Education through Self-Mastery, 260
Jews, and the Jews in England, ix, 256
'Juvenile Delinquency and Sex,' iv
Man: An Indictment, 75 n17, 247, 260
Man's Descent from the Gods, 258, 260
Nietzsche: His Life and Works, 198 n11
Night Hoers, The, 309
Personal Reminiscences of Auguste

Rodin, ix, 81, 268
Quest of Human Quality, The, iii, 1 n1, 216 n26, 238, 240, 243, 254
Religion for Infidels, 248, 258, 260, 309, 311
Sanctity of Private Property, The, 248
Secret of Laughter, The, 272, 273, 274
Truth about Childbirth, The, 260, 280
Truth about Marriage, The, an unpublished work, 317 n6
Violence, Sacrifice and War, 248
Who is to be Master of the World?, 182
Woman: A Vindication, 75, 297, 306

WORKS (NOVELS)
Catherine Doyle, 262-63
French Beans, 264-65
Goddess that Grew Up, The, 49, 264
Mansel Fellowes, 28, 88, 154, 202, 214, 250, 262
Poet's Trumpeter, 267-68
Taming of Don Juan, The, 35-36, 49, 125, 265
Too Old for Dolls, 214, 262
What Woman Wishes, 267

WORKS (TRANSLATIONS)
Antichrist, The (or *Der Antichrist*), 88, 324
Ecce Homo, 88, 88 n31
Eternal Recurrence, 86, 323
Letters of a Post-Impressionist, The, 98, 109
Notes to Zarathustra, 323
Selected Letters of Friedrich Nietzsche, 199 n12
Thoughts Out of Season (or *Unzeitgemässe Betrachtungen*), 88 n31
Twilight of the Idols, The (or *Götzendämmerung*), 88 n31, 323
Will to Power, The (or *Der Wille zur Macht*), 88 n31, 90, 324

WORKS (ILLUSTRATIONS)
Duke of Berwick: A Nonsense Rhyme, The, 26, 26 n1

WORKS (ONLINE)
his books on the Internet, 333
his will on the Internet, iii n1
details of Edinburgh University Library's Ludovici papers on the Internet, iv n3

Ludovici, Carl Guenther, 2 n3
Ludovici, Christianus Theophilus, 2 n3
Ludovici, Dorothy *or* Dolly (AML's sister), 29, 31-34
Ludovici, Edward (AML's brother), 29, 34-38, 52
Ludovici, Elsie F. (AML's wife); see Elsie F. Buckley
Ludovici, George (AML's brother), 3, 13, 29, 30-31, 39, 52; death of, 31 n34
Ludovici, Jacob Friedrich, 2 n3
Ludovici, Lily (AML's sister), appearance of, 13, 21; artistic and literary gifts of, 5, 20, 21, 52; consumption of, 23, 25, 26, 28; death of, 23, 25, 26-28; in love with Frederick Hobday, 22-25, 28-29; logical French mind of, 8; personality of, 20, 21, 40-41, 46, 47; very close to AML, 13, 20, 45, 158, 161, 322
Ludovici, Marie (AML's mother), ancestry of, 2; appearance of, 10, 11, 54; a born actress, 21; death of, 52, 60, 61; described by Dr G. T. Wrench, 61-62; dislikes Schopenhauer, 79; eloquence of, 5; excellent memory of, 5; illnesses of, 52-57; literary gifts of, 5, 49; loathes Germans, 65, 79; personality of, 21, 44, 48, 61; president of the women's section of the Société Nationale de Professeurs de Français en Angleterre, 47; recitations of, 5, 21, 43; repelled by James McNeill Whistler, 229; sees her daughter Dolly choke to death,

31–33; sings to her children, 5, 43; stays with AML in France when he is secretary to Rodin, 60, 82; teaches her children French, 21, 24, 63; tends her dying daughter Lily, 25–26, 28; very close to AML and her daughter Lily, 20, 39, 48, 60, 61–62, 159, 322
Lymington, Lord (later the 9th Earl of Portsmouth), 135, 152, 256

M
Macaulay, Lord, 48
MacAuliffe, Léon, 11
Mace, Dr David, 301–2
Machen, Mr, 186–89
Mackenzie, Mr, 131
Mackenzie, Compton, 275
Magnus, Laurie, 203
Magnus, Leonard, friendship with AML of, 202–3
Magnus, Sir Philip, 203 n17
Mairet, Philip, 201
Mahomet, 141
Male and Female, 76 n18
Malherbe, François de, 34
Malory, Thomas, 50, 80
Man and Society, 246 n40
Man and Woman, 292 n109
Manet, Edouard, 230
Mannheim, Professor Karl, 244, 246–47
Manon Lescaut, 225, 227
Mann, Detective, 153–54
Marlow, Louis, 157 n15
Marx, Karl, 104
Mastery of Life, The, 206, 296 n15
Mating, Marriage and the Status of Women, 75, 306
Matson, Major, 127
Maugham Enigma, The, 146
Maugham, Somerset, 68, 87
Maxims (by Duc de La Rochefoucauld), 145 n13
May, Edna, 10
Mead, Margaret, 76, 77

Medwin, T., 145
Méhaye, Marie (AML's maternal grandmother), 2
Meistersinger von Nürnberg, Die, 140
Mémoires (by Duc de St Simon), 60
Mémoires (by Cardinal de Retz), 103 n8
Memoirs (by Alexander von Humboldt), 167
Mercer, The Right Rev. J. E., Bishop of Tasmania, 270
Meredith, George, 50, 51, 77, 225
Mersey, Viscount, 146
Mew, Egan, 21
Mill, John Stuart, 291, 293
Millet, François, 164
Milner, Viscountess, 16
Milton, John, 65
Mist Procession, The, 182 n3
Molière (Jean Baptiste Poquelin), 43
Monde où l'on s'ennuie, Le, 47
Monro, Dr D. H., 272, 275
Montaigne, Michel de, dislikes sweetmeats, 12; believes health the most important thing, 46, 256; bored by his work as a doctor, 194; devoted to his father, 318; finds his illness hardening his nearest and dearest, 60; not studied by AML in youth, 65; prefers authorship to parenthood, 224–25; profound insight of, 46, 249; thinks children disloyal to their parents, 316; would live his life over again in exactly the same way, 315–16
Montesquieu, Charles Louis de, 151, 296
Moore, George, 51, 167, 226, 234, 235, 235 n1, 238, 271
Morale de l'amour, La, 254 n2
Morgan, Charles, 51
Morillon, Madame, 117–20, 122, 123

Morley, Lord, 150
Morning Post, The, 229
Morrison, Lord, 18
Mr Wu, 60
Mügge, Dr Maximilian, 198
Murry, John Middleton, 244
Music, Classical, Romantic and Modern, 232 n16
Mussolini, Benito, 135, 196
My Flesh and Blood, 300
My Picture Gallery, 17 n23
My Political Life (by L. S. Amery), 146

N
Napoleon Bonaparte, 113, 140, 141
Neale, Rev. J. M., 92
New Age, The, 98, 104, 105, 109, 110, 110 n12, 110 n13, 112
New Age circle, the, 90, 100, 103, 135, 179, 194
New English Weekly, The, 107, 109, 112, 201, 201 n15,
New Statesman, The, 275
Newman, Chaim, 153 n31, 256
Nicholas Nickleby, 172
Nicol, Sir William Robertson, 66
Nicolas, M. P., 198–200
Nicolson, Nigel, 240 n1
Nietzsche, Friedrich, discussed by AML and Goebbels, 137; discussed by AML and Hitler, 139; Ferdinand Schmidt first arouses AML's enthusiasm in, 84; lectured on by AML, 60, 87; read by AML's friend, Sidney H. Wright, 182; studied by AML, 84; translated by AML, 88–89, 198, 324; see also Anthony Mario Ludovici: Opinions: Friedrich Nietzsche
Nietzsche circle in England, the early, 100, 194, 195
Nietzsche à Hitler, De, 198
Nineteenth Century and After, The, 116, 116 n18, 126
Nippel, Alma, 190, 191

Nippel, Frau, 84, 190
Nippel, Hedwig, 191
Nursing Homes in England and Wales, 172

O
Offenbach, Jacques, 43
Ohnet, Georges, 78
Old Friends, 226 n8
Old School, The, 166, 166 n10
'On the Conduct of Life: Advice to a Schoolboy,' 183
'On the Feeling of Immortality in Youth,' 48 n10
Opposite Sexes, The, 291 n107
Orage, A. R., 90, 104–8, 110, 112
Orders of the Day, 270 n5
Origins of Wit and Humour, The, 275
Orioli, G., 112, 112 n15
Orthodoxy, 270 n76
Our Towns, 16
Ouspensky, P. D., 105–7

P
Page, Dr, 259–60
Pailleron, Edouard, 47
Palissier, Bernard, 165
Pantagruel, 296 n116
Parerga und Paralipomena, 78, 297
Pascal, Blaise, 161, 318
Patterns of Anti-Democratic Thought, 243 n35
Paysans, Les, 225
Peau de chagrin, La, 225
Penjon, Auguste, 8
Pensées (by Blaise Pascal), 161 n6
Pensées diverses (by Charles Louis de Montesquieu), 296 n117
People and Parliament, 240 n34
People of Ship Street, The, 304 n132
Perrault, Charles, 43
Perronet, Amélie, 21
'Petit doigt de maman, Le,' 44
Philip Magnus: Victorian Educational Pioneer, 203 n17
Phillpotts, Eden, 77
Philo, 251

Picture of Life, A, 146
Plaisirs et les jours, Les, 213 n21
Plantade, Charles Henri, 231
Plea for Liberty, A, 16 n19
Poems of E. B. Browning, 146
Politics (by Aristotle), 252 n53, 295 n114
Polner, Tikhon, 150 n29, 228 n11
Pope, Alexander, 50
Porson, Richard, 225
Posthumous Works (by Thomas de Quincey), 128 n24
Powys, John Cowper, 146, 271
Praeterita, 126 n23
Prévost, Abbé, 225
Price, Ward, 139
Priestley, J. B., 275
Pritt, D. N., 10
Proctor, Richard A., 77
Prometheus myth, 258, 259
Prometheus Unbound, 250
Proudhon, Pierre Joseph, 166
Proust, Marcel, 159, 213
Puck of Pook's Hill, 225

Q
Quinault, Mlle, 310 n150

R
Rabelais, François, 35, 65, 296
Racine, Jean, 43
Ramsay, Captain, 149
Rapp, Albert, 275
Reade, Charles, 50
Recollections of the Table-Talk of Samuel Rogers and Porsoniana 195 n2
Réflexions morales (by François de La Rochefoucauld), 160 n4
Réflexions et maximes (by Marquis de Vauvenargues), 316 n5
Regulation 18B, 149, 151, 219
Rémusat, Madame de, 296
Renan, Ernest, 17
Renouvier, Charles, 8
Republic (by Plato), 45 n7
Return to Philosophy, 220 n12

Retz, Cardinal de, 103
Revue des deux mondes, La, x
Rhonda, Lady, 163
Ribbentrop, Joachim von, 137
Right Club, 148, 149, 150
Rilke, Rainer Maria, 81
Rink, Max, 250, 251
Rink, Mrs Max, 162, 251
Rire, Le, 8 n7
Rise and Fall of the Third Reich, The, 143
Roberts, Dr Ffrangcon, 274
Robinson Crusoe, 6, 271
Robinson, E. Arnot, 166, 166 n10
Robinson, Kenneth, 146
Robinson, Mrs Rowan, 164
Rodin, Auguste, ix, x, 60, 81–82, 189,
Roman de deux jeunes mariées, Le, 74
Romanes, George, 77
Rome, 295
Romulus, 303 n131
Röpke, Professor Wilhelm, 244, 245, 248
Rosset, Charlotte, 54
Rosset, Germaine, 54
Rosset, Madame, 53, 55, 56
Rossetti, Dante Gabriel, 68
Rossiter, G., 254
Rothschilds, the, 253
Rousseau, Jean-Jacques, ascribes bravery to vanity, 128, 129, 130; claims that democracy works only for gods, 239; dislikes mixing with people from a different class, 215; his great *Confessions* a work without humour, 271; mistrusts ex-friends when talking about each other, 219; realises that everyone is motivated by self-interest, 239; spontaneity of his *Confessions*, 51
Ruskin, John, 127–28, 128 n23, 230, 235, 293
Russell, Bertrand, 17

Russell, Mrs Bertrand, 163

S
Saint-Beuve, Charles Augustin, 81
Salisbury (by A. L. Kennedy), 146
Salt and his Circle, 269 n75
Sanders, C. R., 146
Sanders, Lloyd C., 149
Sanderson, William, 135, 137, 138
Santayana, George, 239
Saturday Review, The, 275
Saxe-Coburg, Duke of, 138
Schebsmann, Annetta, 183
Schiller, Friedrich, 64, 65, 77, 79
Schirach, Baldur von, 137
Schmidt, Ferdinand, 84; friendship with AML of, 84, 189–91, 194, 321
Schmidt, Dr Otto, 84, 191
Schopenhauer, Arthur, an anti-feminist, 297–98; greatly influenced AML, 65, 77, 78, 79, 228; influenced Nietzsche, 78, 228; insight of, 77, 78, 228; often anticipates Freud, 77
Schopenhauer as Educator, 78 n28
Schültze, Dr Oskar, 292
Search for Good Sense, The, 8, 51 n14
Sesame Club, 100
Seven Friends, 167 n15
Sexuelle Not, Die, 75, 75 n16, 276 n93, 306
Shakespeare, William, 65, 80, 318
Shaw, George Bernard, 86, 104, 225, 227
Sheldon, William H., 140
Shelley, Percy Bysshe, 146, 258, 259
Shirer, William L., 143
Shorter, Clement, 66, 68
Shute, Nevil, 220, 245–46, 248
Sidgwick, Henry, 293
Siècle de Louis XIV, Le, 128
Simpson, William, 200; friendship with AML of, 222
Slesser, Sir Henry, 253
Smollett, Tobias, 50, 87
Social Contract, The, 239

Social Purposes of Education, The, 304 n133
Social Statics, 290 n106, 293
Socrates, 45, 67, 92, 257, 292
Something of Myself, 146
Sorrows of Young Werther, The, 79
Soufar, Dr K. A., 278
Sparrow, Judge Gerald, 17
Sparta, 320–21
Spencer, Herbert, 16, 65, 77, 191, 269, 290
Spenser, Edmund, 50, 80
Spitz, Dr David, 243
Springs of Laughter, The, 269
St Simon, Duc de, 60
Stalin, Joseph, 270
Standard, The, 229
Stein, Charlotte von, 80
Stendhal (Marie Henri Beyle), 192, 228
Sterne, Laurence, 50
Sternthal, Friedrich, 79
Stirling, Colonel W. F., 132, 148, 149
Story, Thomas Waldo, 235,
Story of the Gadsbys, The, 321 n8
Strachey Family, The, 146
Study of Sociology, The, 290
Sunday Times, The, 268
Supplément au siècle de Louis XIV, 218 n28
Swift, Jonathan, 50
Swiss Family Robinson, The, 6
Symonds, Percival M., 140

T
Talleyrand, Charles Maurice de, 271
Telegraph, The, 229
Temple, Archbishop, 146
Ten O'Clock, 98, 231, 235, 236
Tennyson, Alfred Lord, 6, 251
Thackeray, William Makepeace, 50, 77, 225
Thénard, Madame, 47
Theogony, 260
Thomas, Rowland, 17

Thoreau, Henry David, 320
Thoughts on War, 129
Through the Looking-Glass, 6–9, 196
Thus Spake Zarathustra, 89, 198, 208 n20, 228
Times Literary Supplement, The, 268, 272, 287
Times, The, 144, 229, 234, 254, 268, 278, 307
Tolstoy and his Wife, 150 n29, 228 n11
Tolstoy, Count Leo, 150, 228
Tolstoy, Madame, 289
Tourville, Henri de, 153
Townsend, Peter, 172
Toye, Francis, 15
Trahison des clercs, La, 200
Travers, R. M. W., 233 n18
Trêve, Jacques, 161, 162
Truly Thankful, 15
Twain, Mark, 51

U
Über naive und sentimentale Dichtung, 79
Unto this Last, 128 n23

V
Valentine, C. W., 302, 303
Valentine, David, 267
Valentine Vox, 172
Vanity Fair, 225
Vansittart, Lord, 182
Vauvenargues, Marquis de, 316
Veblen, Thorstein, 14, 15, 218
Vernon, G. F. Carr, 63
Victoria, Queen, 19
Voltaire (François Marie Arouet), 128, 129, 130, 151, 218, 310

W
Wace, Dr Henry, 77
Waggets, the, 101
Wagner, Richard, 86, 140, 197, 200, 228
Wahlverwandtschaften, Die, 79
Walker, Dr Joseph V., 301, 305

Walker, Dr Kenneth, 106
Walker, Miss Mary, 44–45, 47, 64
Walker-Smith, Derek, 142
Wallach, Dr, 97
Wallich, Dr Nathaniel, 184
Wallich, Horace, friendship with AML of, 184–85
Wallich, Mrs, 184–85
Walpole, Hugh, 270
Warburton, Mr, 112, 112 n15
Ward, Miss, 173
War of Belgian Independence, see World War I
Warren, Major (later Colonel) Leonard E., friendship with AML of, 222, 321
Way of My World, The, 218
Webb, Miss, 210
Weber, Professor Alfred, 244
Weib in anthropologischer und sozialer Betrachtung, Das, 292 n2
Welch, Colin, 143
Wellington, 1st Duke of, 141
Wellington, 5th Duke of, 149
Wells, Bombardier Billy, 60
Welt als Wille und Vorstellung, Die, 78
Wertheimers, the, 250
Wheel of Health, The, 258, 261
When I was a Boy, 146
Whetham, C., 249
Whetham, W. C. D., 249
Whistler, James McNeill, 98–100; aesthetic doctrines of, 229–33, 234–37
Why Exhibit Works of Art?, 233 n17
Wilde, Oscar, 191, 235, 235 n20
Wilhelm II, Kaiser, 112
Wilkie Collins (by Kenneth Robinson), 146
Wilkie Collins, Le Fanu and Others, 146
Williams, R. Lester, friendship with AML of, 222
Williamson, Dr J. A., 255
Wilson, Geoffrey, friendship with AML of, 135 n4

Winstin, Stephen, 269 n75
Winterton, Earl, 270 n80
Wittels, Dr Fritz, 75, 276, 305–6
Wolf, Simon, 253
Woman (by Dr Bernard A. Bauer), 291 n108
Women in Love, 74 n13
Woodroffe, Caroline, 172
Woolf, Virginia, 163
Wordsworth, William, 50, 79, 225
World War I, 100–13, 125, 127, 128, 129, 130, 138, 143, 147, 164, 171, 194, 221, 265, 301, 321
World War II, 50, 112, 115, 116, 123, 129, 132, 147–48, 171, 213, 219, 221, 285
World, The, 98, 231
Wrench, Dr G. T., admires Mussolini, 196; admits his Nietzscheanism might stem from inferiority feelings, 209; appearance of, 206–7; approves of miscegenation, 212; bored by his work as a doctor, 194–95, 206; claims the English cannot fathom women, 296; death of, 207, 213; exaggerates importance of diet, 261; fails to understand the Alexander method, 209–10, 213; friendship with AML of, 194, 207–11, 213–14, 321; his letter to AML about his late mother, 61; likes AML's translations of Nietzsche, 88; marries a Jewish woman, 211, 212; observes AML's romance with a waitress, 262; personality of, 207, 208, 209, 210, 211; portrayed in a novel by AML, 214, 262; praises AML's work on Prometheus, 258; settles in Karachi, 212; values Freud, 195; wonders how AML could be devoted to his mother yet an antifeminist, 212–13, 287, 311
Wright, Sidney H., acquaints AML with the English classics, 49–50; AML pawns his gold watch and chain for, 180; appearance of, 64, 183, 209; death of, 183; dislikes Nietzsche, 183; friendship with AML of, 49, 180–81, 182, 184, 186, 321, 322; religious interests of, 64, 181–82; teaches AML, 50, 64, 65, 180, 181
Wuthering Heights, 66–75, 77, 225; the greatest work of European fiction, 66, 271
Wynne, G. W. L., friendship with AML of, 222

Y
Yet Again, 271 n83
Yonge, Charlotte M., 46 n8
Youssoupoff, Prince Felix, 161–62

Z
Zola, Émile, 231

ABOUT THE AUTHOR

In the first decades of the twentieth century, Anthony Mario Ludovici (1882–1971) was one of Britain's most celebrated intellectuals.

One of the first and most accomplished translators of Nietzsche into English and a leading exponent of Nietzsche's thought, Ludovici was also an original philosopher in his own right.

In nearly 40 books, including eight novels, and dozens of shorter works, Ludovici set forth his views on metaphysics, religion, ethics, politics, economics, the sexes, health, eugenics, art, modern culture and current events with a clarity, wit and fearless honesty that made him famous.

Ludovici was a passionate, principled defender of aristocracy and conservatism and a fierce, uncompromising critic of egalitarianism in all its manifestations: Christianity, liberalism, Marxism, socialism, feminism, multiculturalism, crass commercialism, a debased popular culture, and the denial of innate and unalterable biological differences between individuals, the sexes and the races.

ABOUT THE EDITOR

John V. Day was born in 1961 and educated at the University of Edinburgh and Queen's University of Belfast, where he received a doctorate in prehistory. He is the author of the highly praised book *Indo-European Origins: The Anthropological Evidence* (Washington, D.C.: Institute for the Study of Man, 2001) and a number of articles. He is the editor of *The Lost Philosopher: The Best of Anthony M. Ludovici* (Berkeley, Cal.: Educational Translation and Scholarship Foundation, 2003) and the creator of an online Ludovici archive, www.anthonymludovici.com, that makes available many works by and about Ludovici.

www.ingramcontent.com/pod-product-compliance
Lightning Source LLC
Chambersburg PA
CBHW030816190426
43197CB00036B/498